the sketchbook of
·LOISH·
art in progress

3dtotalPublishing

Correspondence: publishing@3dtotal.com
Website: www.3dtotal.com

Every effort has been made to ensure the credits and contact information listed are present and correct. In the case of any errors that have occurred, the publisher respectfully directs readers to the **www.3dtotalpublishing.com** website for any updated information and/or corrections.

First published in the United Kingdom, 2018, by 3dtotal Publishing. 3dtotal.com Ltd, 29 Foregate Street, Worcester WR1 1DS, United Kingdom.

Reprinted in 2022 by 3dtotal Publishing.

Soft cover ISBN: 978-1-909414-54-9
Printing and binding: Leo Paper Products Ltd.
www.leo.com.hk

Visit **www.3dtotalpublishing.com** for a complete list of available book titles.

Editor: Annie Moss
Proofreader: Melanie Smith
Lead designer: Imogen Williams
Cover designer: Matthew Lewis
Managing editor: Simon Morse

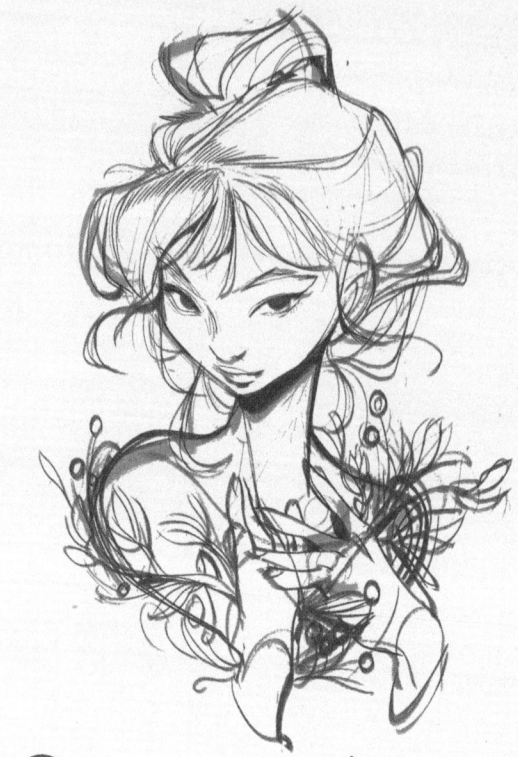

One tree planted for every book sold

OUR PLEDGE

From 2020, 3dtotal Publishing has pledged to plant one tree for every book sold by partnering with and donating the appropriate amounts to re-foresting charities. This is one of the first steps in our ambition to become a carbon neutral company with carbon neutral publications, giving our customers the knowledge that by buying from 3dtotal Publishing, we are working together to balance the environmental damage caused by the publishing, shipping, and retail industries.

· contents ·

· introduction ·

The book you have in your hands right now is my second art book. I have been thinking about creating this book for quite some time. When putting together my first art book, *The Art of Loish*, my favorite part was gathering images for the *sketches & studies* chapter. I dug up old sketchbooks and browsed through the pages, rediscovering sketches and doodles that I had long since forgotten. I found piles of A4 sheets and school notes with drawings in the margins. I browsed through the work I had created during my studies as an animation student, and I found unfinished sketches in my digital art folders. It all felt so much more playful and fun than my more finished pieces. There was a lot to share, and ever since then, I have wanted to create a new book just for these works.

The reason I have a personal preference for sketches and rough work is because they tend to be more raw and authentic. They are the first thing the artist creates; whether it is just for practice, or the first step in the creation of a digital painting or animation project. In this sense, they are pure: the first visualization of an idea or process. For the same reason, they are also more varied than my finished work. A lot of my sketches are the result of experiments, practice, and trying out new things, so you will see a much wider range of styles and subject matter than you will find in my digital paintings.

The main reason rougher work can be more interesting is the insights they provide into a creative process. Sketches are often the first step in a larger process, not only for digital paintings, animations, or other large productions, but also in the overall artistic evolution of an artist. Rough works can be the puzzle piece that reveals the bigger picture of an artist's thoughts, philosophy, and ideas.

These preliminary works can be especially interesting when seen in the context of digital art, since the creation process is often seen as mysterious and complex by those who are unfamiliar with digital art techniques. Seeing the sketches and works in progress behind a digital art piece can demystify the process by showing the evolution from the first lines to a finished piece.

I hope that by reading this book you will be able to get a closer look at who I am as an artist. Not only will you see how my style and skills have changed over time, but also see my mindless doodles, first ideas, concept art, and first steps in creating more complex artwork. You will also find tips and tutorials that show the role of speed painting and sketching in the creation of my digital paintings. Most of all, I hope you enjoy browsing through the pages, and that it feels a little bit like browsing through my personal sketchbook!

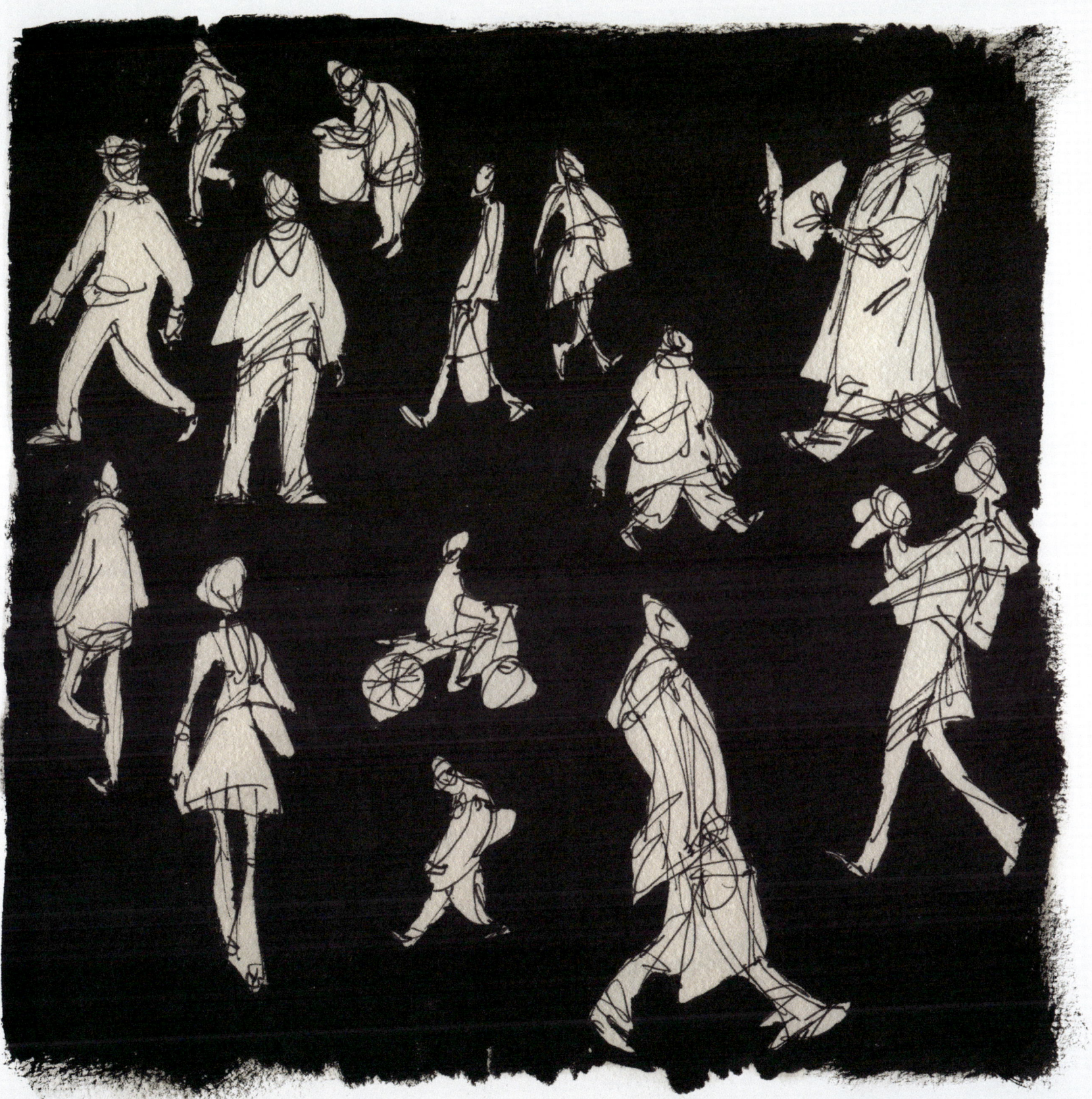

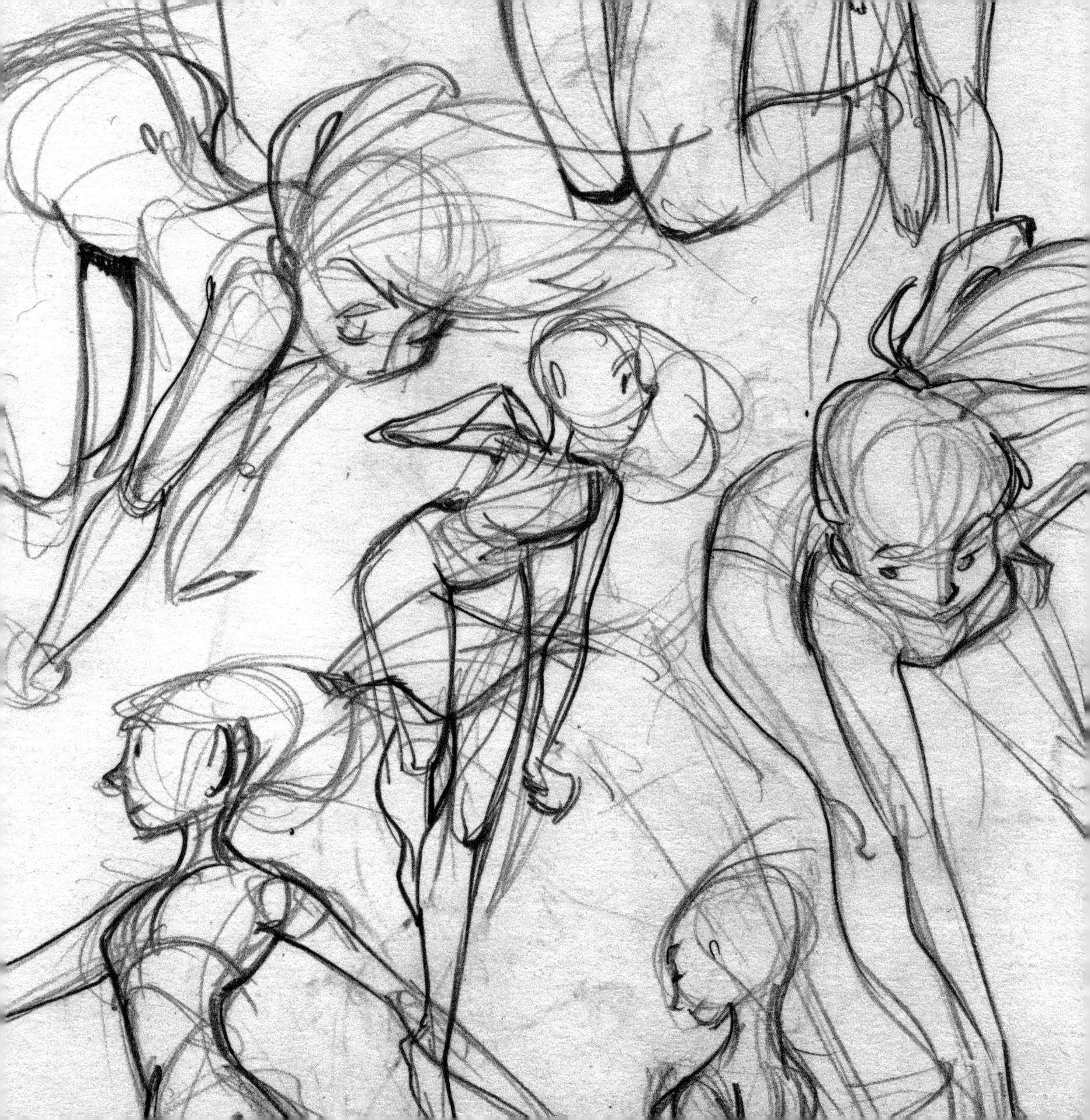

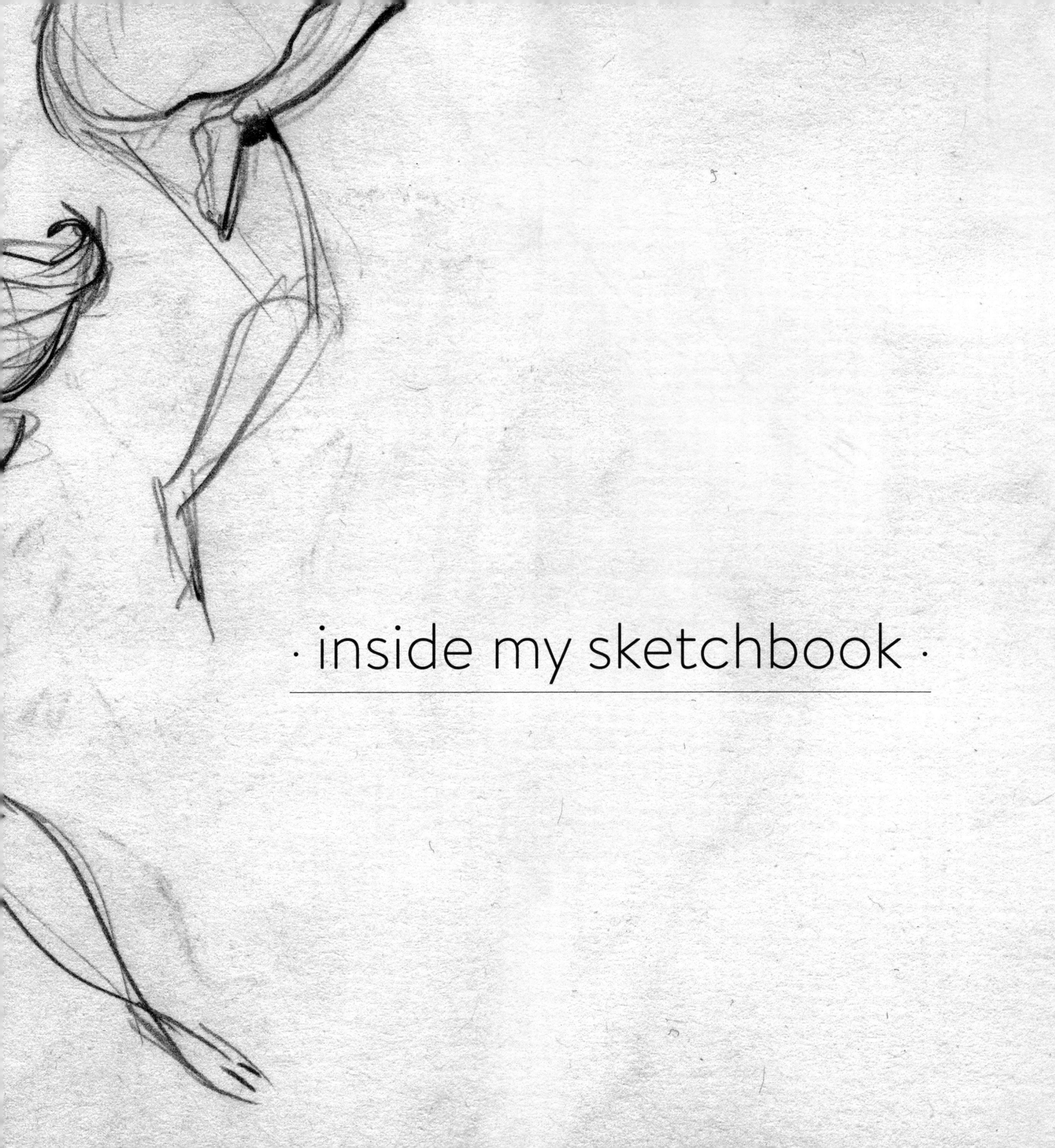

· inside my sketchbook ·

· learning through sketches ·

I feel that sketching is where we all start out as artists. When I was a toddler, long before I ever learned to create finished drawings, I would grab pencils, crayons, markers, or anything else that was lying around and doodle whatever came to mind. This was usually princesses, dinosaurs, or a combination of both.

As we get older, we tend to lose the ability to draw so freely, despite how important this freedom is to our creative process. In order to preserve this skill, it is essential to create an emotional space in which we can experiment, learn, and play around; just as we did when we were younger.

That freedom to experiment is what sketching is to me. However, I have never been the type of artist to regularly draw in a physical sketchbook until it is filled. As a digital artist, I jump from traditional to digital media all the time, and my rough work is scattered all over the place. Sometimes a simple sketch is just a simple sketch. Sometimes I see more potential in the rough lines and turn it into a digital painting, which takes days to complete, while the sketch disappears under layers of digital paintwork.

At times I draw on loose sheets of paper, and at other times I draw on the computer. My definition of "sketch" can include pencil sketches, speed paints, and rough digital paintings. What unites these rough works is that I create them with the mindset of working freely. I allow myself to let go of the pressures of trying to creating my strongest piece, and instead, I enjoy being in a creative flow.

The most important benefit of sketching, to me, is how it allows me to learn. Through my rough work, I have developed my grasp of proportions, understanding of anatomy, and ability to stylize my drawings. As a child, I took art lessons that taught me to draw from life and photo reference, which had a huge impact on my ability to draw a range of subjects.

When I was eleven, I discovered cross-hatching, a technique that allowed me to create shading with lots of little lines drawn over each other.

Opposite: Drawings from my third grade journal, 1993

8

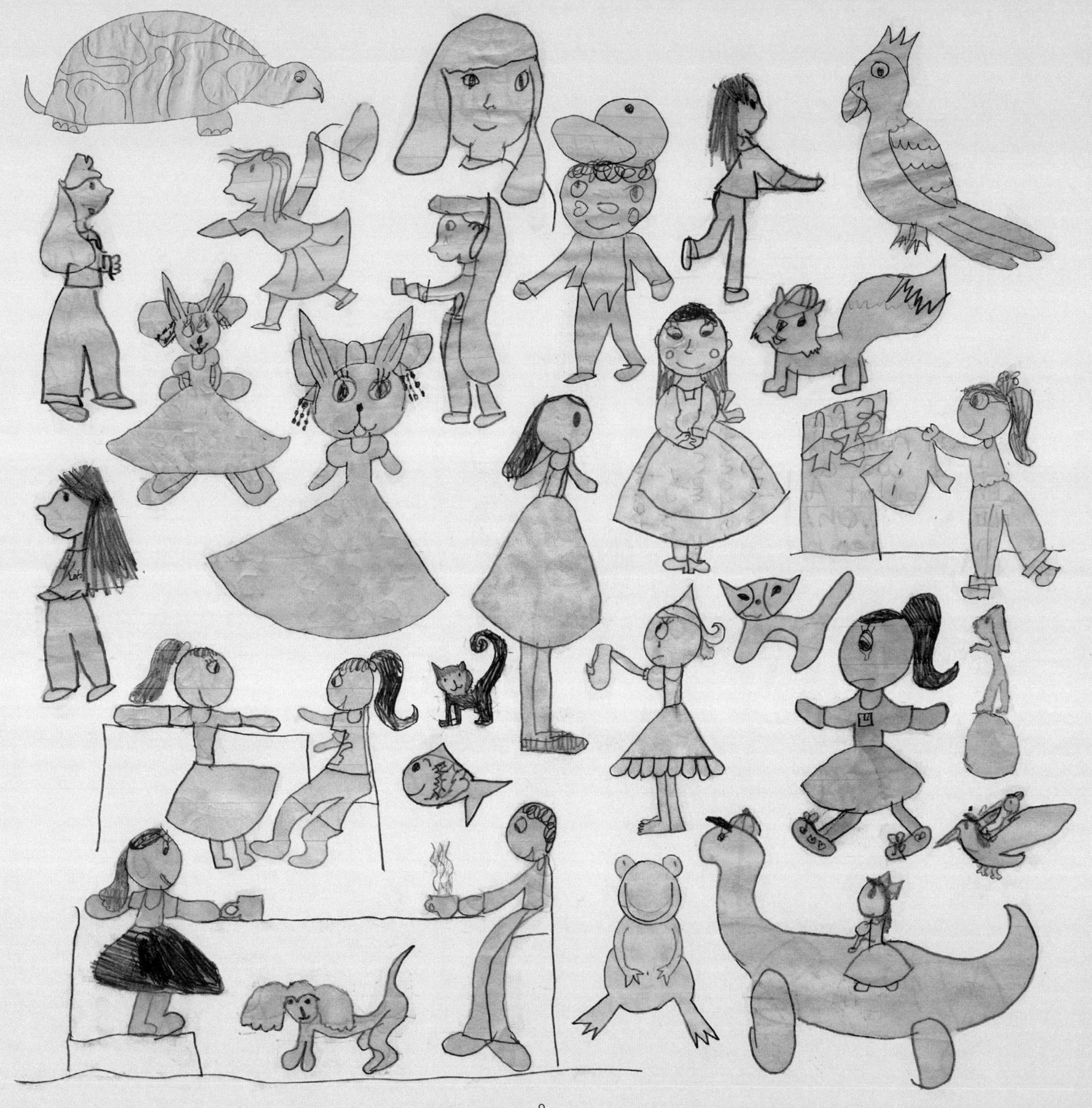

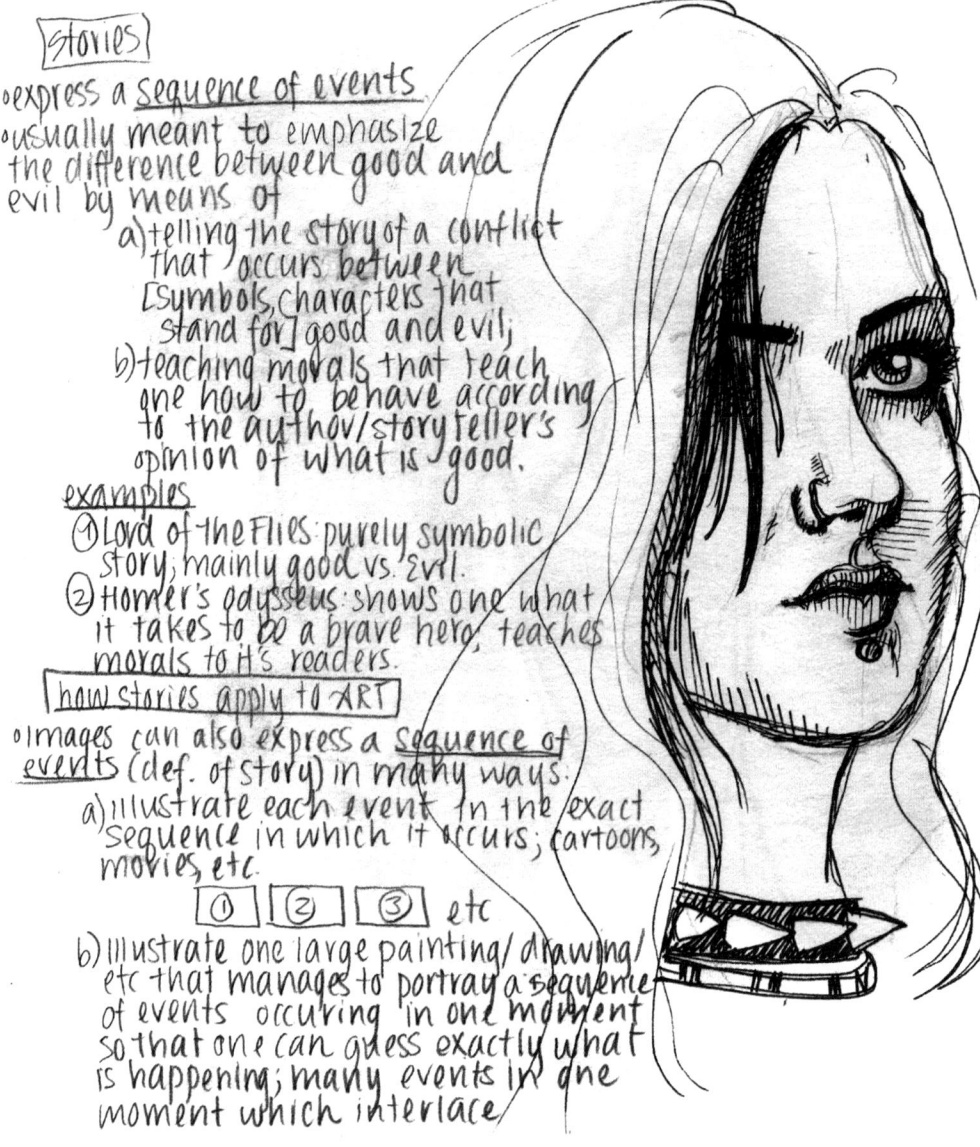

stories
o express a sequence of events
o usually meant to emphasize
the difference between good and
evil by means of
    a) telling the story of a conflict
       that occurs between
       [symbols, characters that
       stand for] good and evil;
    b) teaching morals that teach
       one how to behave according
       to the author/storyteller's
       opinion of what is good.
examples
 ① Lord of the Flies: purely symbolic
    story; mainly good vs. evil.
 ② Homer's Odysseus: shows one what
    it takes to be a brave hero, teaches
    morals to it's readers.
how stories apply to ART
o Images can also express a sequence of
  events (def. of story) in many ways:
    a) illustrate each event in the exact
       sequence in which it occurs; cartoons,
       movies, etc.

       ① ② ③ etc

    b) illustrate one large painting/drawing/
       etc that manages to portray a sequence
       of events occuring in one moment
       so that one can guess exactly what
       is happening; many events in one
       moment which interlace

Above: A sketch in my school note margins, 2001

Opposite: Various sketches I drew from 2003-2004

I really loved the texture that cross-hatching created, and I used it for everything. It became the defining aspect of my drawing style at the time, and today, creating texture through brush and pen strokes is still an important part of how I draw.

In the years before I discovered digital art, I was not particularly passionate about my sketches progressing to a more finished level with color. Instead, I preferred to draw with a pen or pencil and just leave it at that. At most, I would finalize my artwork with colored pencils, but keep the sketchy cross-hatching look.

I found painting to be quite difficult; blending colors to get anything other than mud-brown was particularly challenging, especially given my preference for bright candy colors. If I had lived in a world without computers, I would probably have overcome this hurdle earlier in life, since my desire to work with color was growing. Instead, at the age of fifteen, I discovered Photoshop and digital art, which meant I could indulge in my desire to play with color without using real paint.

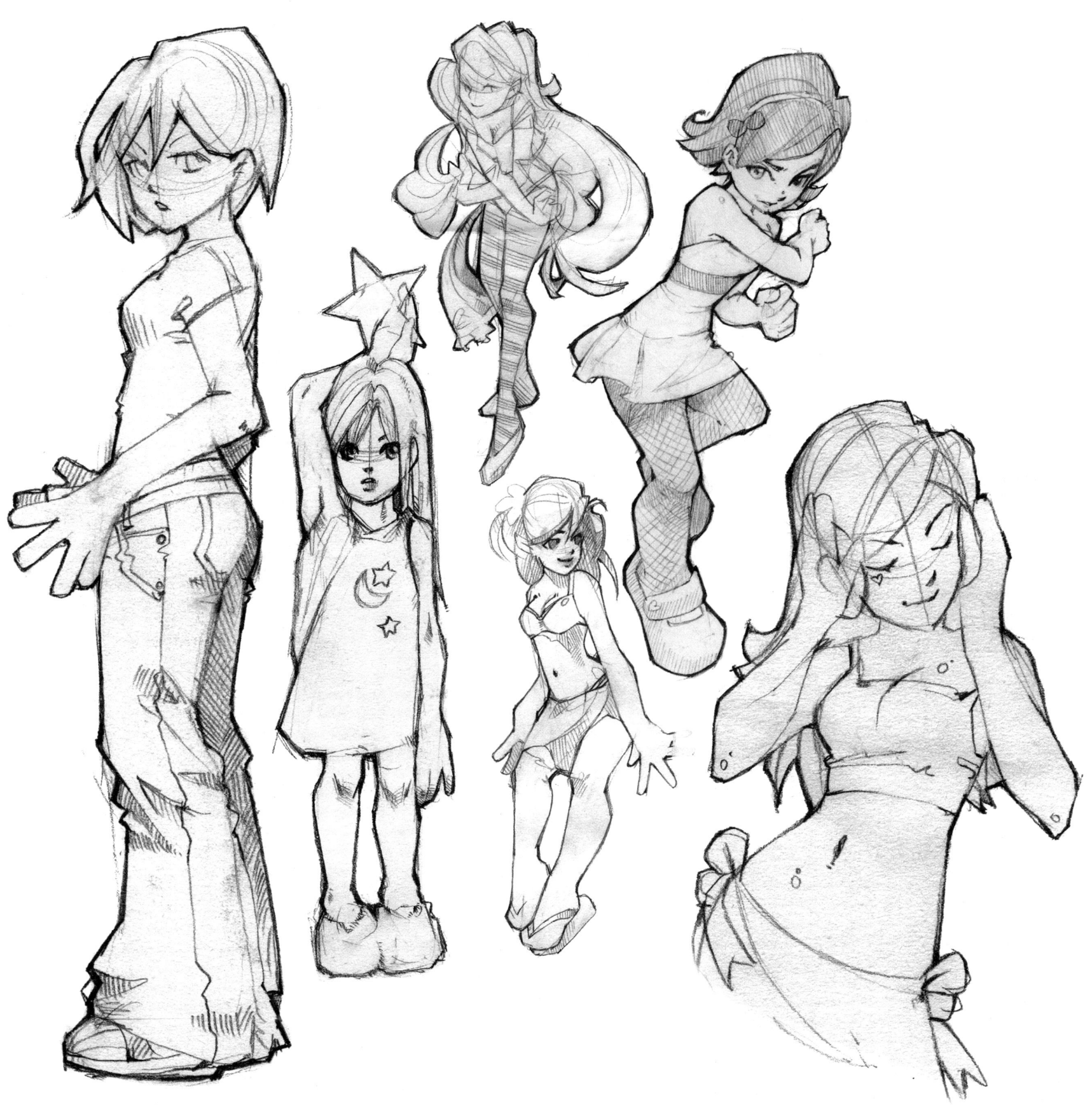

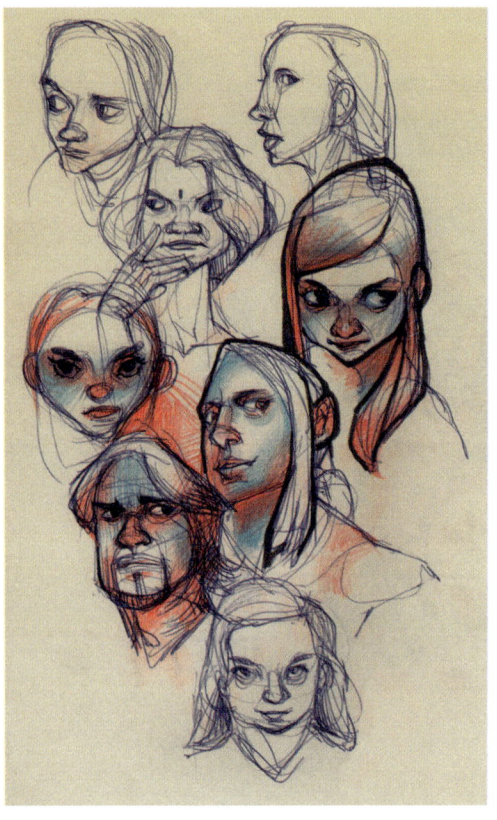

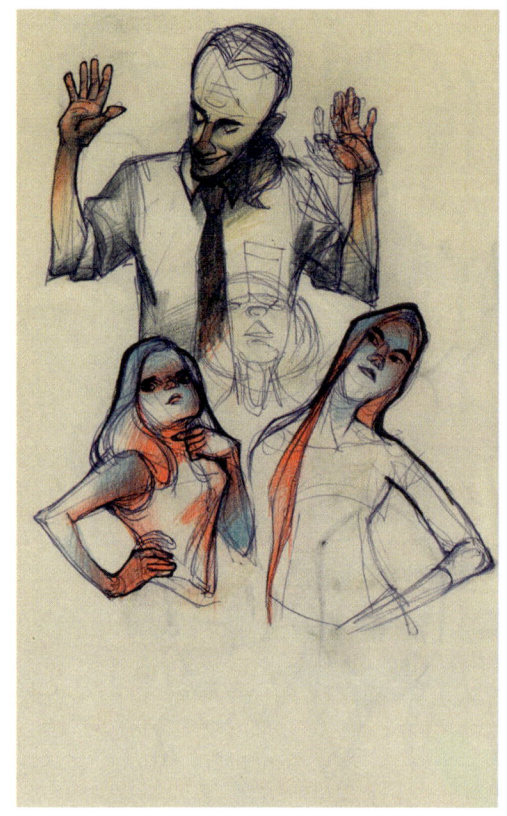

I was amazed and immediately hooked by the possibilities of Photoshop! When I first started, I never spent more than a few hours on one drawing. There was so much to learn that I wanted to quickly move on to my next digital creation. I was very impatient and excited. I started making a lot of quick digital pieces on a tiny, pixelated canvas every day and sketching in the margins of my school notes. I also started to translate my digital drawing techniques onto paper, using markers to create line art and mimic the shaded cel look where shade is shown as blocks of color, rather than a smooth gradient. I learned so much during this time.

It was only later that I started to spend longer and longer on one drawing, and developed a workflow for my digital paintings. It was then that I learned how to render and add detail to my artwork. However, the more time consuming my process got, the more I craved the freedom of drawing quickly and intuitively. That impatient feeling of wanting to create faster and learn more always returns.

This is a repeating cycle in my life as an artist; I have always gone through phases where I start to feel stuck in my style and bored with my workflow. The solution is always the same: get a sketchbook; make some speed paints; and doodle whatever comes to mind. Essentially, I repeatedly return to the basics of sketching, whether that is on paper or digitally. Not only has this brought me to where I am today, but it also keeps me inspired, motivated, and is often the beginning of a new phase of creativity and excitement.

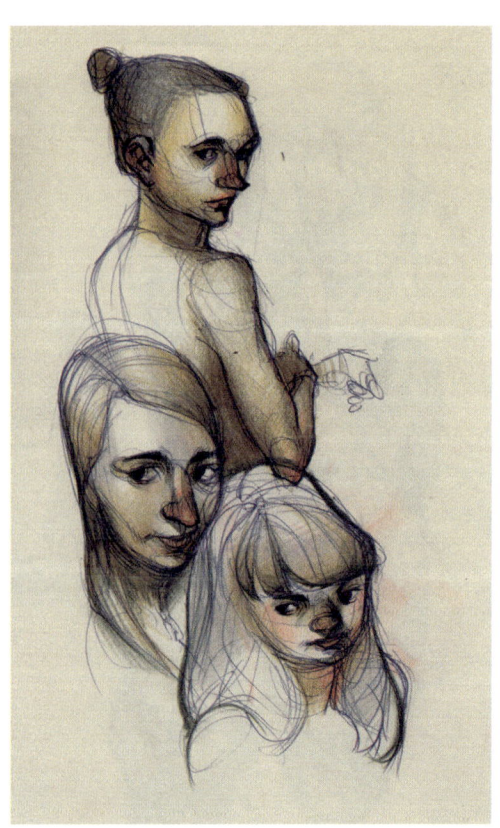

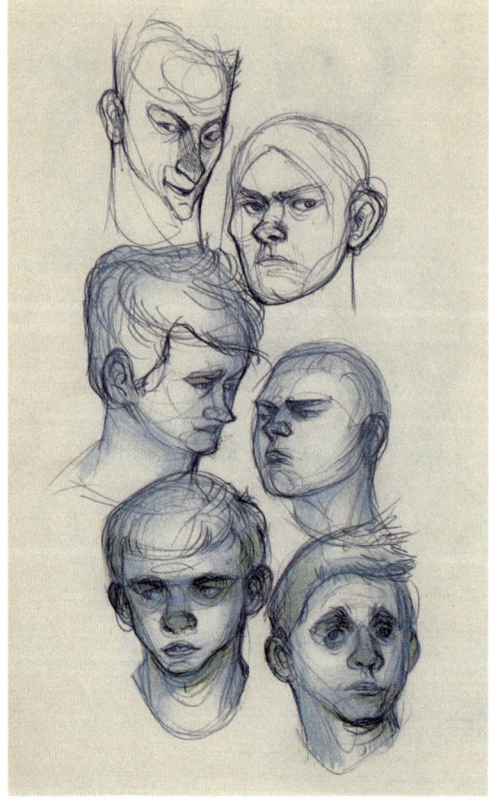

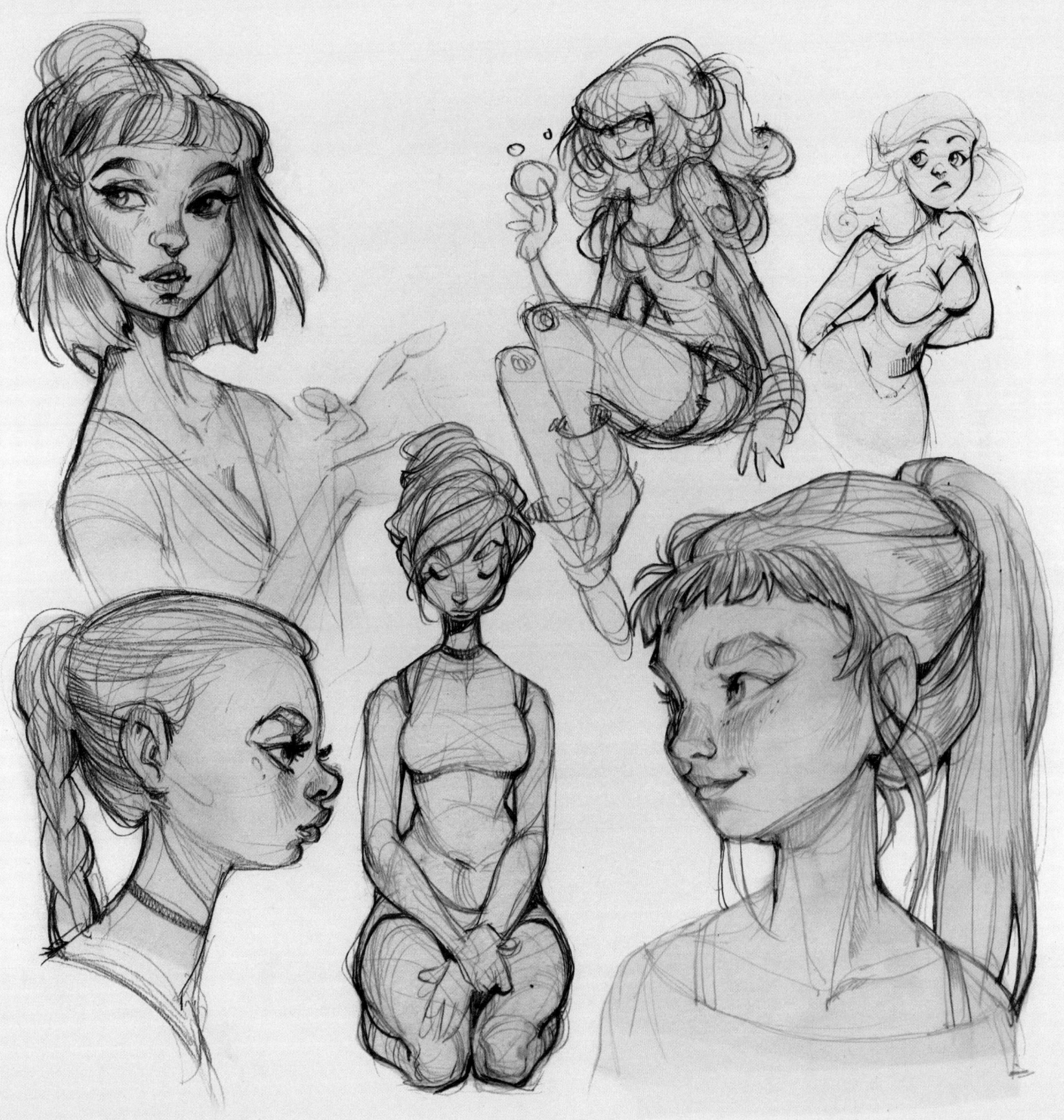

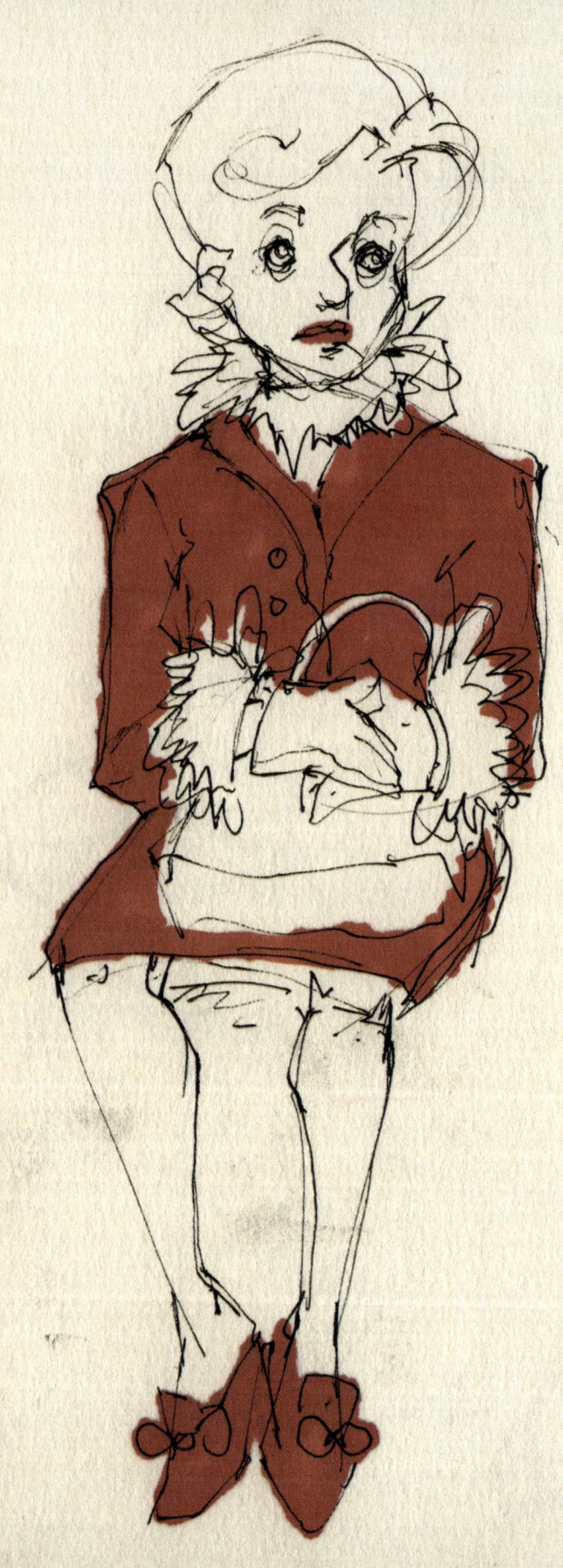

· sketching & animation ·

When I was eighteen, just graduated from high school, I went to my first day of animation school and received the instruction: keep a sketchbook. We were expected to maintain this sketchbook over the entire course of the school year – our grade even depended on it! This was my first introduction to how important sketching is for animators. As the year progressed, the sketchbook became crucial to developing my skills. I learned to draw quickly and capture the gesture of animals and people within seconds. I learned to explore my style by exaggerating forms and trying different tools, and to think of my drawings as scenes in a story.

Animation school had a huge effect on my drawing ability. Before, I would draw in a very chunky, blocky style. I loved thick, heavy lines and angular forms, and I always outlined my characters with a thick black line which further encased them inside this chunky aesthetic. My animation teachers criticized this style; I remember feeling very attacked and not understanding their dislike of it. I thought it looked great!

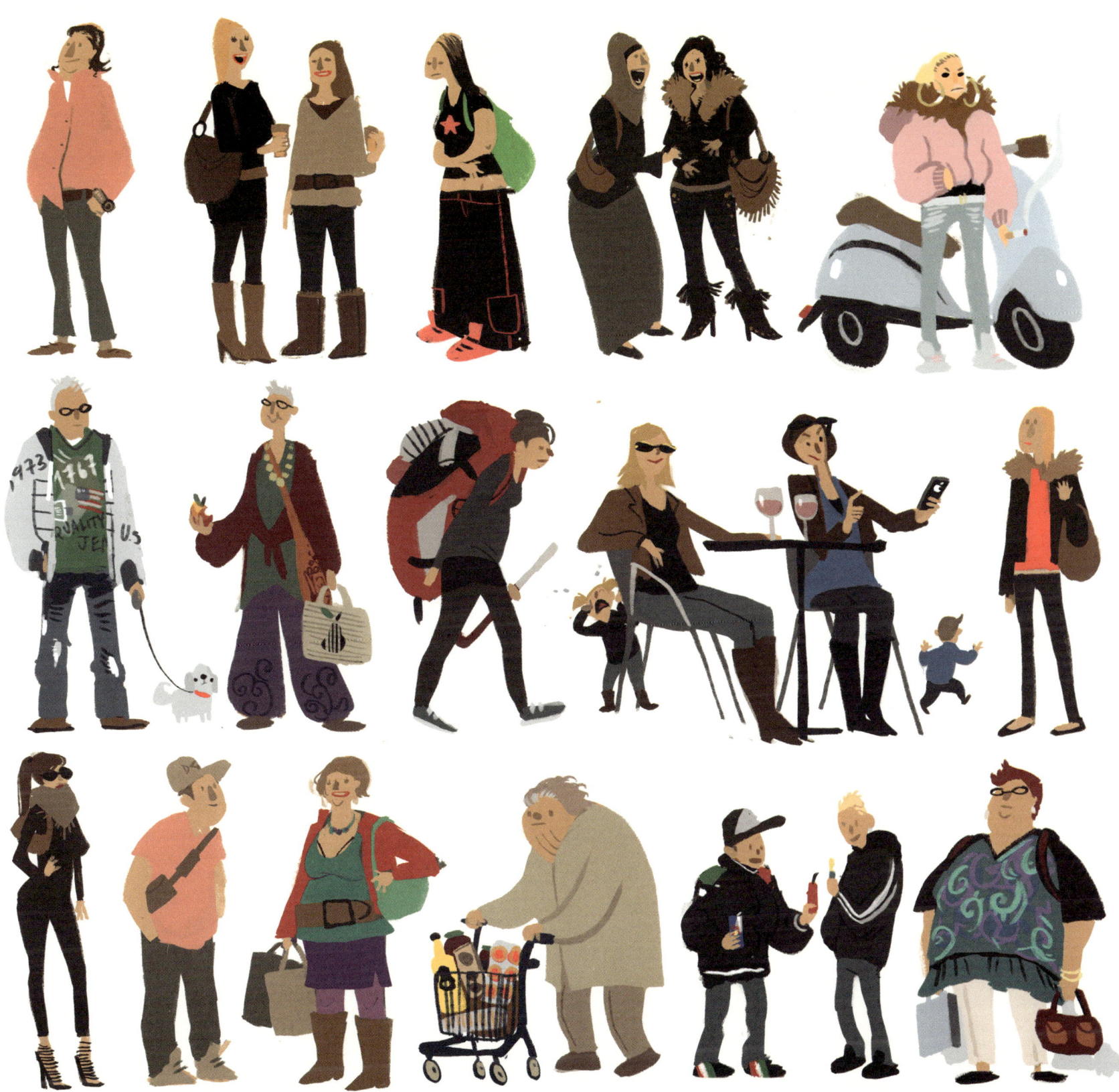

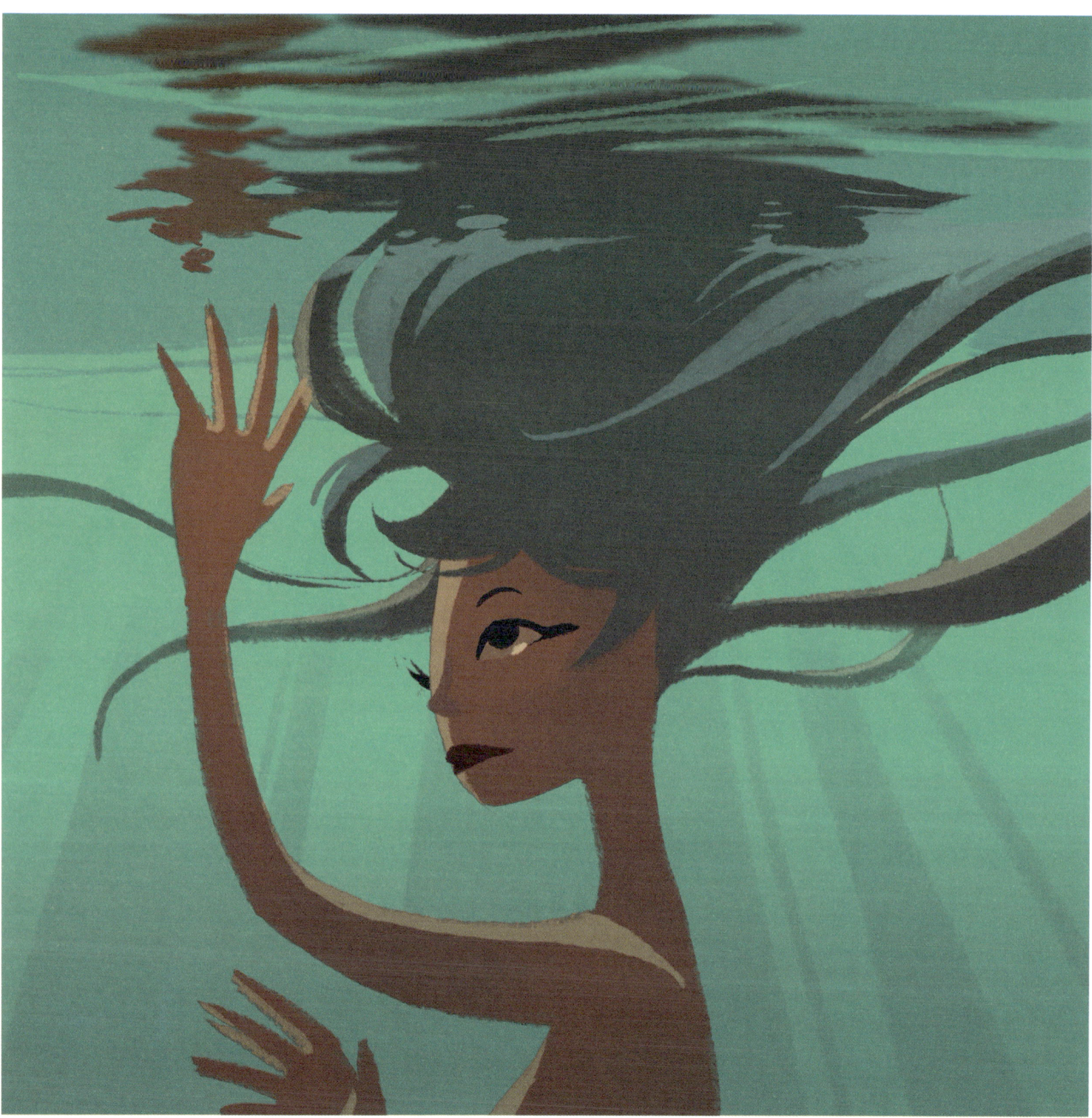

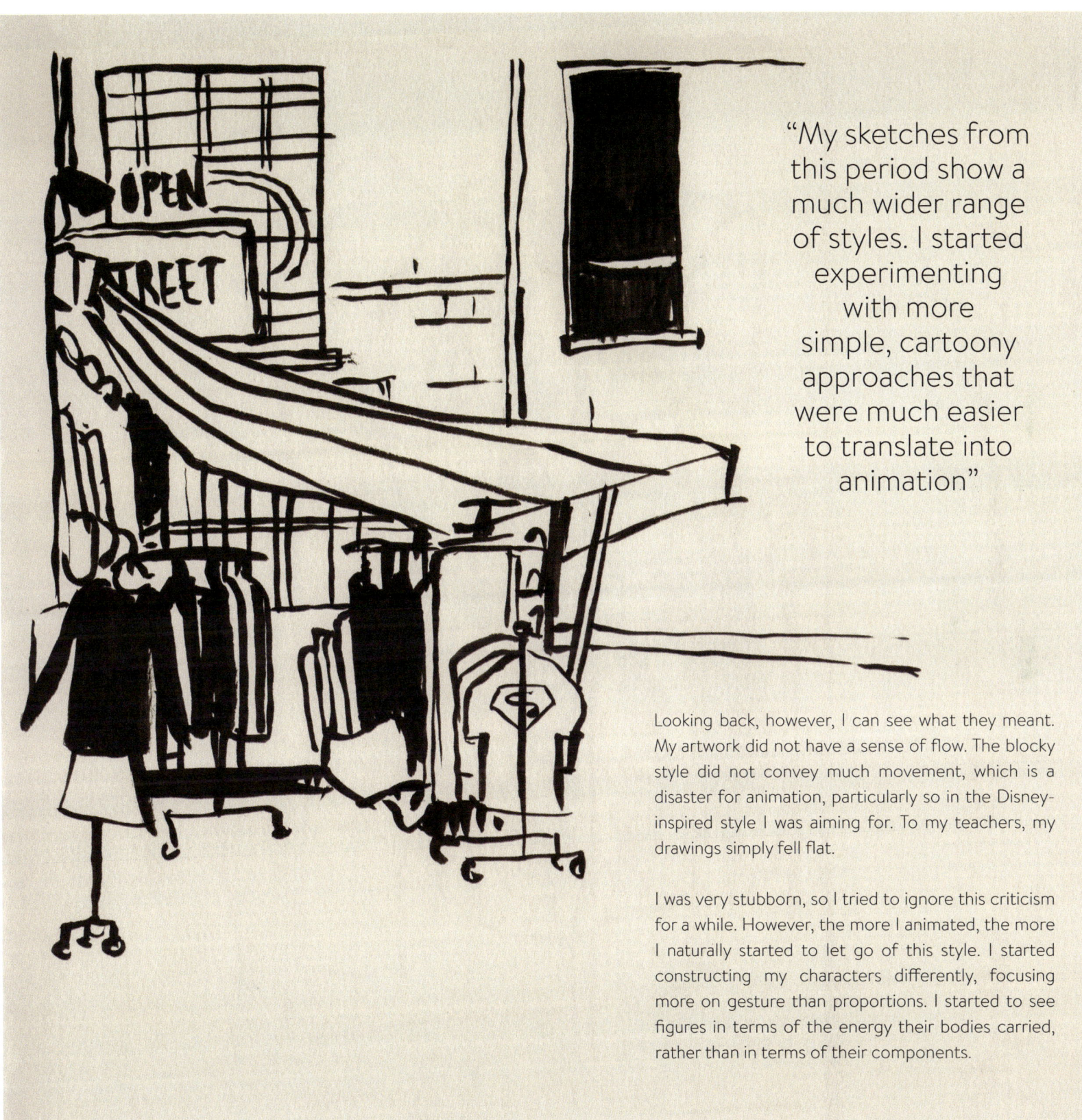

"My sketches from this period show a much wider range of styles. I started experimenting with more simple, cartoony approaches that were much easier to translate into animation"

Looking back, however, I can see what they meant. My artwork did not have a sense of flow. The blocky style did not convey much movement, which is a disaster for animation, particularly so in the Disney-inspired style I was aiming for. To my teachers, my drawings simply fell flat.

I was very stubborn, so I tried to ignore this criticism for a while. However, the more I animated, the more I naturally started to let go of this style. I started constructing my characters differently, focusing more on gesture than proportions. I started to see figures in terms of the energy their bodies carried, rather than in terms of their components.

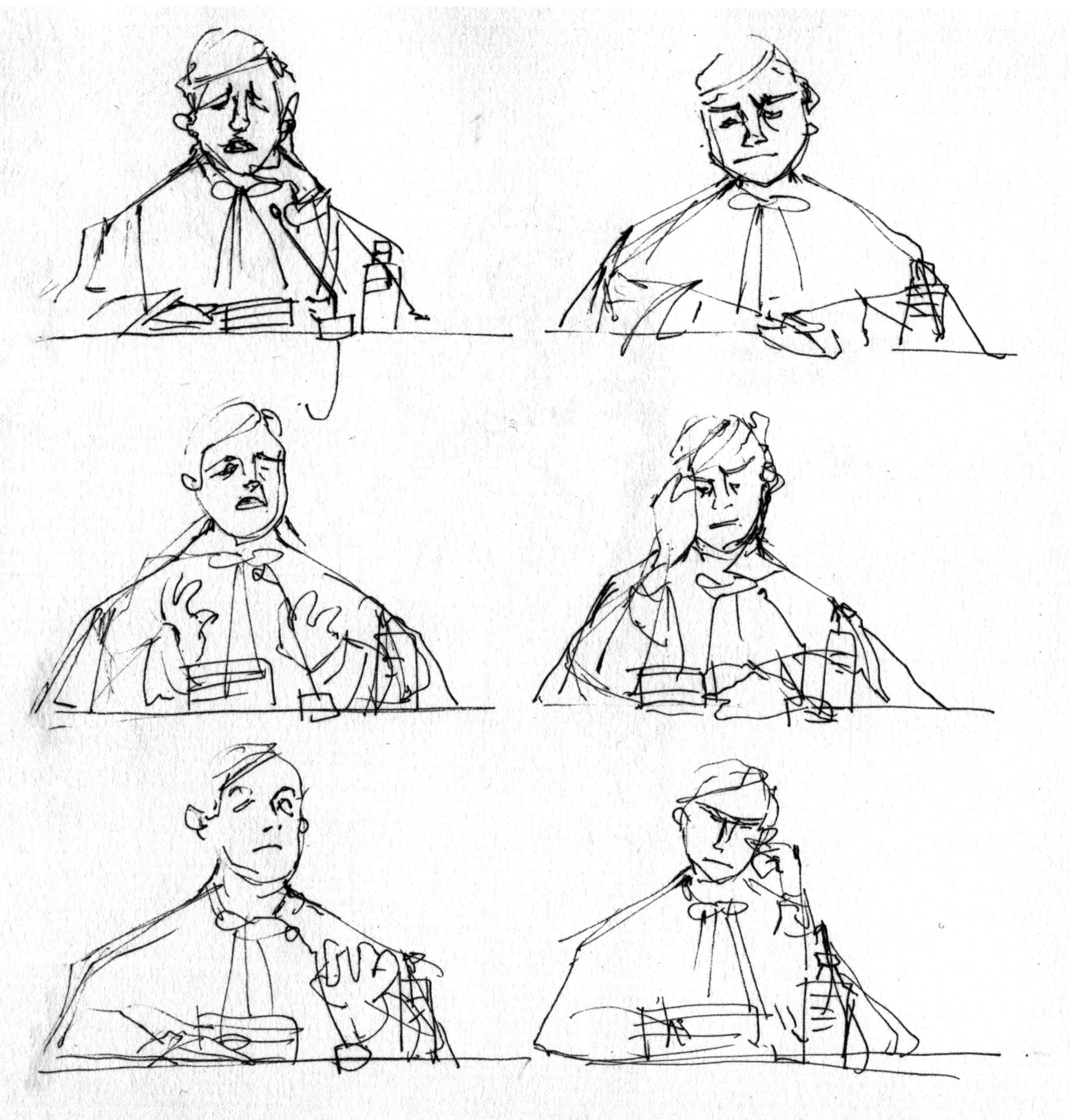

In this sense, studying animation truly changed the way I saw the world around me. Today, capturing a sense of flow and movement is one of my main priorities while drawing.

Studying animation also challenged me to experiment with the level of detail in my style. In 2D animation, every single frame needs to be drawn individually, and in animation school, the animations we created were usually twelve frames per second. Any animator can tell you that this is an enormous amount of work. As a result, animators seek out an efficient style. They have to make careful choices about the level of detail in their characters, as well as picking a style that can be easily replicated over many frames. Animators tend to work with basic construction shapes, which help the character to appear consistent throughout the animation.

As a response to these practical limitations, my sketches from this period show a much wider range of styles. I started experimenting with more simple, cartoony approaches that were much easier to translate into animation. I also tried more efficient rendering techniques, and started exaggerating shapes more.

I will never know what my style would have looked like if I had not gone to animation school, but looking back, I can definitely say that it was an essential step in the development of my drawing style and skills. Most importantly, it taught me the significance of rough work and sketching, something I think is an essential component of my artistic practice to this day.

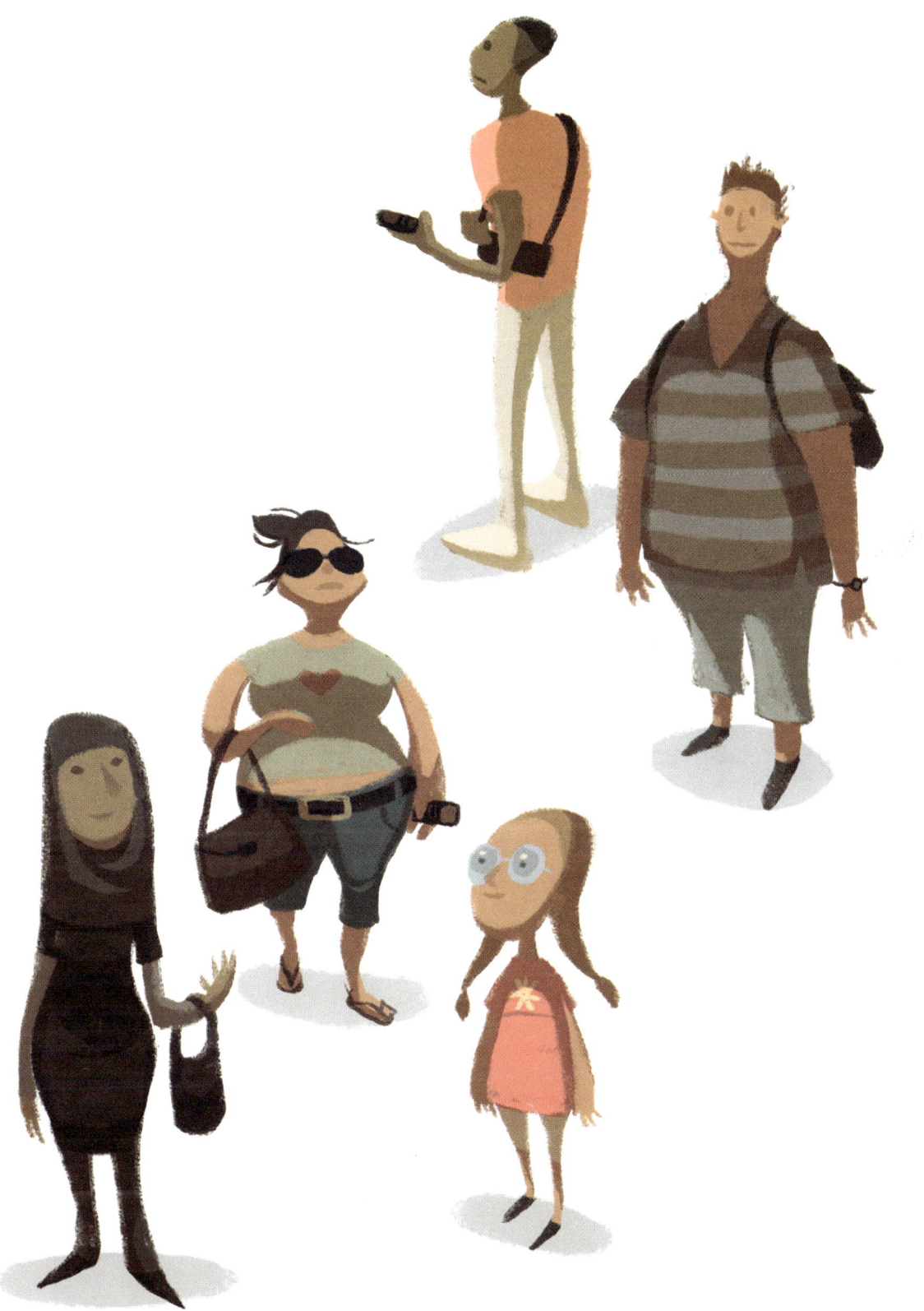

· gesture sketching & anatomy ·

As a character artist, my ability to draw anatomy and the human form is crucial to my work. However, for the most part, I am a self-taught artist. I have always drawn in my free time and developed the majority of my drawing skills outside a formal art education. As a result, I never really learned to draw anatomy in the classical sense.

From the outset, my approach to drawing the human form was heavily stylized. My first drawings of characters were cartoons, inspired by what I can only describe as a generic late-90s cartoon style with huge bubble eyes. Later on, I was inspired by a mix of French comics, Disney, and Japanese Manga, which became the foundations of my current style. My goal

was to create characters that were cartoons, but had moderately realistic body proportions. I wanted the bodies to feel "real" and have a sense of mass, despite being stylized.

I have experimented with different approaches to this ambition throughout the years, such as drawing in a more cartoony way – I had a "huge hands and feet" phase when I was eighteen – or instead aiming for a more streamlined and realistic look. I have always tried to balance stylization with realism.

It was only when I attended animation school that I started drawing from life and this is where the limitations of my angular, chunky style started to show.

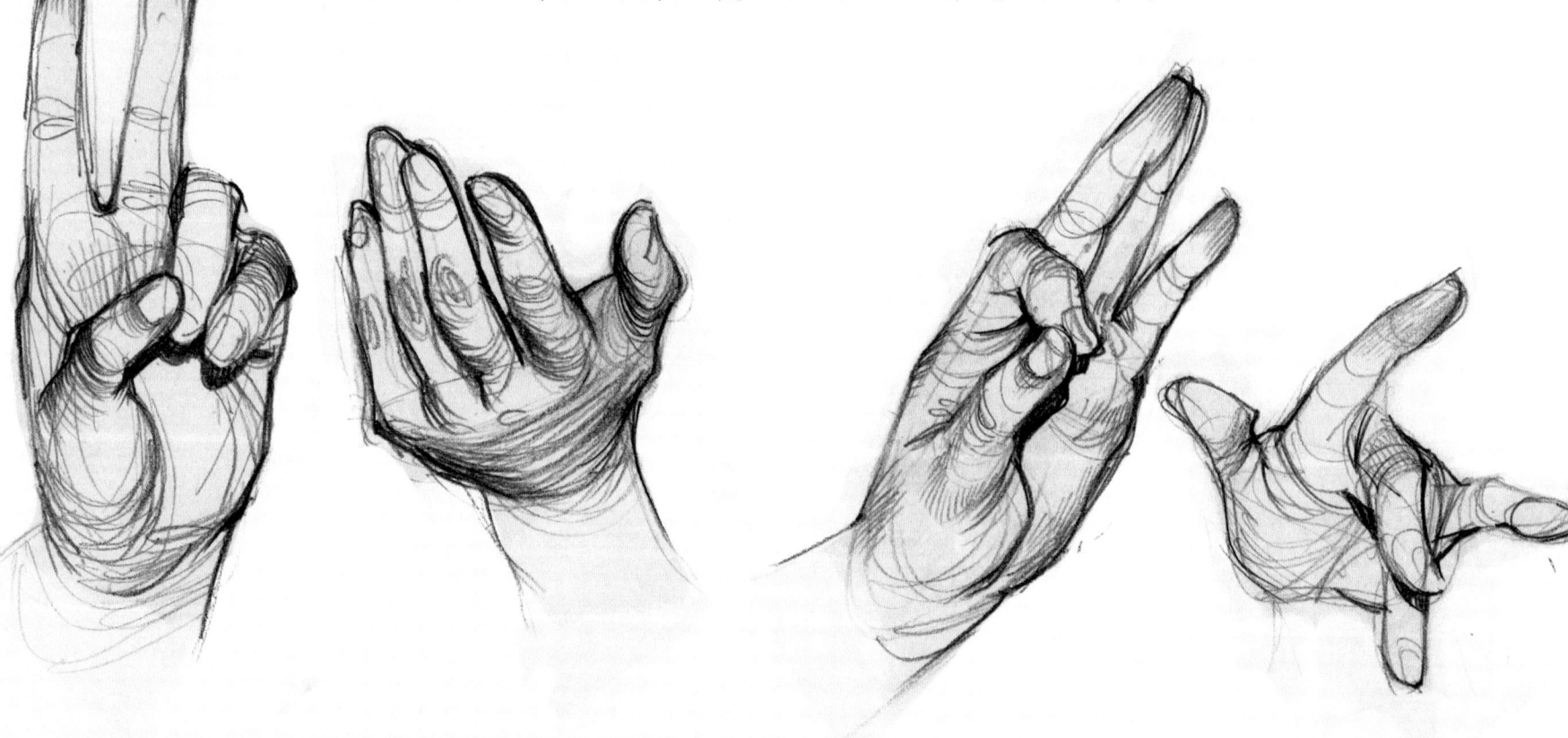

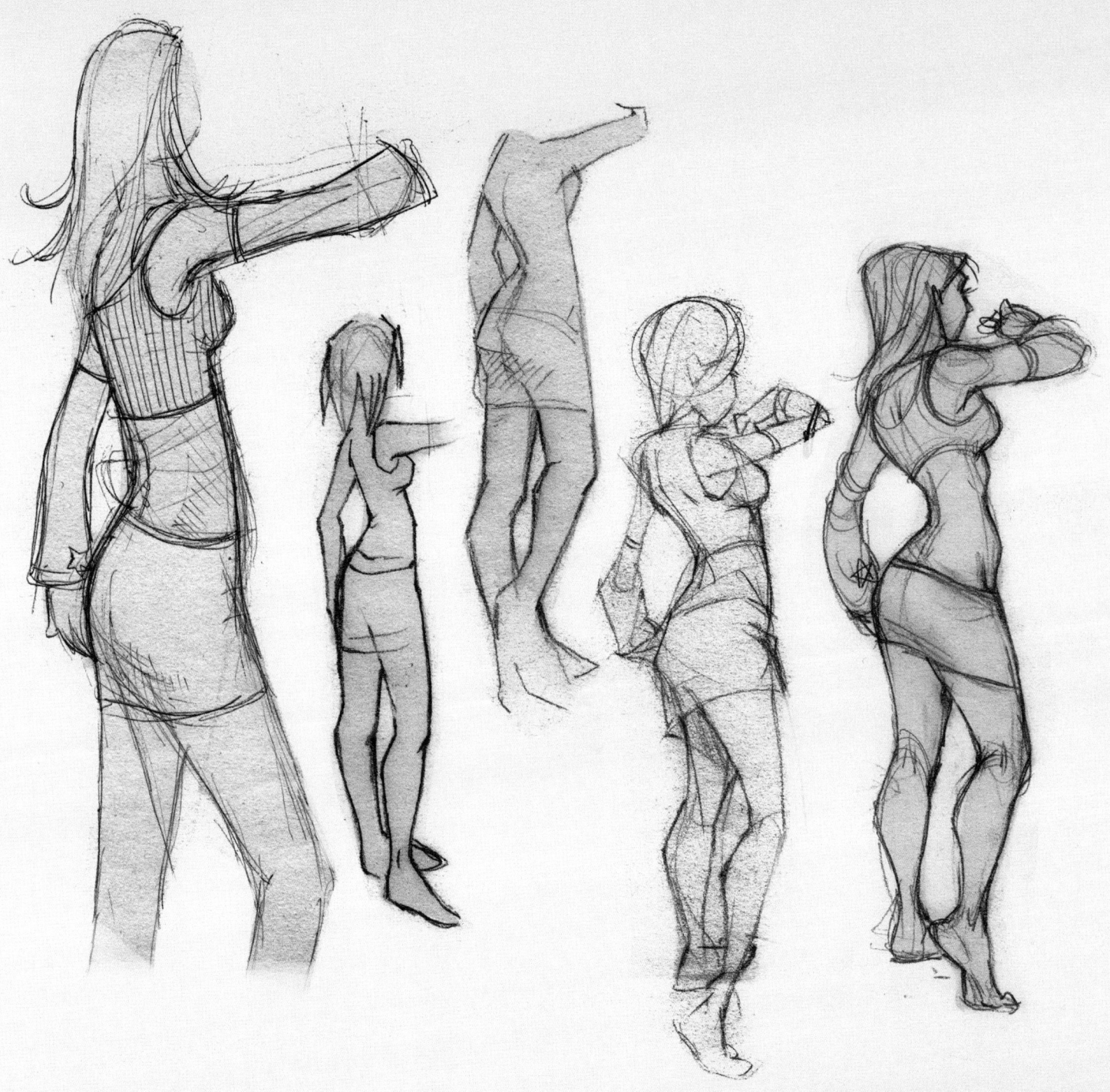

These sketches show the same pose drawn over the span of eleven years. When I first drew the pose aged fifteen, I had no idea what I was doing and really struggled to draw the human form. I did not know how to create a sense of gesture and mass, especially in a pose where the character is turned away from the viewer. I just could not rely on the tricks I used for forward-facing poses. I returned to the sketch every now and then, each time with a slightly different style.

I continued to find it very frustrating for many years, often leaving out the character's head or feet because I felt the sketch was not working. It was only in 2012 that I finally felt I was able to capture the pose as I had originally intended, with a sense of gesture and mass, and more confidence in my style. While these sketches are not my strongest works, they are an interesting example of how long it took me to reach a level I was happy with.

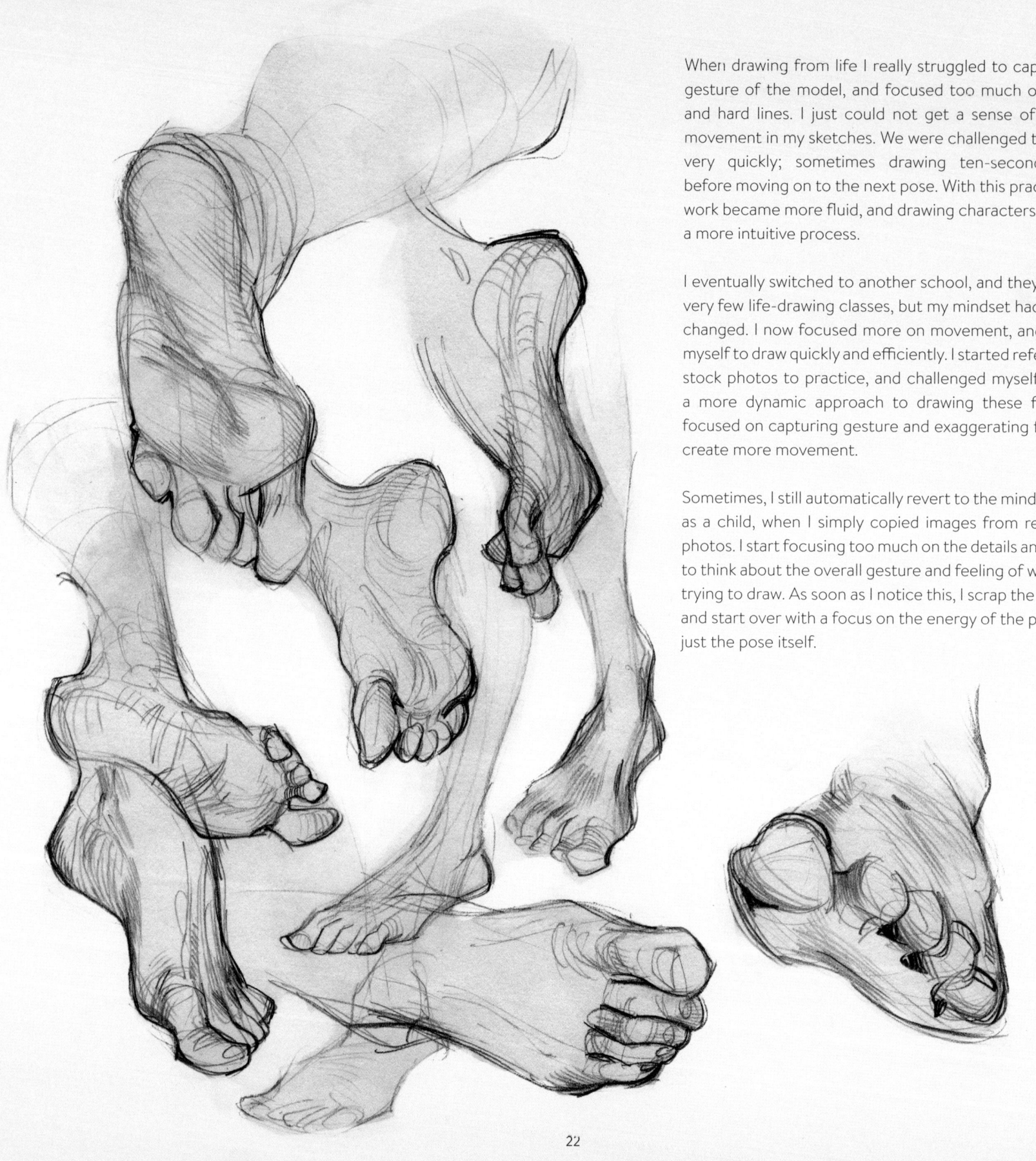

When drawing from life I really struggled to capture the gesture of the model, and focused too much on angles and hard lines. I just could not get a sense of life and movement in my sketches. We were challenged to sketch very quickly; sometimes drawing ten-second poses before moving on to the next pose. With this practice, my work became more fluid, and drawing characters became a more intuitive process.

I eventually switched to another school, and they offered very few life-drawing classes, but my mindset had already changed. I now focused more on movement, and forced myself to draw quickly and efficiently. I started referencing stock photos to practice, and challenged myself to take a more dynamic approach to drawing these figures. I focused on capturing gesture and exaggerating forms to create more movement.

Sometimes, I still automatically revert to the mindset I had as a child, when I simply copied images from reference photos. I start focusing too much on the details and forget to think about the overall gesture and feeling of what I am trying to draw. As soon as I notice this, I scrap the drawing and start over with a focus on the energy of the pose, not just the pose itself.

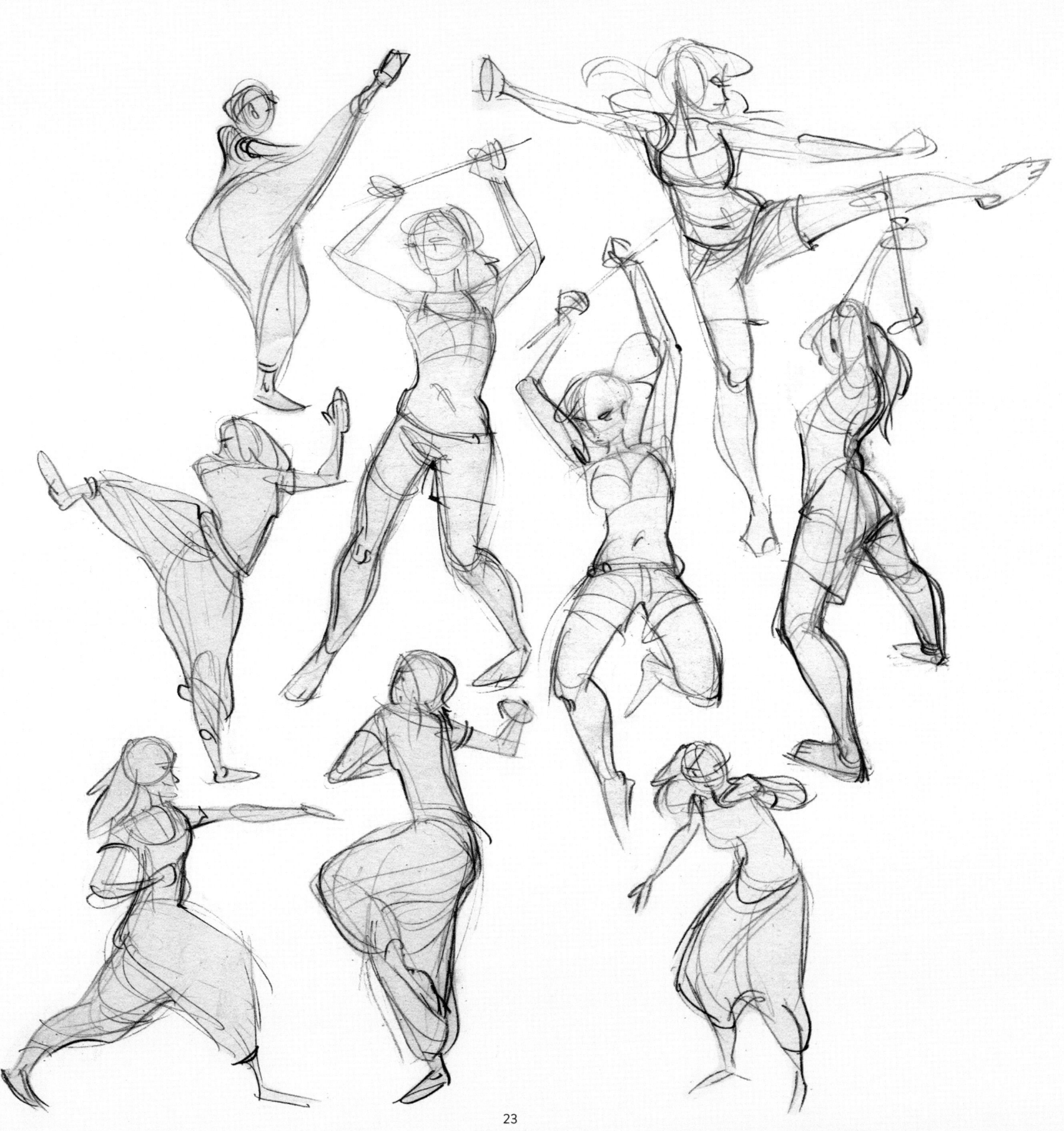

· stylization ·

When creating a finished digital painting, I put a lot of pressure on myself to create a strong finished piece. I do not strive for perfection in the proportions and detail, but I want the overall image to have appeal and a strong impact on the viewer. I allow myself some room to play around, but not too much, as I do not want to waste hours and hours on a potentially failed experiment. This pressure can motivate me to do my absolute best, but it can also be exhausting.

When I am working on rough drawings, however, I do not have this pressure. I avoid spending too much time on one sketch, so I do not worry whether the work is worth all of the time that I am putting into it. When adding color and details I spend less time polishing the initial sketch, so much more of the initial energy is preserved. This leaves much more room for experimentation; I can try new things and approach my drawing process with a more playful mindset. There is more room for what I call "lucky coincidences"; lines, shapes, or brush choices that happen to work out nicely, which I would not have tried otherwise.

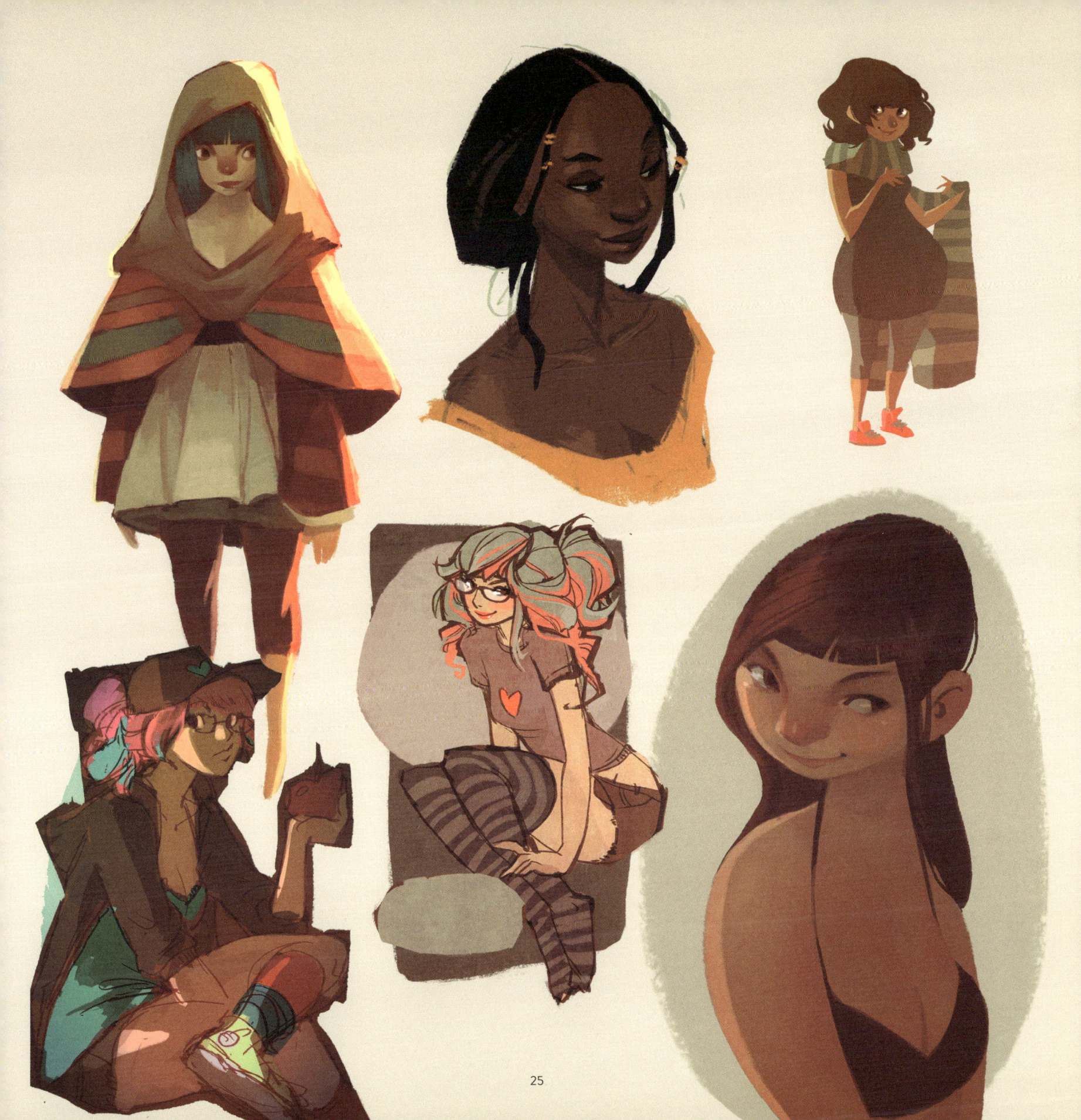

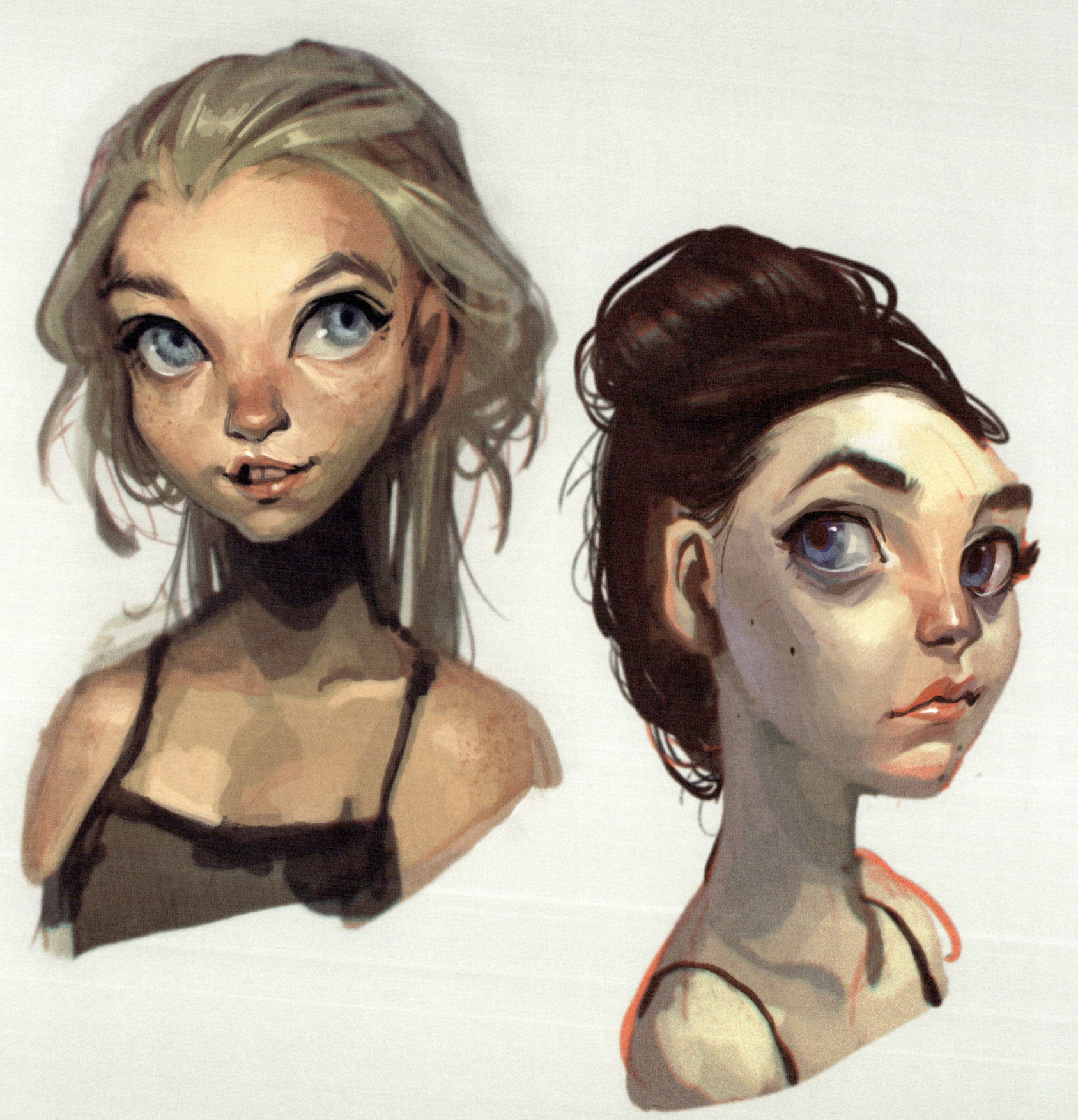

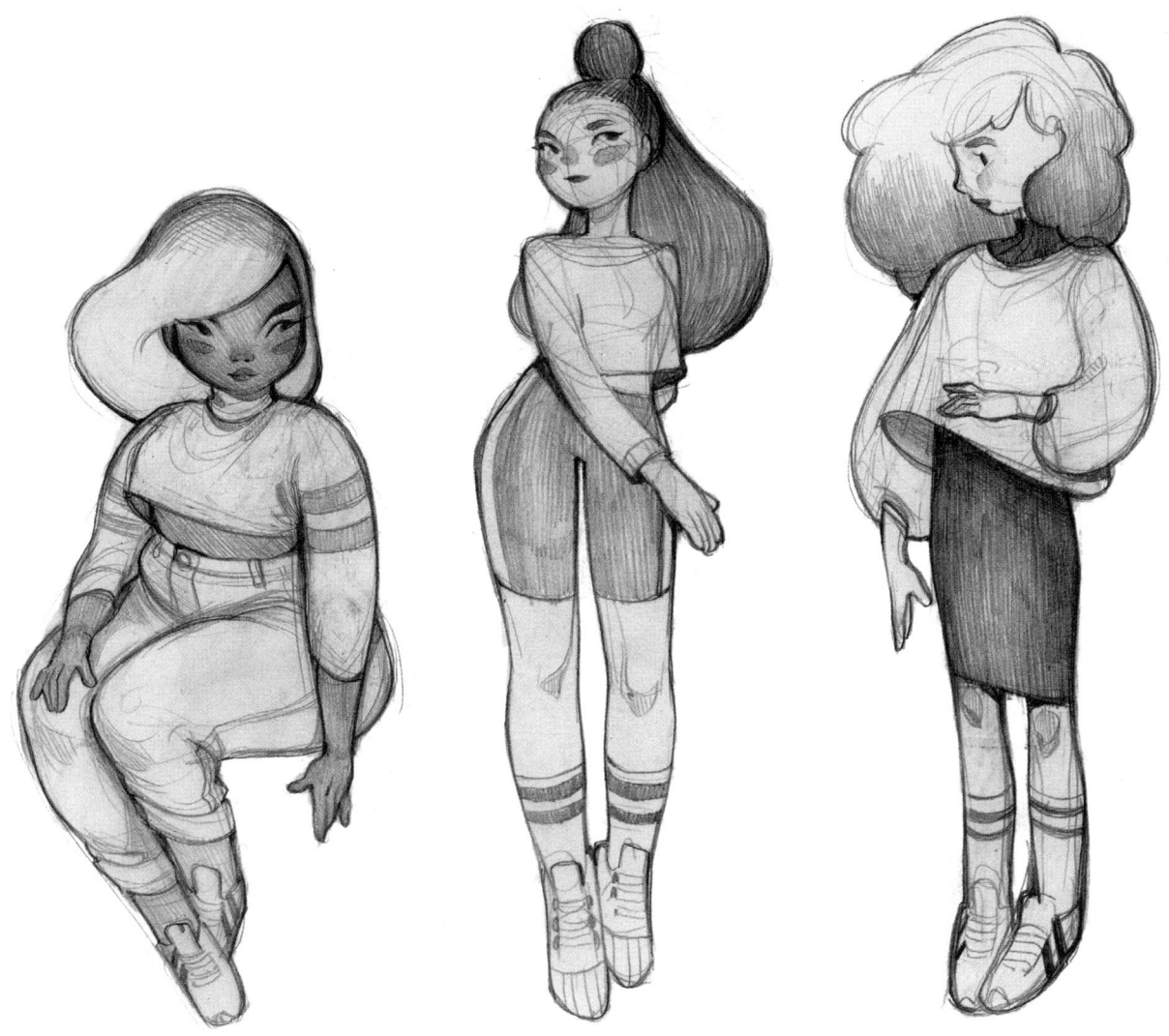

It is in this opportunistic mindset that I am able to experiment with my style. I am happy to exaggerate proportions more than I normally would, or try a different technique for shading. I might also introduce stylistic approaches that I have not tried before, like simple dots for eyes, or exaggerated shapes for the body. I allow myself to take a different course, and let go of any expectations for the end product. For me, this is truly drawing for fun.

This approach to drawing has yielded so many results! I try not to pressure myself by seeing my rough drawings as really important to my artistic growth, but in truth, they are. They have introduced me to new ways of working that are now part of my digital painting workflow, and to new visual elements to my drawing style. They have also attracted the attention of potential clients and led to paid work opportunities. However, I try not to think about all of this while sketching!

I think that a freedom to explore is one of the most important benefits of sketching for artists who are crafting their own style. It is the ideal situation in which to discover new techniques, and push your style a little further than you normally would. This is the space in which an artist's unique touch flourishes.

· sketching digitally ·

Many artists use digital tools exclusively for finished pieces, and stick to sketching on paper for their rougher work. This is understandable as the feeling of a pencil on paper is unmatched by any technology. I also find myself reaching for paper and pencil quite often. However, I think there are a lot of benefits to sketching digitally, especially given the increasing rate at which digital tools can mimic traditional drawing tools.

For me, the main benefit of sketching digitally is that it enables you to add color quickly and easily. Because of this, you are not limited to working only with lines; you can create color studies or experiment with new color schemes too. You can also choose from a wide range of brushes that bring different textures and personality to the brushstrokes.

Most importantly, digital tools allow the sketch to evolve in any direction. You can pile on as much detail as you like, or even turn the sketch into a finished piece.

I have often started a simple doodle with the intention of spending half an hour on it, only to spend days polishing it into a finished work. This is what I love about working digitally: there is so much flexibility and room to be spontaneous.

During the digital sketching process, it is important for me to keep my expectations low, and let the drawing evolve in its own way. Sometimes those initial sketch lines are unsuccessful and do not inspire me to move forward. This is fine though, since both failures and successes are part of the creative process.

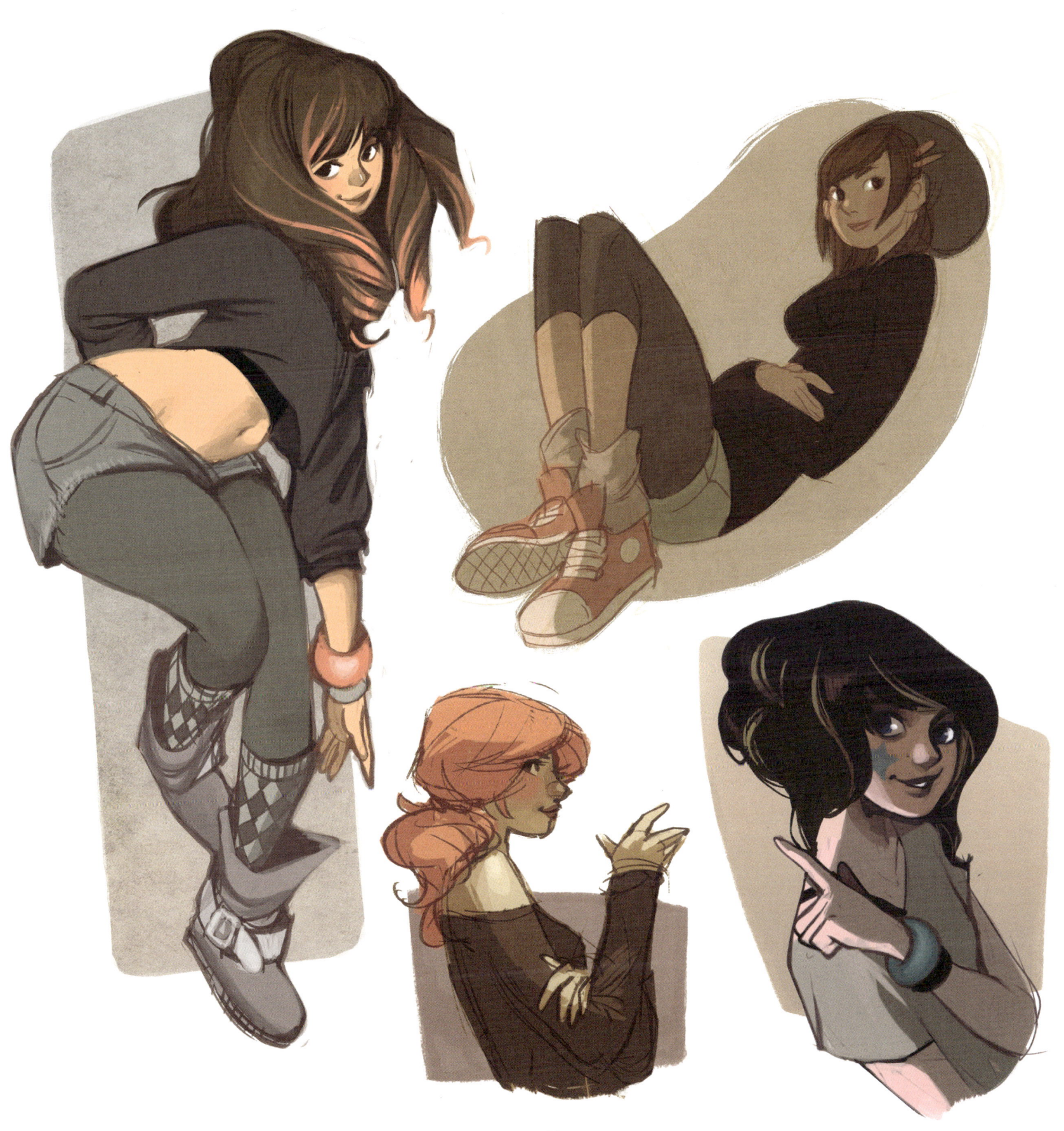

· speed painting ·

As a character artist, I work with a line-based approach by constructing my character in lines and develop the image from there. Because of this, it can be really refreshing to do speed paintings. This technique involves blocking in color and working as quickly as possible. As you can see in my speed painting tutorial on page 128, it is a very different workflow from the one I use to draw characters.

With digital paintings it is very tempting to apply a high level of detail over the whole image. Many people hold the belief that the more detailed a painting is, the better it must be. Some artists also believe that the more time they put in, the more rewarding the final work will be.

I have learned the hard way that this belief is not always true! There are various drawings that I spent a long time working on, only for the finished piece to lack the intended impact. The effort I had invested did not show through.

I have learned that the impact of a finished piece does not depend on the level of detail, but on the distribution of detail. It needs to be placed in such a way that it can be seen and appreciated. This is a skill I practice with speed painting.

By limiting the time I spend on one piece, I also limit the amount of detail I can apply. I have to be selective with what I spend time on, which is a handy skill for my overall workflow. The focus is on efficiency and expression.

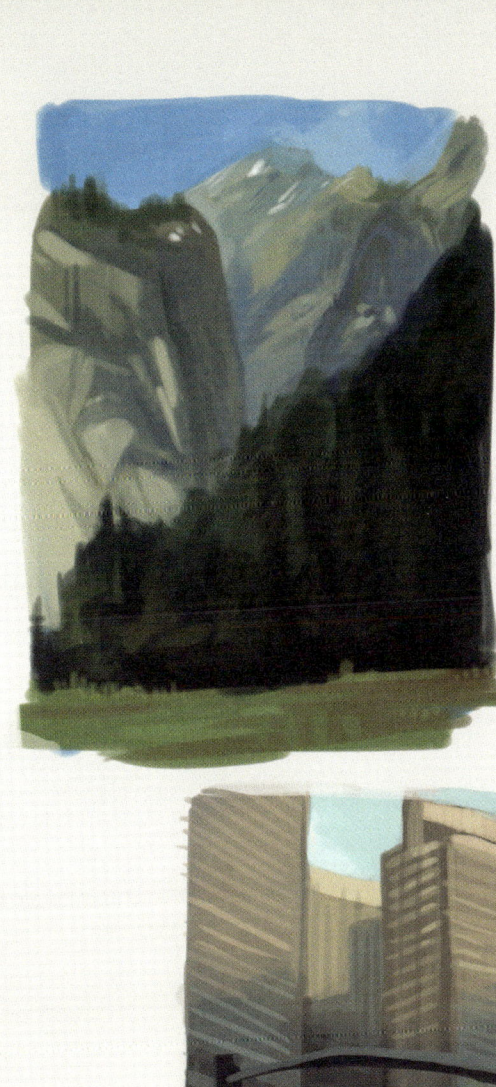
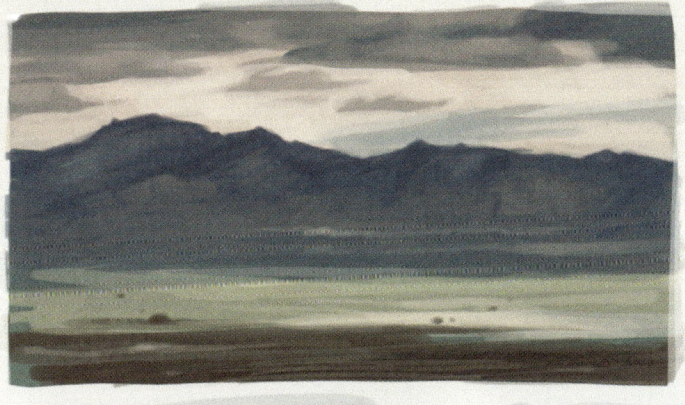
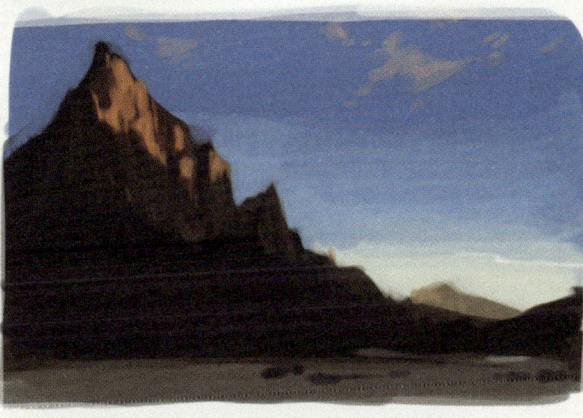
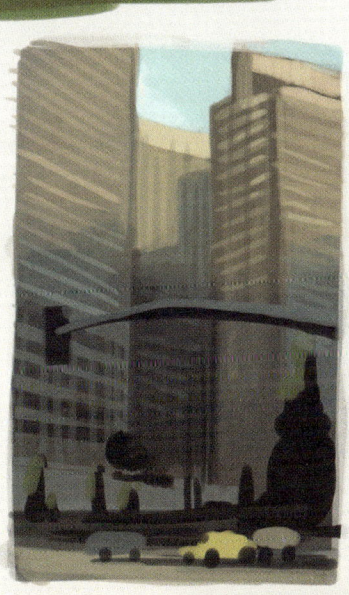
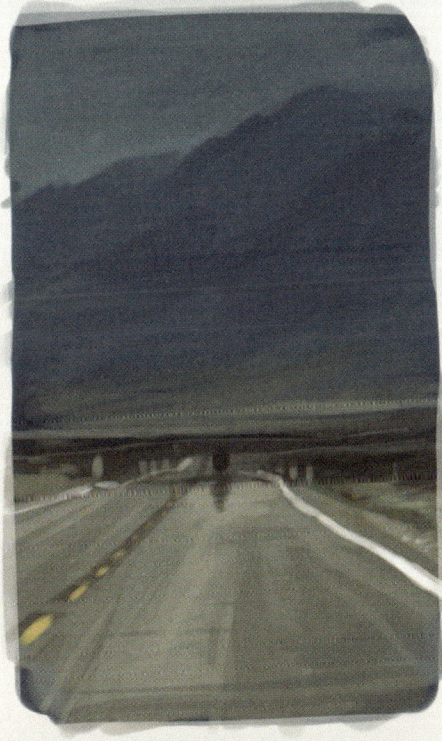
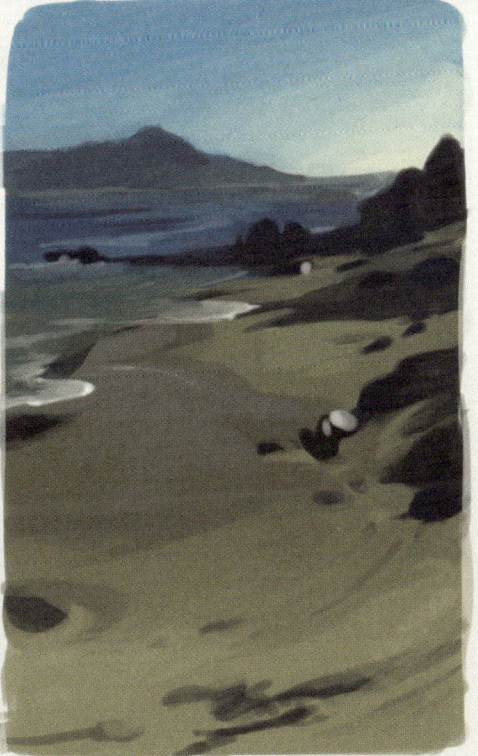
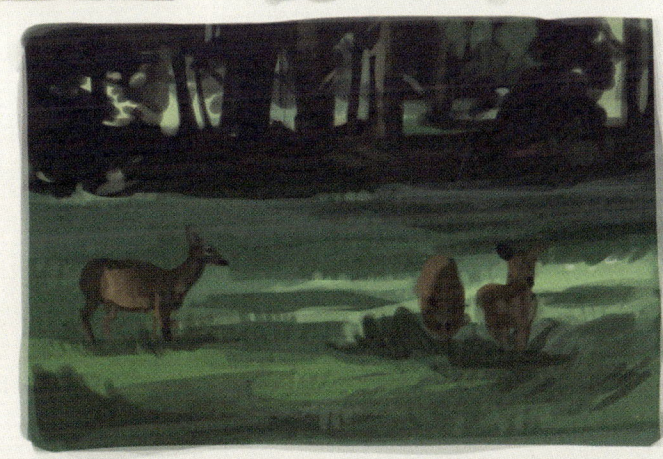

· mindset ·

I am not someone who rigorously insists on sketching every day. The reason for this is because I think it is important to have a relaxed mindset when sketching. There needs to be room to play around and learn new things. I use sketching as a way to relieve the pressure I put on myself when creating client work or finished digital pieces, which is why I leave sketching until the moment is right. If I forced myself to sketch daily, I would risk losing some of the spontaneity I need to create rough work.

So, rather than forcing myself to develop a regular sketching habit, I try to prioritize having time between projects in which I am free to draw whatever I want. It is only when my schedule is calm that I can clear my mind and think about what it is that I want to draw: a landscape, gesture sketch, or just a mindless sketch session on the couch. I only know when that time comes, and when that moment arrives, it always helps rekindle my creativity and motivation to create.

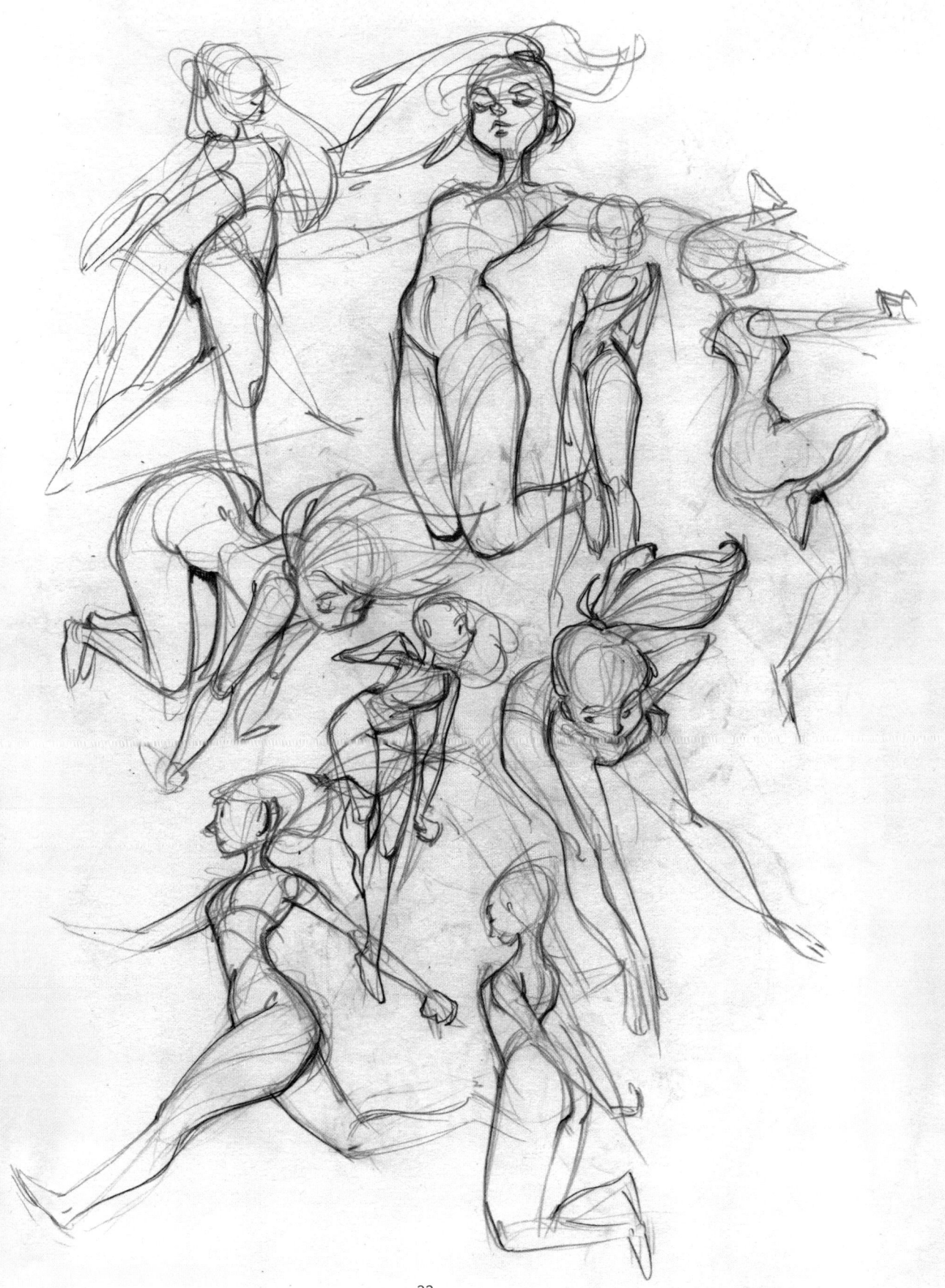

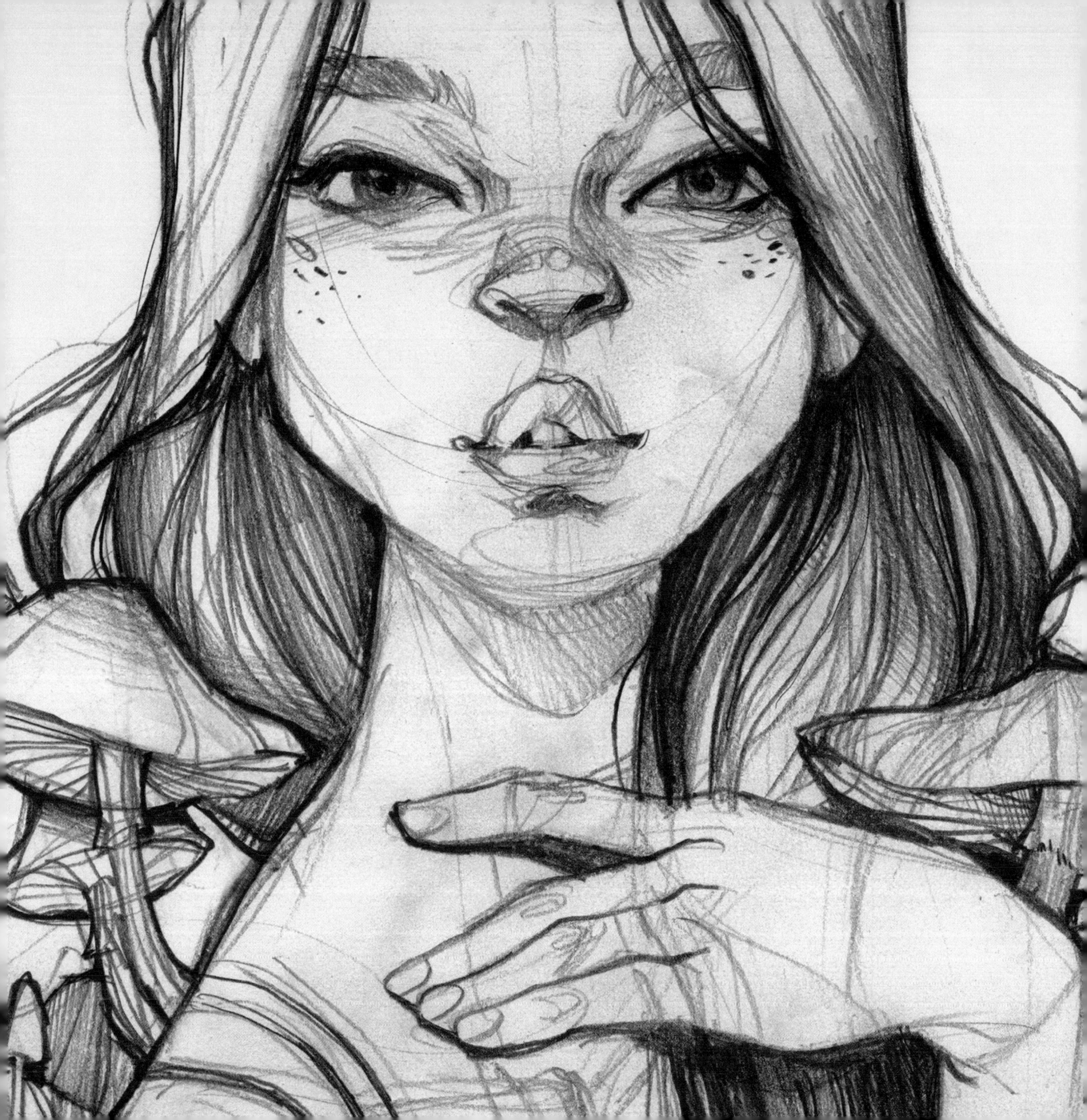

· character sketches ·

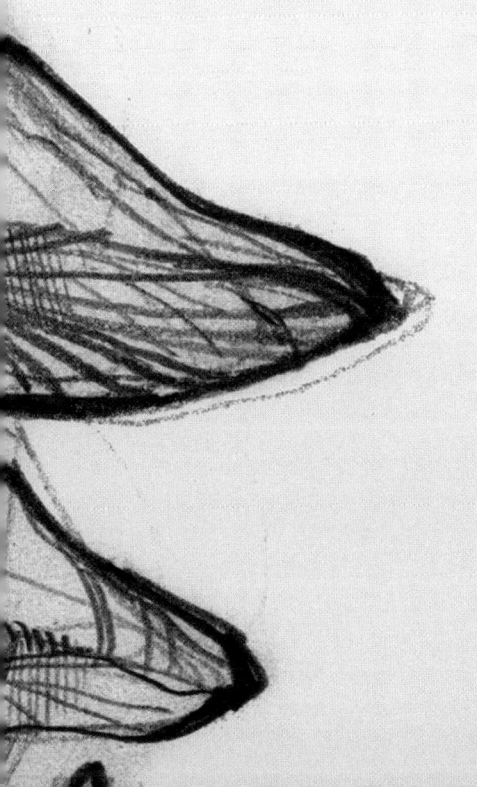

· character sketches ·

Ever since my first doodles as a toddler, I have loved to draw people. They were, and still continue to be, what inspire and motivate me the most. As a child I drew people I knew, such as my family and friends, but also characters I imagined like princesses, mermaids, and the cartoon characters that I loved to watch in animated films. In that sense, my artistic focus has not changed very much over the years!

When I discovered Art Nouveau and Japanese Manga as a teenager, I felt so excited by the stylistic elements that could be used to convey these beautiful and ethereal people. This motivated me to learn more about character design, and still spurs me on today.

My main inspirations are Disney and Alphonse Mucha's Art Nouveau posters, so it has always felt natural to me to draw mostly feminine characters. It is the type of artwork that draws me in the most and really sparks my imagination. To me, these characters are beautiful and inspiring, but also warm and friendly. They radiate confidence, but also sensitivity and kindness.

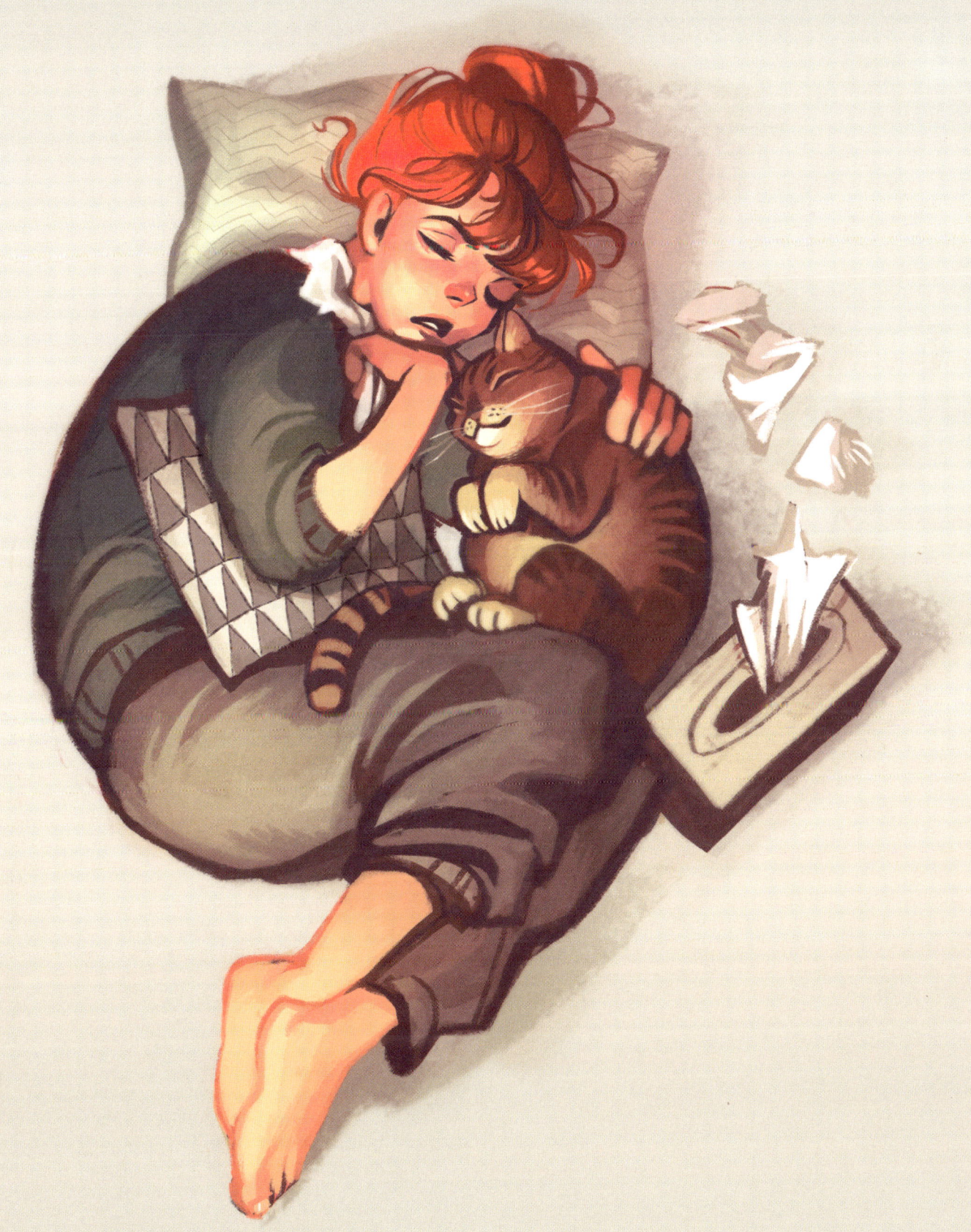

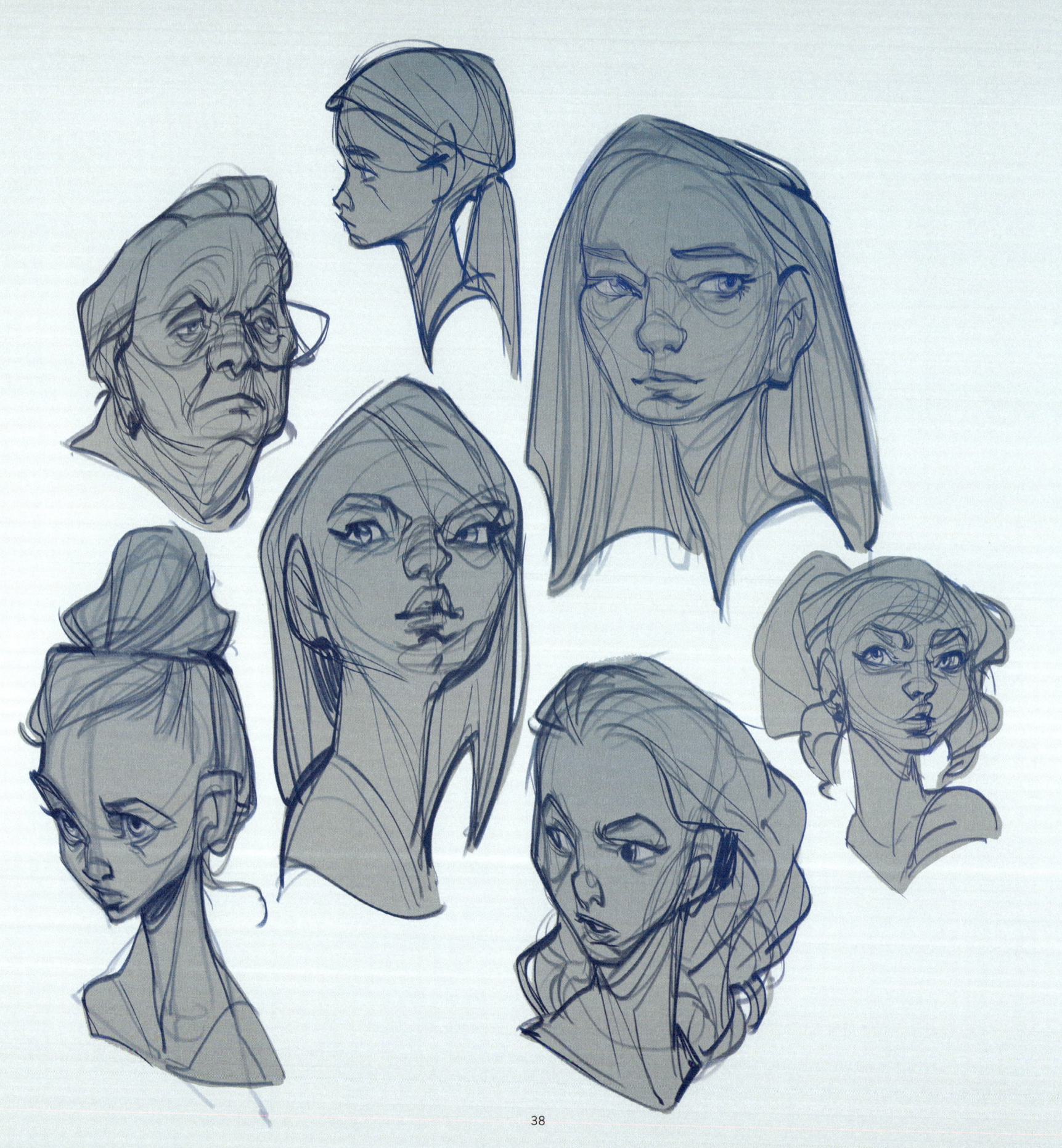

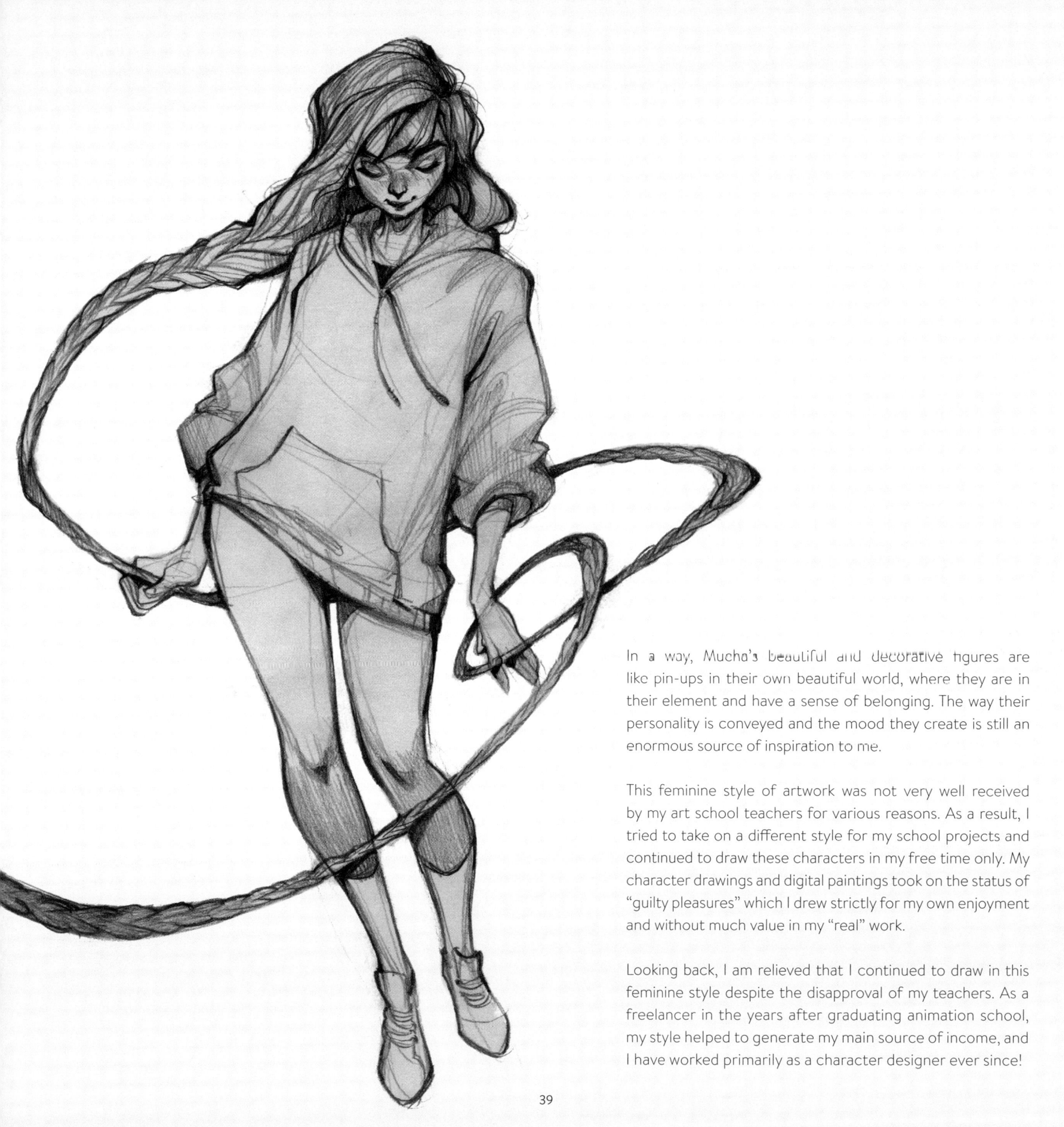

In a way, Mucha's beautiful and decorative figures are like pin-ups in their own beautiful world, where they are in their element and have a sense of belonging. The way their personality is conveyed and the mood they create is still an enormous source of inspiration to me.

This feminine style of artwork was not very well received by my art school teachers for various reasons. As a result, I tried to take on a different style for my school projects and continued to draw these characters in my free time only. My character drawings and digital paintings took on the status of "guilty pleasures" which I drew strictly for my own enjoyment and without much value in my "real" work.

Looking back, I am relieved that I continued to draw in this feminine style despite the disapproval of my teachers. As a freelancer in the years after graduating animation school, my style helped to generate my main source of income, and I have worked primarily as a character designer ever since!

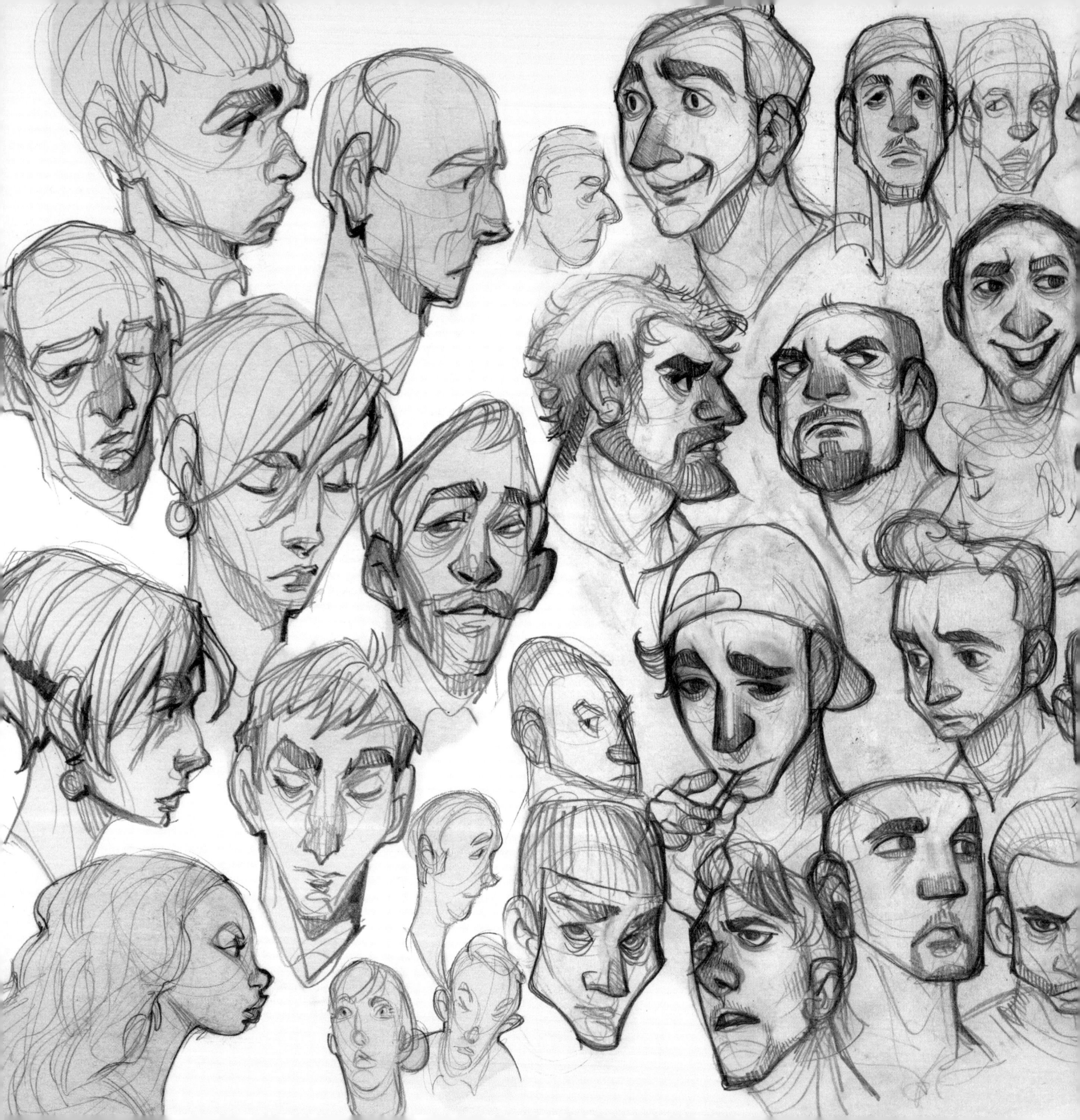

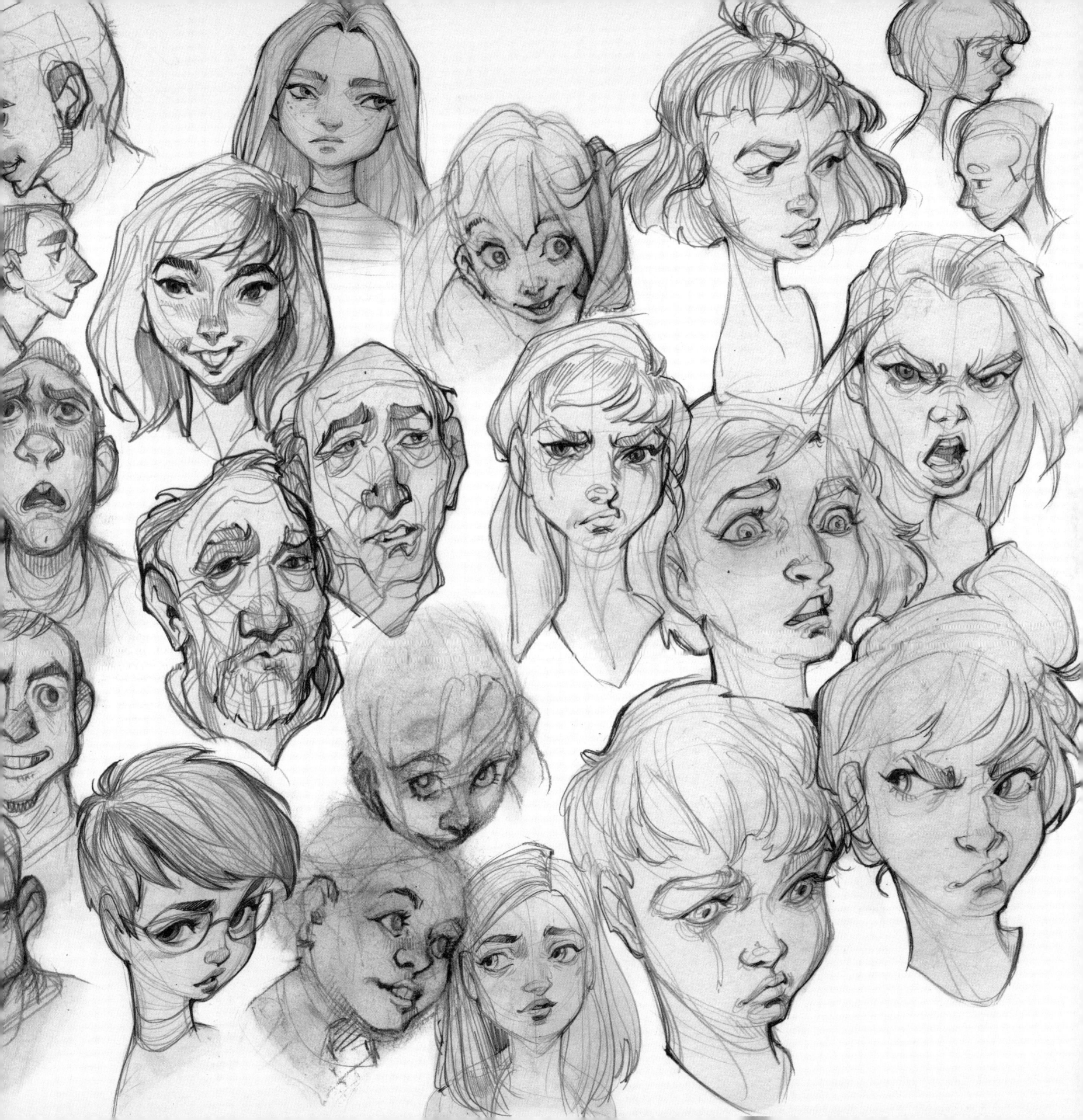

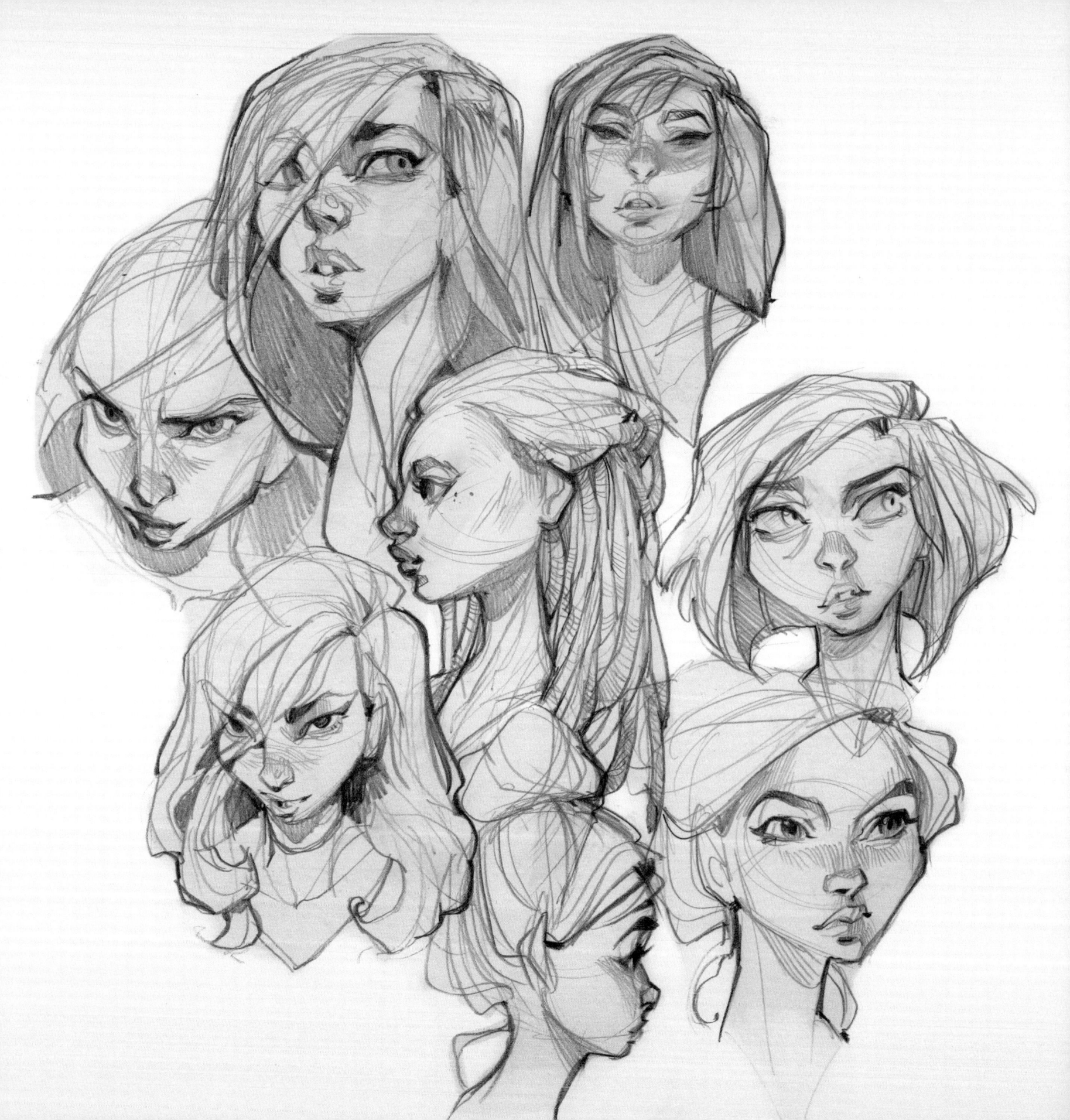

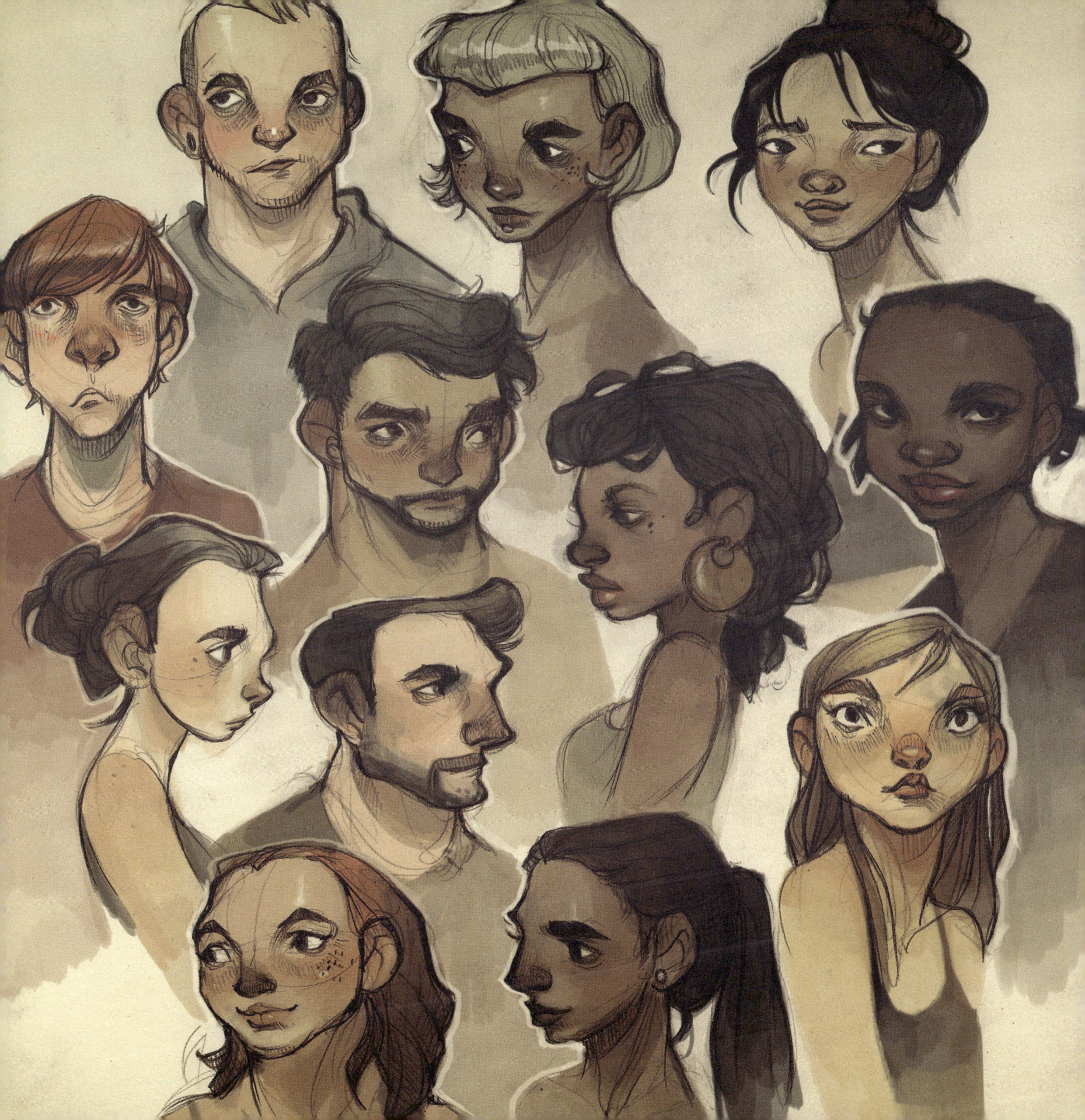

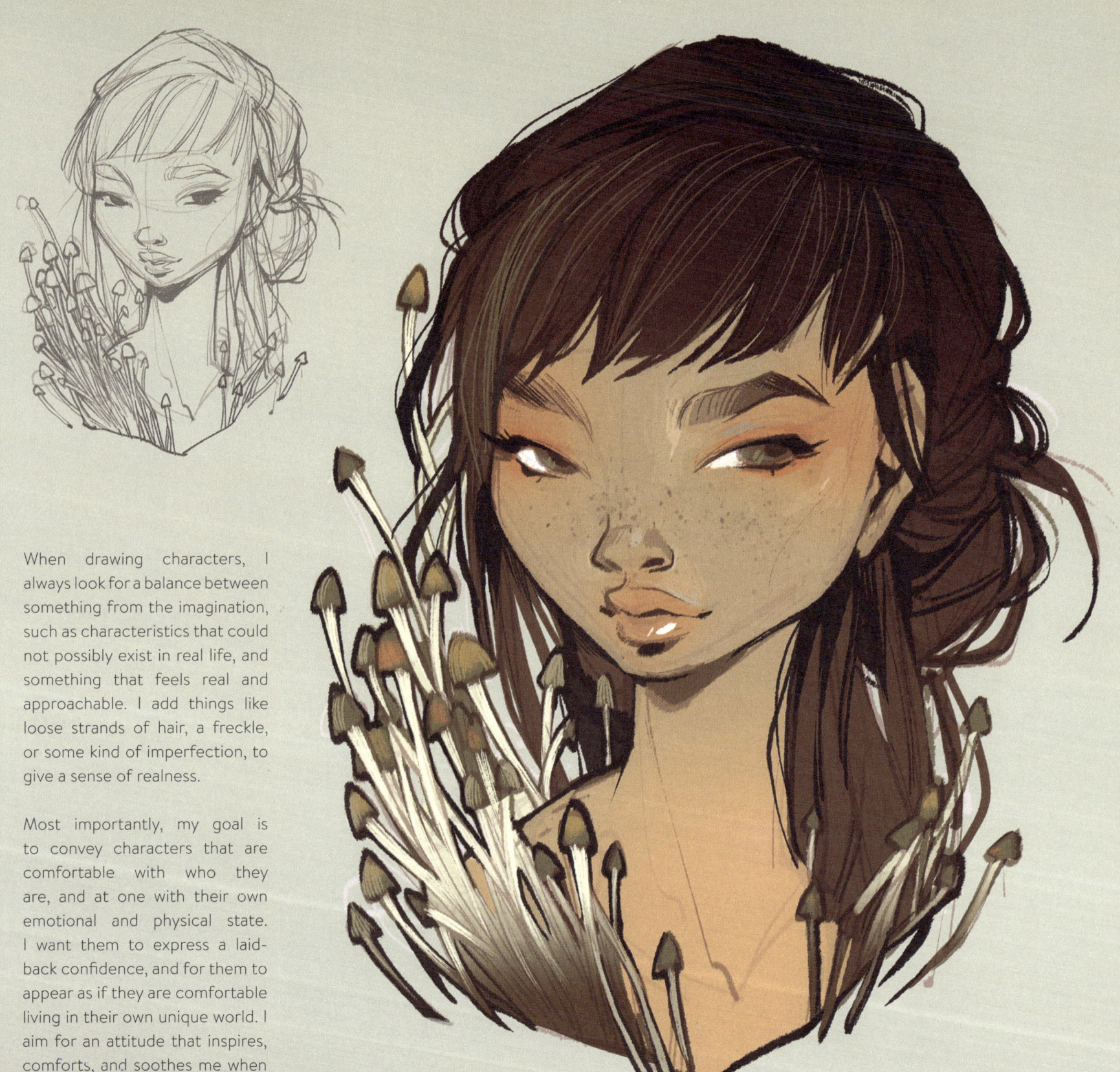

When drawing characters, I always look for a balance between something from the imagination, such as characteristics that could not possibly exist in real life, and something that feels real and approachable. I add things like loose strands of hair, a freckle, or some kind of imperfection, to give a sense of realness.

Most importantly, my goal is to convey characters that are comfortable with who they are, and at one with their own emotional and physical state. I want them to express a laid-back confidence, and for them to appear as if they are comfortable living in their own unique world. I aim for an attitude that inspires, comforts, and soothes me when I see it in others.

44

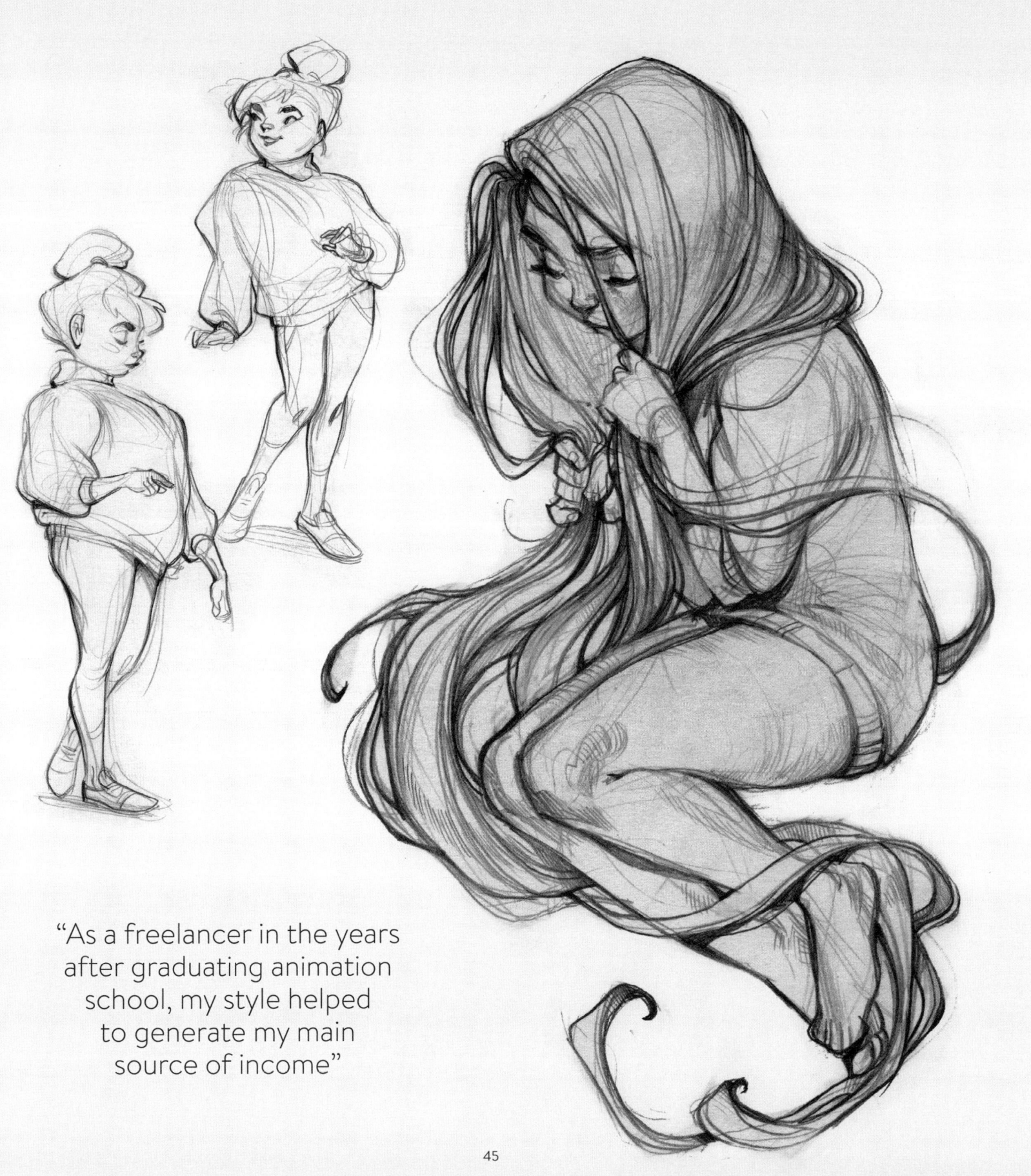

"As a freelancer in the years after graduating animation school, my style helped to generate my main source of income"

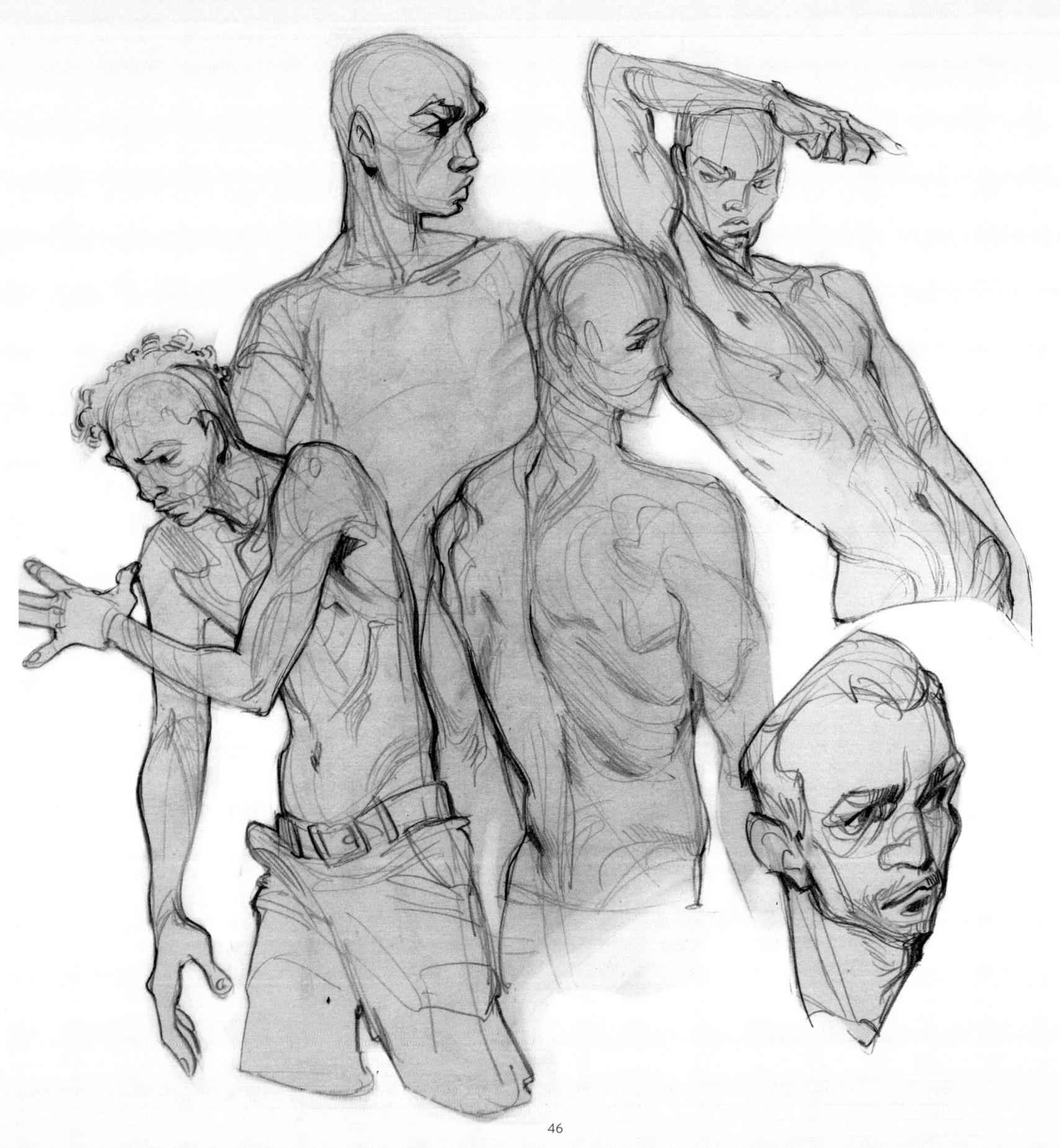

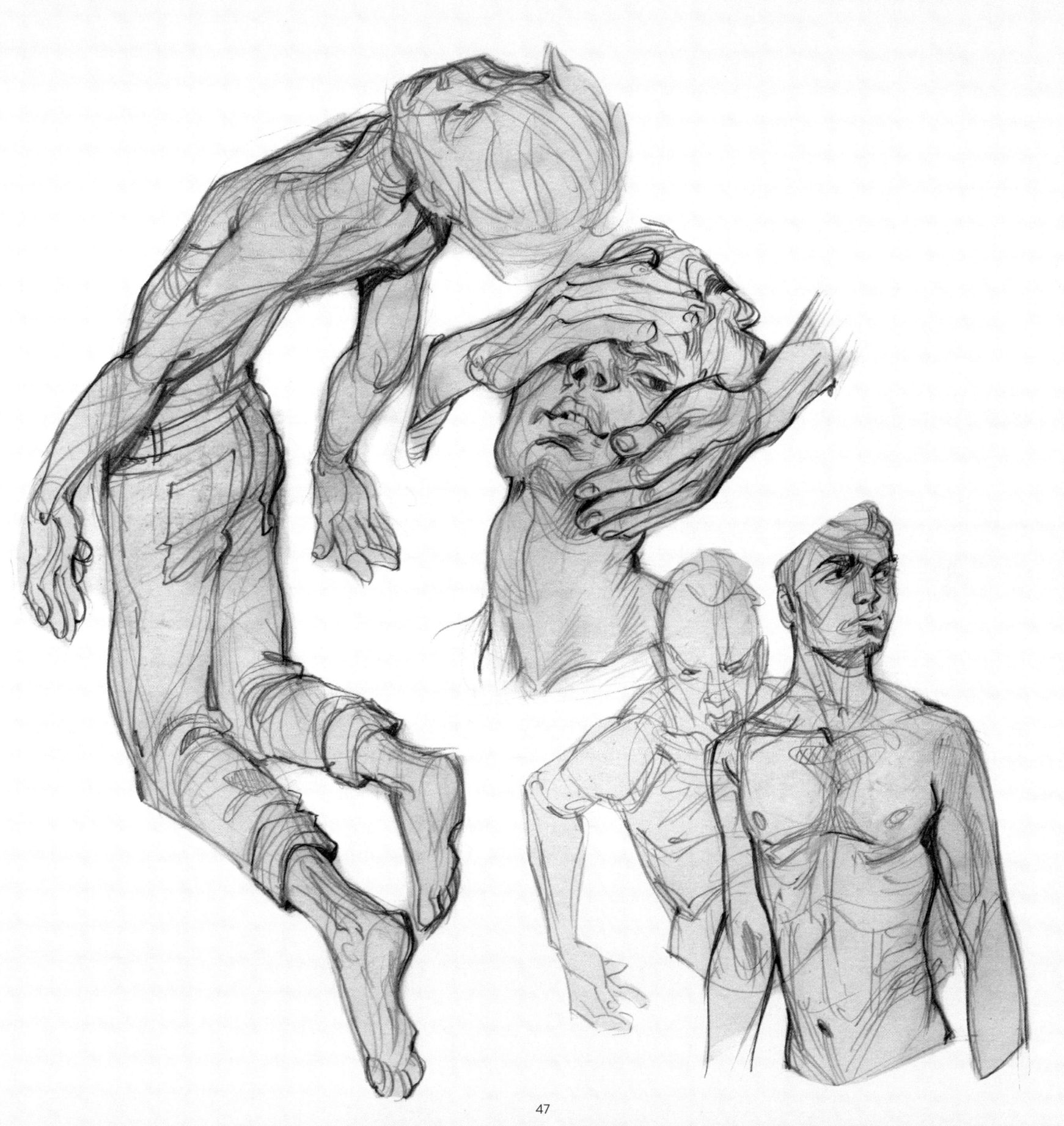

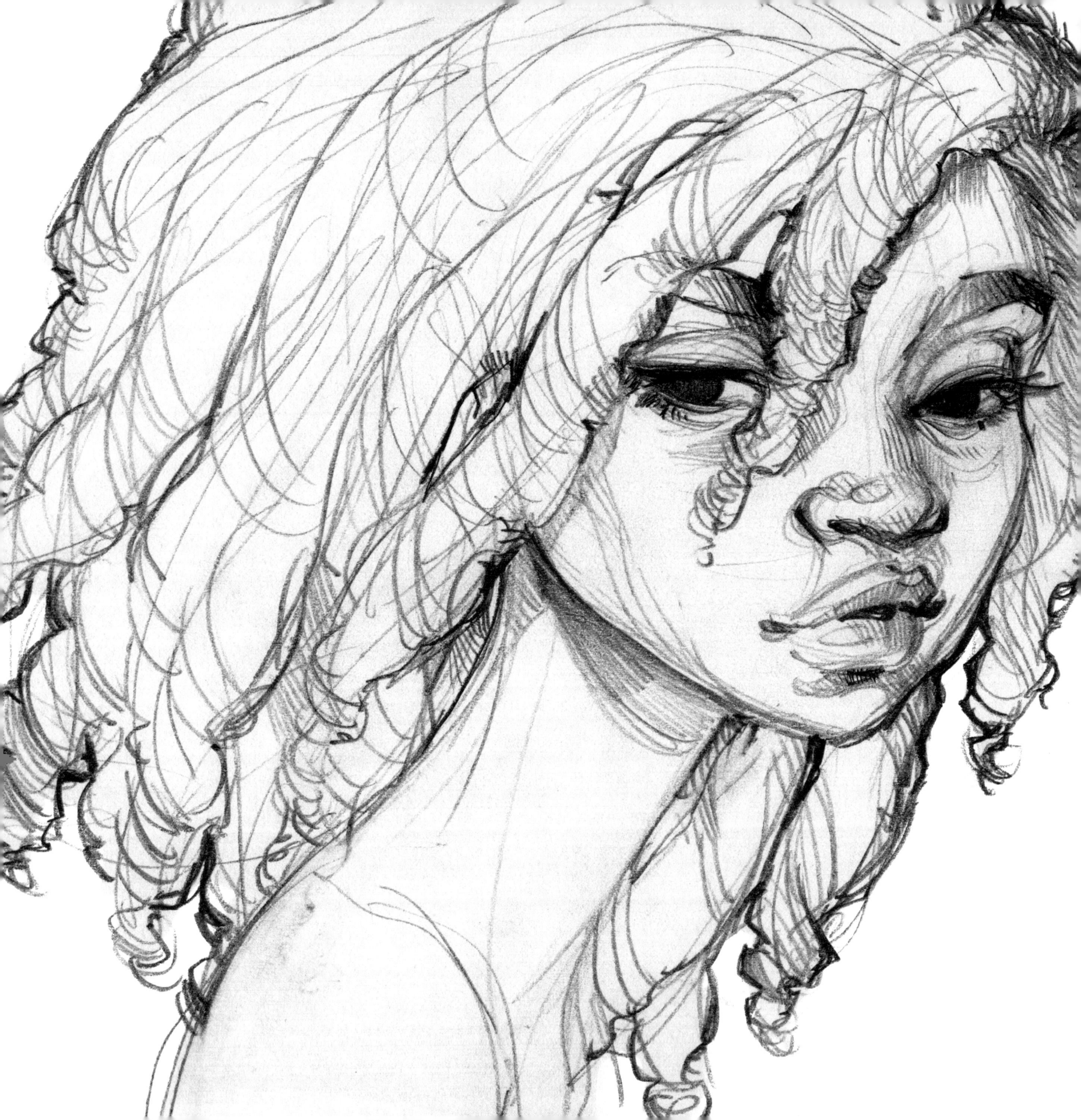

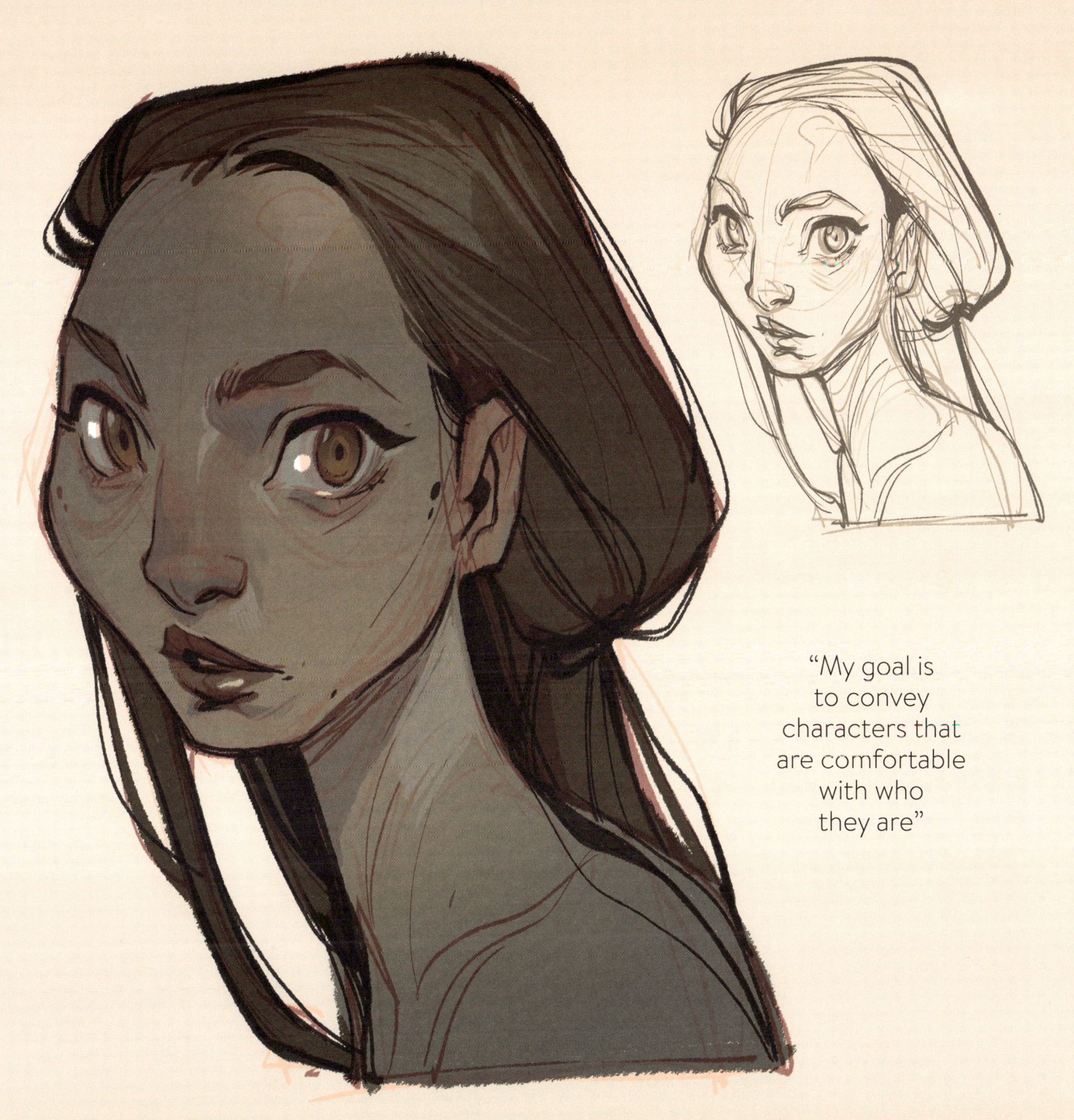

"My goal is to convey characters that are comfortable with who they are"

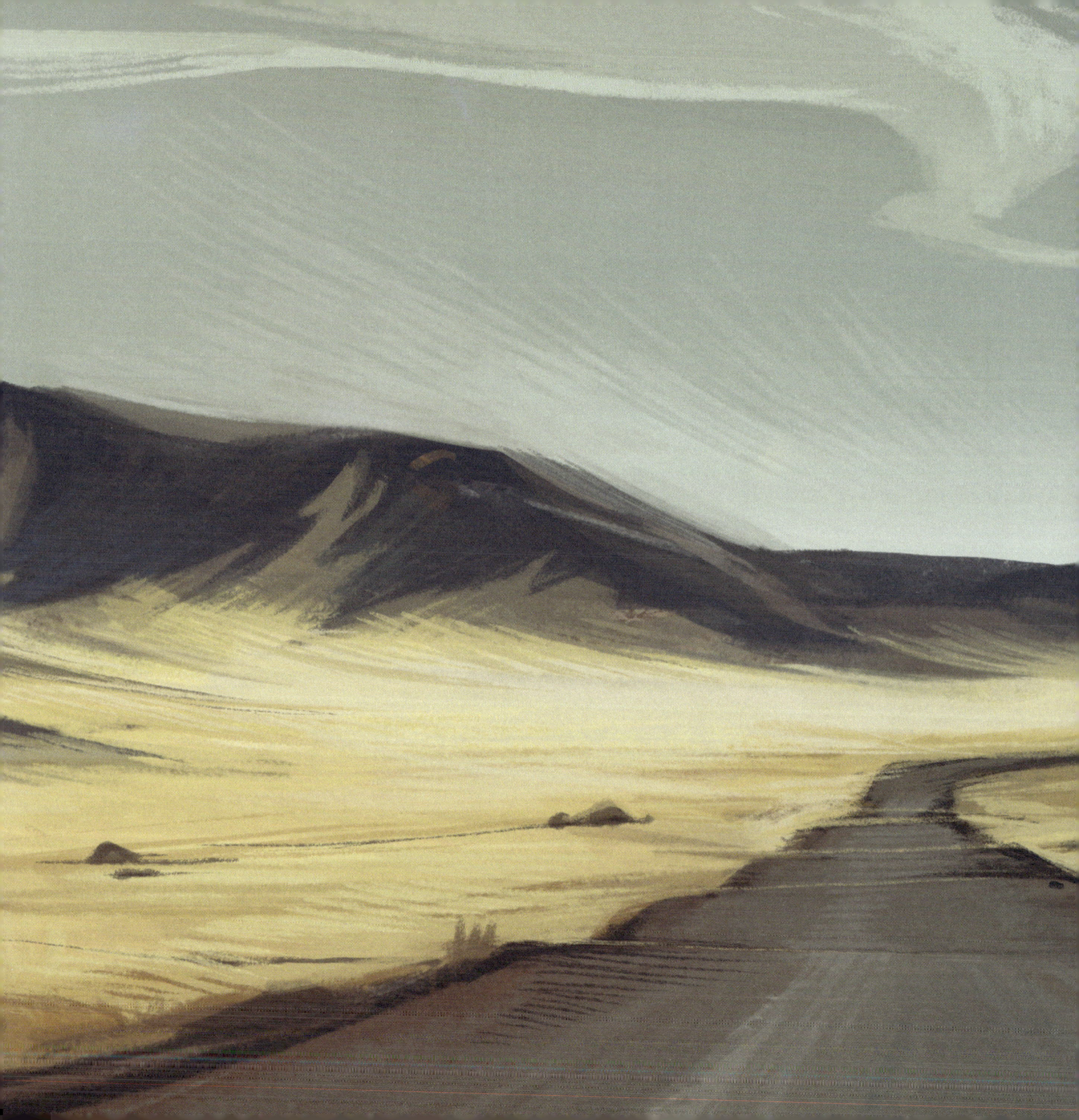

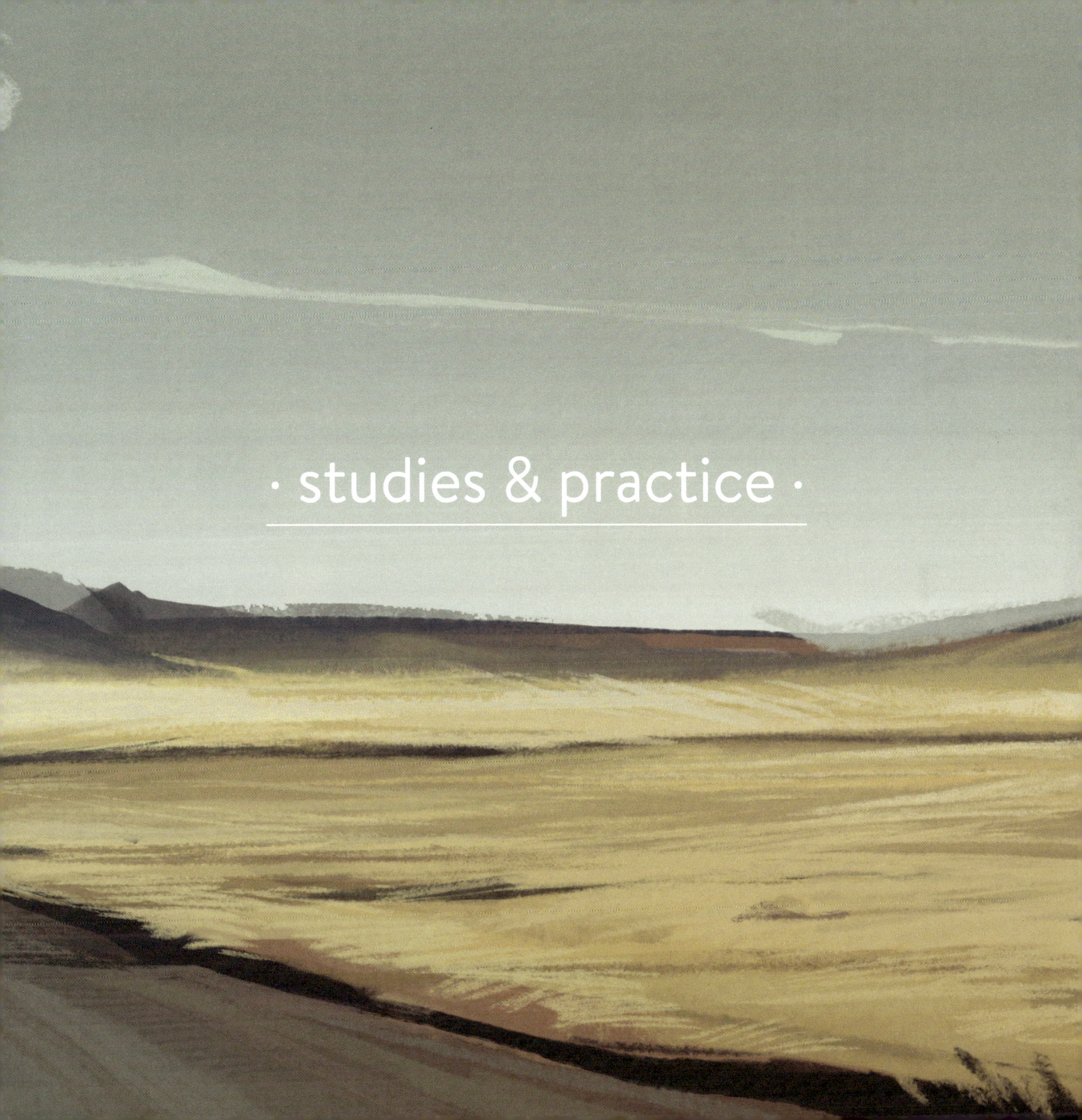

· studies & practice ·

· studies & practice ·

For me, creating studies and sketches from reference is a welcome break from my usual workflow. Drawing from the imagination is fun but also quite challenging, especially when you are staring at a blank canvas, racking your brain for ideas on what to draw. When you use references, the first step has already been taken: the subject for the drawing already exists. In this case the artist is a translator, converting the original material into a new creation. I find it a relief from the pressure of generating ideas from scratch.

I choose to do sketches and studies for a variety of reasons. Sometimes, it is because I am not sure how to draw a certain thing from memory, like an animal or a specific type of plant. By studying it, I can learn the new shapes and forms, and introduce them into my visual vocabulary.

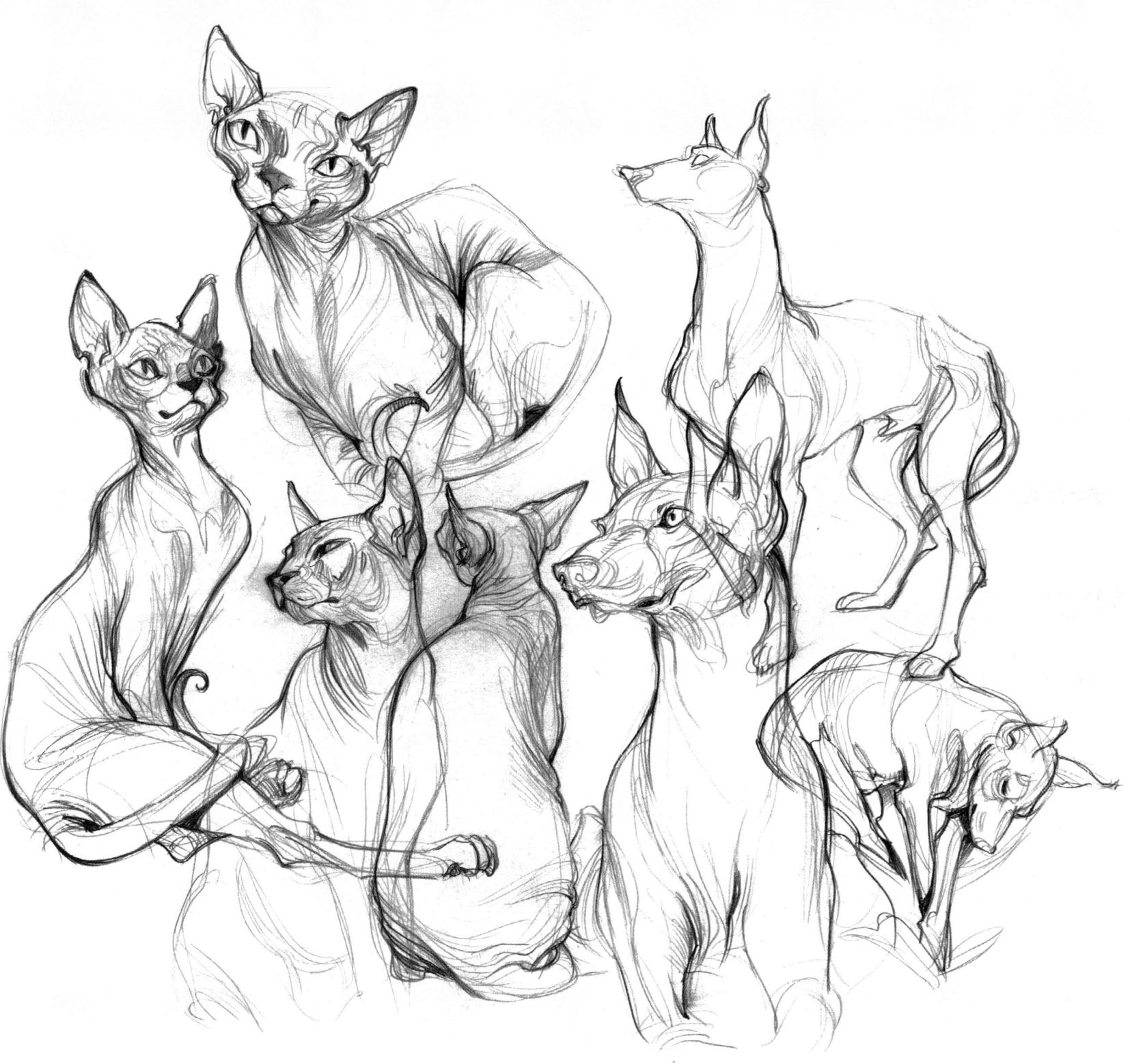

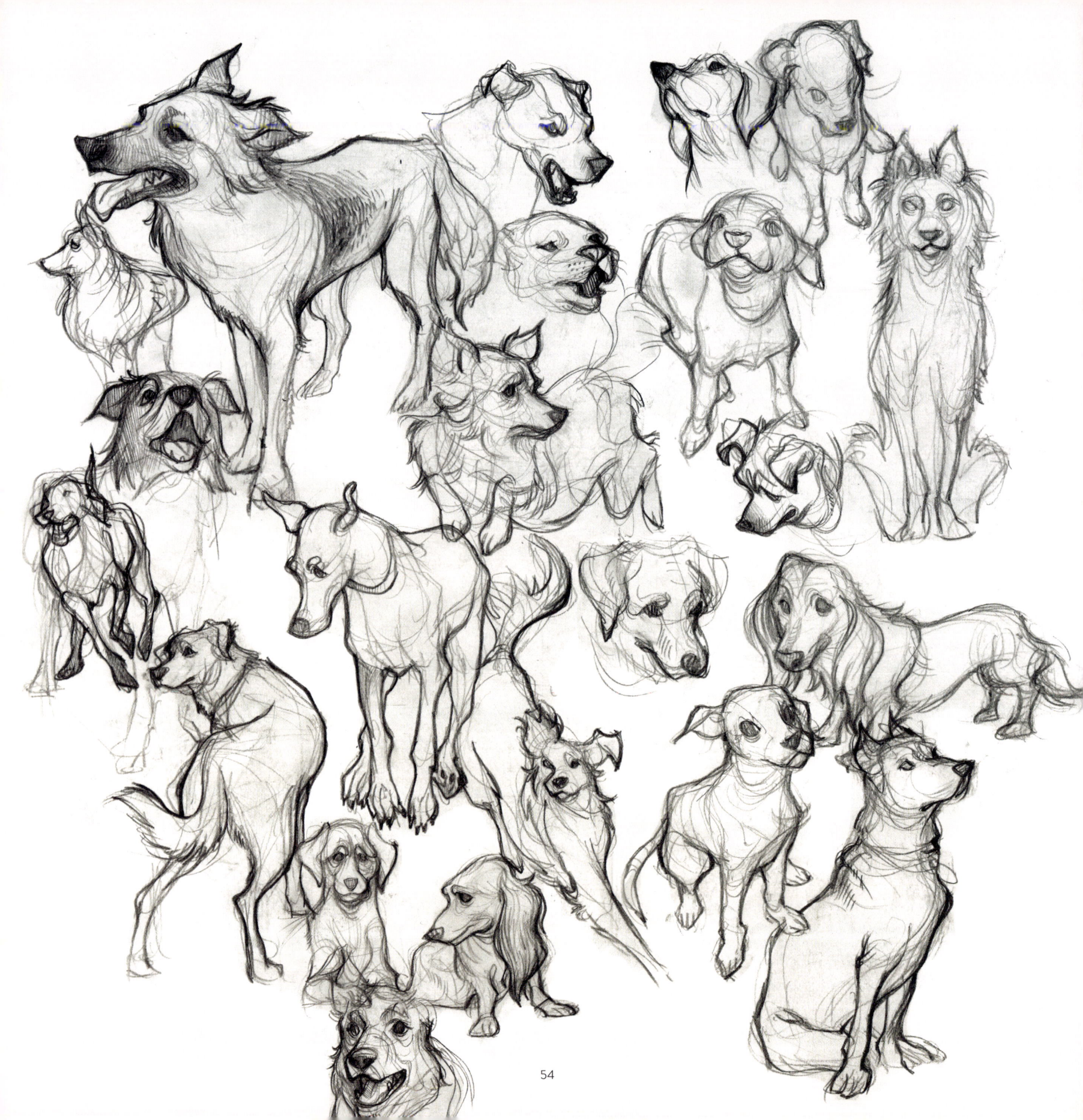

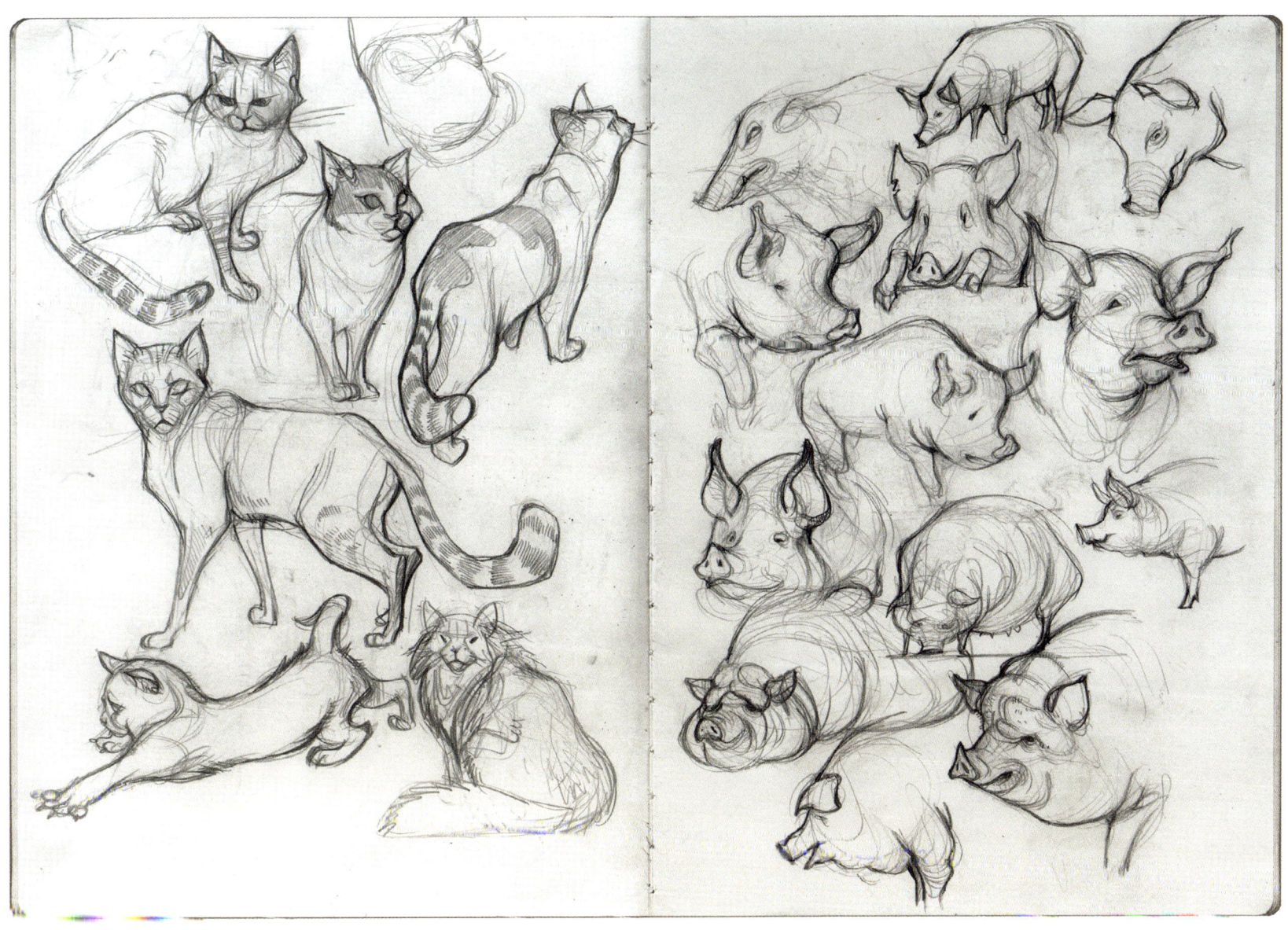

At other times, I study something that I draw often such as faces, bodies, and hands, to extend my knowledge further. Over time, I have gradually been able to increase the level of detail in my drawings as a result of learning from these studies.

As someone who learned how to draw by using references, my brain tends to default to creating a close copy of my reference image. However, when I get into this mindset, I tend not to learn anything new because I have been drawing that way since I was very young. It is almost like drawing on auto pilot. Because of this, I always try to set a specific challenge for myself before drawing from reference, which helps me to train my eye to look more critically at the reference image. Instead of making photo studies of people, I think of them as skin tone studies or gesture sketches. Rather than just drawing environments in general, I think of these studies in terms of lighting exploration or ways to capture depth.

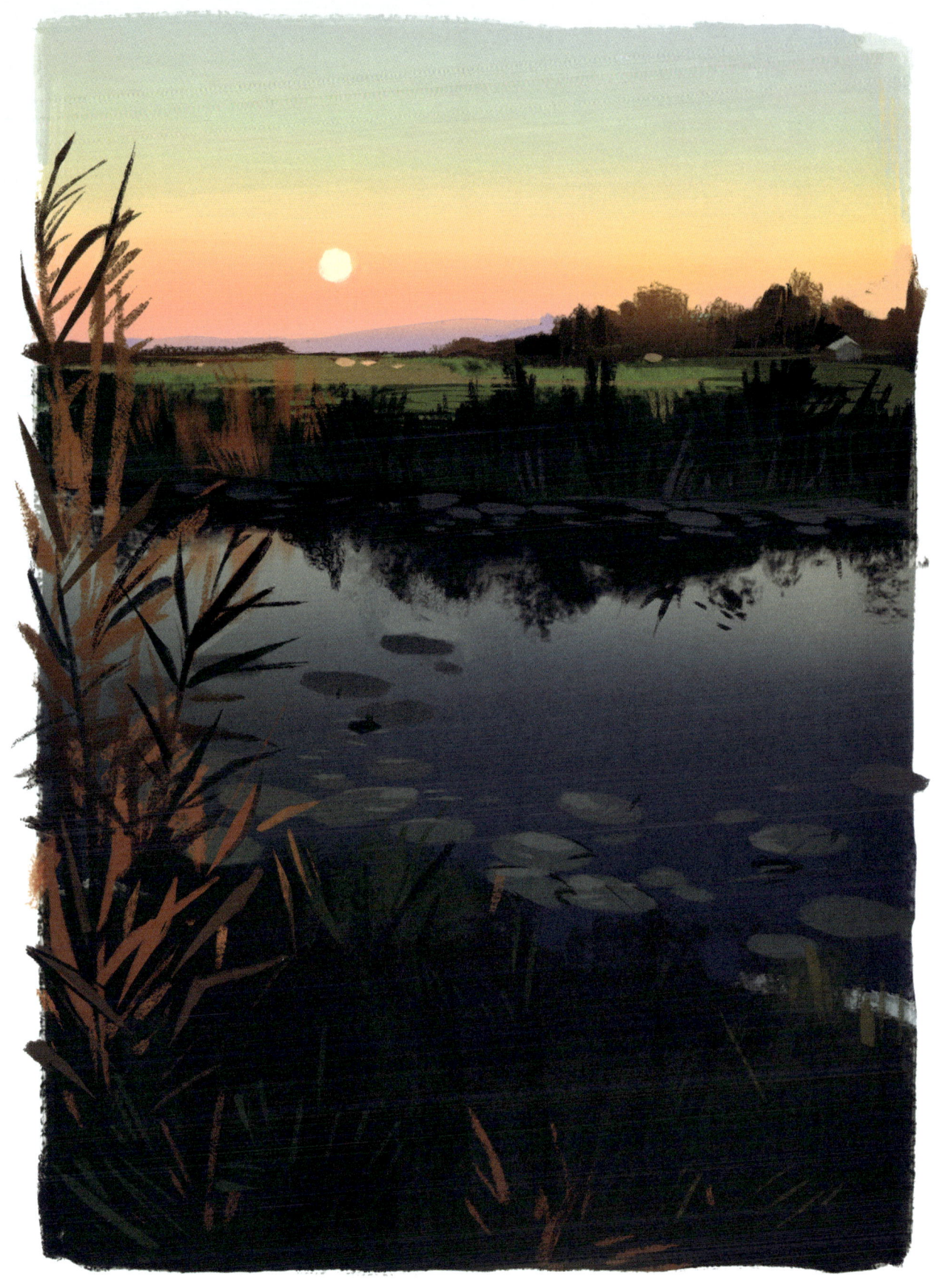

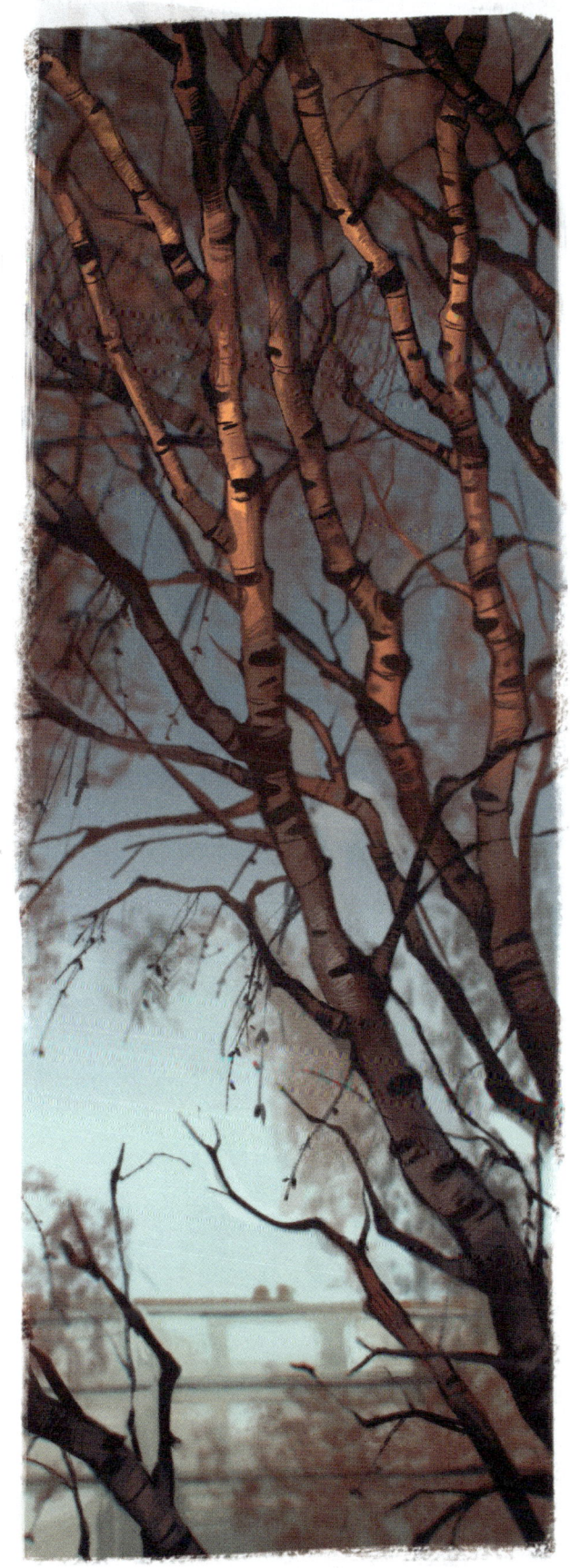
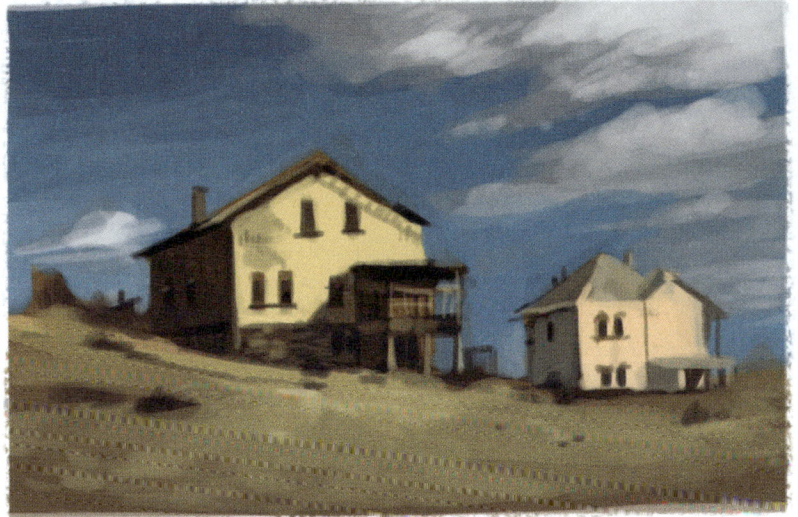
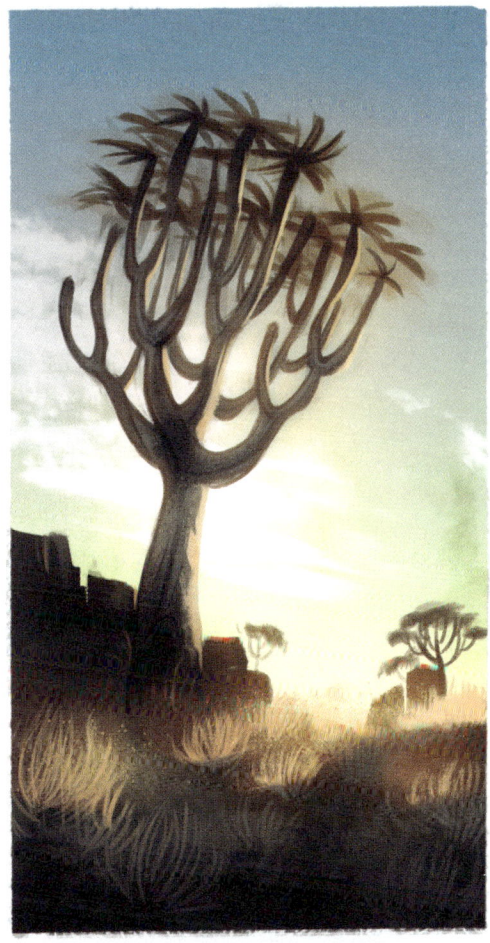
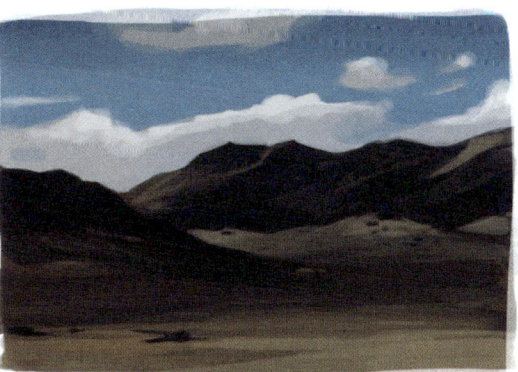
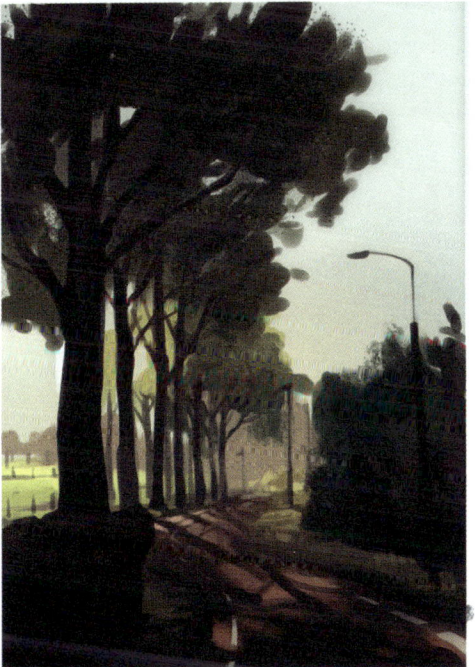
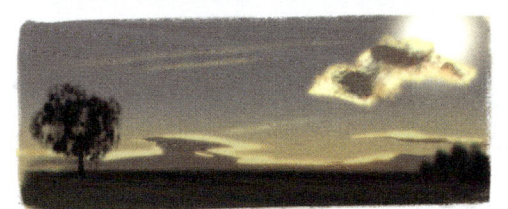

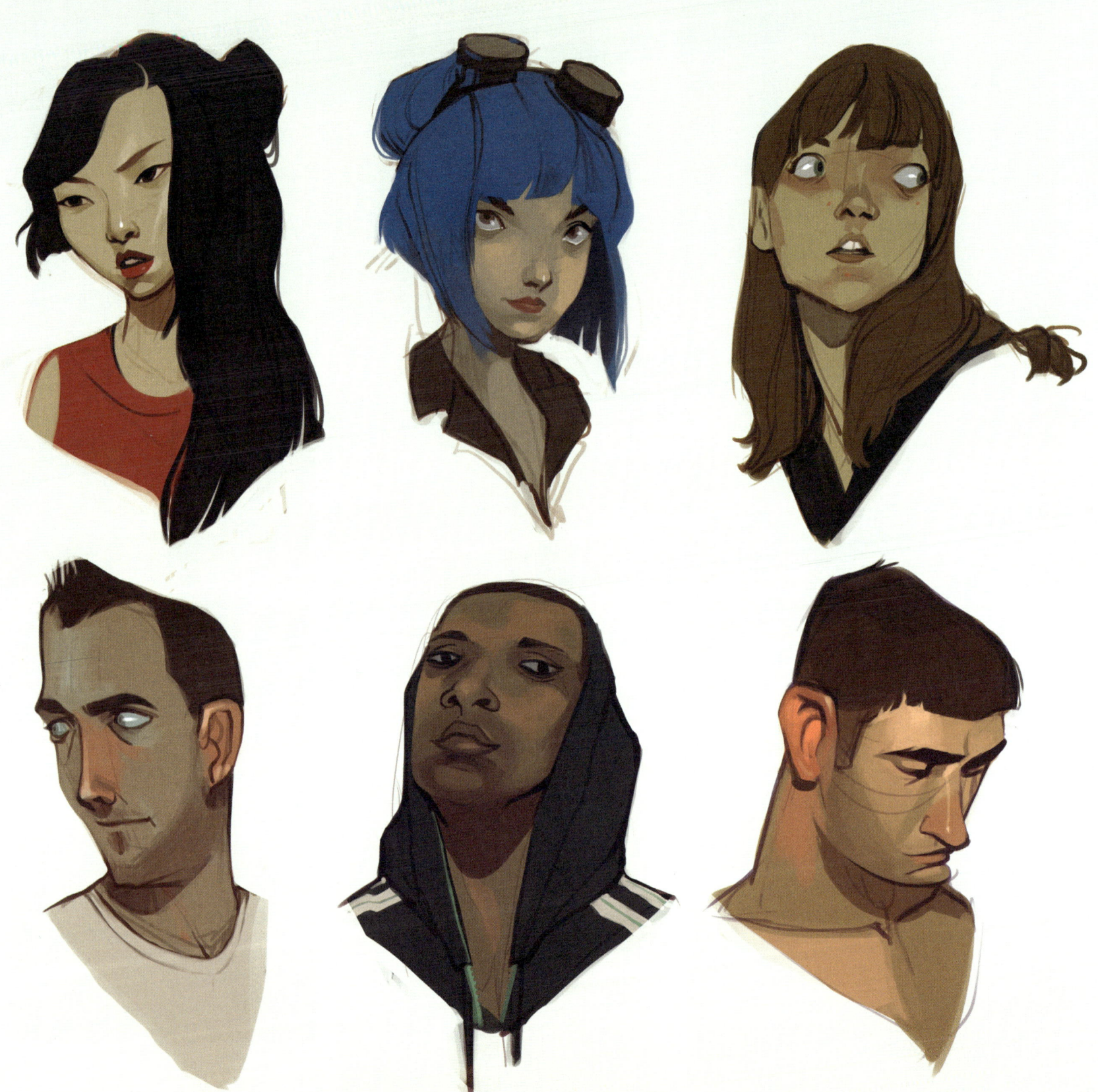

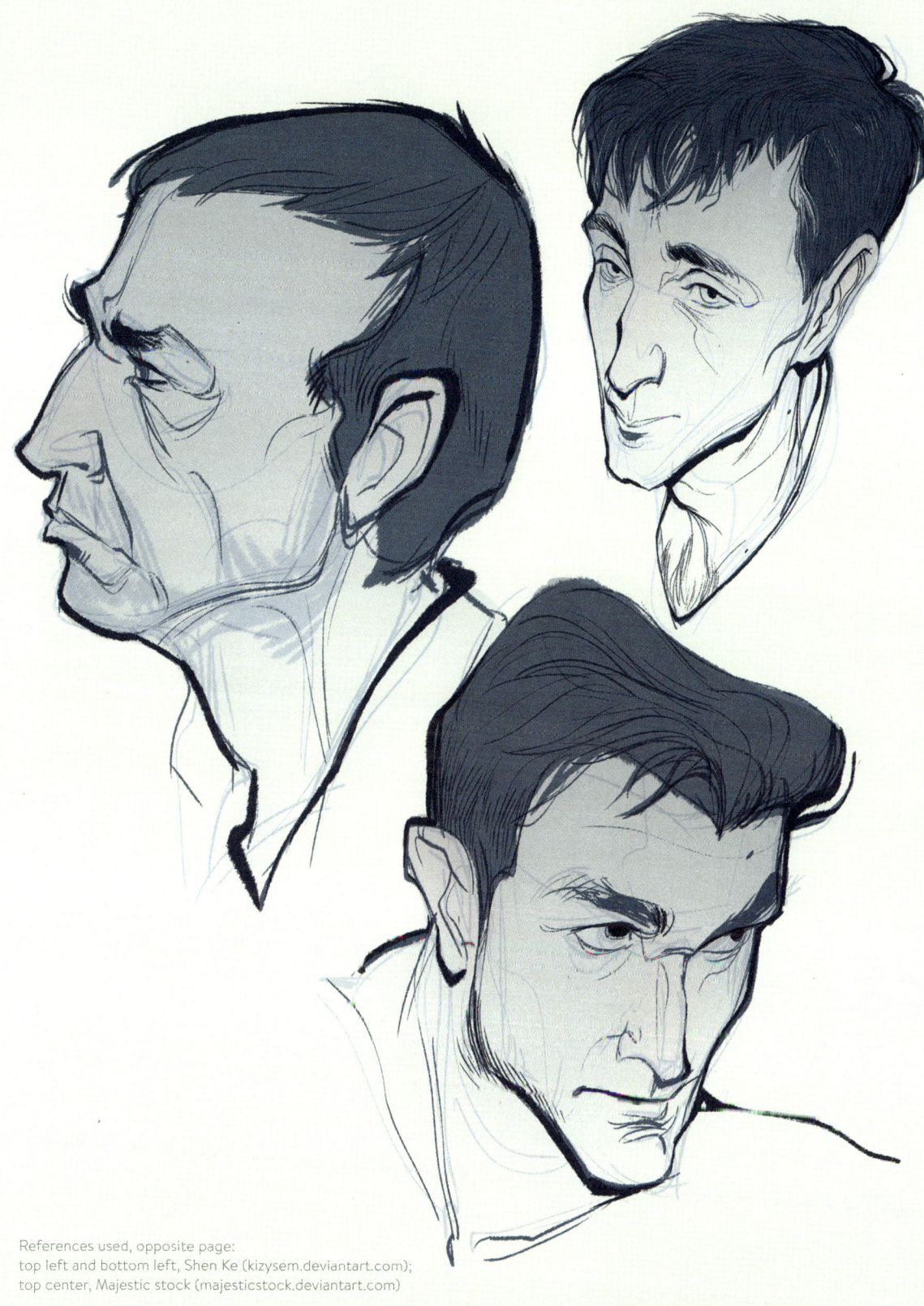

As a character artist, I often focus on portraying people and, as a result, I tend to skip backgrounds and environments. To restore some balance, I love making speed paintings of landscapes and settings that inspire me in my daily life, which you can see in this chapter. It is an ongoing challenge for me to modify my painting style to something that suits an environment, especially given the unique variety of textures, shapes, and perspectives that can be found in nature.

Most importantly, doing studies and speed paintings of landscapes and nature helps me to understand color. I learn how depth is created through color perspective, how different color temperatures interact, and how different times of day change the intensity and warmth of daylight.

Creating studies is a way for me to practice the act of translating my style onto different subjects. I try to find a balance between falling back into my usual artistic comfort zone, and challenging myself to draw and see in a different way. In this sense, it is not just a way for me to practice my skills, but it is also an essential step in the creation and development of my own visual style.

References used, opposite page:
top left and bottom left, Shen Ke (kizysem.deviantart.com);
top center, Majestic stock (majesticstock.deviantart.com)

Reference used above left: Jade Macalla (jademacalla.deviantart.com)

Rerences used right and top right: SenshiStock (senshistock.com)

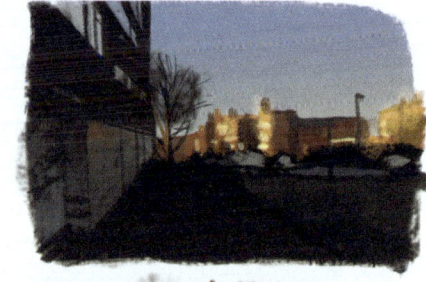
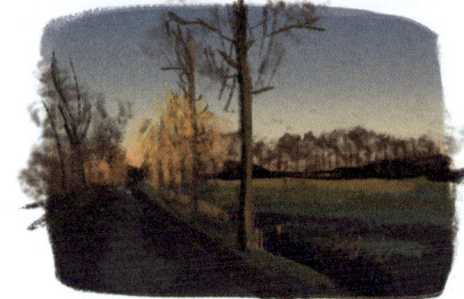
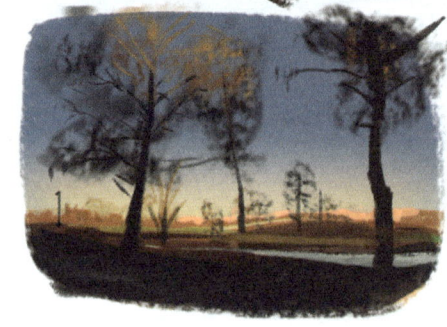
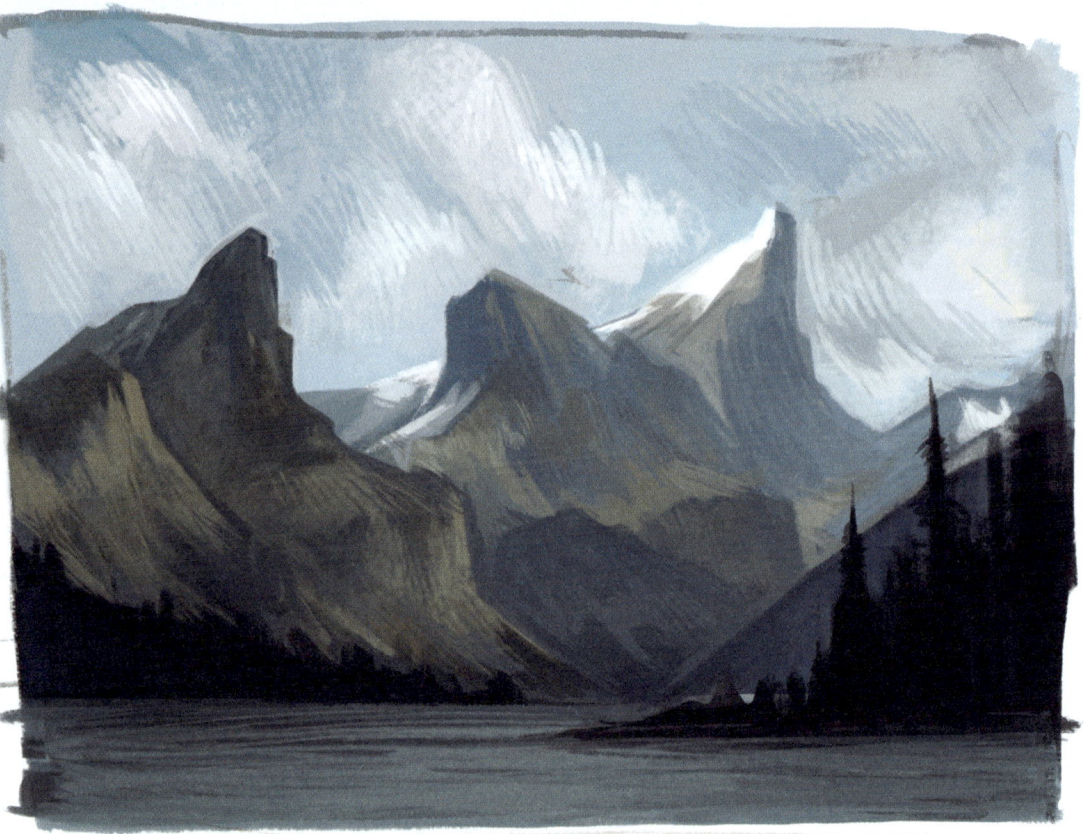
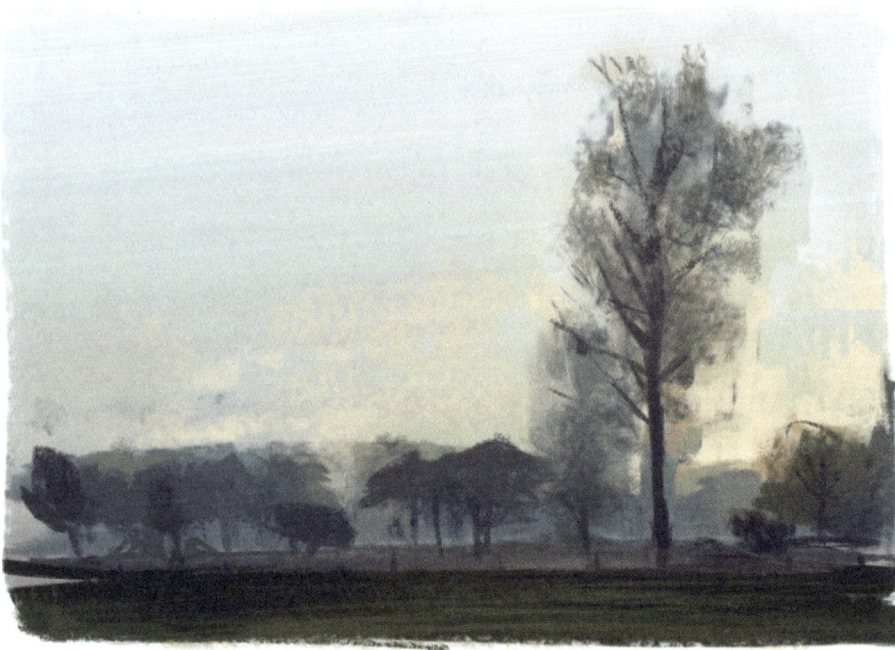
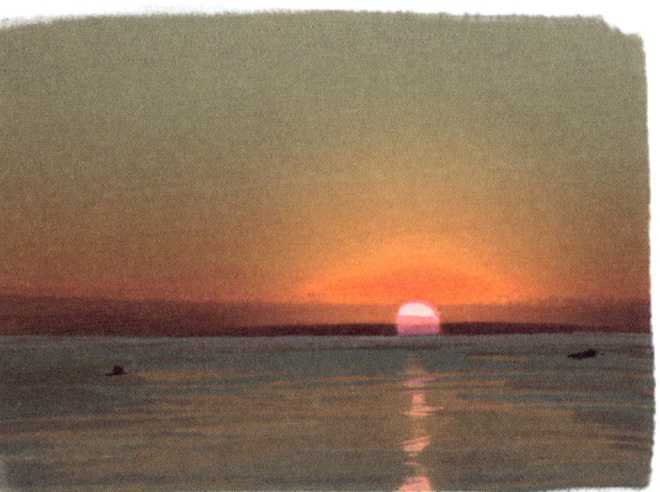

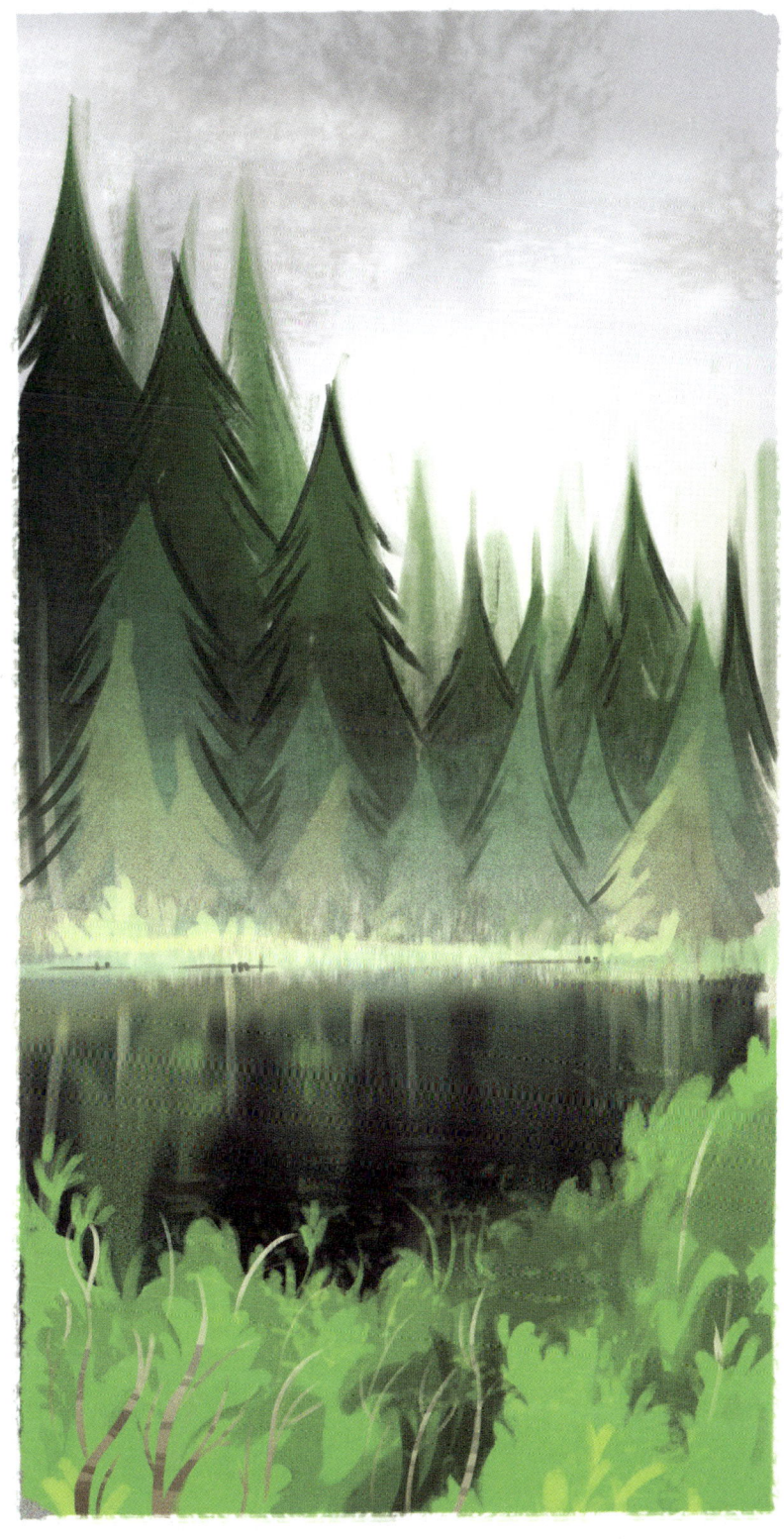
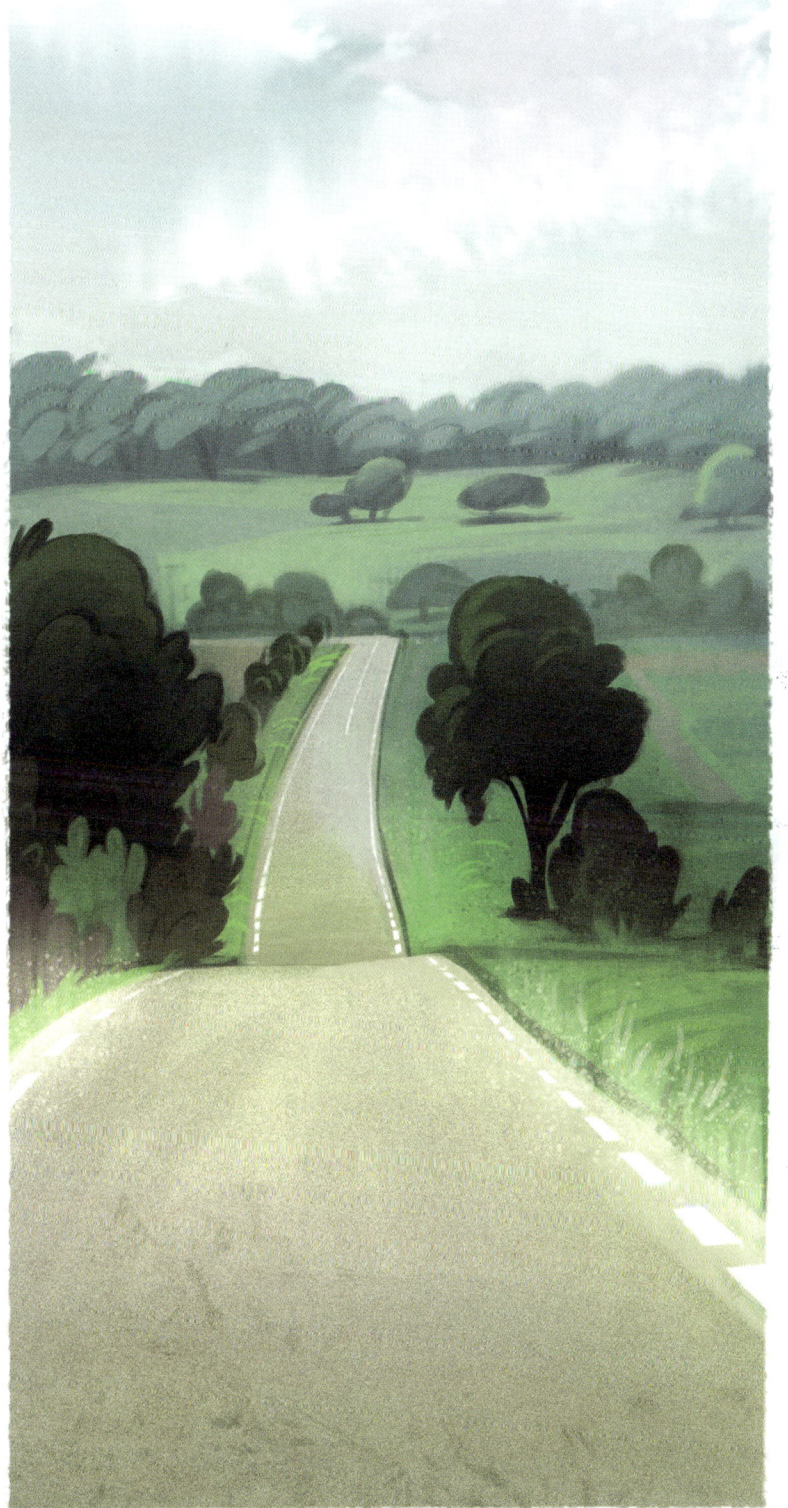

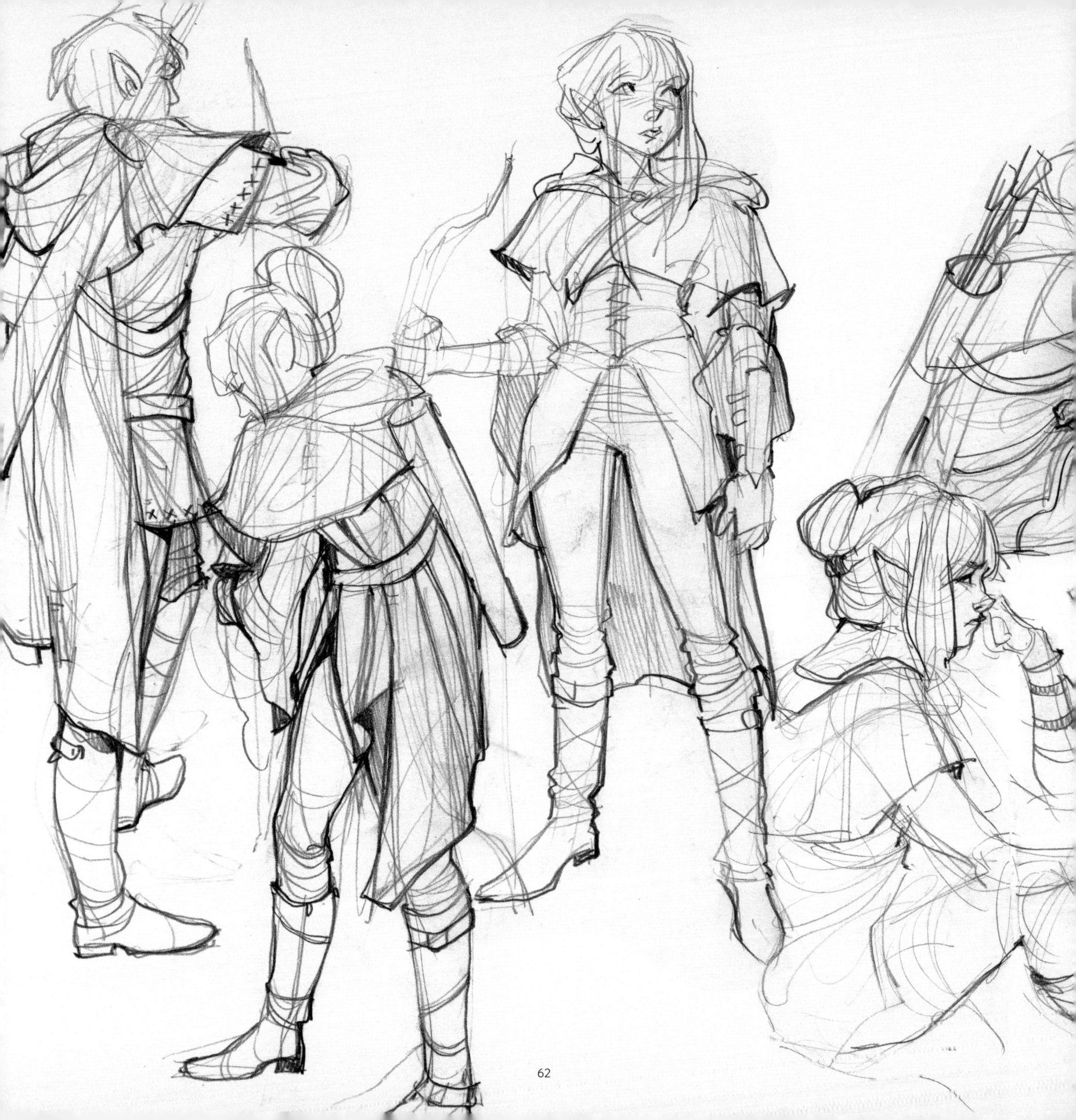

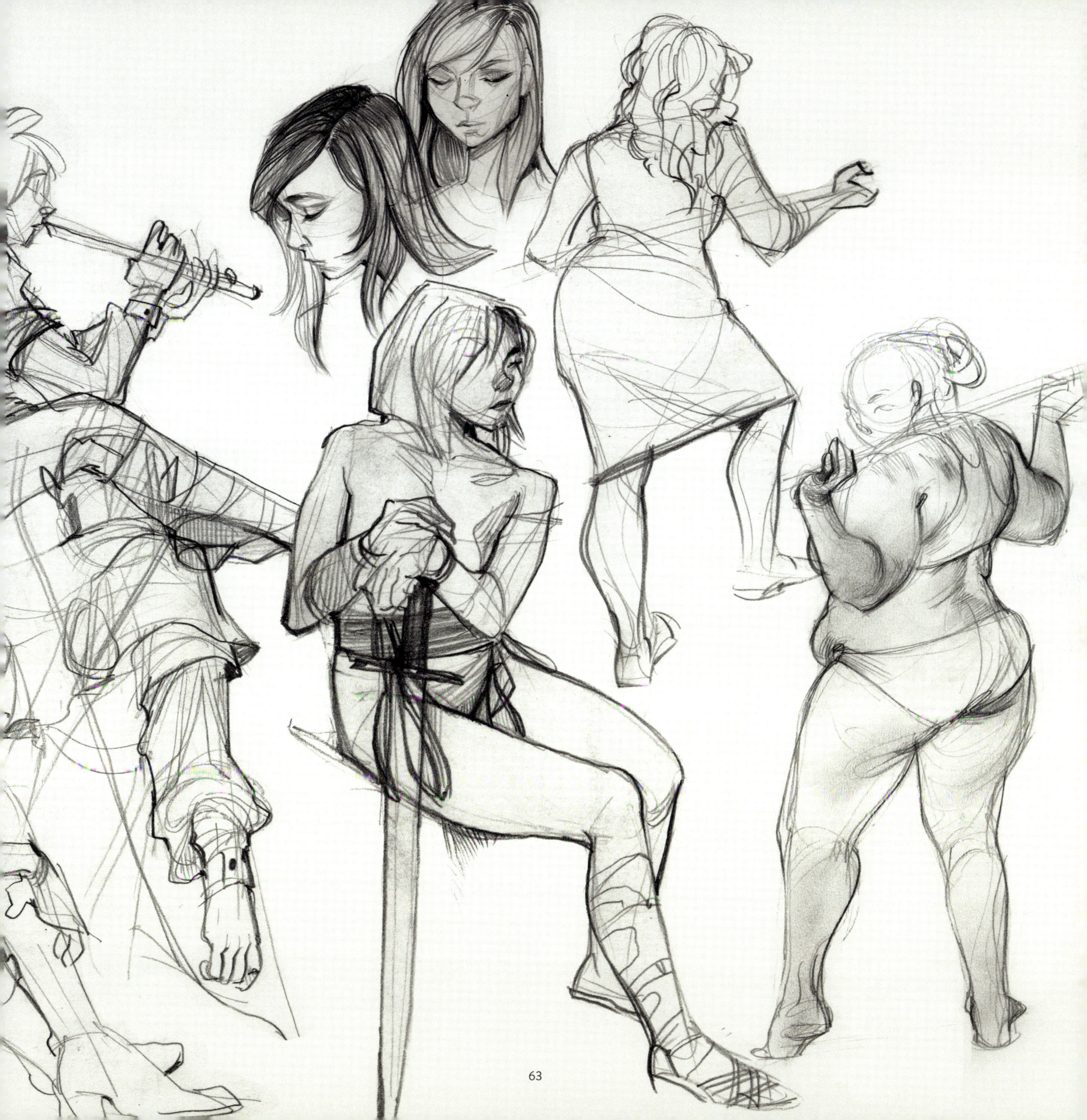

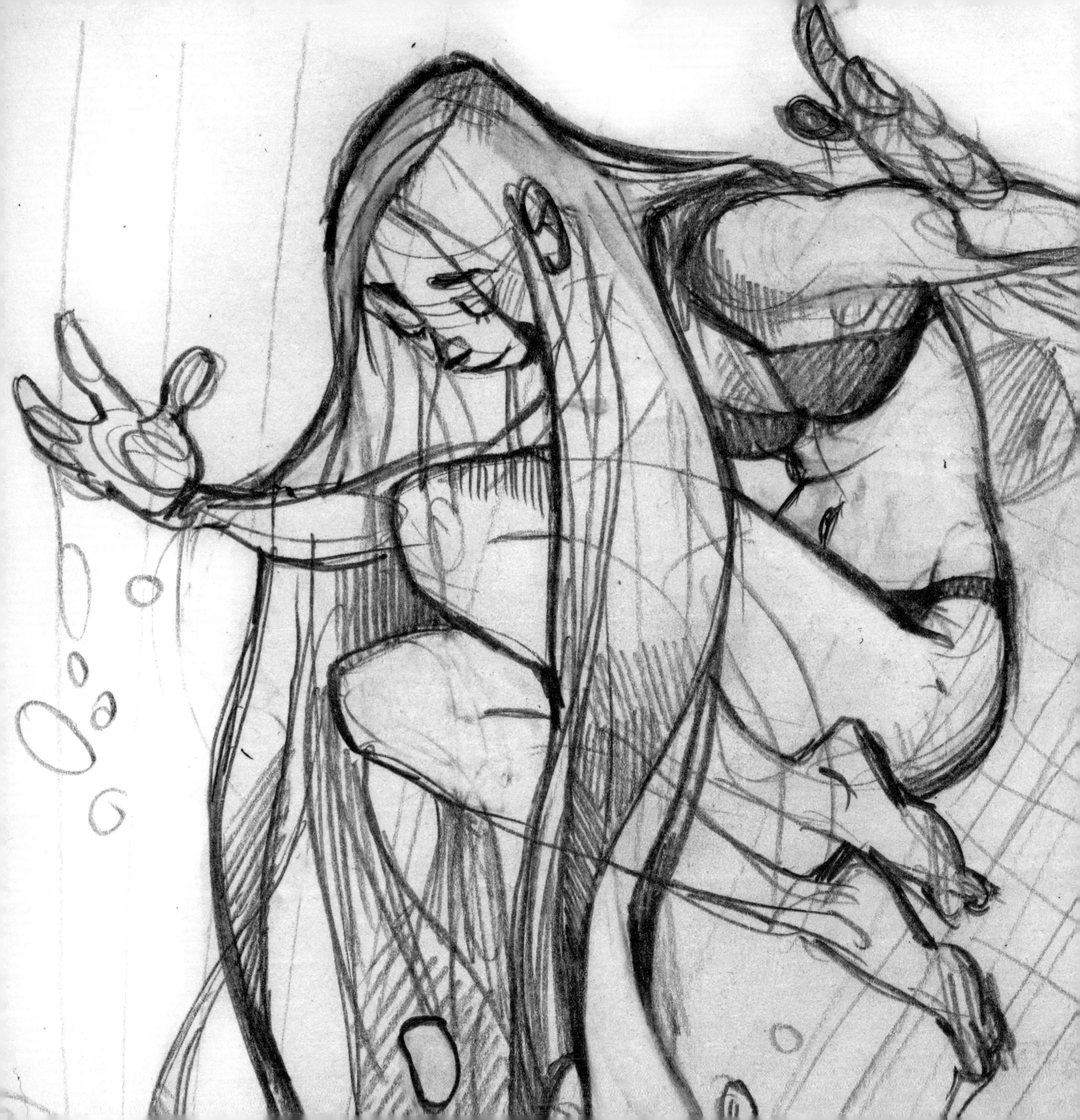

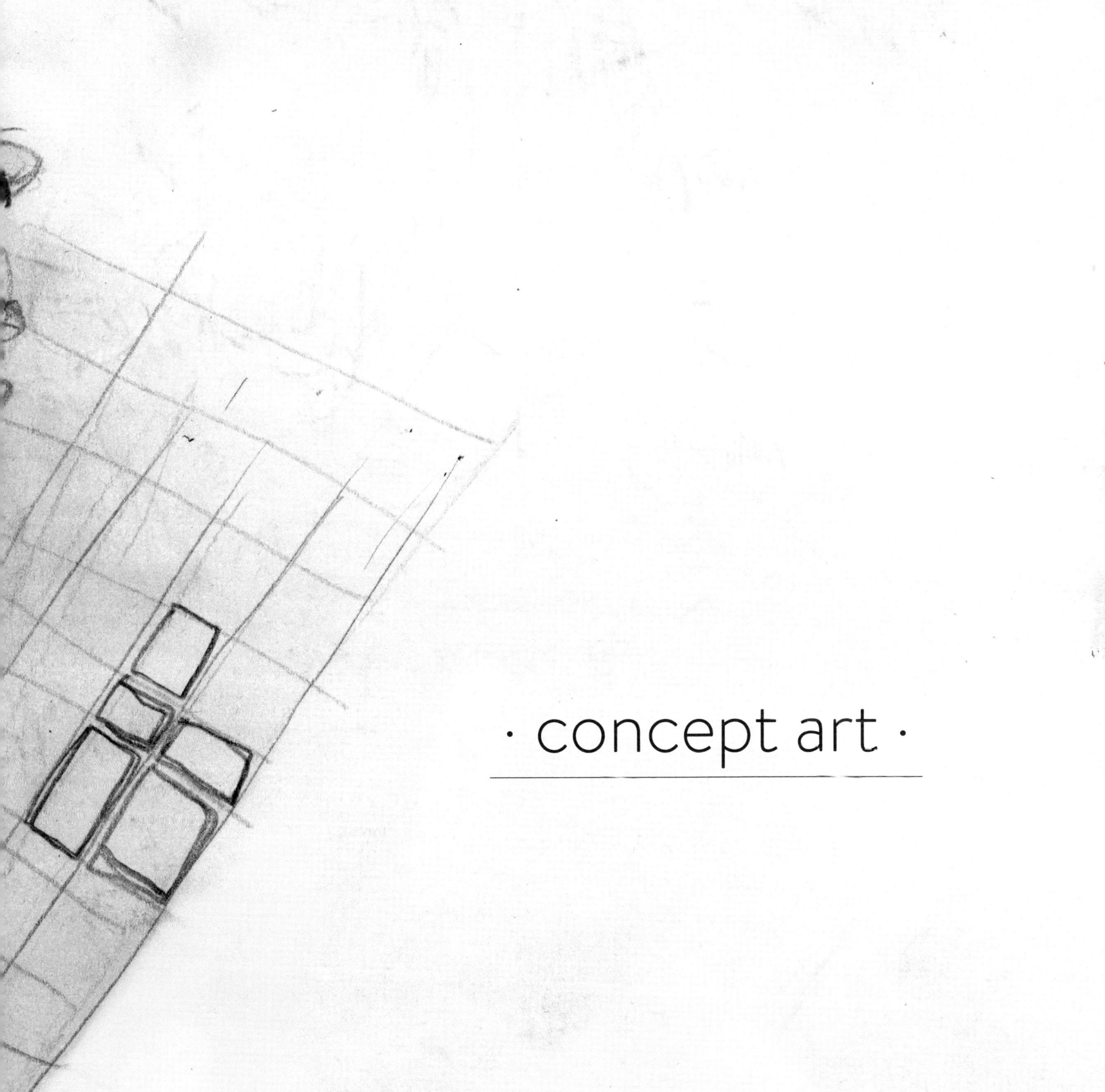

· concept art ·

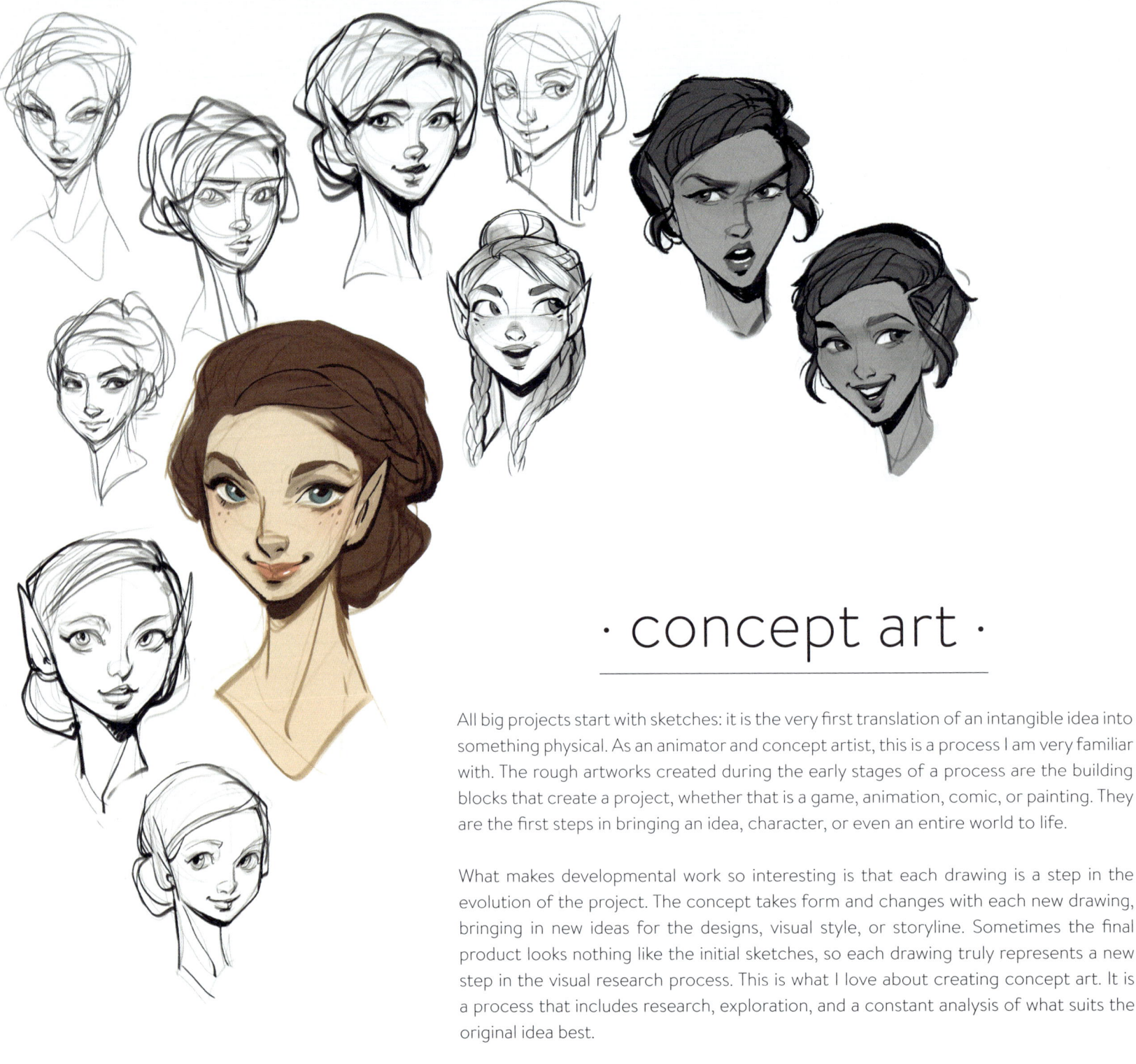

· concept art ·

All big projects start with sketches: it is the very first translation of an intangible idea into something physical. As an animator and concept artist, this is a process I am very familiar with. The rough artworks created during the early stages of a process are the building blocks that create a project, whether that is a game, animation, comic, or painting. They are the first steps in bringing an idea, character, or even an entire world to life.

What makes developmental work so interesting is that each drawing is a step in the evolution of the project. The concept takes form and changes with each new drawing, bringing in new ideas for the designs, visual style, or storyline. Sometimes the final product looks nothing like the initial sketches, so each drawing truly represents a new step in the visual research process. This is what I love about creating concept art. It is a process that includes research, exploration, and a constant analysis of what suits the original idea best.

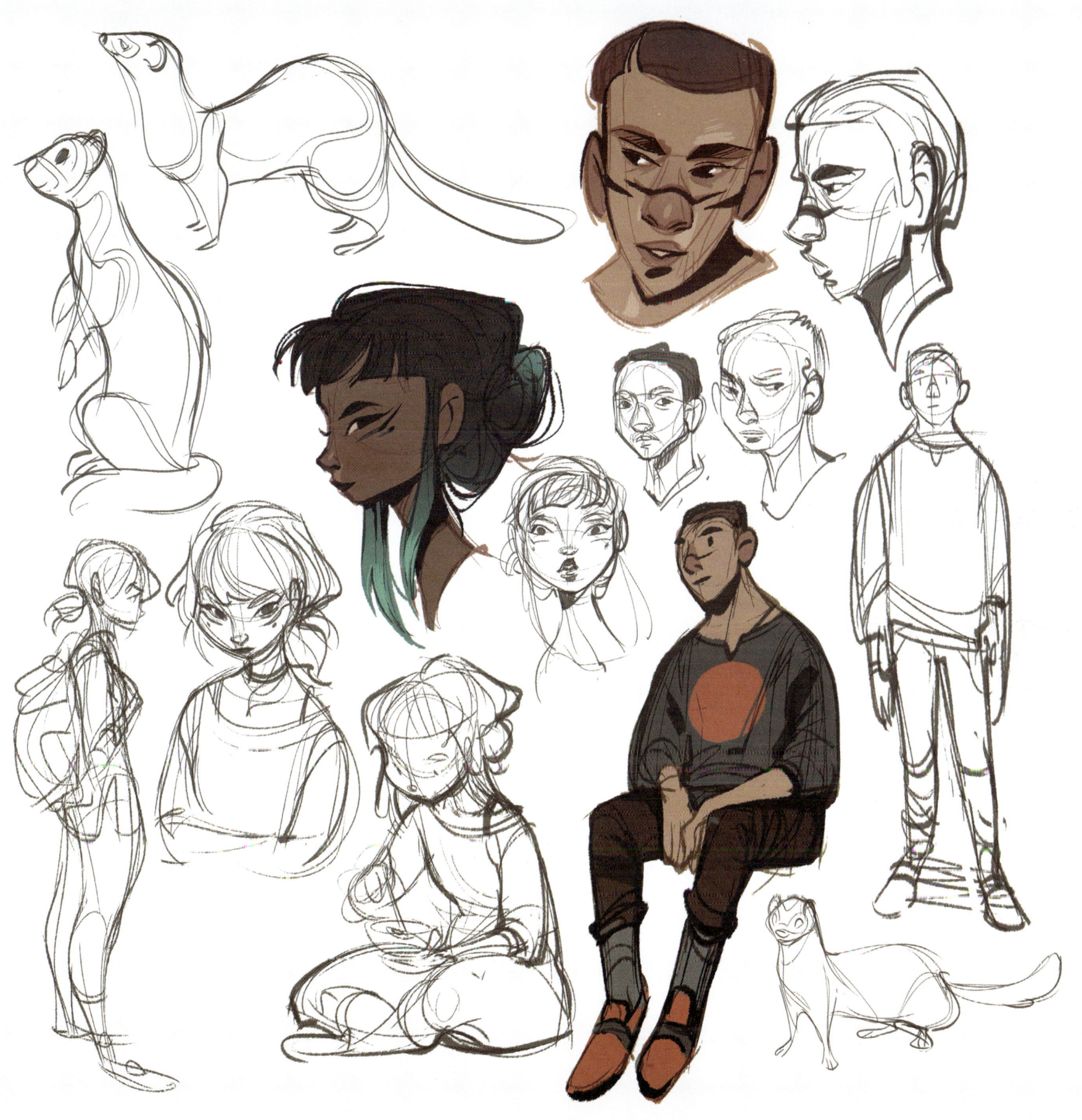

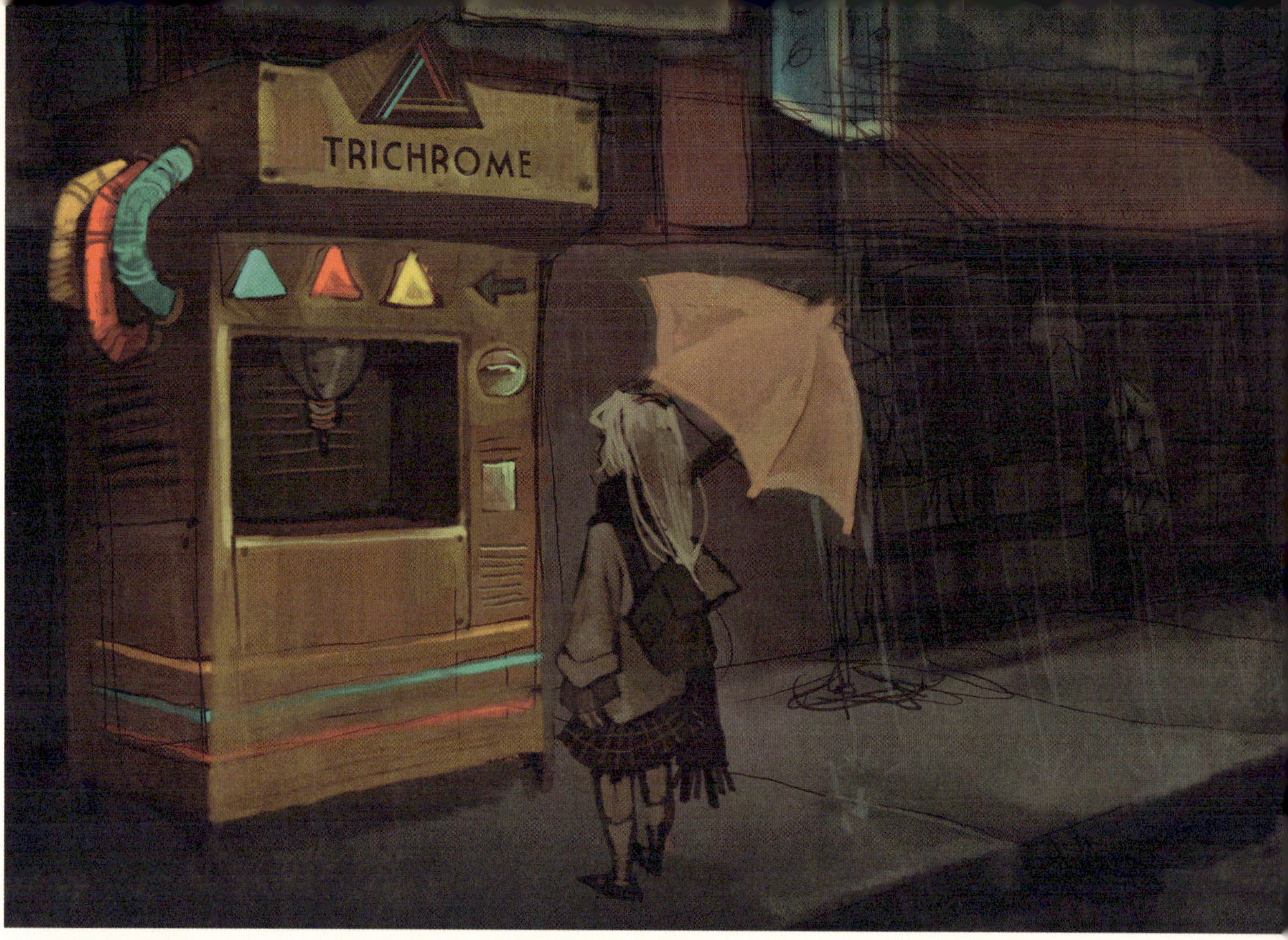
TRICHROME

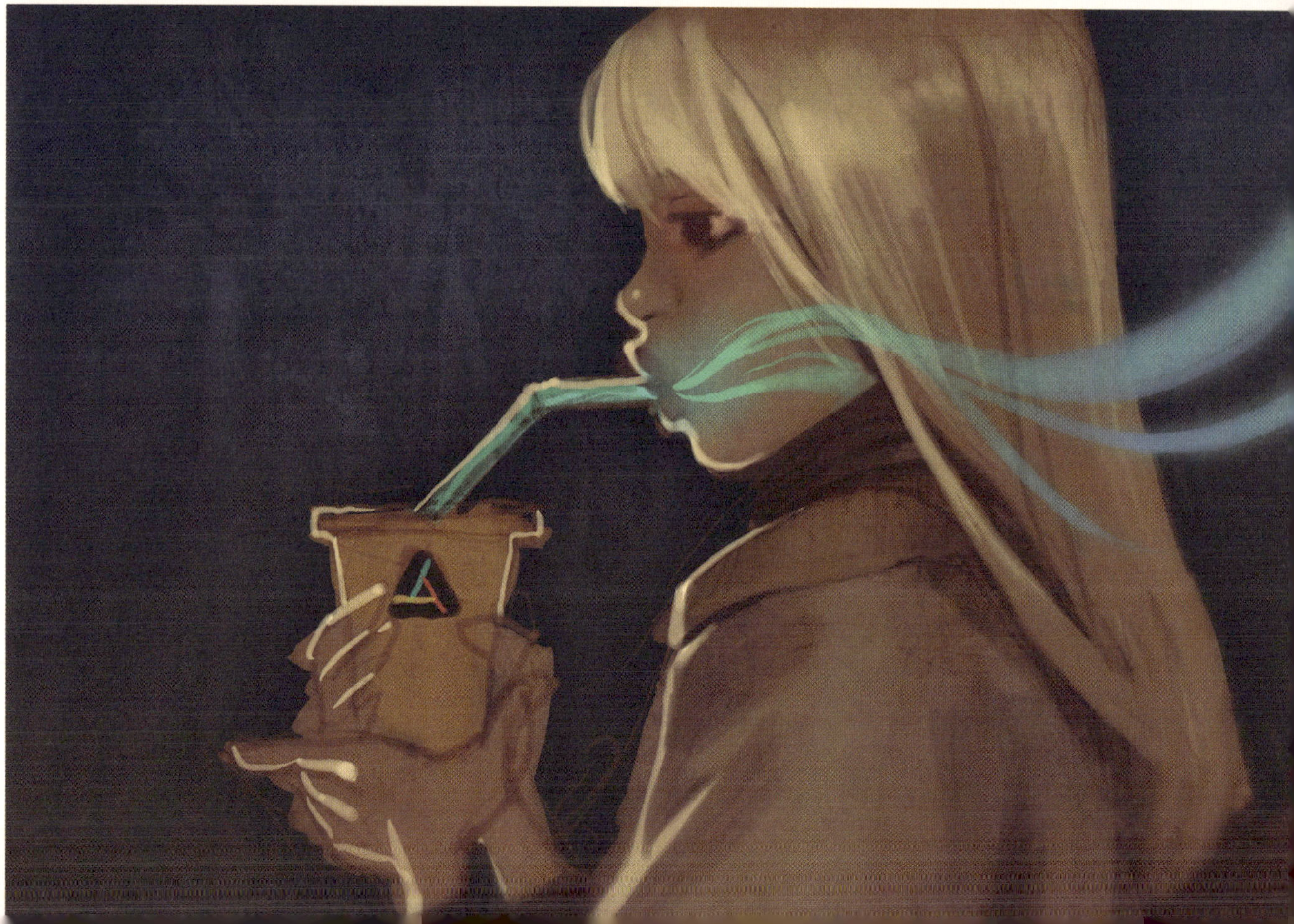

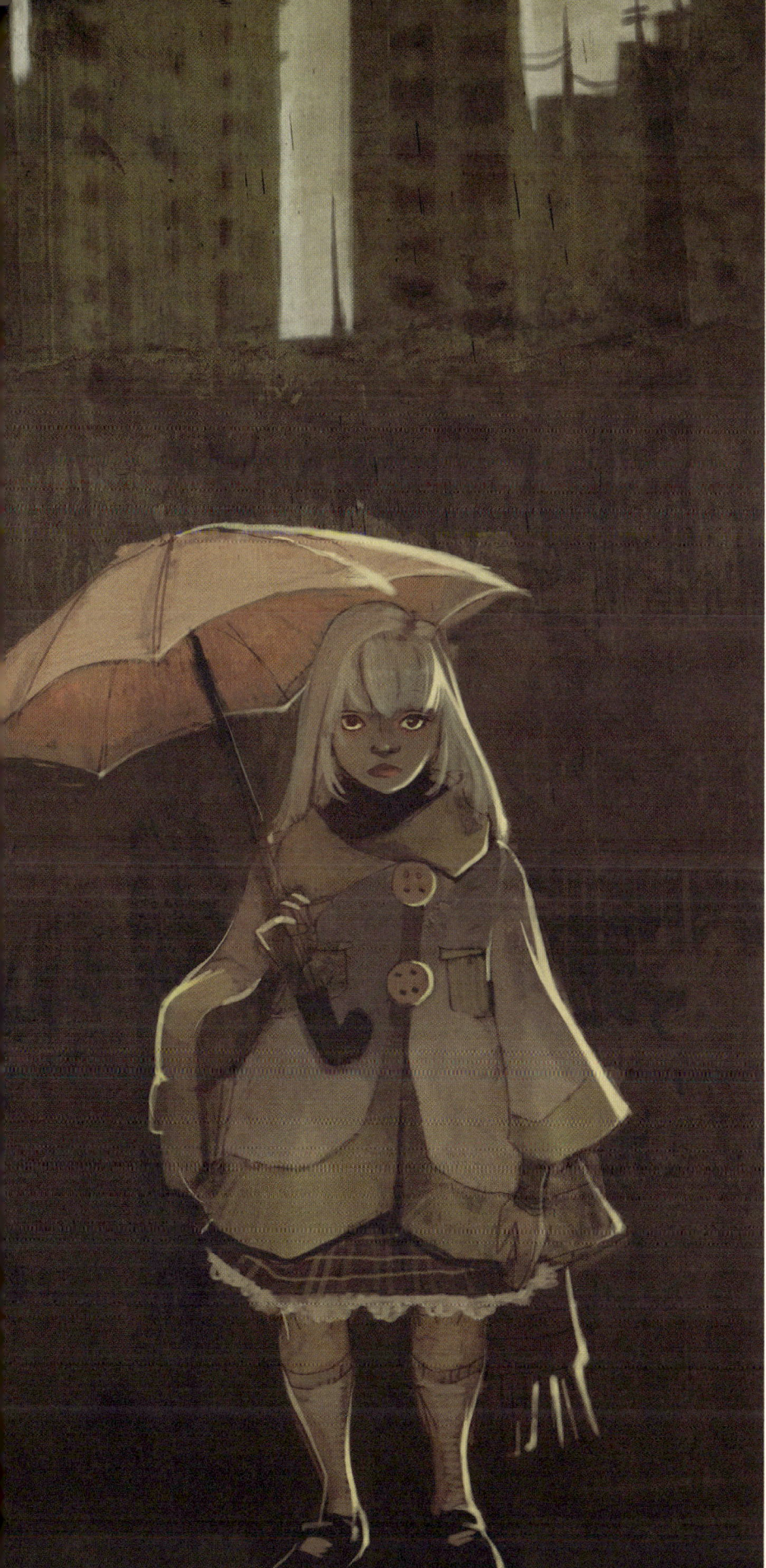

"The concept takes form and changes with each new drawing, bringing in new ideas for the designs, visual style, or storyline"

Most of my client work consists of creating concept art, particularly character designs. When creating concept art for clients, my main approach is to cast a wide net, starting with a large quantity of sketches. I work with the first ideas that come to mind and try not to delve too deeply into very specific ideas at the beginning. This gives the client a lot of flexibility to indicate which elements they feel work, and which do not.

It is often surprising how different a client's idea of a character design is from my own. I can be convinced that a certain drawing completely captures what they are looking for, but then find that they had something different in mind. This feedback process can lead to incredible results. It can be so inspiring to be pushed forward by another person's vision and creativity.

When I create concept art for my own projects, I usually start drawing before I have the concept worked out in detail. I usually need a visual spark to get my ideas flowing. I always feel that the first step is the hardest, so I jump straight into the sketching process and try to keep it simple in the beginning. This helps me to get past that phase as quickly as possible.

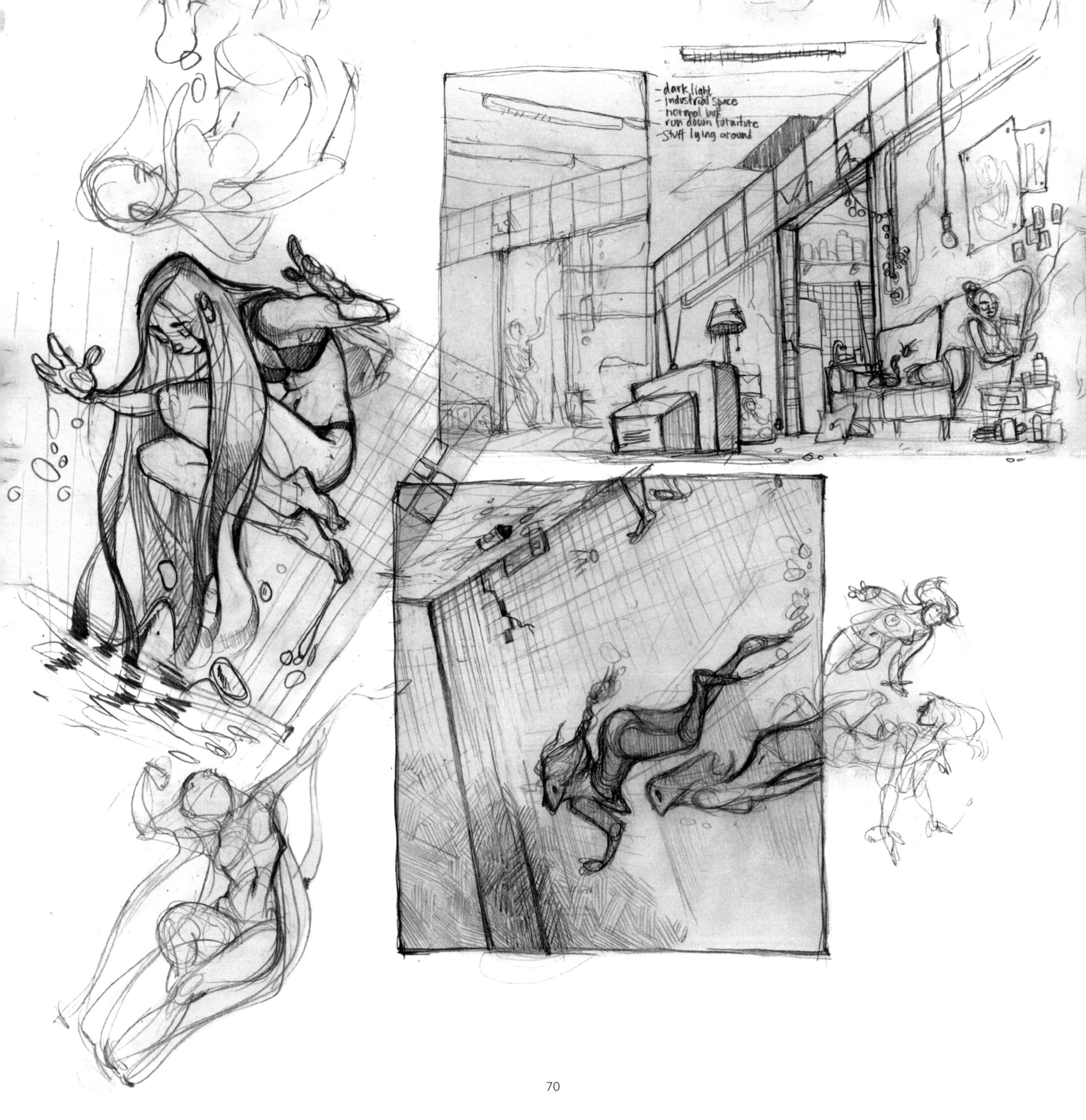

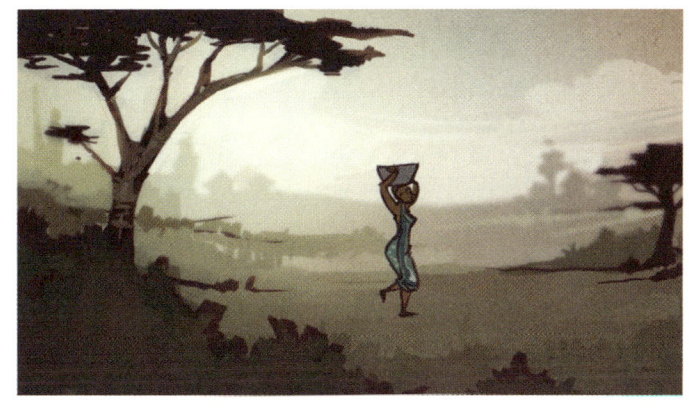
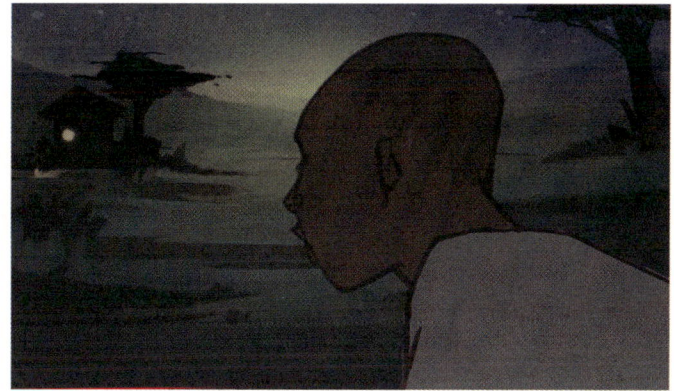
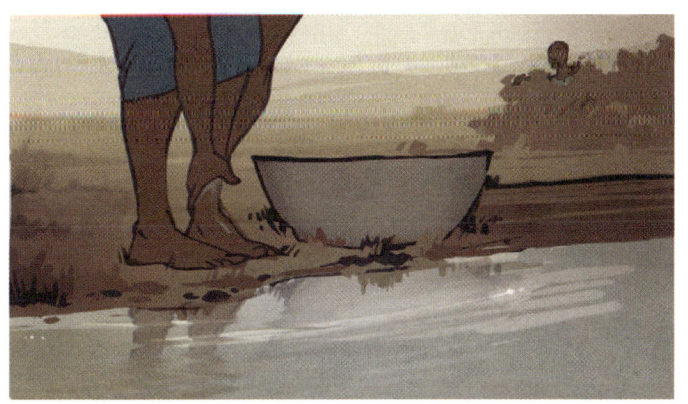
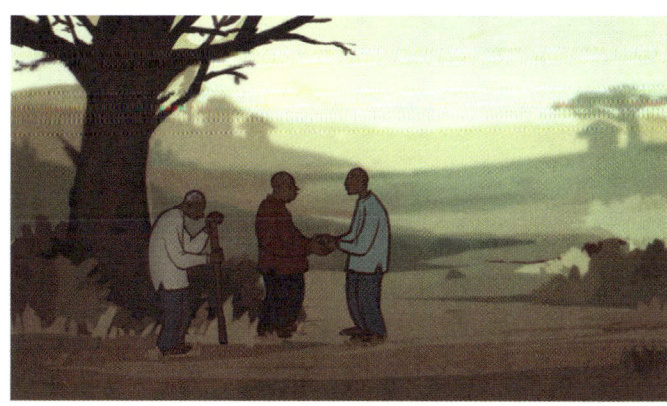
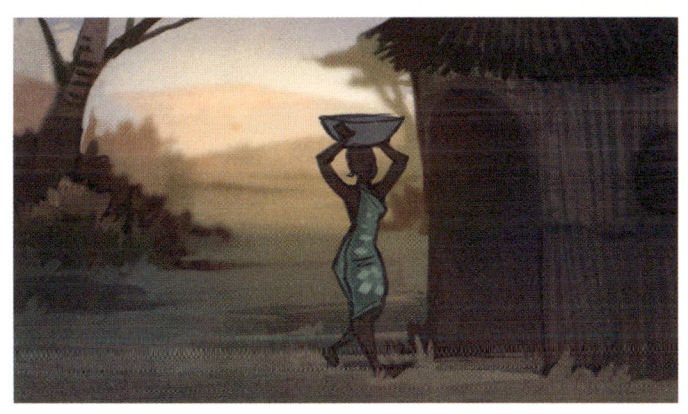
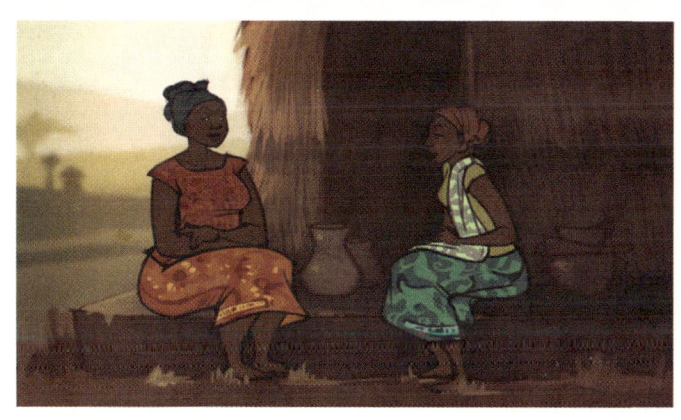
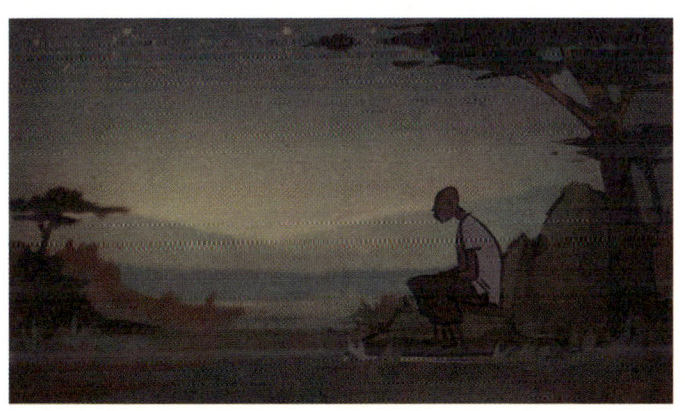
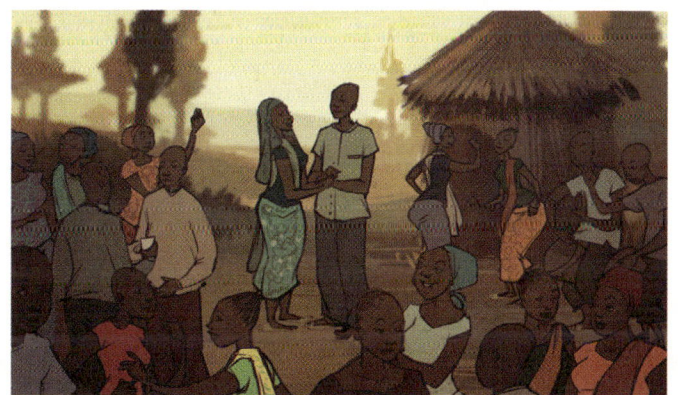

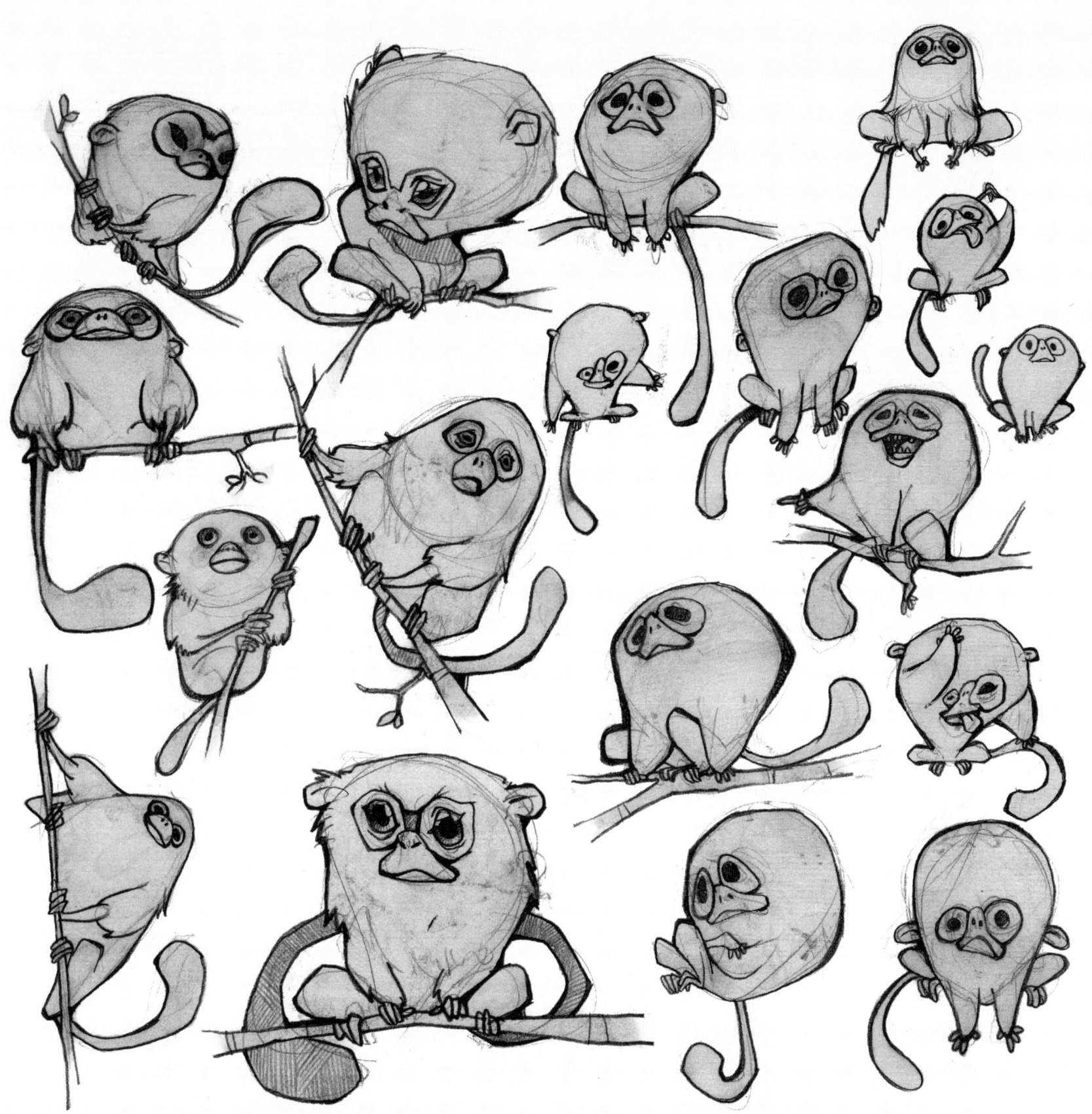

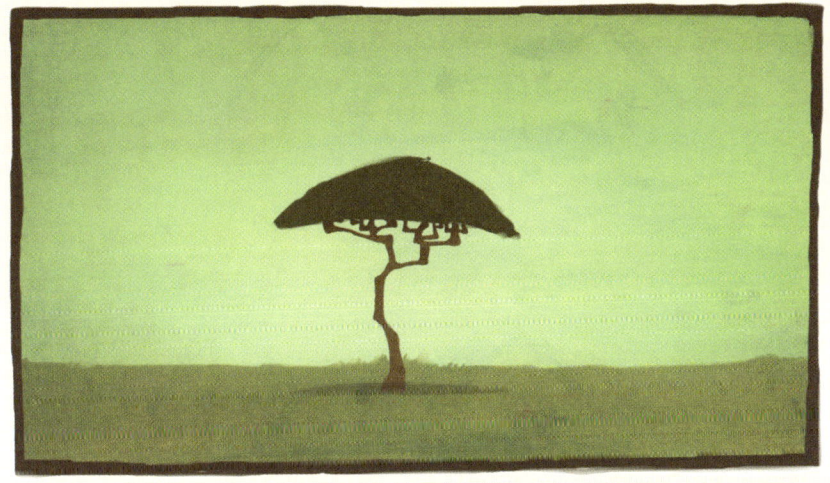
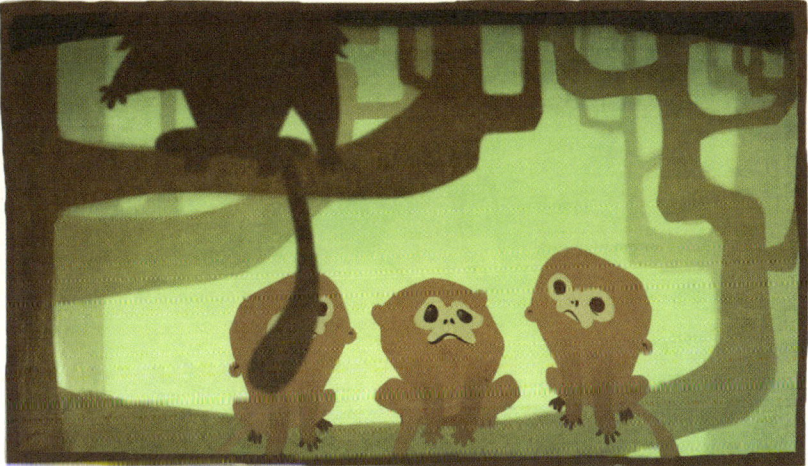
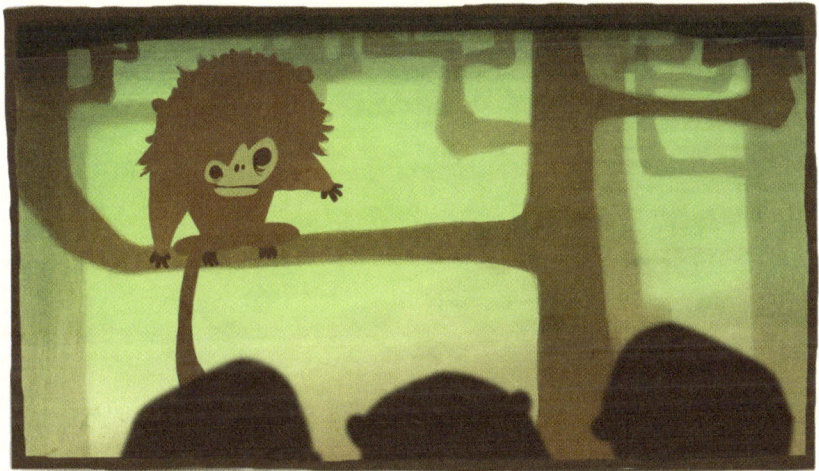
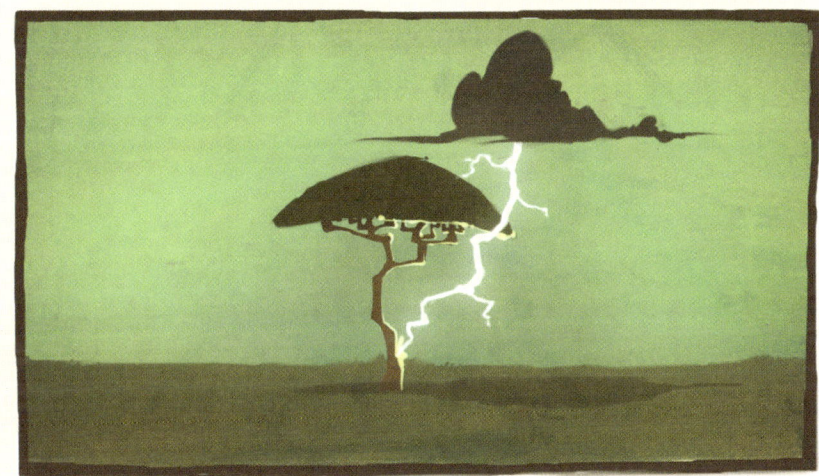

I like to start simple and see where the initial sketches take me, letting the concept evolve naturally as the artwork becomes more complex. Usually the idea continues to develop in my mind as I create more artwork, so for me, the approach that works best is to just get started and see where that takes me, letting the idea develop in any direction that feels right.

"I usually need a visual spark to get my ideas flowing. I always feel that the first step is the hardest, so I jump straight into the sketching process"

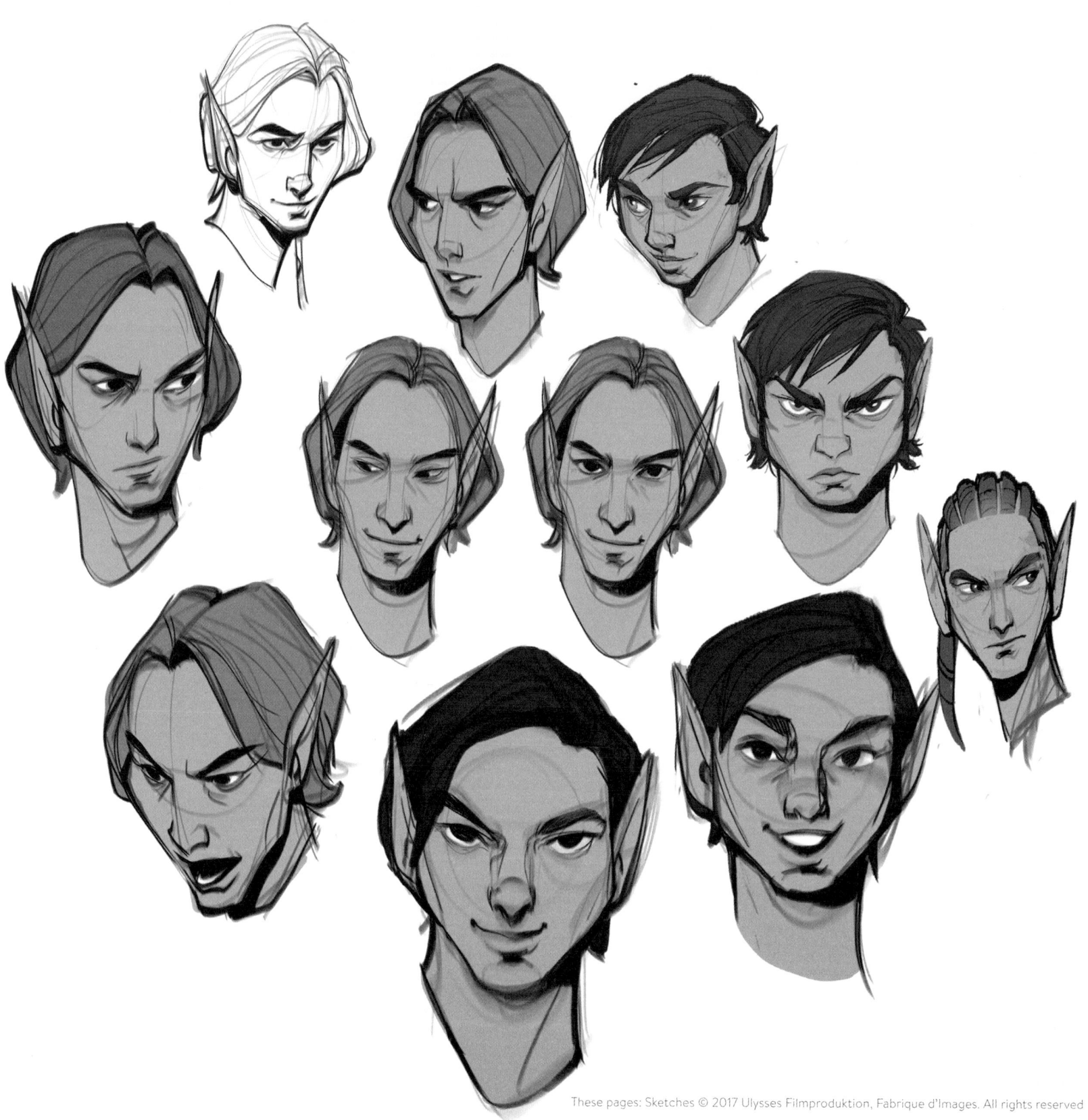

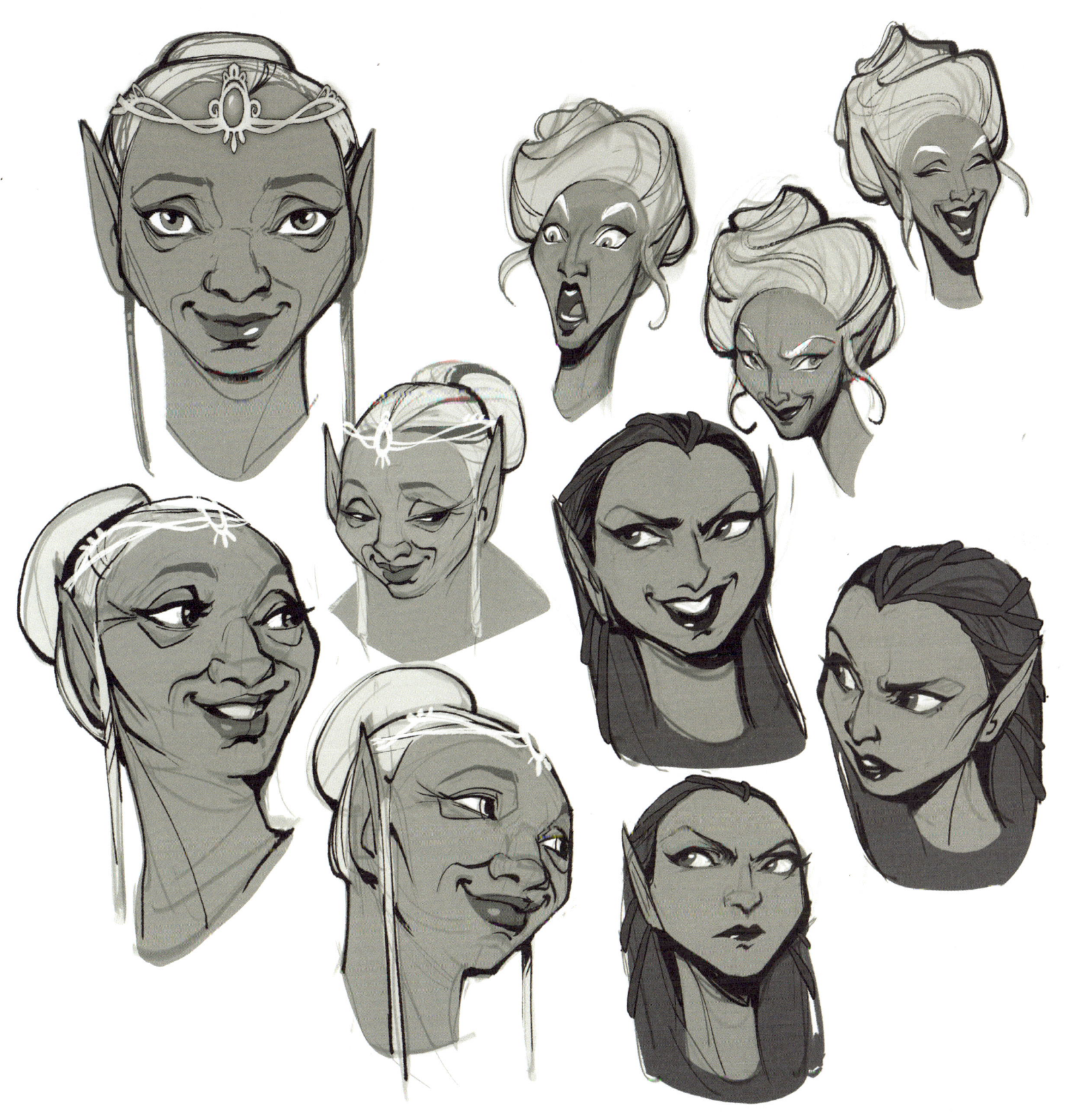

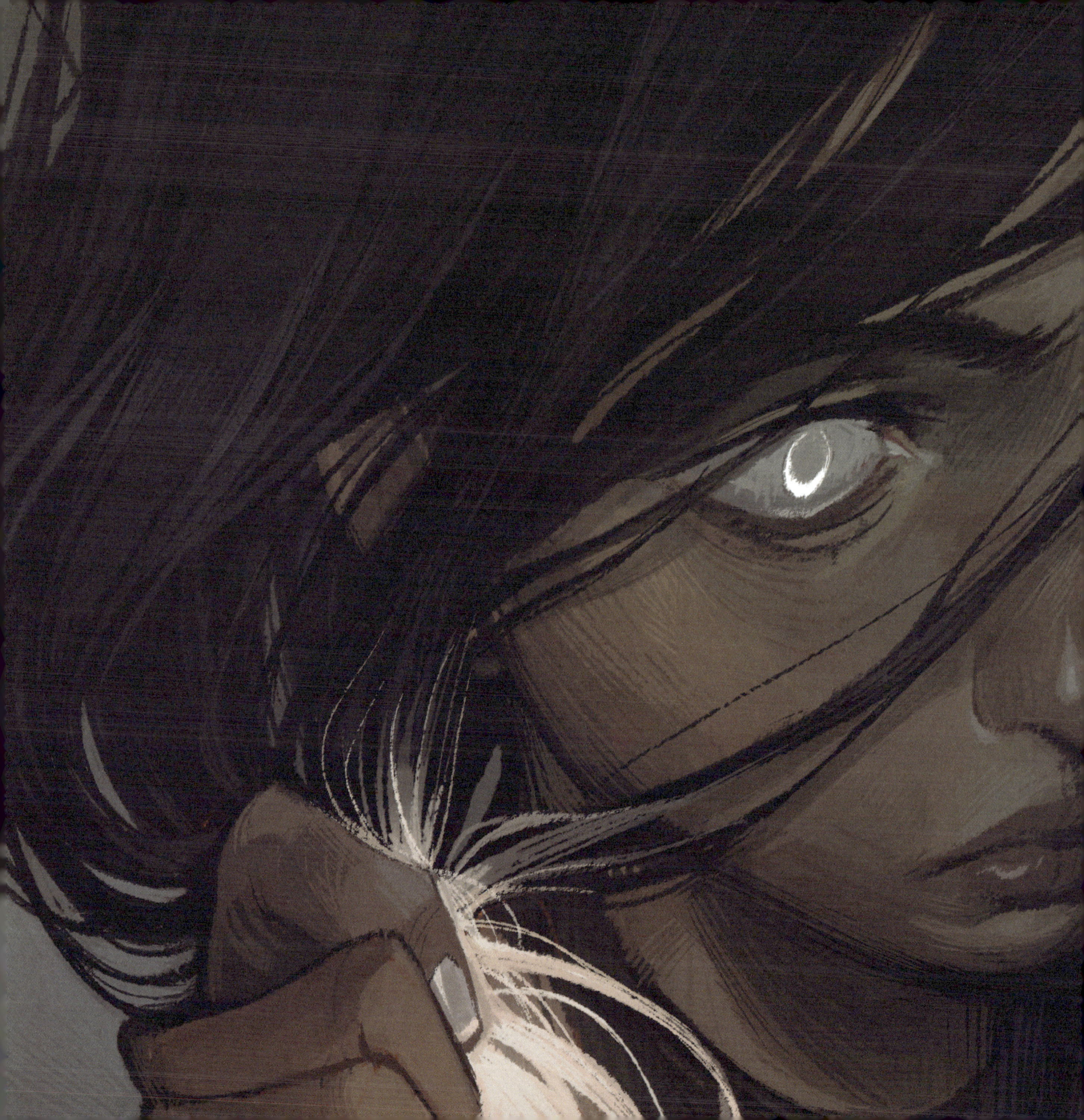

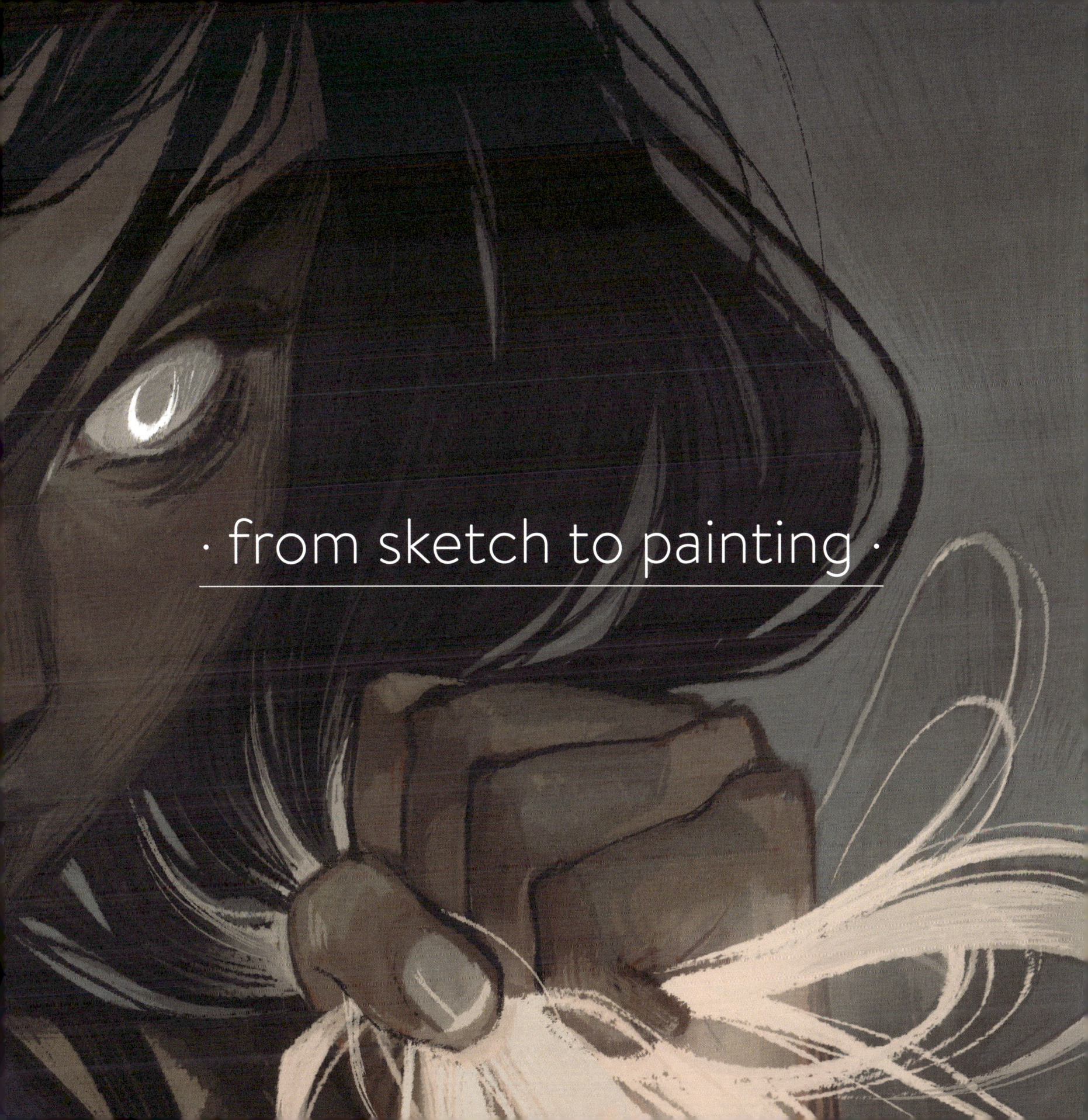

· from sketch to painting ·

· from sketch to painting ·

I love comparing sketches to finished pieces because it reveals a lot about the artist's thought process, as well as the technical steps they take to construct their artwork. For my own digital paintings, one of the most important lessons I have learned is that different phases of the painting process demand different solutions. A rough sketch can look great using a simple rendering style, but as I progress towards a more finished end result, the complexity might change, and so will the style.

It can be really interesting to see how an initial sketch is translated into a painting.

Sometimes it lays down the foundations of the painting, but at other times it changes and morphs into something else as more detail is added.

Occasionally my digital paintings start as sketches in a physical sketchbook, and sometimes the first lines are set with digital tools. The most important thing for me is to get those first lines down and move the painting forward with an open mind. Whenever I create a digital painting, I try to let the piece evolve naturally and see where it takes me, allowing it to develop and change into the final result.

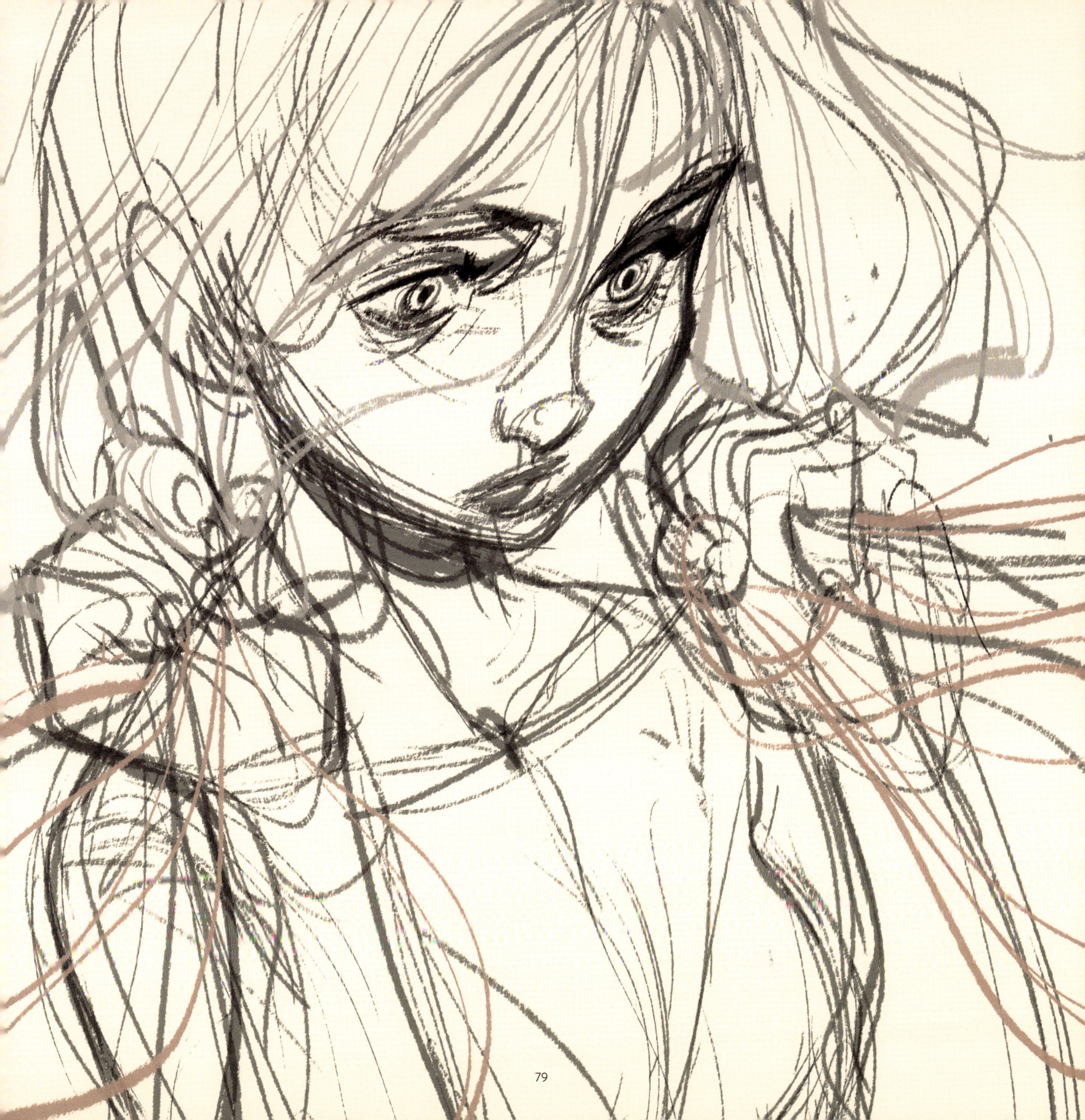

deep

This piece was drawn during a particularly hot week in the summer, at a time where I craved the cool and calm feeling of being underwater. It started as a character sketch on paper, but when I scanned it into Photoshop to turn it into a digital painting, it felt right to make her into some kind of mermaid or underwater spirit. This piece is a good example of how the painting process can transform an idea and atmosphere of a piece, and take the initial sketch in an unexpected direction.

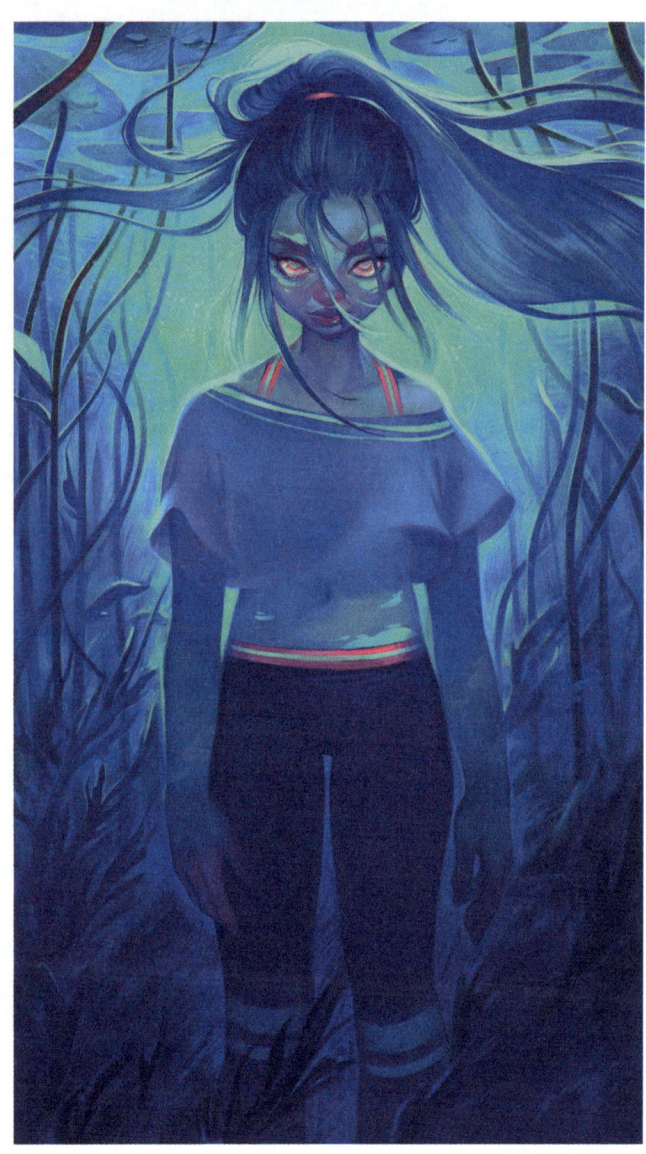

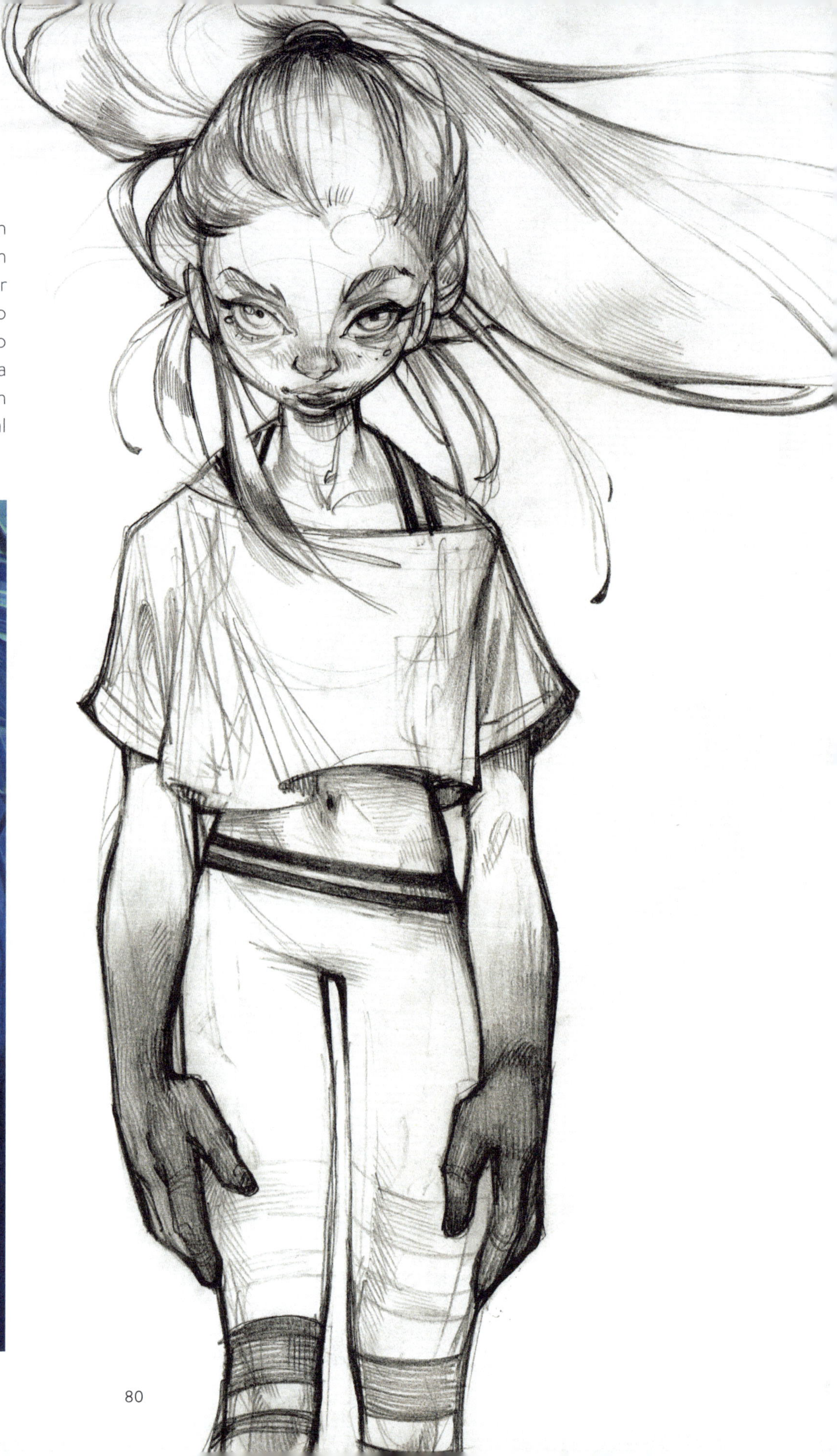

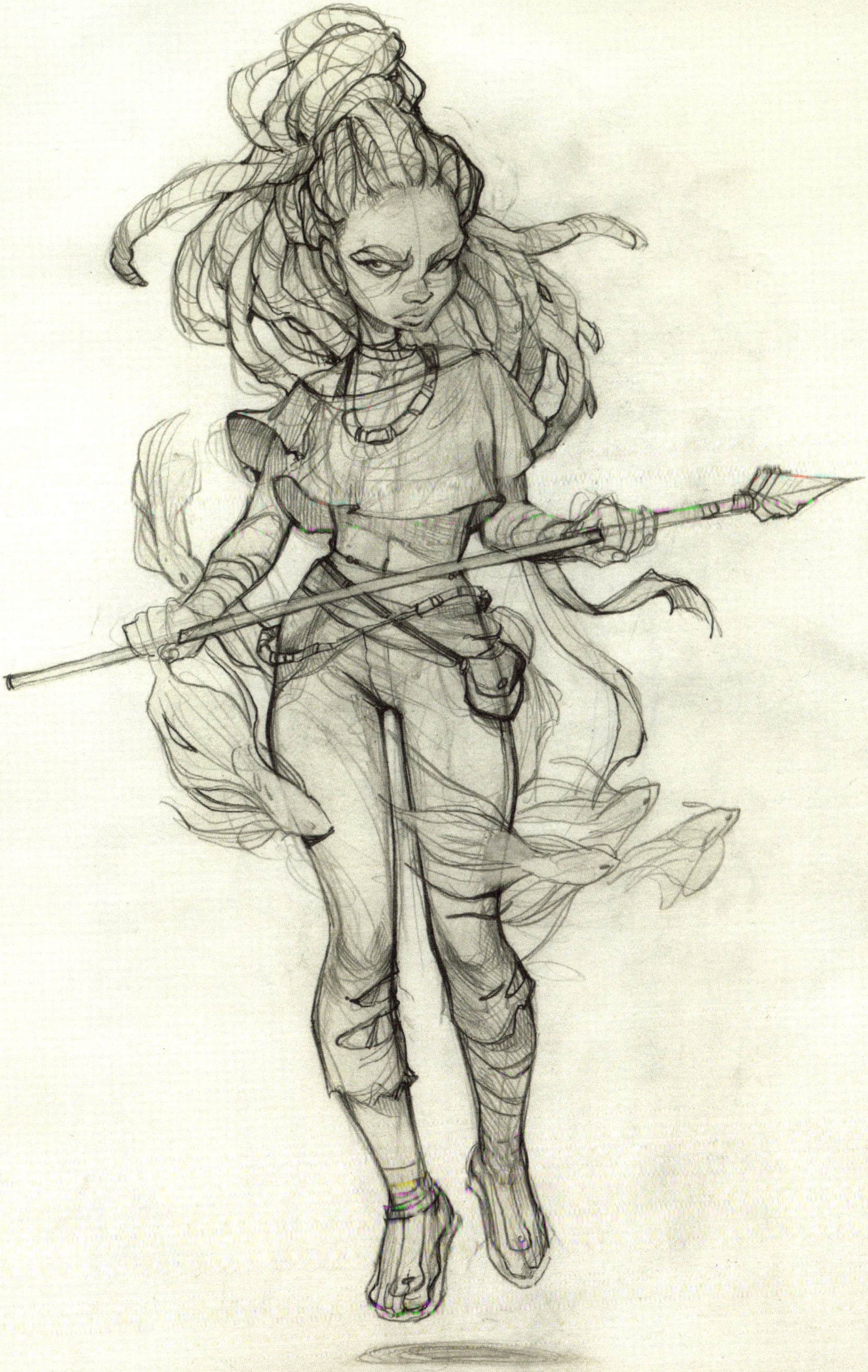

huntress

With this sketch, I wanted to create a character that had a fighting spirit – tough and strong, but without appearing aggressive or dangerous. I wanted her to stand in a defensive pose, ready to take down enemies if need be. The idea popped into my head and I instantly went to my sketchbook to sketch the idea out.

I liked the sketch a lot and decided to finalize it in Photoshop; however, I did not want to lose the texture and spirit of the original sketch. In order to achieve this, I kept the colors minimal, and used a textured brush that had a similar feel to the scanned-in pencil lines.

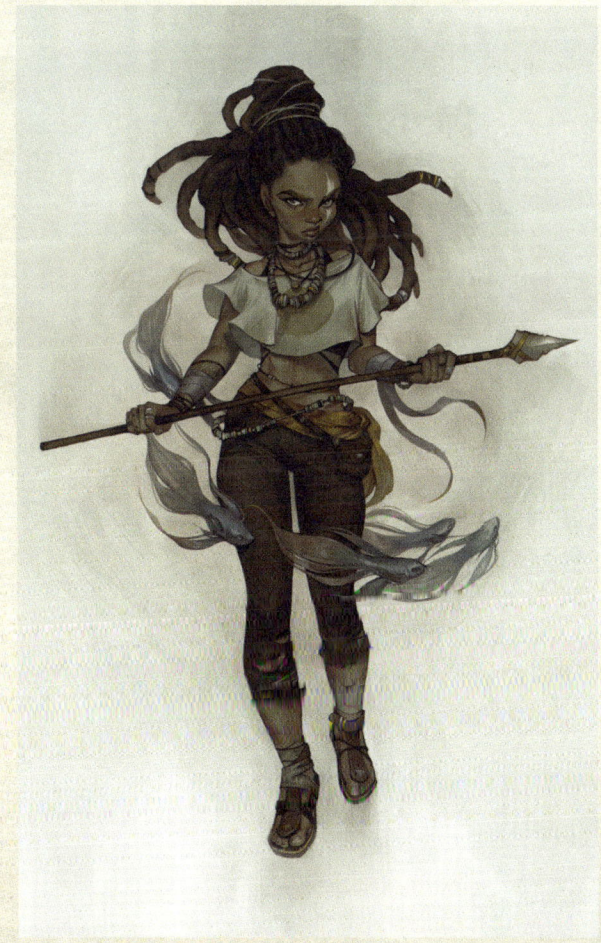

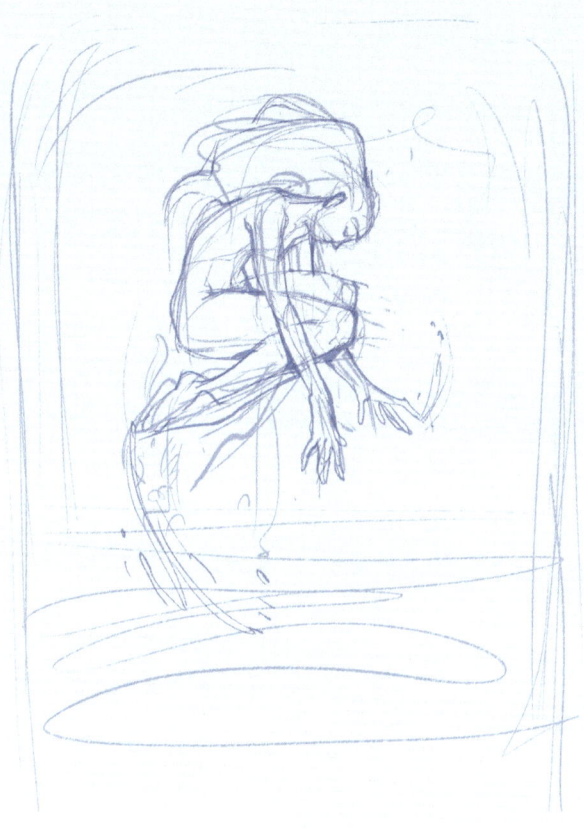

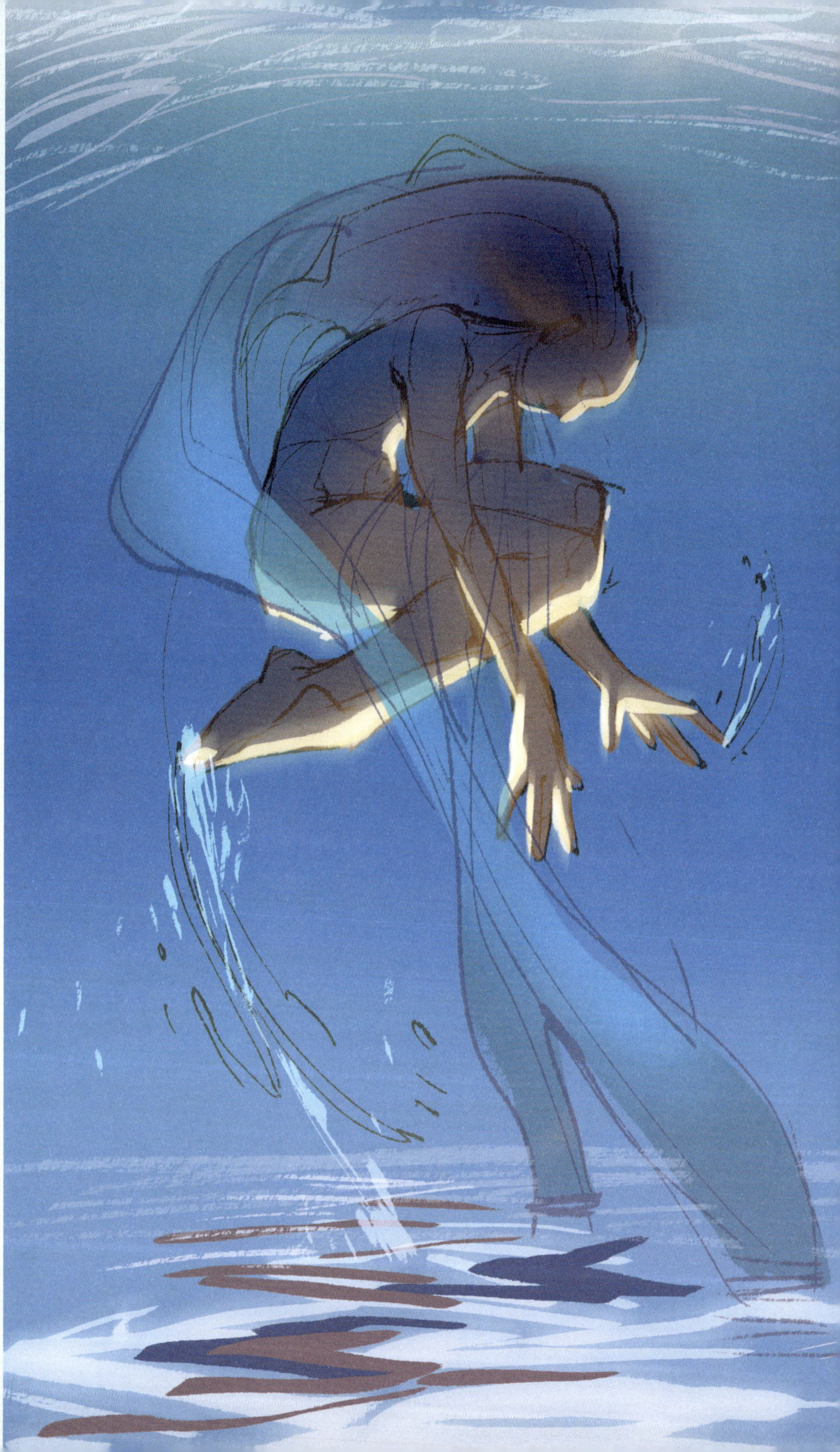

reflection

I love the idea of painting environments that are a metaphor for an emotional space – a space that is not literal, but reflects a mental state in our own mind. With this image, I wanted to convey a space that shows a state of reflection. It needed to communicate a sense of taking a step back and thinking about what we experience. With pieces like this, the idea drives my process. I try to move quickly from sketch to painting so that I can get closer to creating the image I have in my mind.

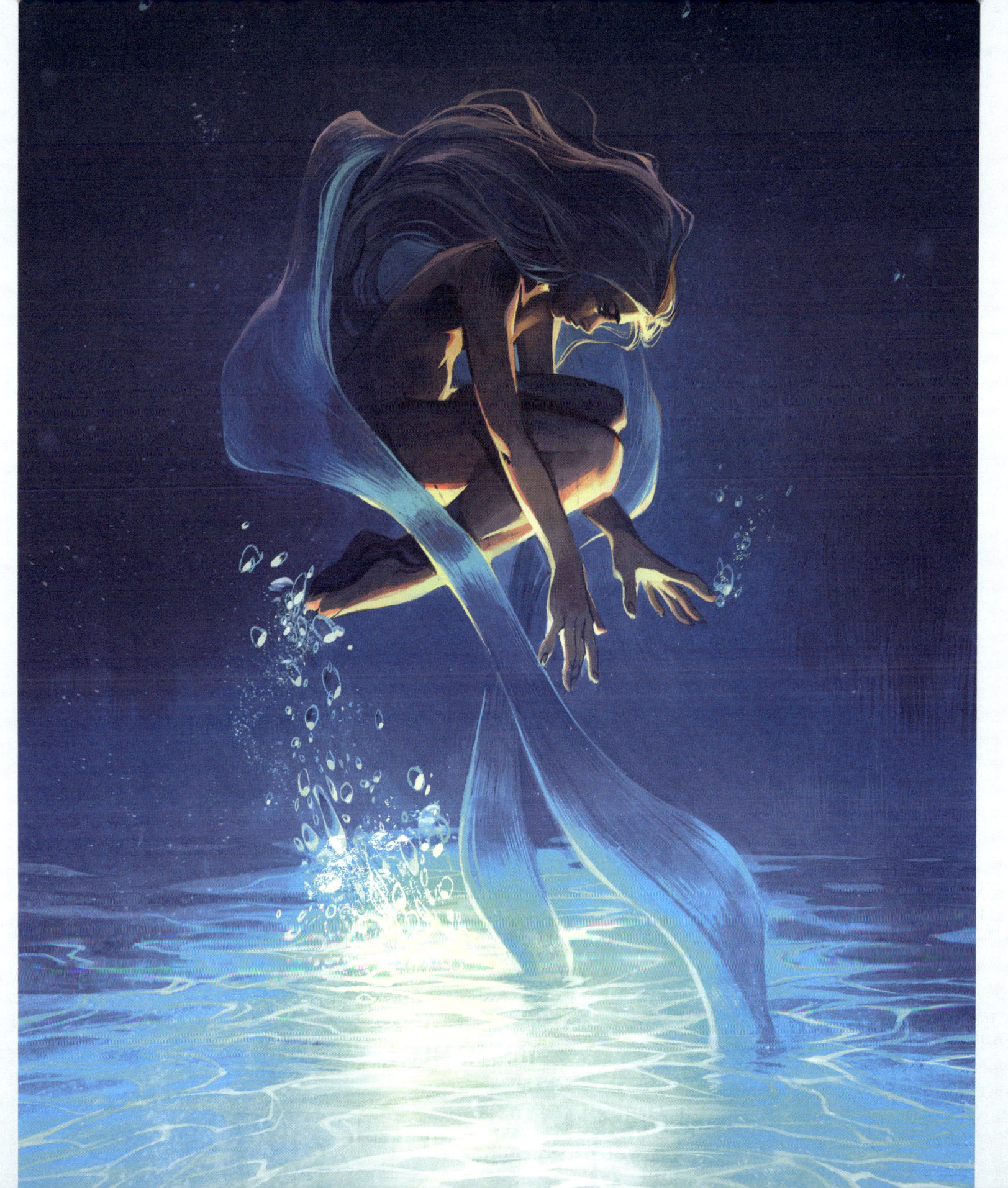

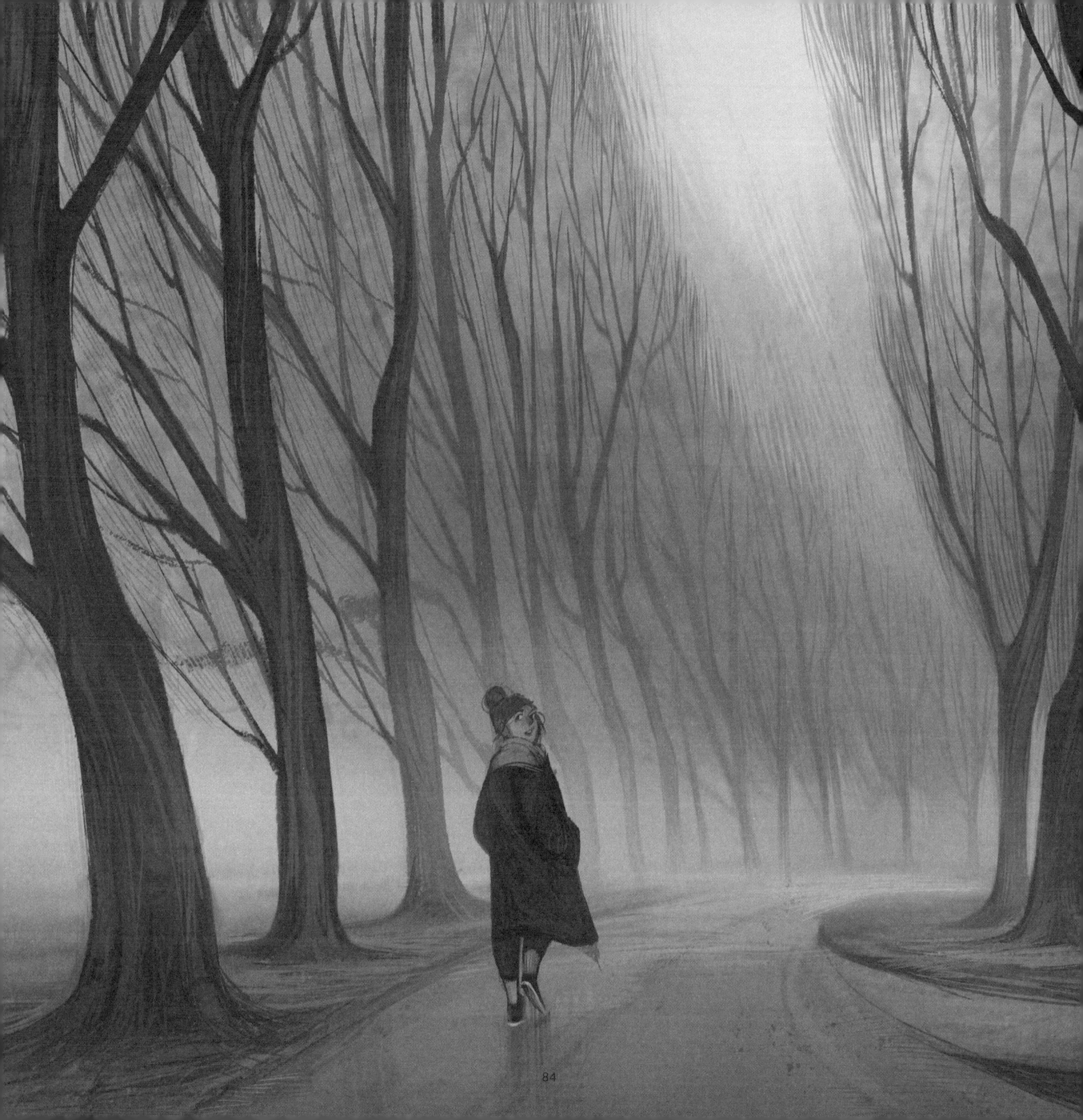

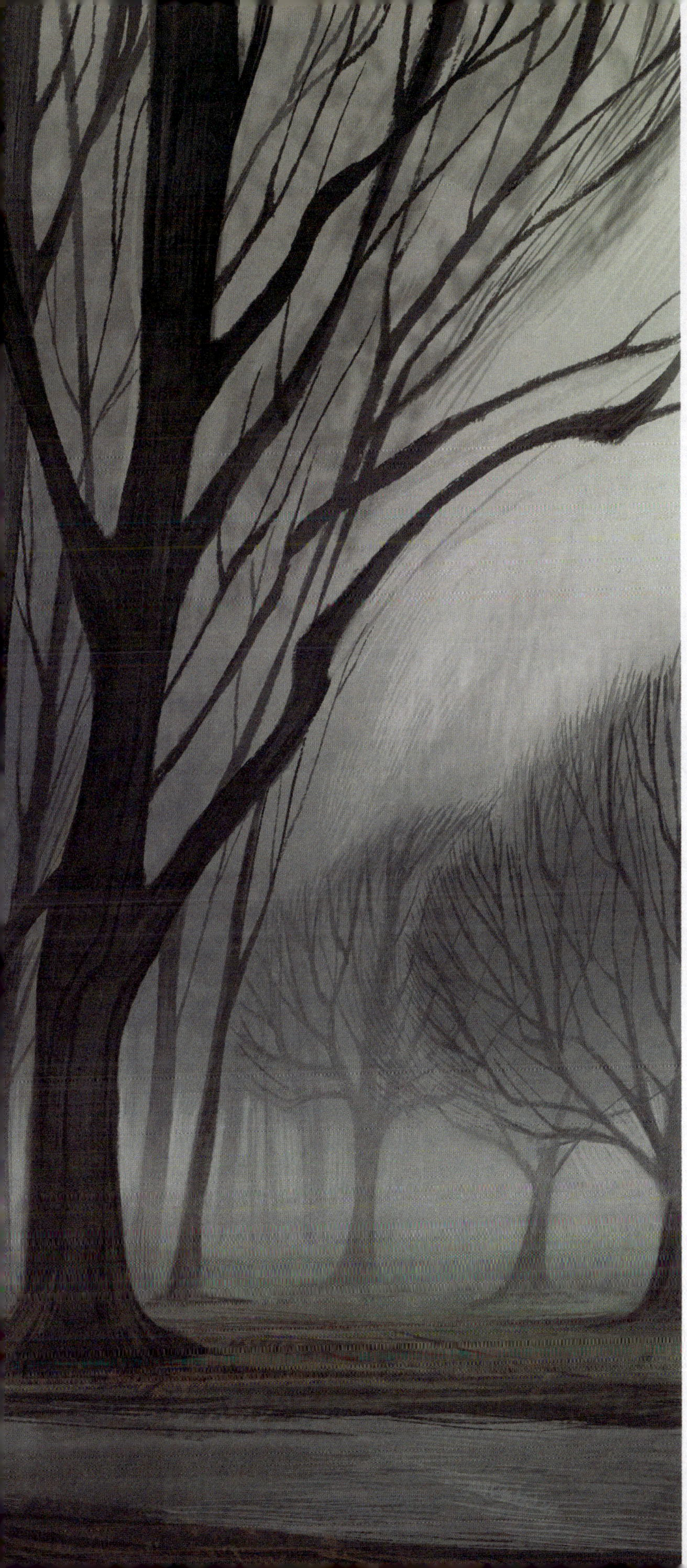

"The most important thing for me is to get those first lines down and move the painting forward with an open mind"

mist

Around the time that I made this painting, there had been a lot of mornings with dense fog in my city. Early one morning, I went to the park near my house and took some pictures of the mist with my phone. This became the inspiration for this painting.

The challenge for me was to take the picture as a starting point, but stylize and exaggerate it so that it was more than just a copy of the reference photo. The result is an artwork with the same feeling of the original photograph, but similar to an illustration in a storybook. There is something in it that speaks to the imagination, which is how I felt that morning while walking in the park.

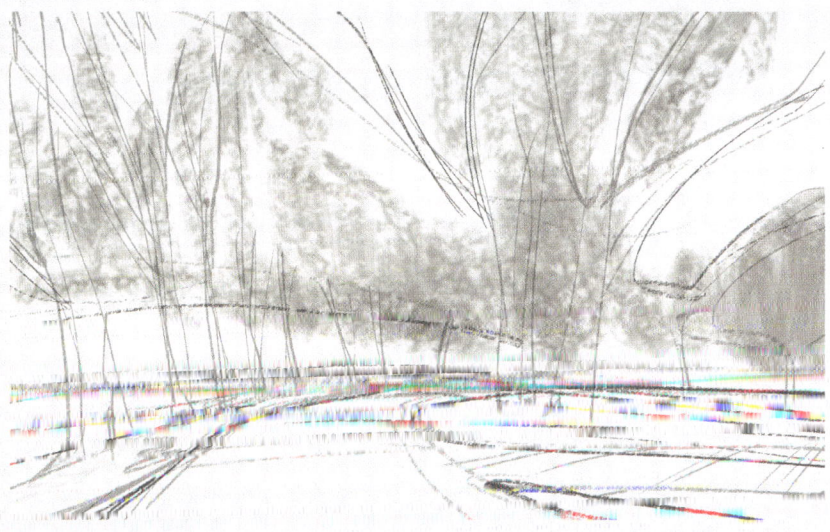

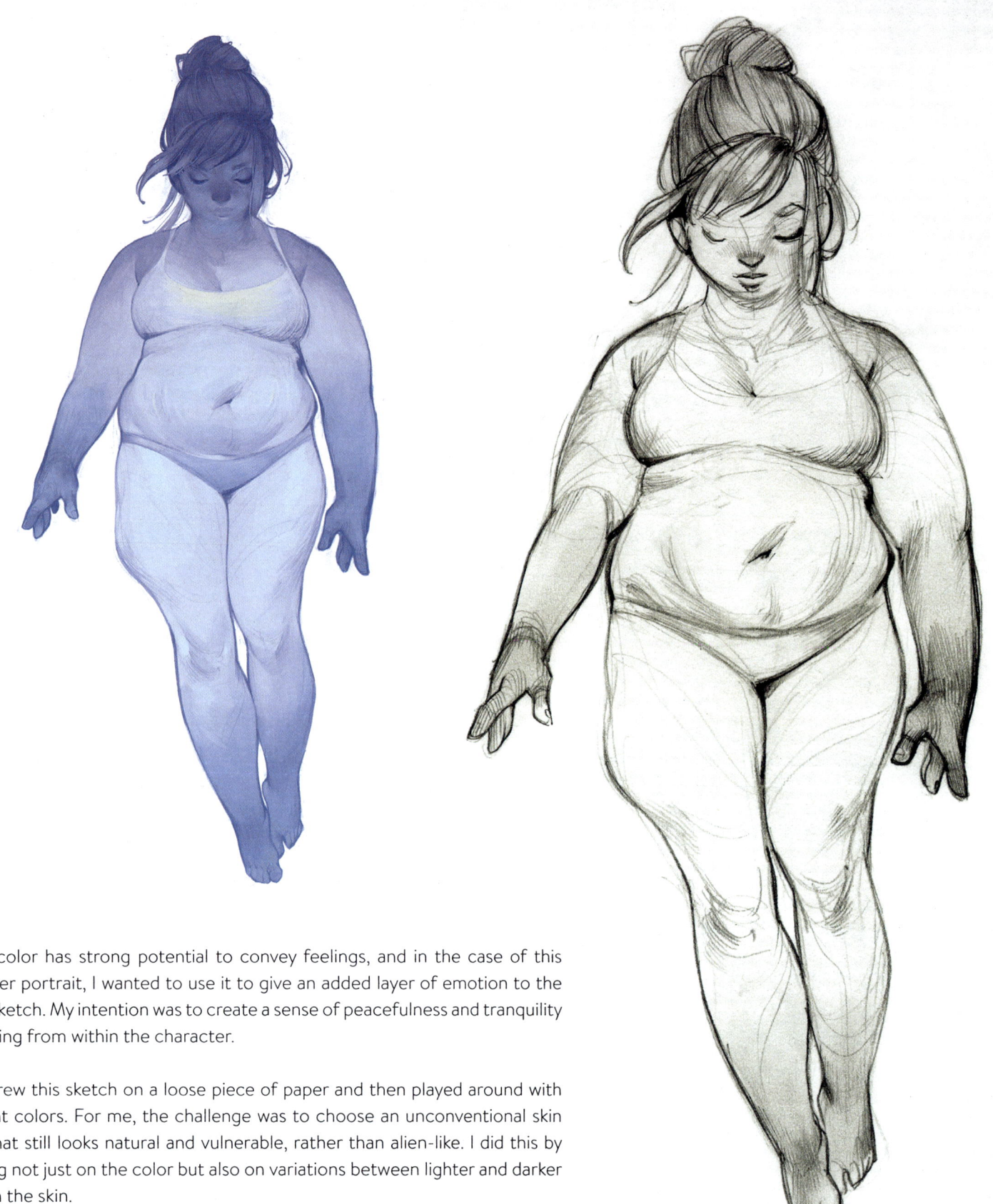

lily

I think color has strong potential to convey feelings, and in the case of this character portrait, I wanted to use it to give an added layer of emotion to the pencil sketch. My intention was to create a sense of peacefulness and tranquility emanating from within the character.

I first drew this sketch on a loose piece of paper and then played around with different colors. For me, the challenge was to choose an unconventional skin color that still looks natural and vulnerable, rather than alien-like. I did this by focusing not just on the color but also on variations between lighter and darker tones in the skin.

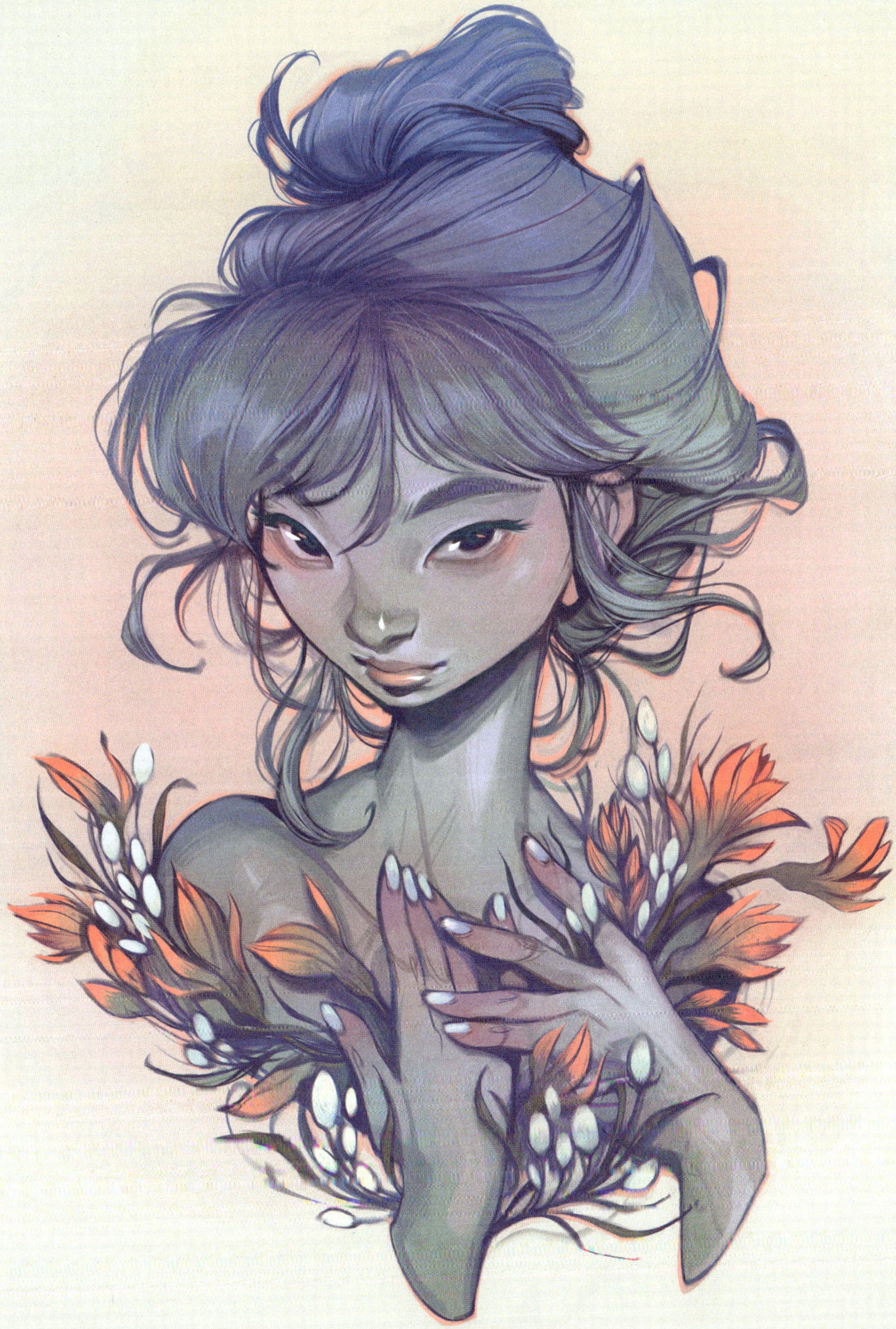

floret

In my digital painting process, sketch lines are very important. Not only do they form the construction of a piece, but I also use them to add texture and color to my work. I use Photoshop's Color Picker to select the line color and use that to add shadows and definition to the piece. Gradually the lines and paintwork merge together.

A lot of artists like to clean their line work and move forward from there, but I think there is a lot to gain from skipping this step and letting the dynamic lines of a sketch bring life to the final painting. Even though the lines are sometimes rough, they can add so much to the finished piece.

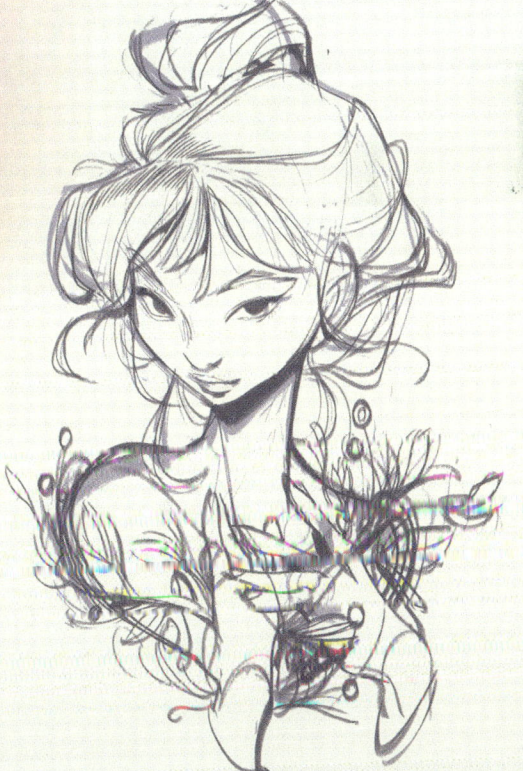

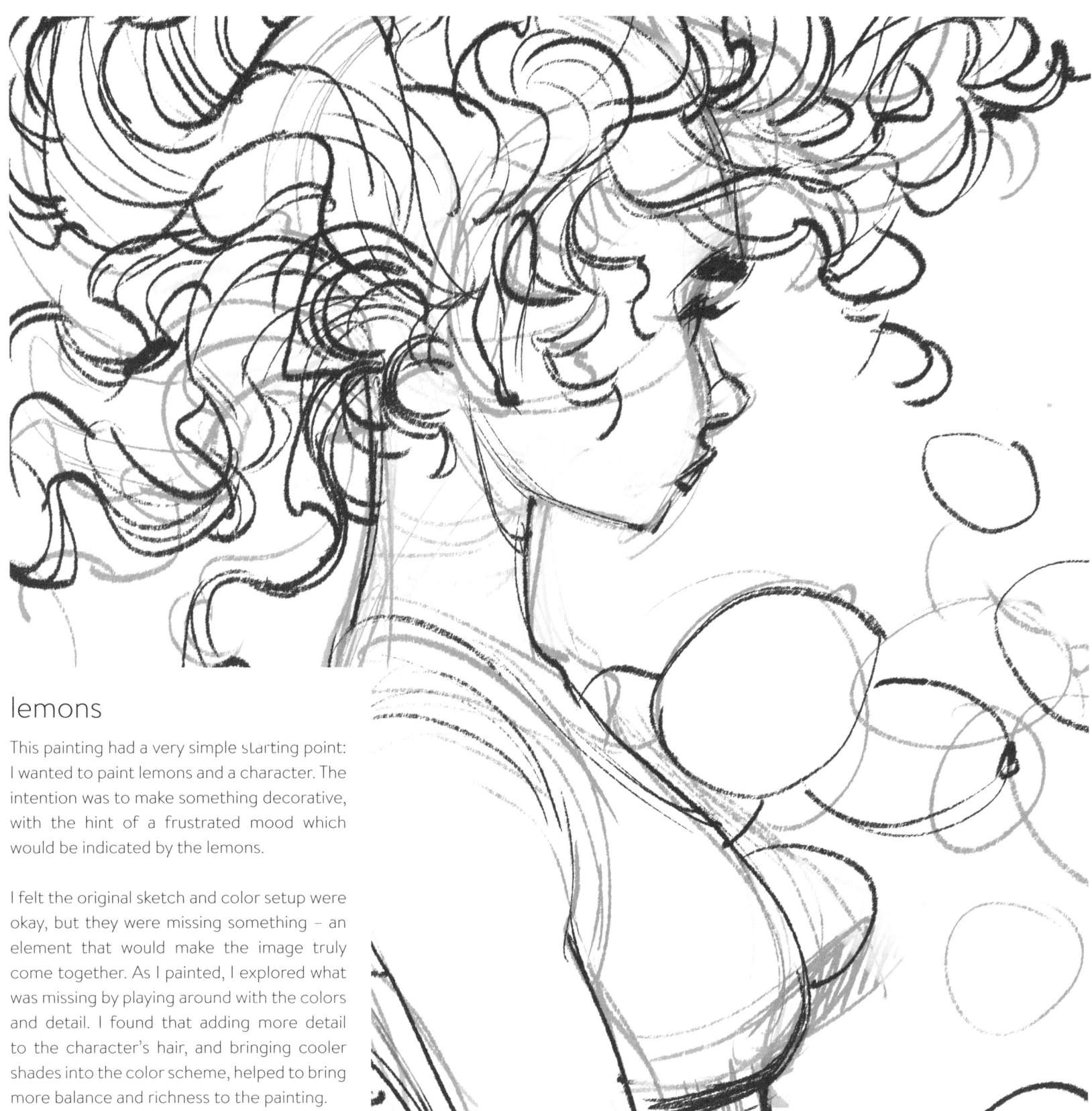

lemons

This painting had a very simple starting point: I wanted to paint lemons and a character. The intention was to make something decorative, with the hint of a frustrated mood which would be indicated by the lemons.

I felt the original sketch and color setup were okay, but they were missing something – an element that would make the image truly come together. As I painted, I explored what was missing by playing around with the colors and detail. I found that adding more detail to the character's hair, and bringing cooler shades into the color scheme, helped to bring more balance and richness to the painting.

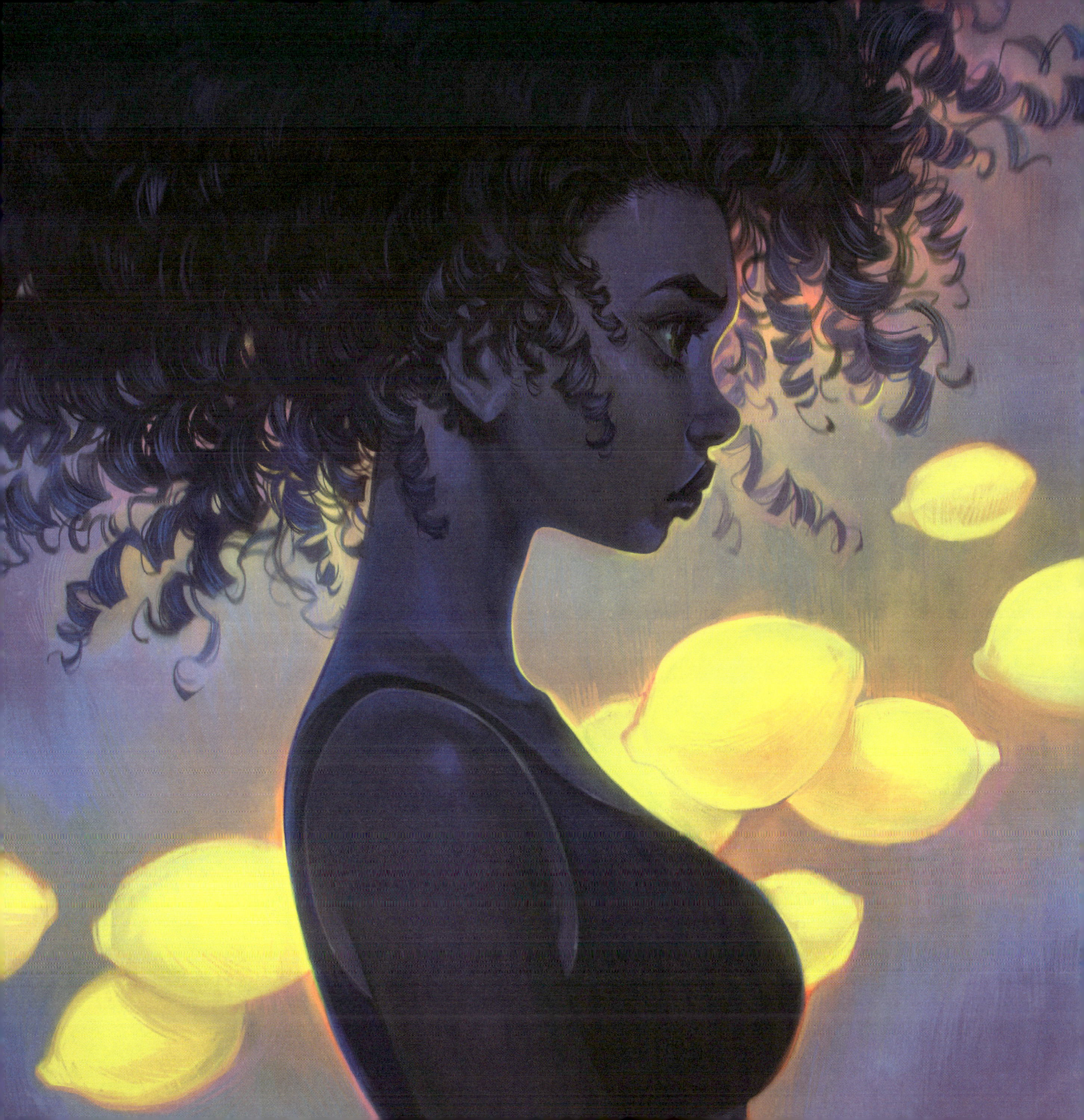

nocturne

This piece is a typical example of a painting that starts as a very simple sketch, and becomes more detailed through the painting process. Sometimes, I feel that it can be more efficient to quickly set up the basic composition and colors, and avoid spending too much time on the construction of an image.

I also find that starting with very cartoony proportions, and then moving towards more realistic proportions during the painting process, can create interesting results for the character. The result in this painting is something in-between a realistic and cartoony style.

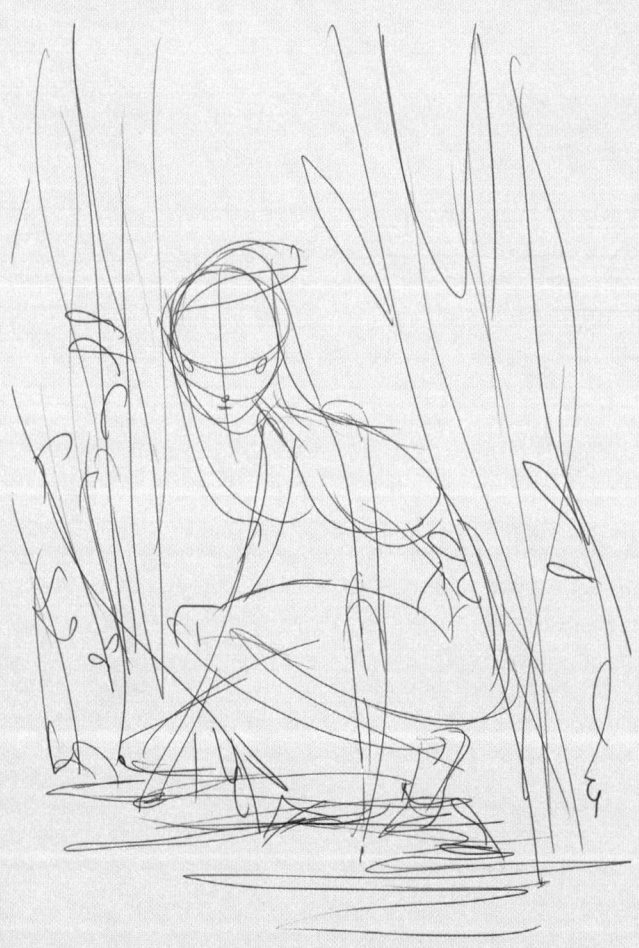

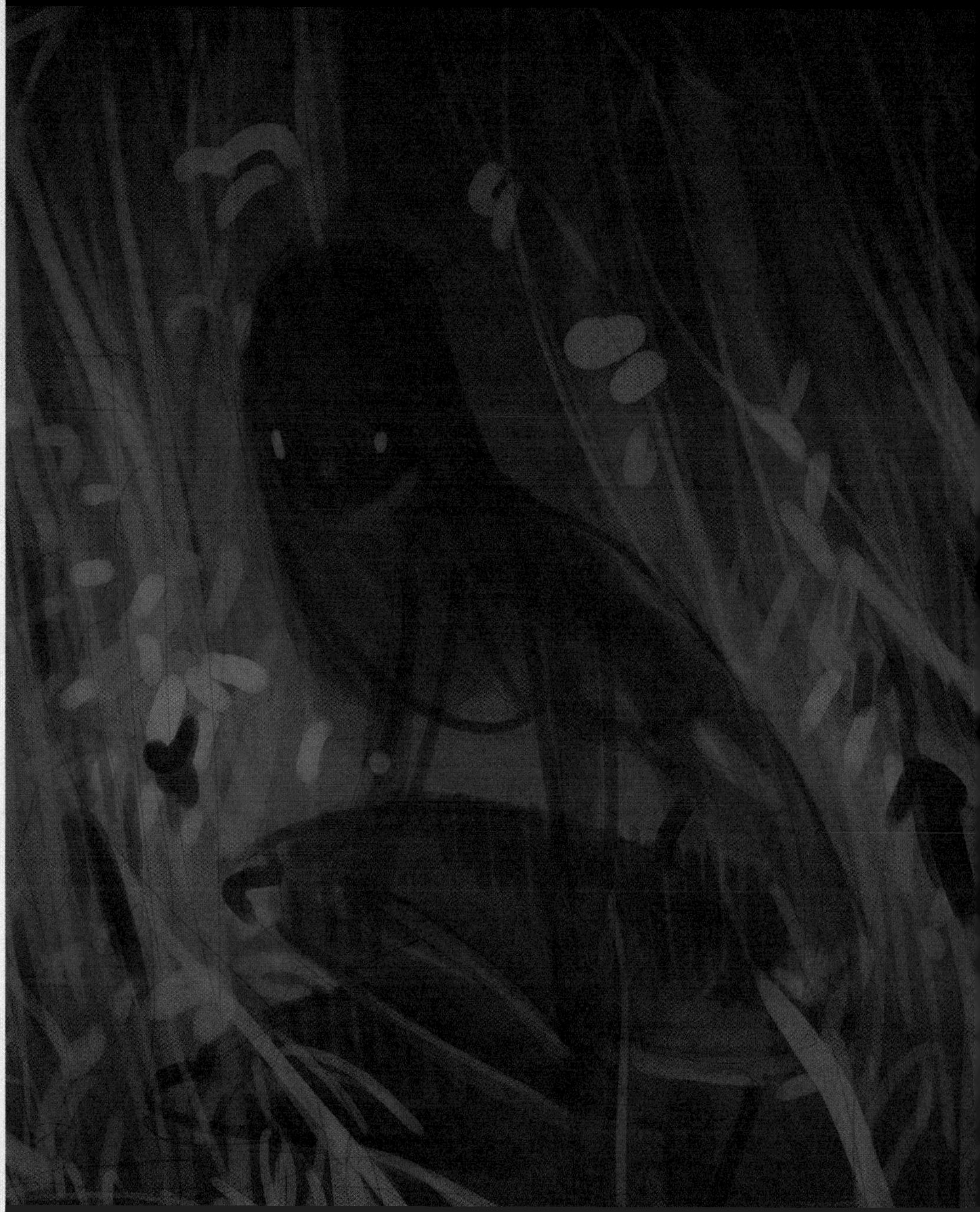

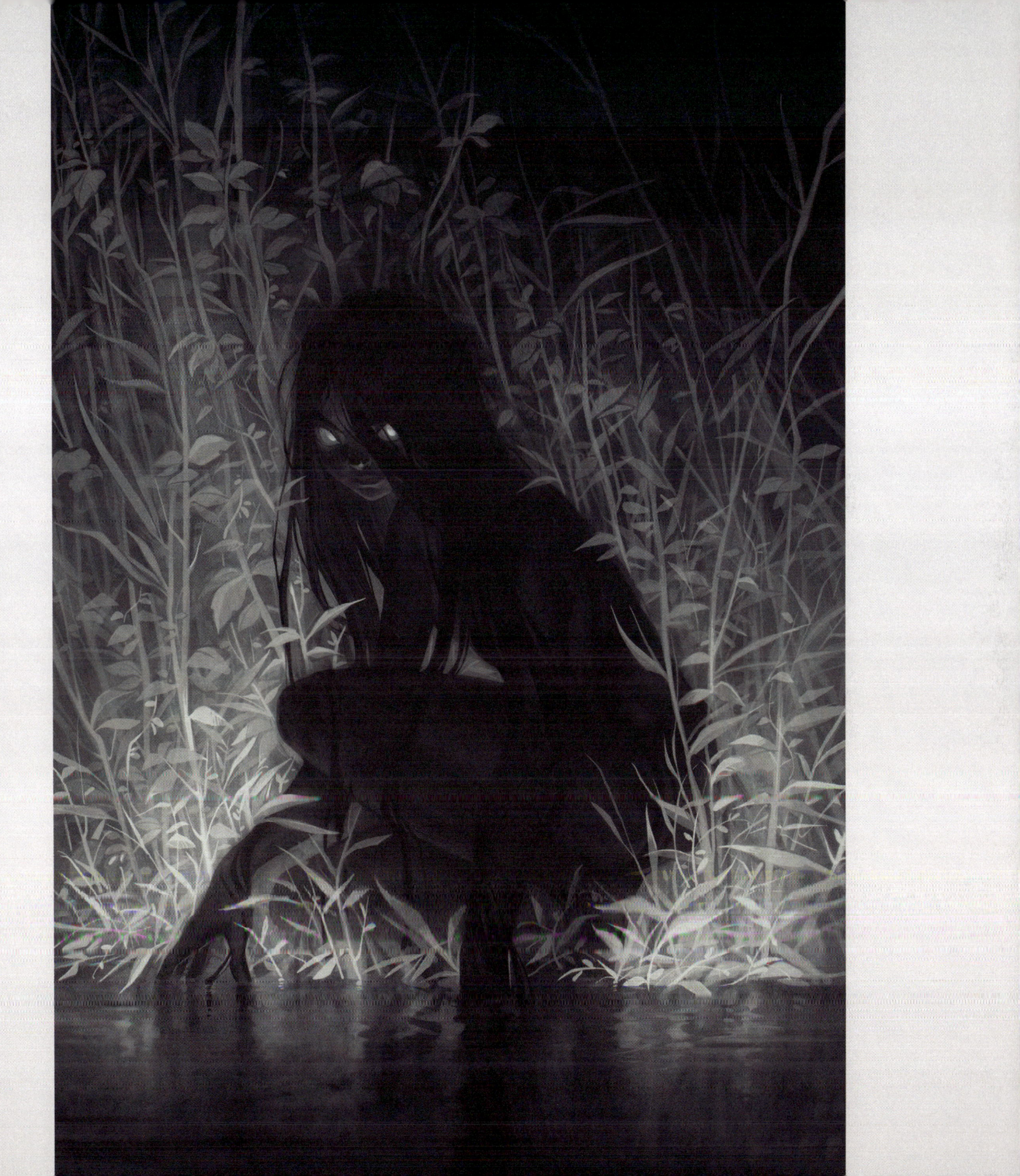

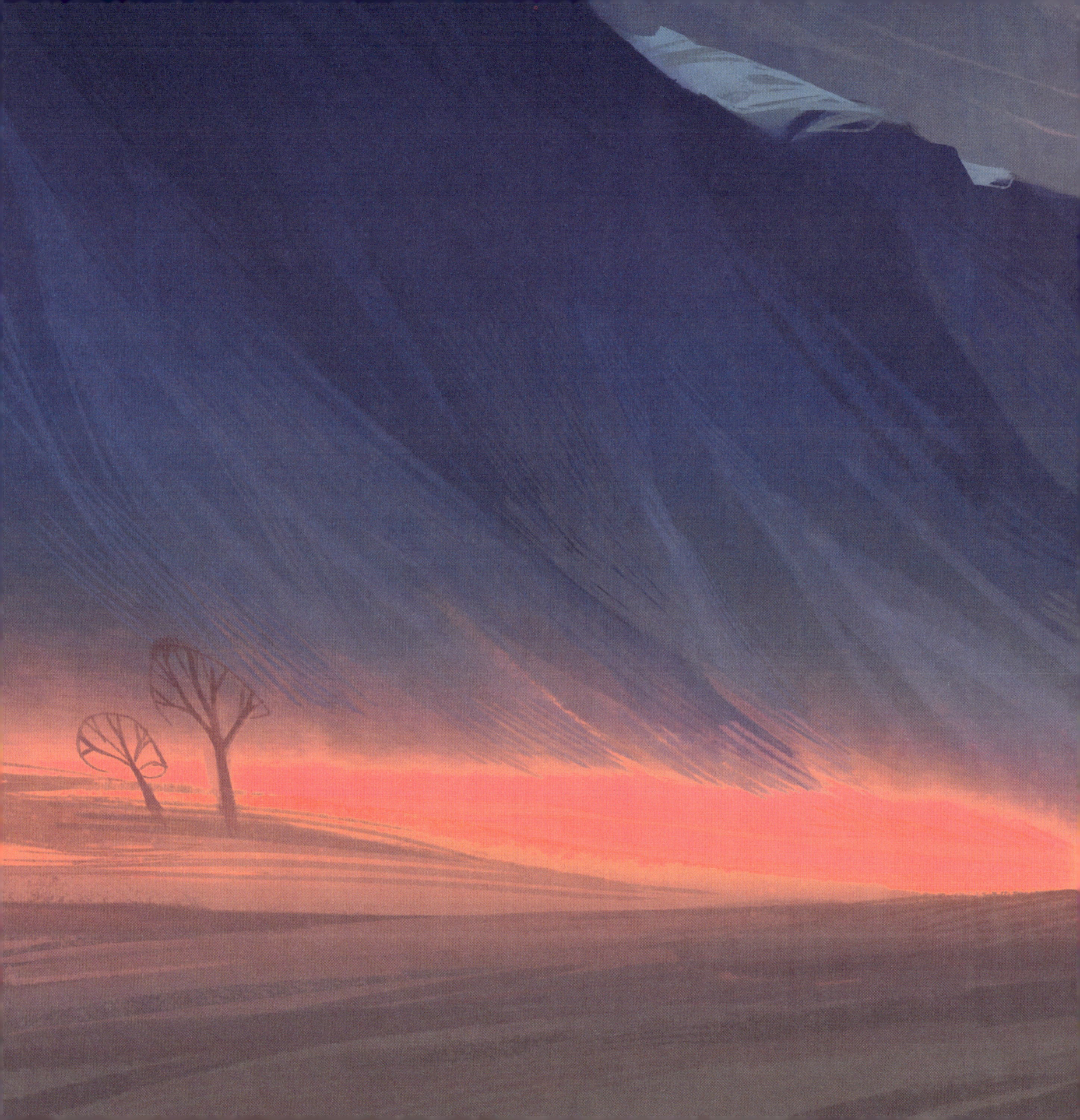

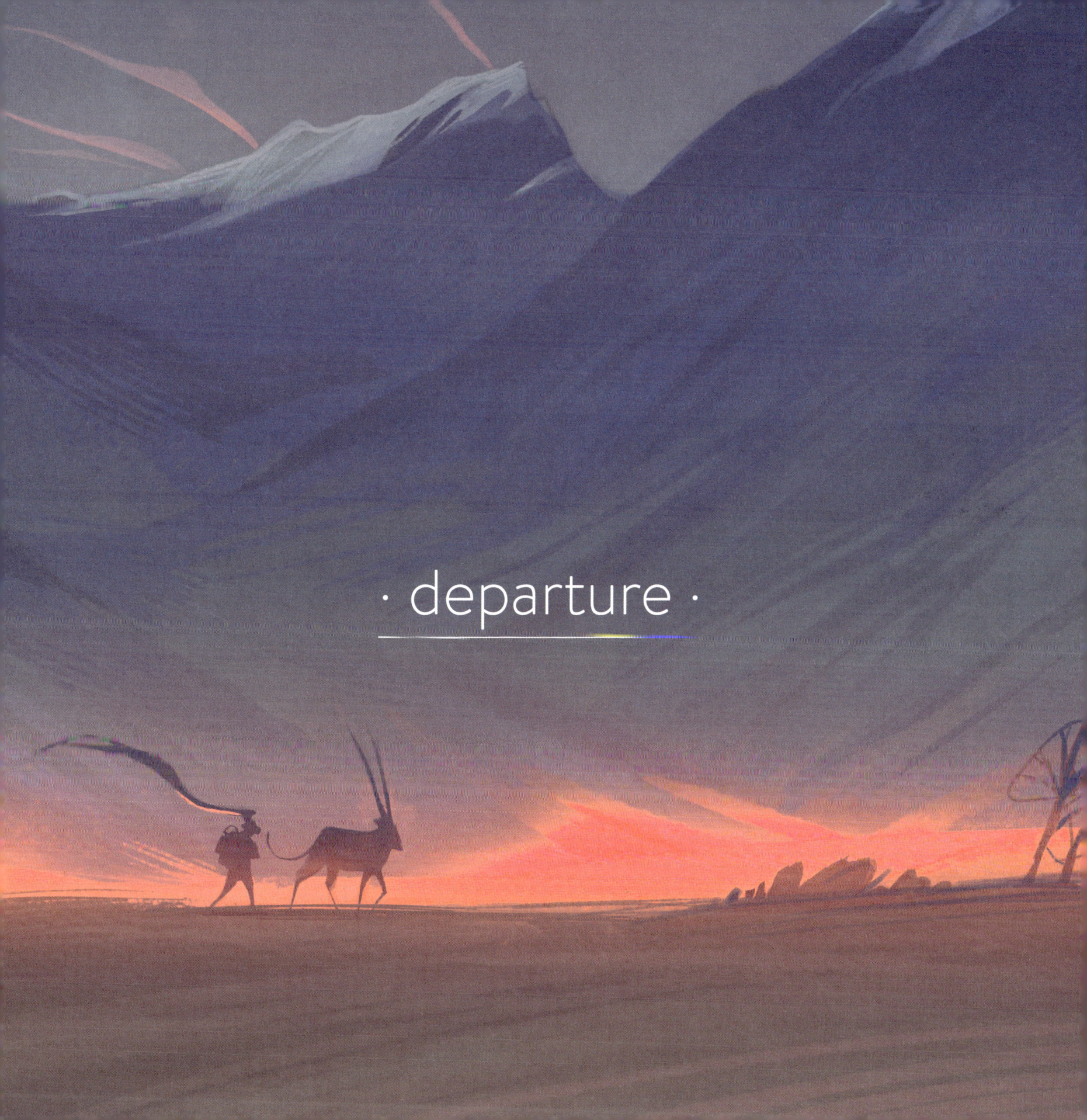

· departure ·

When planning the chapters for this book, the idea of creating a whole new concept from scratch popped into my mind. This would be a way for me to create character sketches, settings, and basically develop an idea from the ground up, just for this book. What I like about this idea is that it shows you not only the rough work that goes into bringing a concept to life, but also my own process from first sketch into a more detailed vision. So I began to develop *Departure*.

As a concept artist, I have worked on many different media projects, from games and animation to comics and illustration. I have learned that it is important to adapt my style to the demands of the medium. However, when I came up with *Departure*, I wanted to create something that could potentially be adapted into any medium, but for now, was not constricted to a specific style or limitation.

My starting point was a sketch from my sketchbook. I drew this sketch long before I started working on *Departure*. When I returned to it, the idea of a character embarking on a journey really resonated with me. With this sketch as my inspiration, I started to develop the idea further.

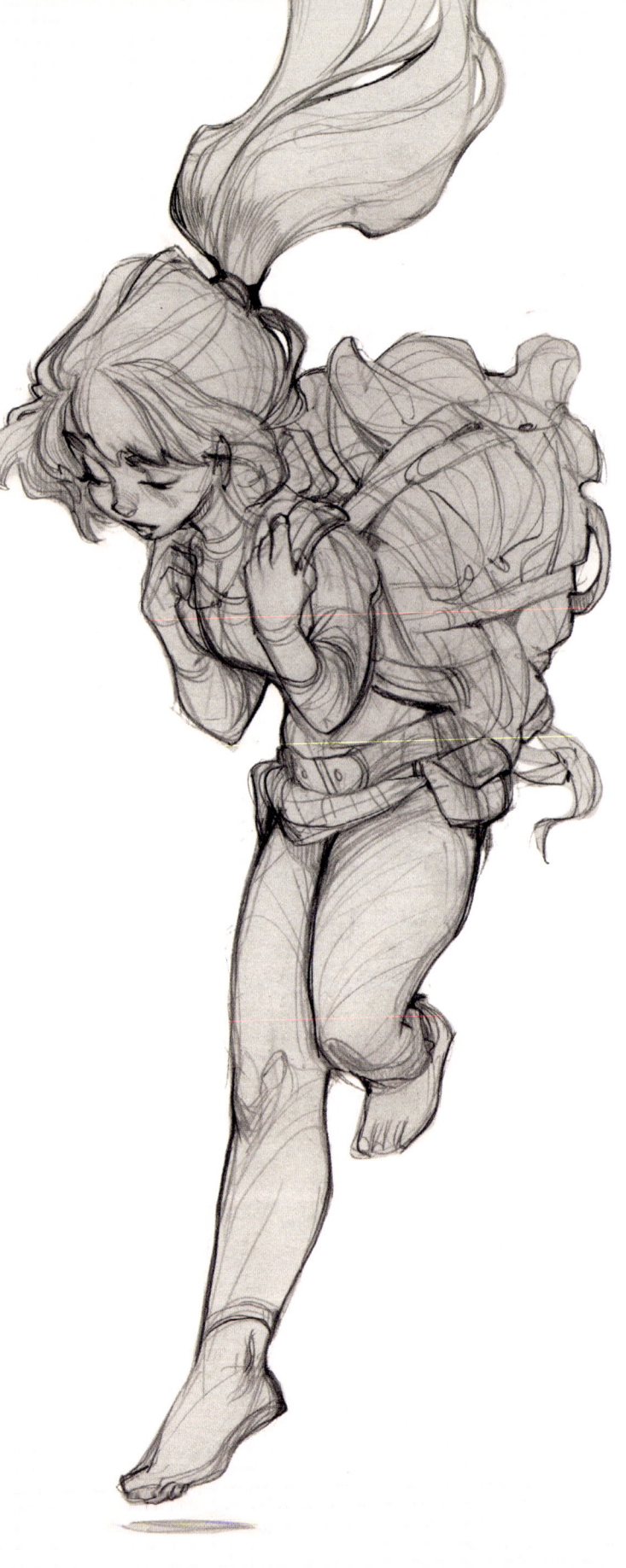

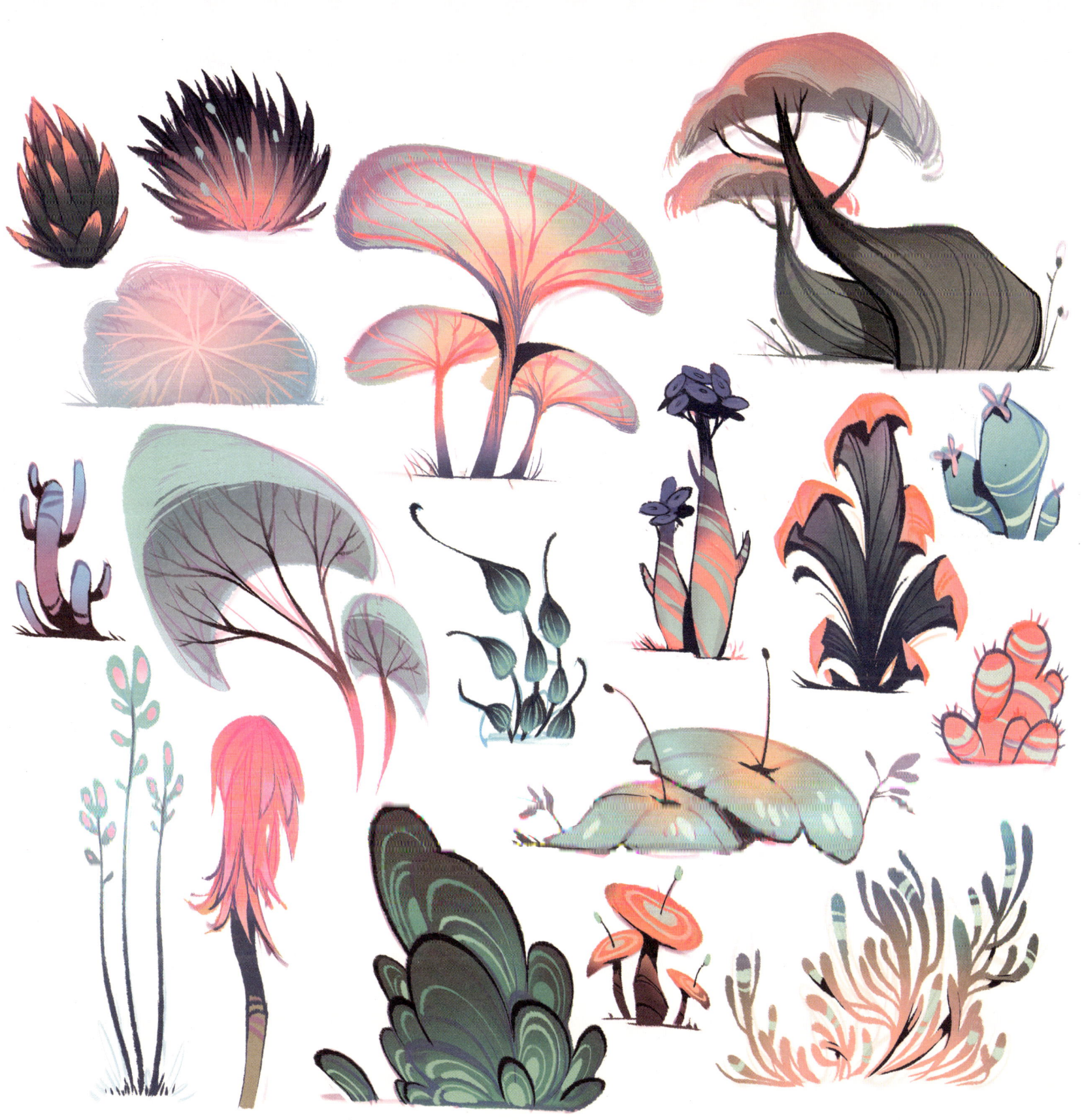

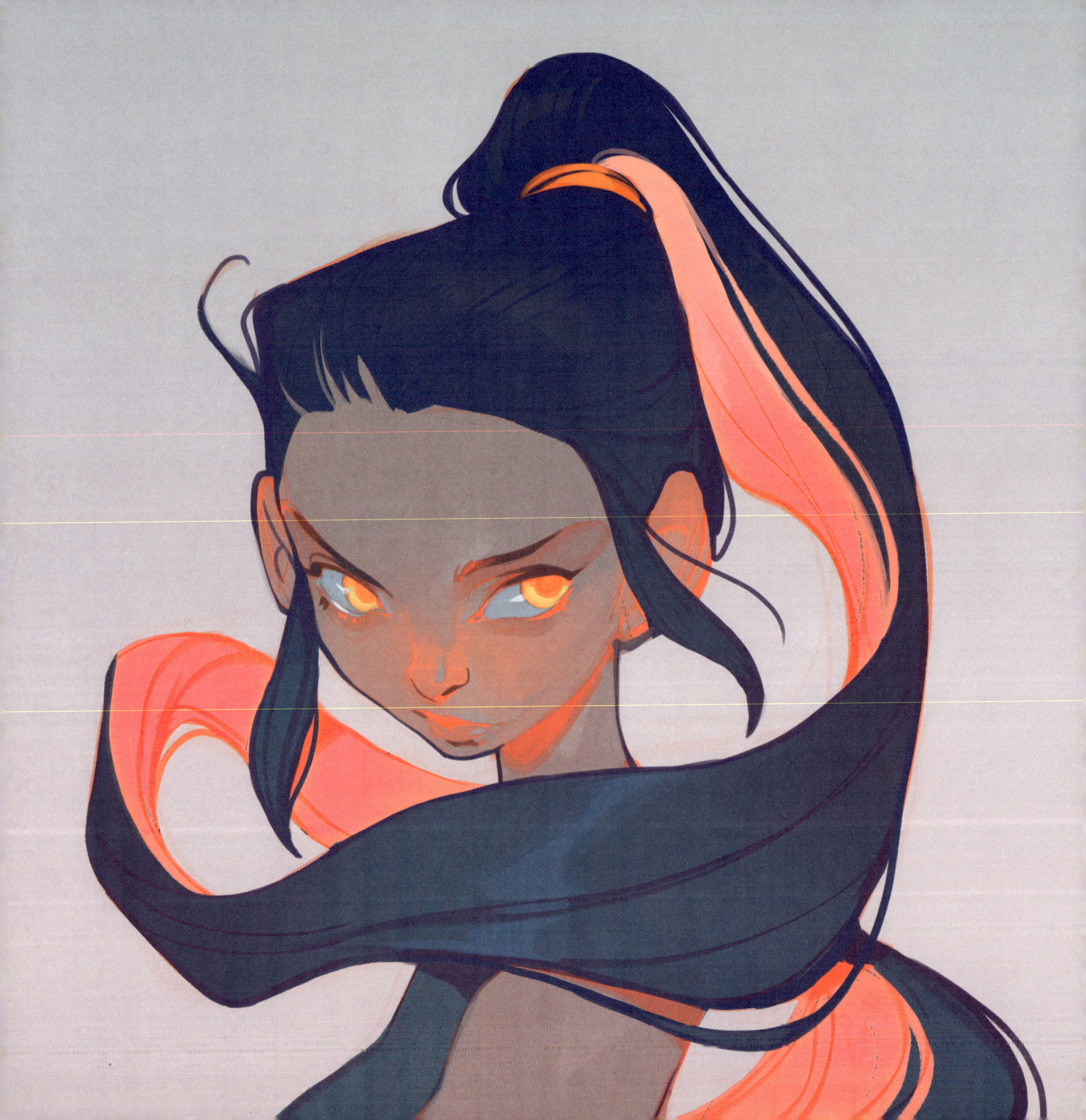

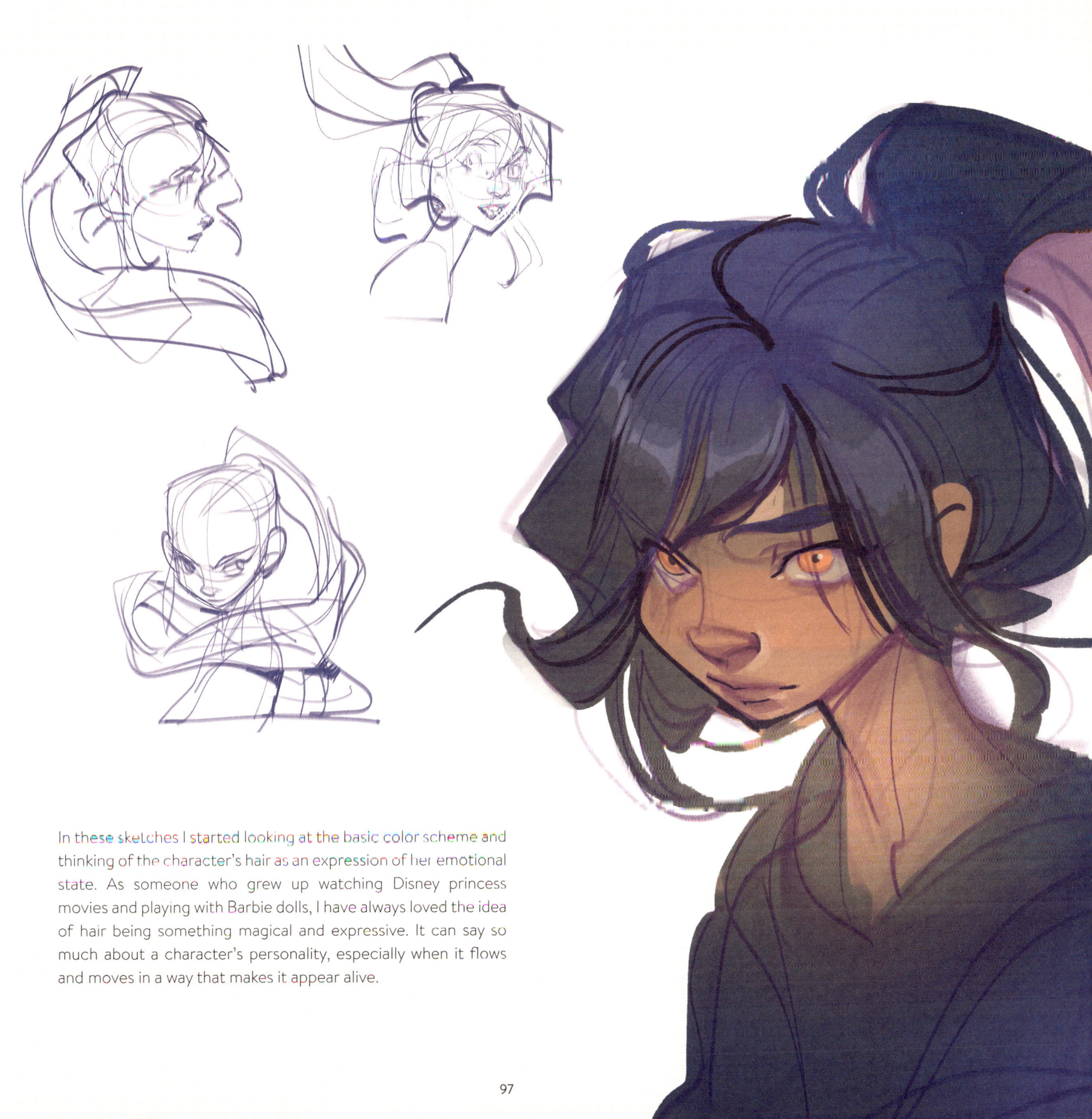

In these sketches I started looking at the basic color scheme and thinking of the character's hair as an expression of her emotional state. As someone who grew up watching Disney princess movies and playing with Barbie dolls, I have always loved the idea of hair being something magical and expressive. It can say so much about a character's personality, especially when it flows and moves in a way that makes it appear alive.

97

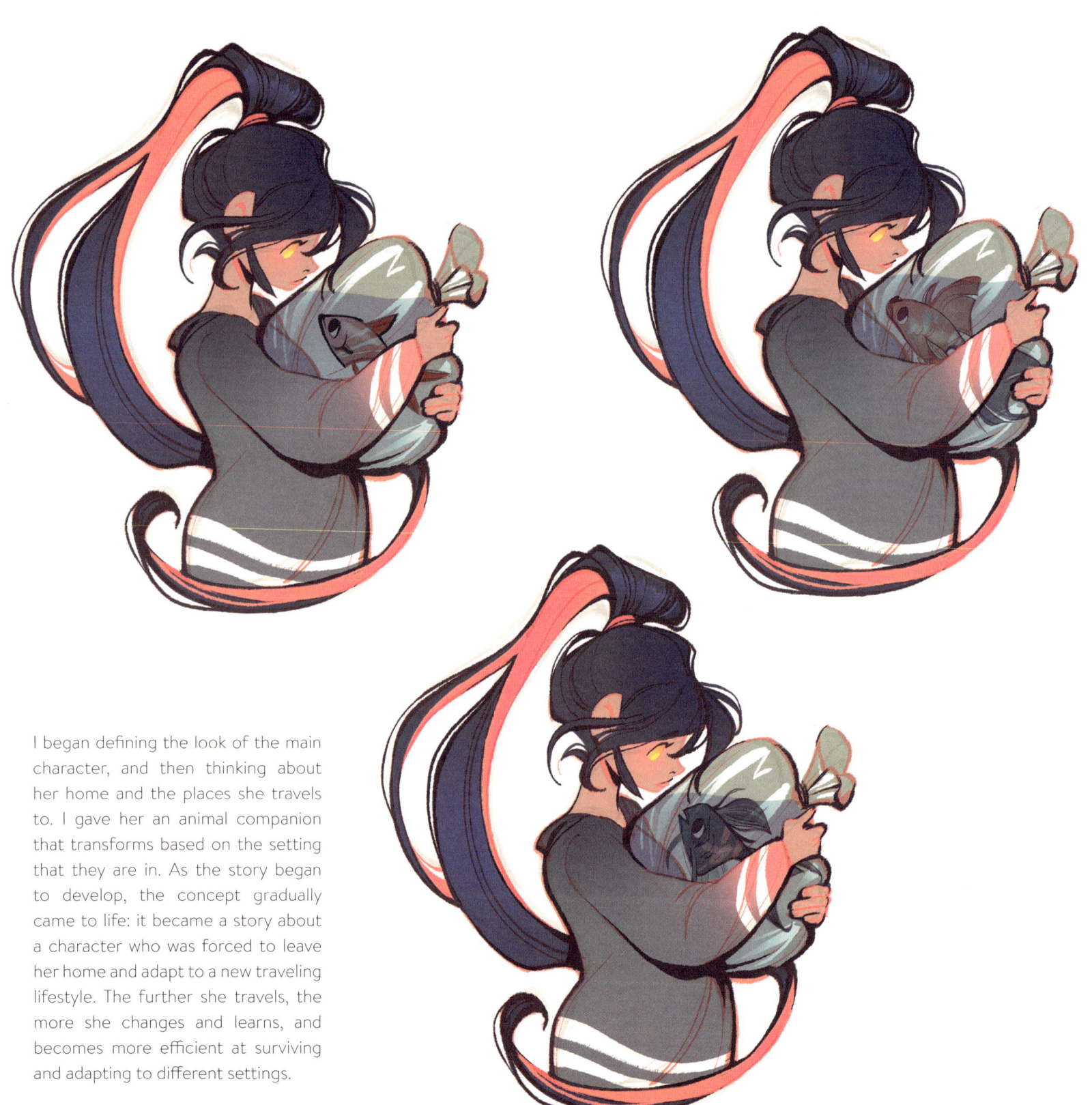

I began defining the look of the main character, and then thinking about her home and the places she travels to. I gave her an animal companion that transforms based on the setting that they are in. As the story began to develop, the concept gradually came to life: it became a story about a character who was forced to leave her home and adapt to a new traveling lifestyle. The further she travels, the more she changes and learns, and becomes more efficient at surviving and adapting to different settings.

> "I let the details form with each new drawing, and gave the concept room to change and evolve"

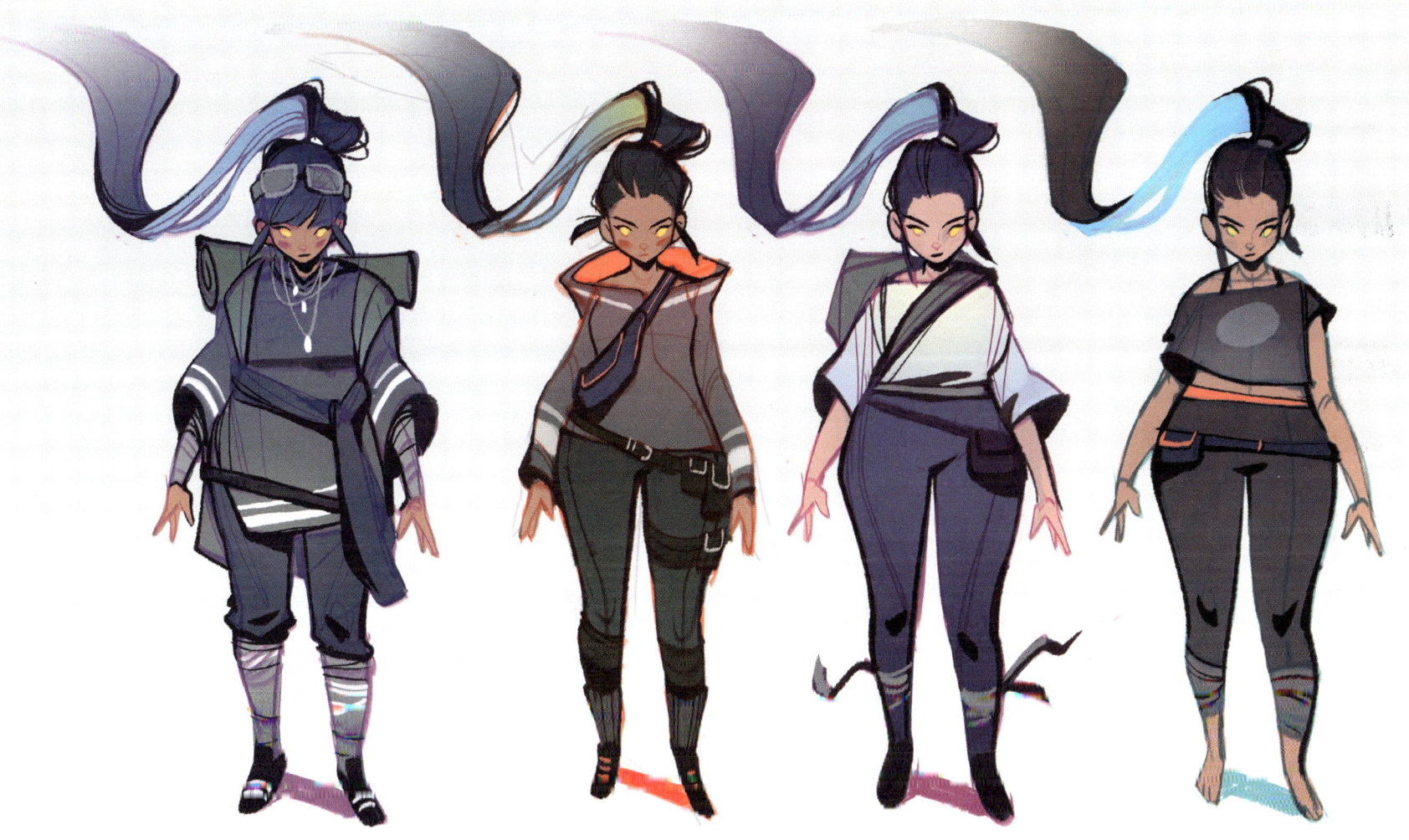

I wanted this character to live in a fantasy world so I included elements of the world we live in, but also elements of an imaginary place. In exploring different outfits, I looked at ways to make her clothing look convenient and comfortable while still having something futuristic and unique in the smaller details.

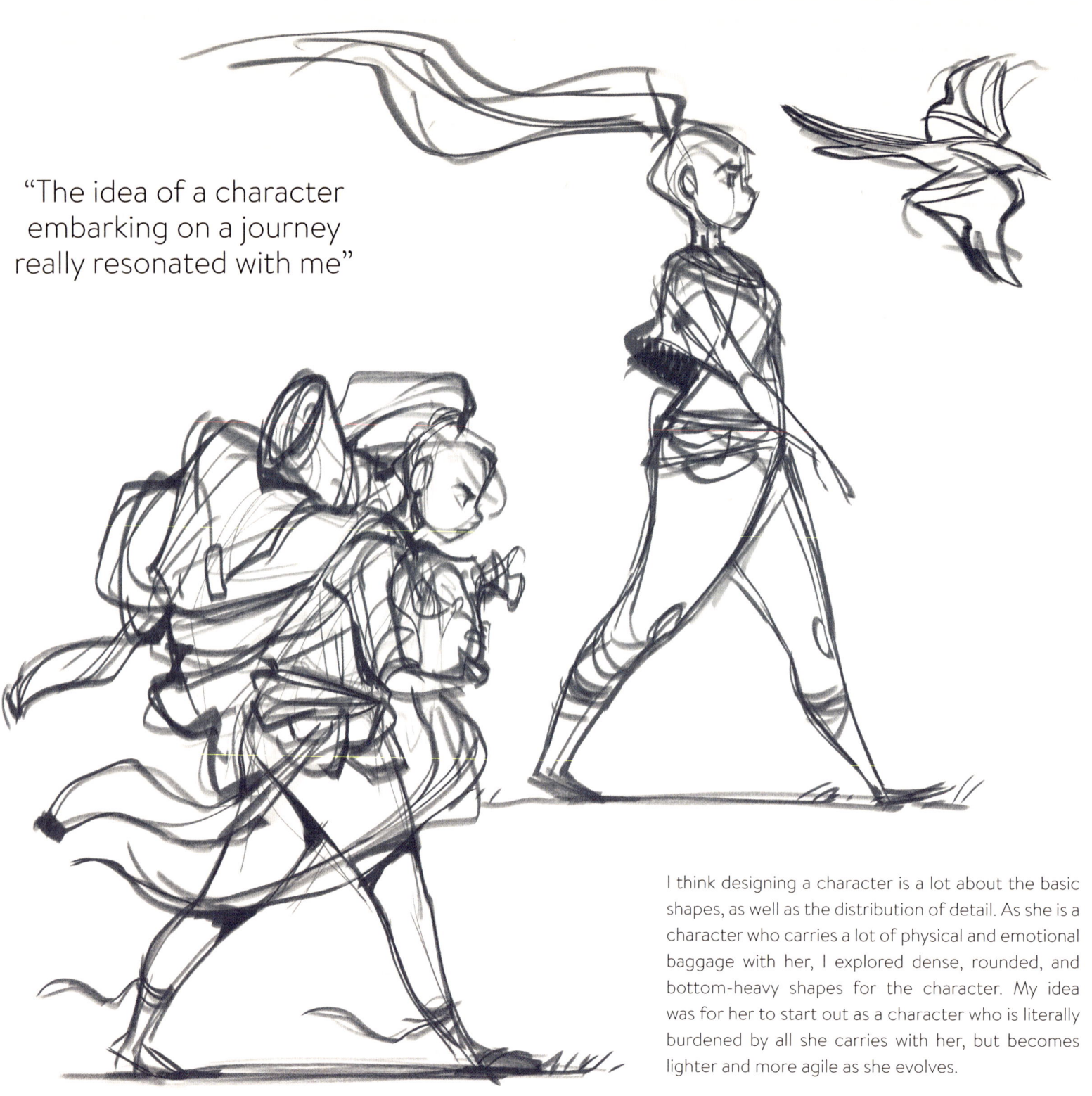

"The idea of a character embarking on a journey really resonated with me"

I think designing a character is a lot about the basic shapes, as well as the distribution of detail. As she is a character who carries a lot of physical and emotional baggage with her, I explored dense, rounded, and bottom-heavy shapes for the character. My idea was for her to start out as a character who is literally burdened by all she carries with her, but becomes lighter and more agile as she evolves.

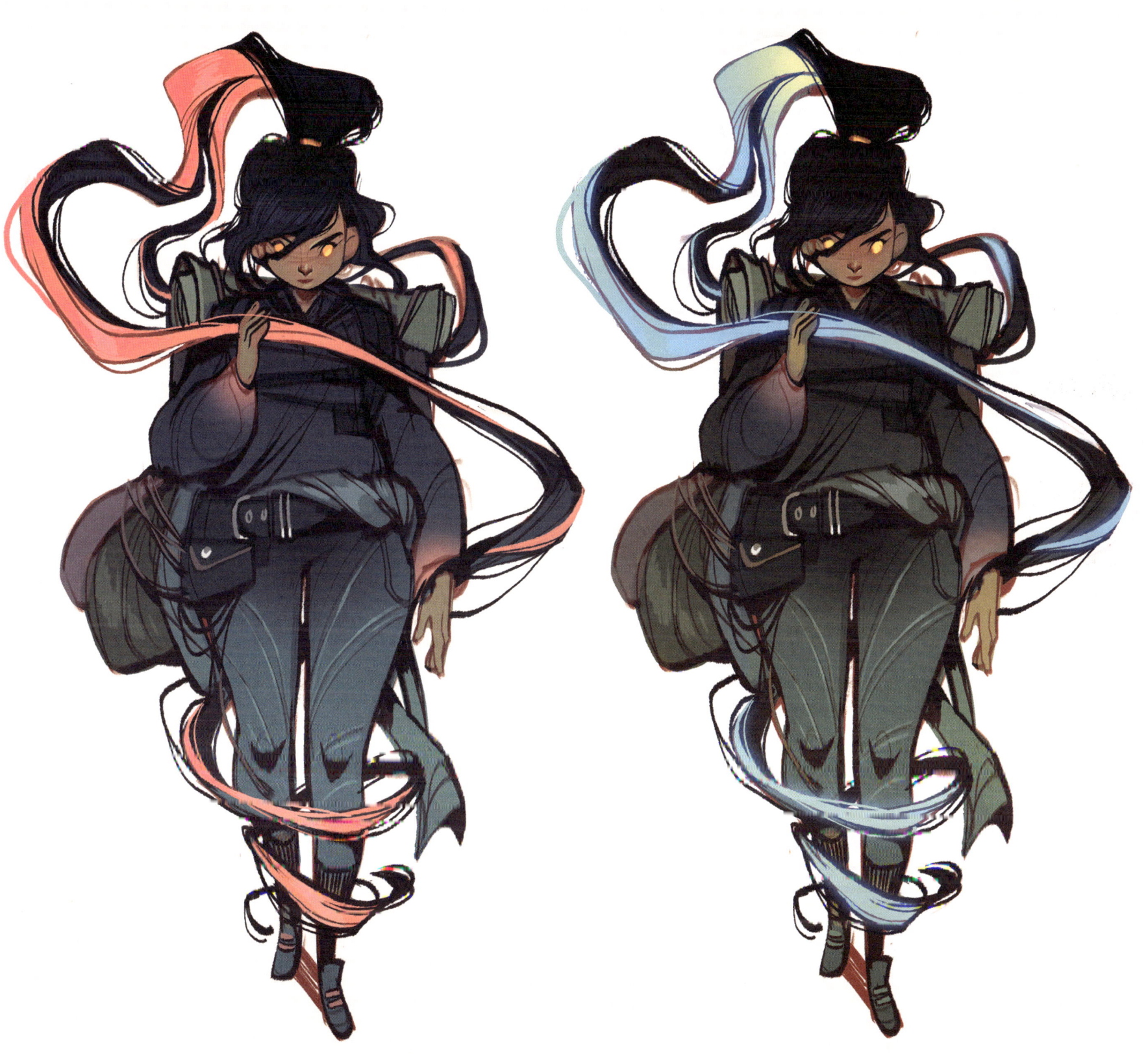

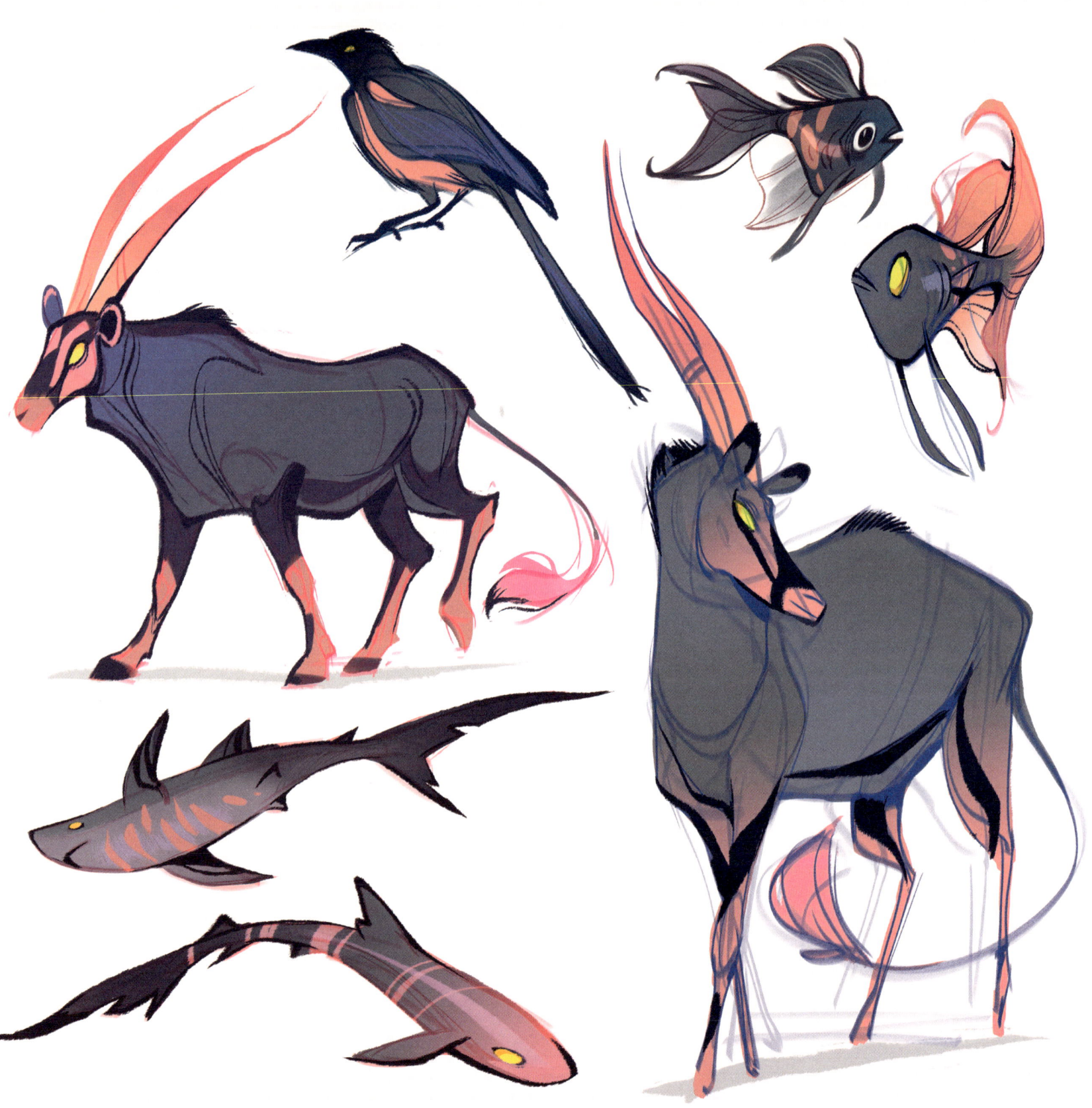

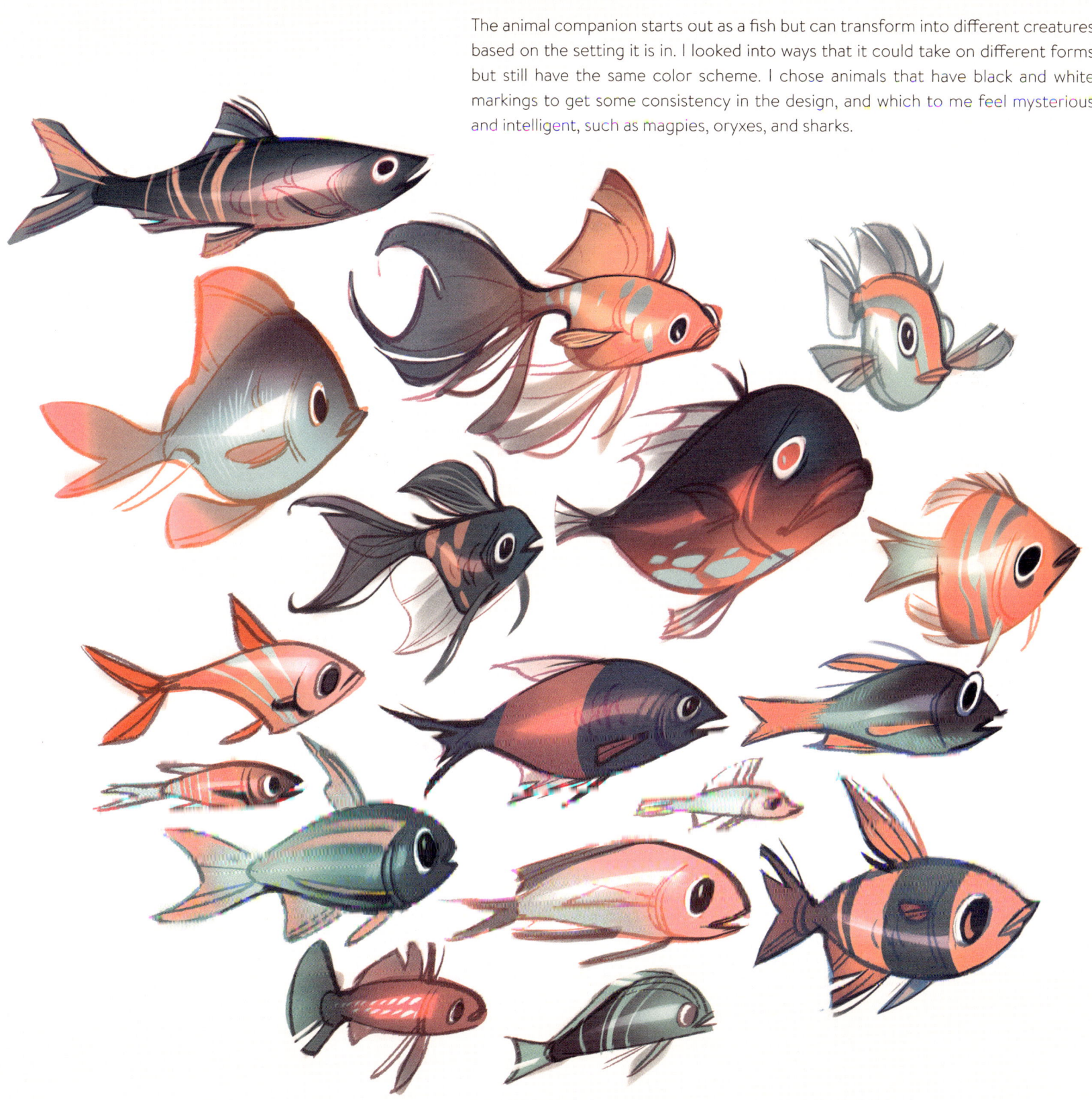

The animal companion starts out as a fish but can transform into different creatures based on the setting it is in. I looked into ways that it could take on different forms but still have the same color scheme. I chose animals that have black and white markings to get some consistency in the design, and which to me feel mysterious and intelligent, such as magpies, oryxes, and sharks.

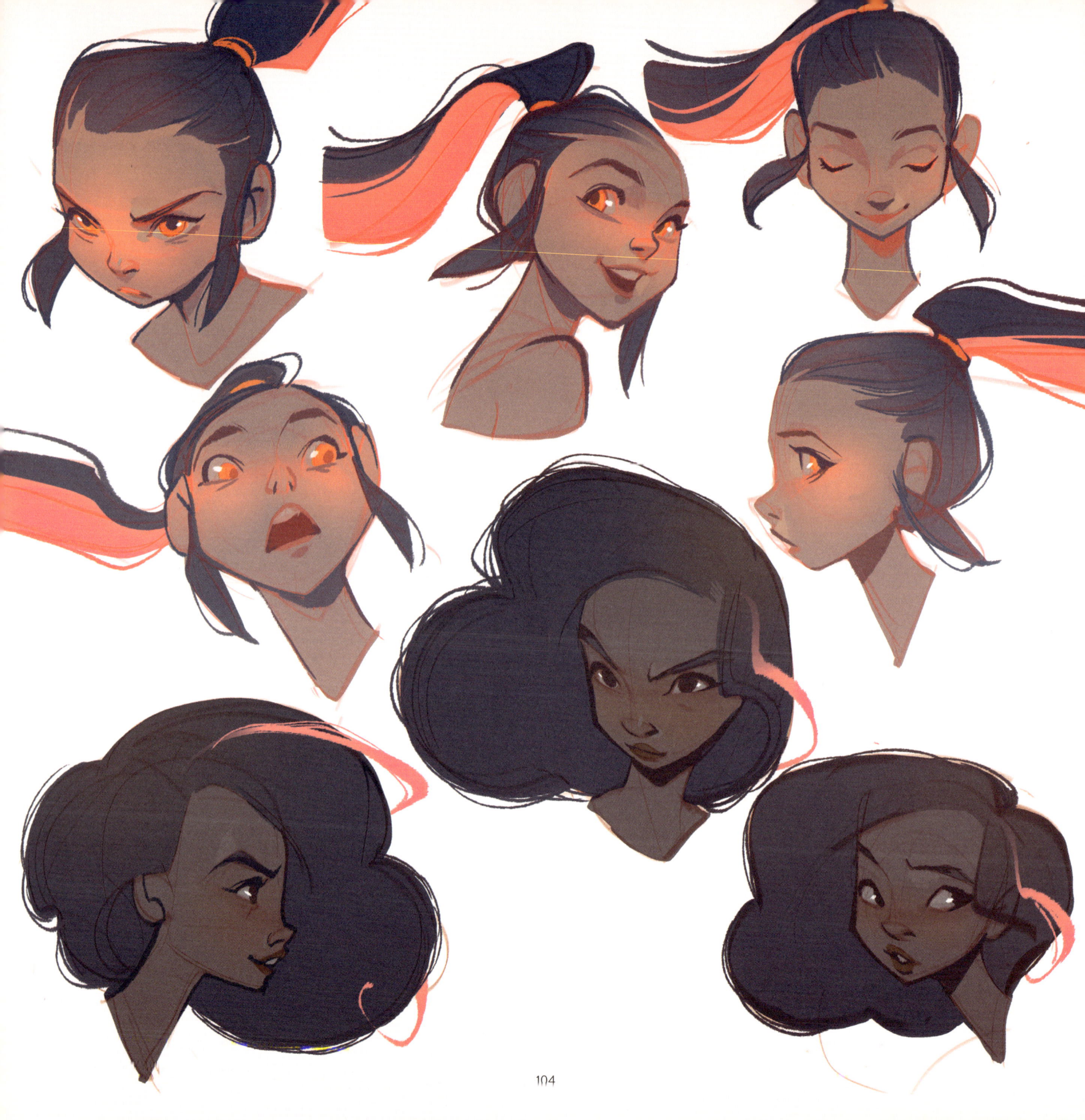

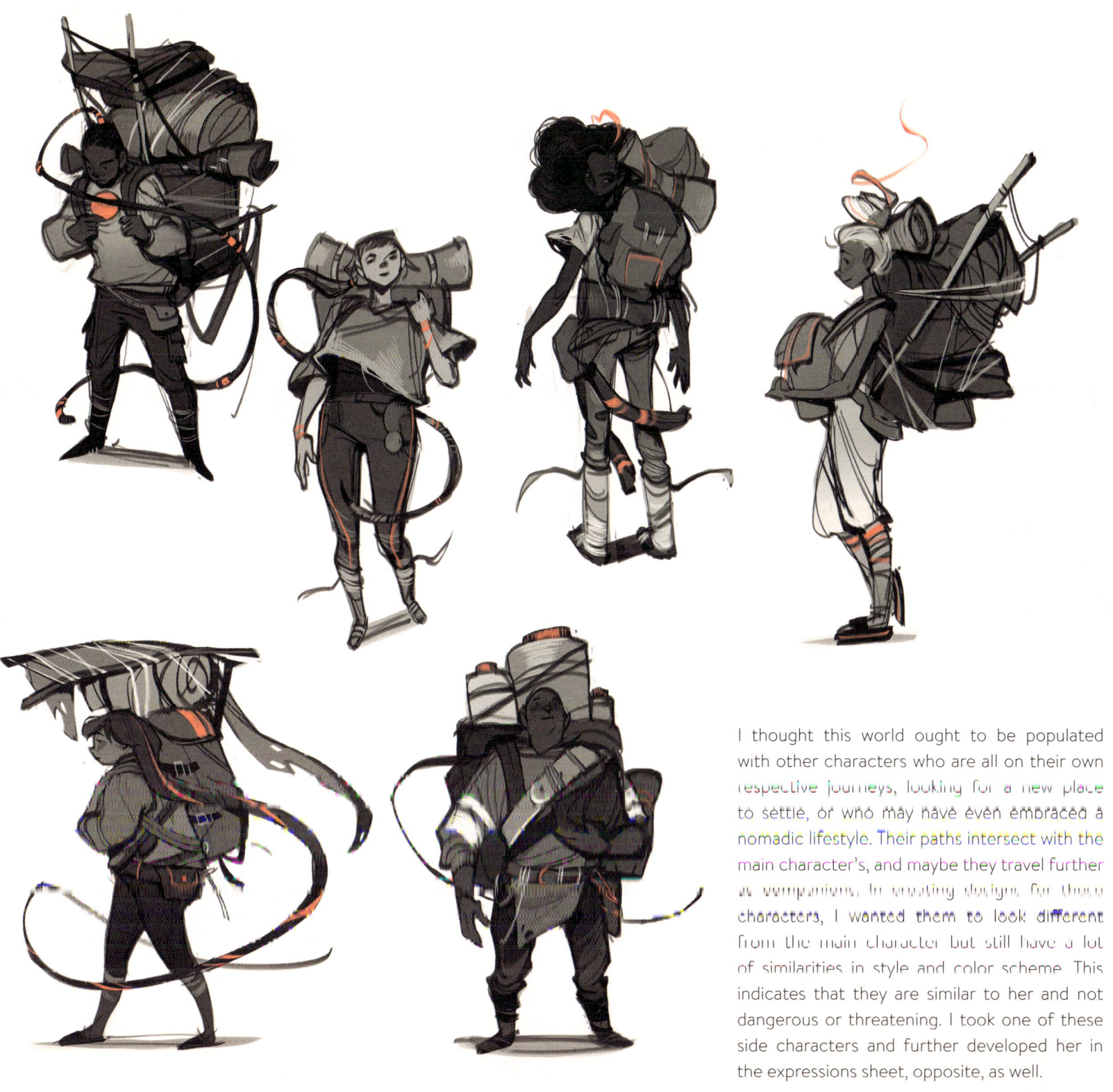

I thought this world ought to be populated with other characters who are all on their own respective journeys, looking for a new place to settle, or who may have even embraced a nomadic lifestyle. Their paths intersect with the main character's, and maybe they travel further as companions. In creating designs for these characters, I wanted them to look different from the main character but still have a lot of similarities in style and color scheme. This indicates that they are similar to her and not dangerous or threatening. I took one of these side characters and further developed her in the expressions sheet, opposite, as well.

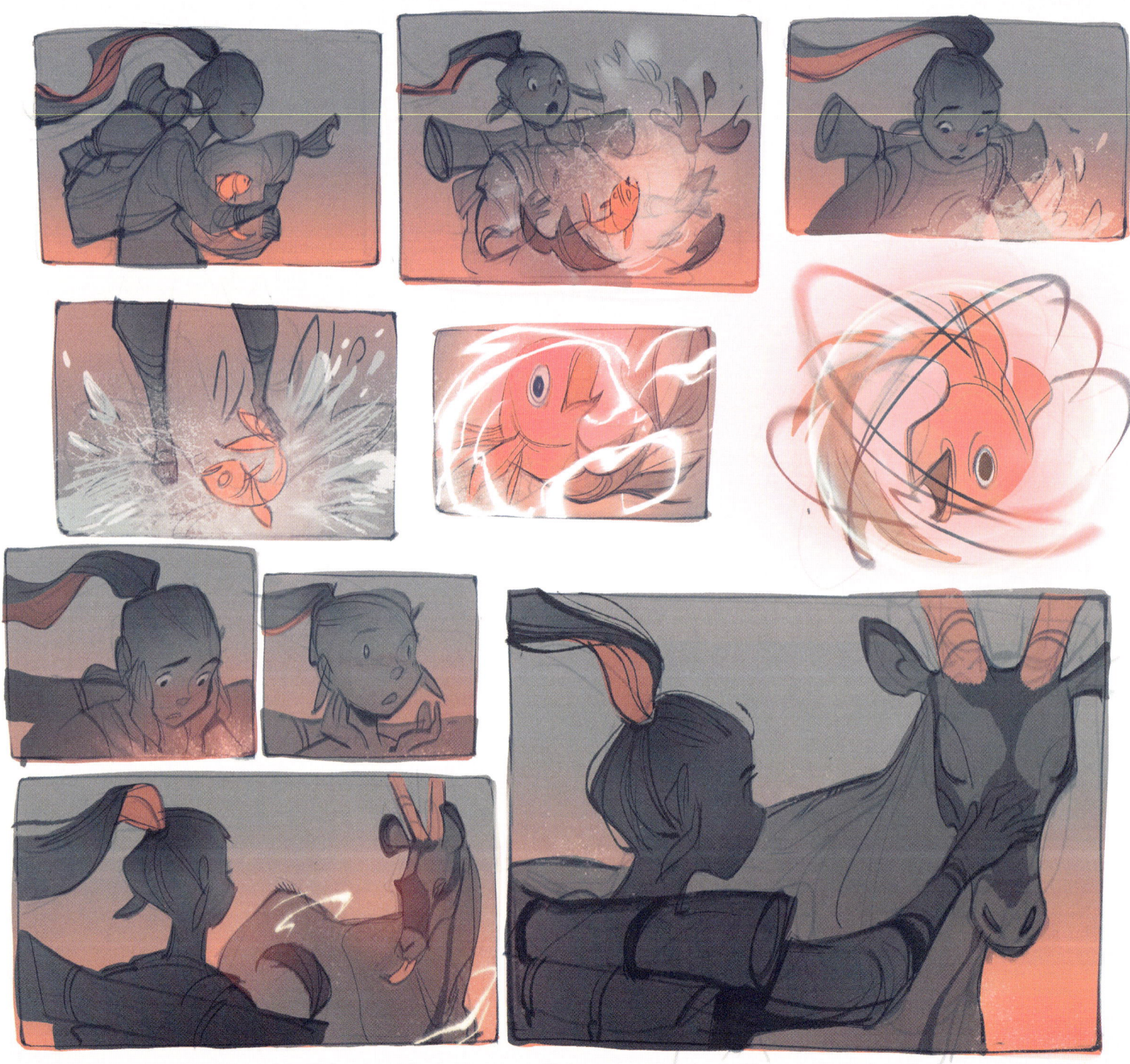

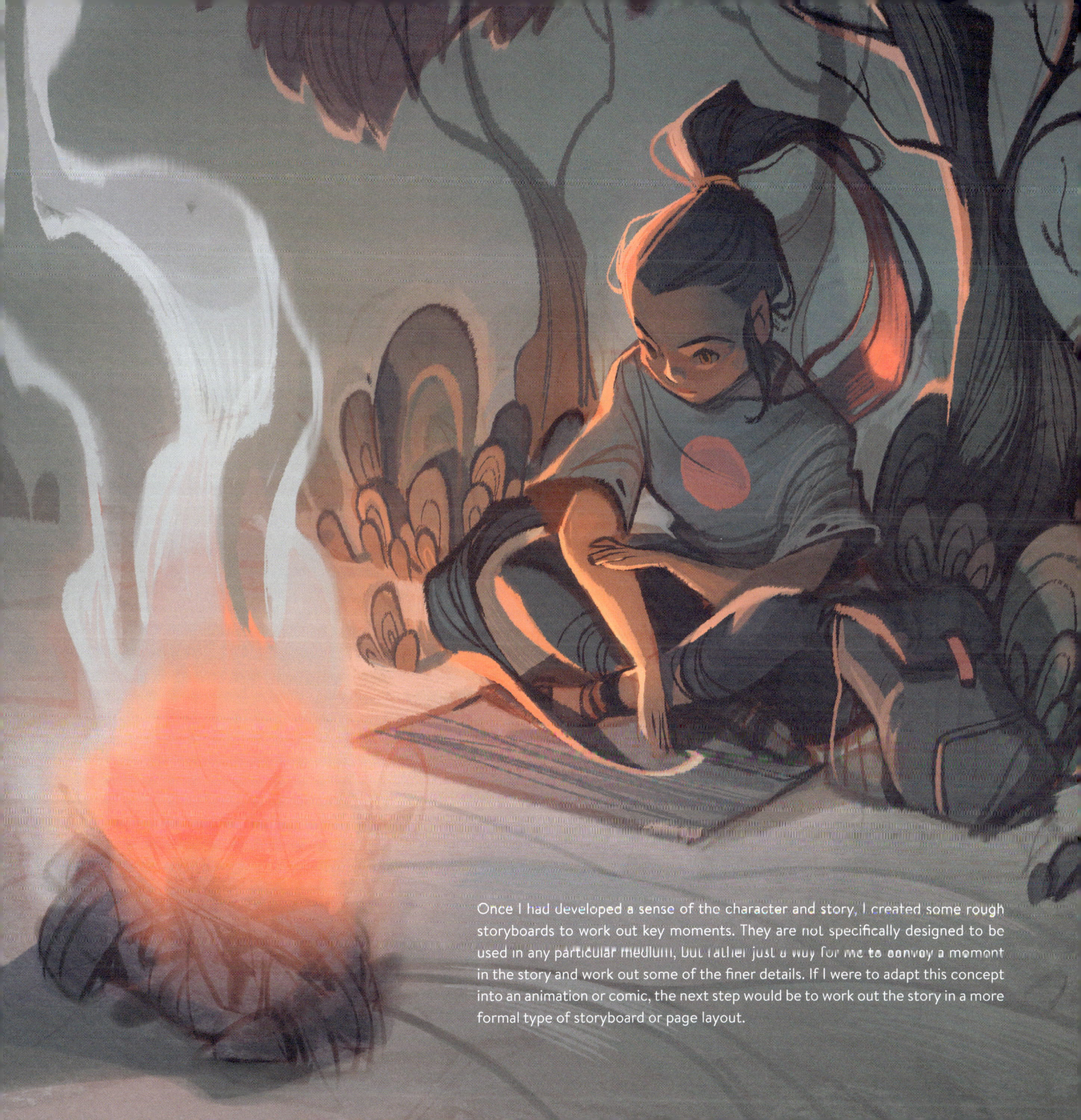

Once I had developed a sense of the character and story, I created some rough storyboards to work out key moments. They are not specifically designed to be used in any particular medium, but rather just a way for me to convey a moment in the story and work out some of the finer details. If I were to adapt this concept into an animation or comic, the next step would be to work out the story in a more formal type of storyboard or page layout.

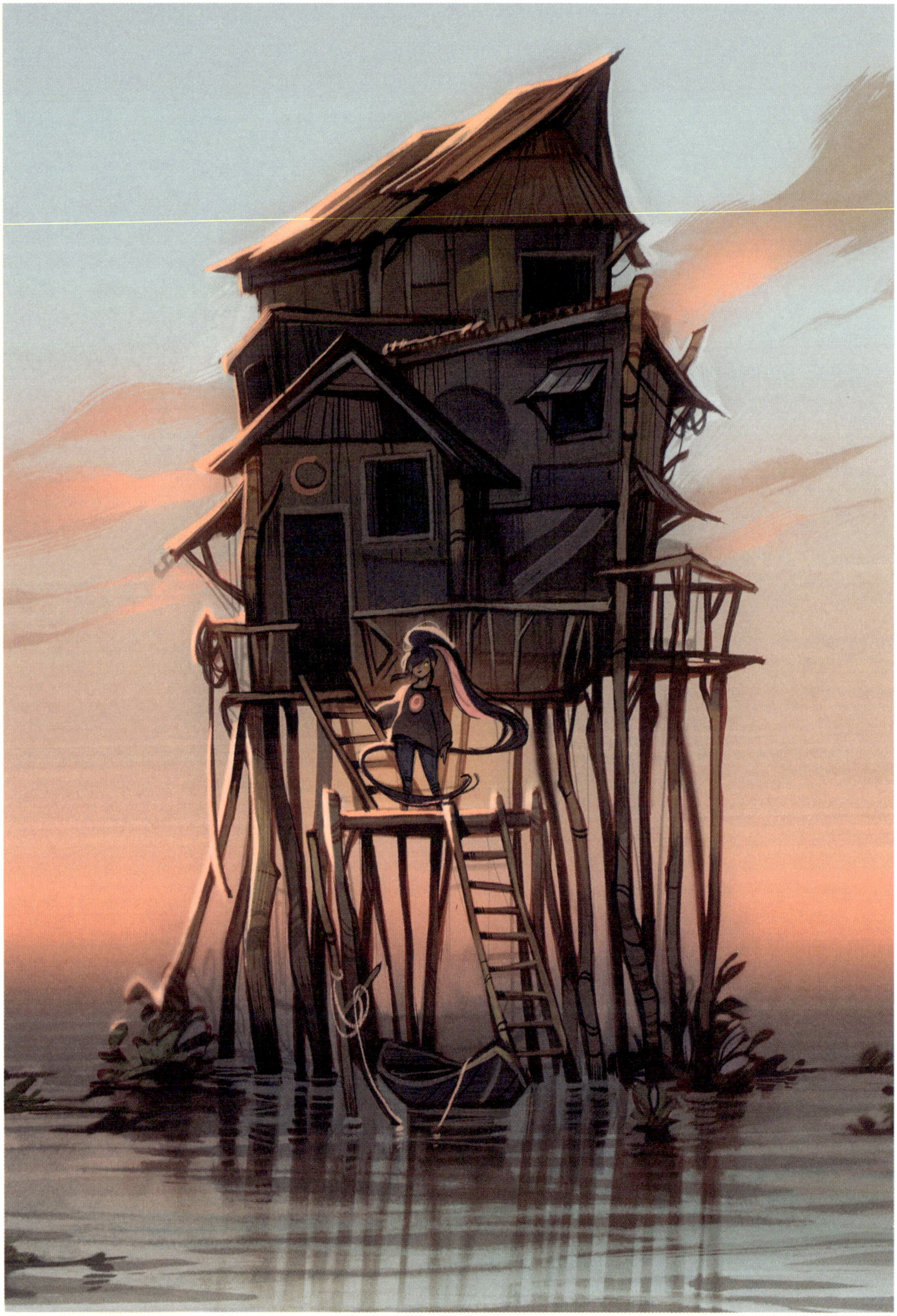

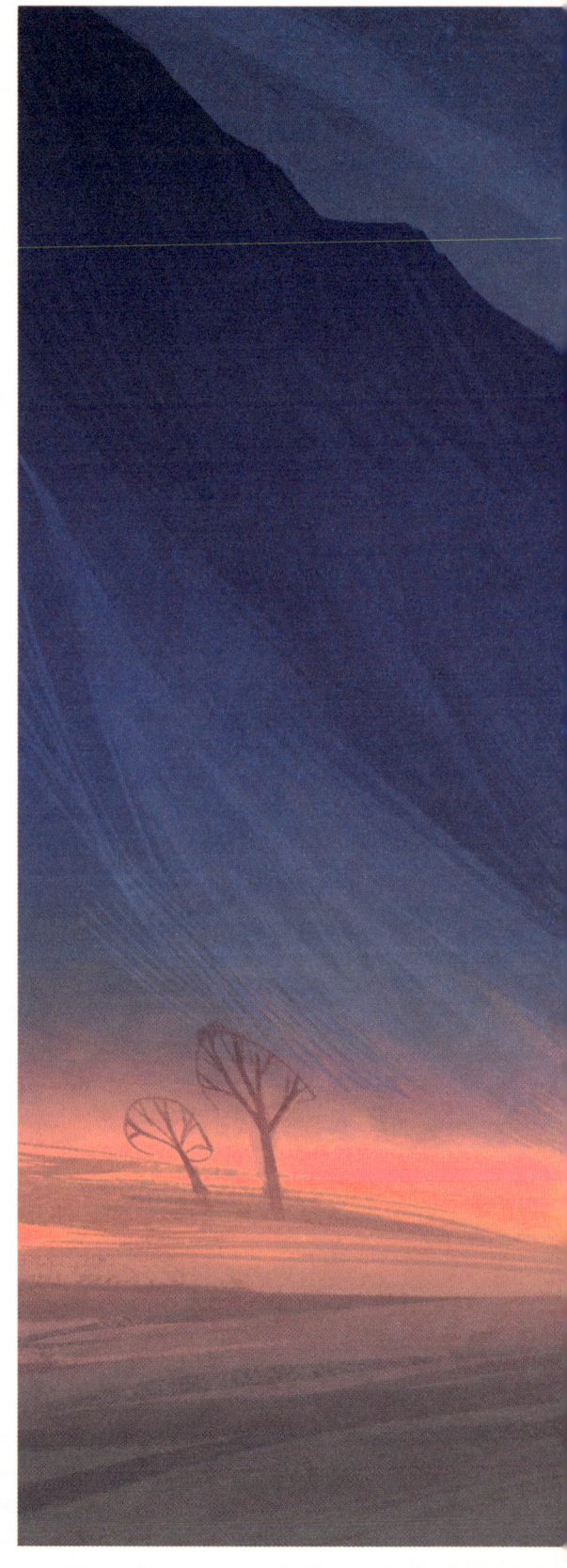

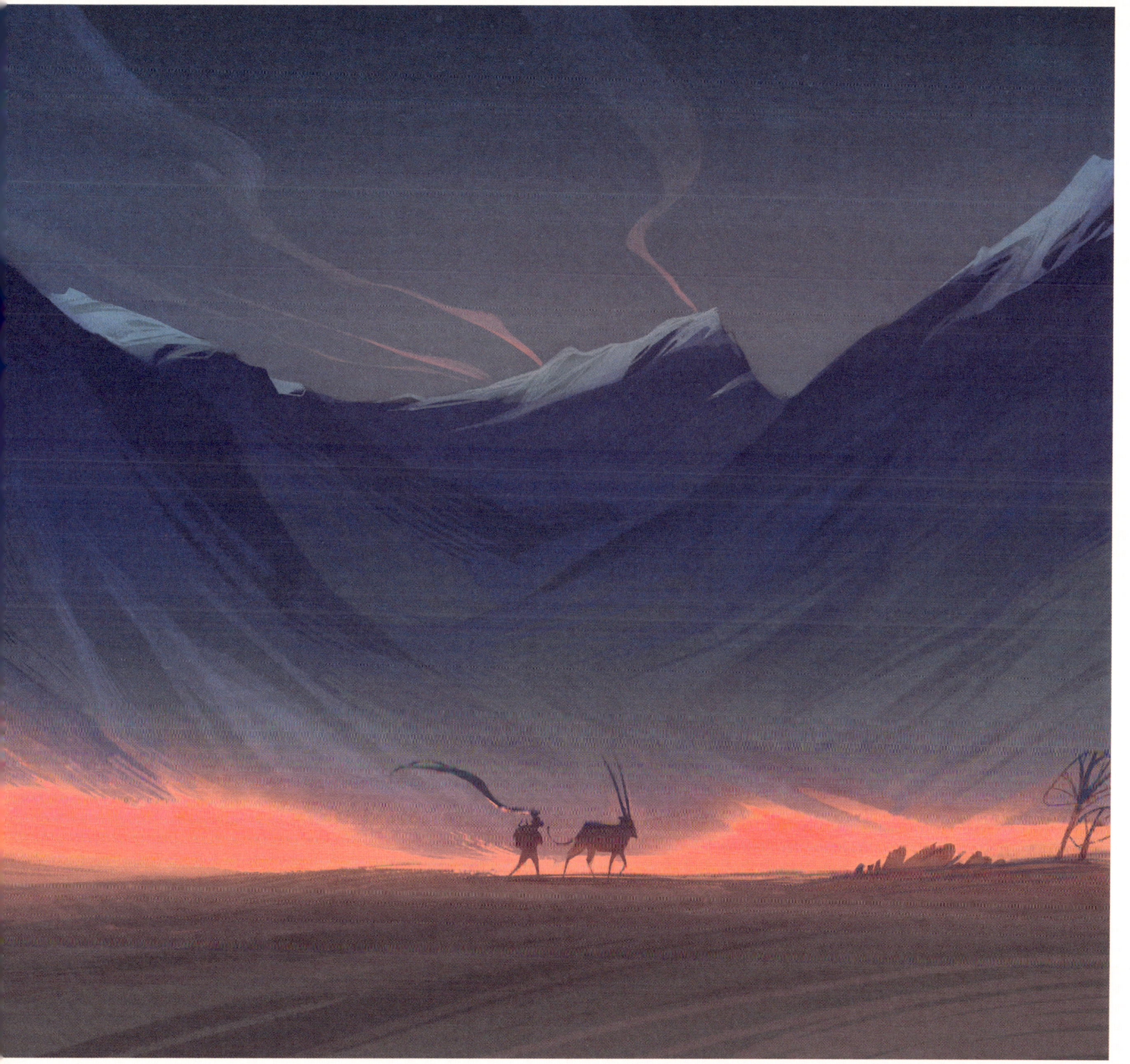

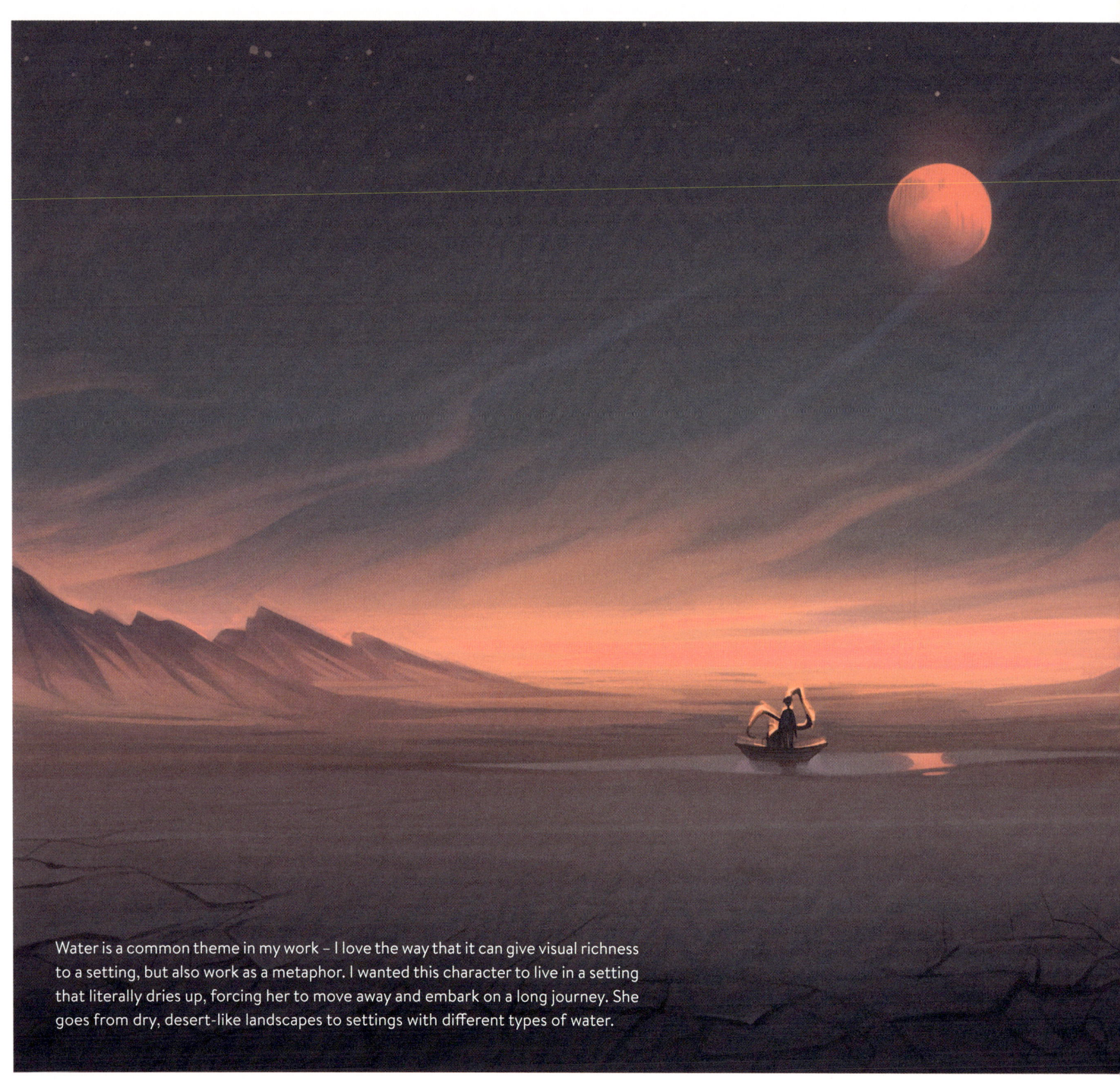

Water is a common theme in my work – I love the way that it can give visual richness to a setting, but also work as a metaphor. I wanted this character to live in a setting that literally dries up, forcing her to move away and embark on a long journey. She goes from dry, desert-like landscapes to settings with different types of water.

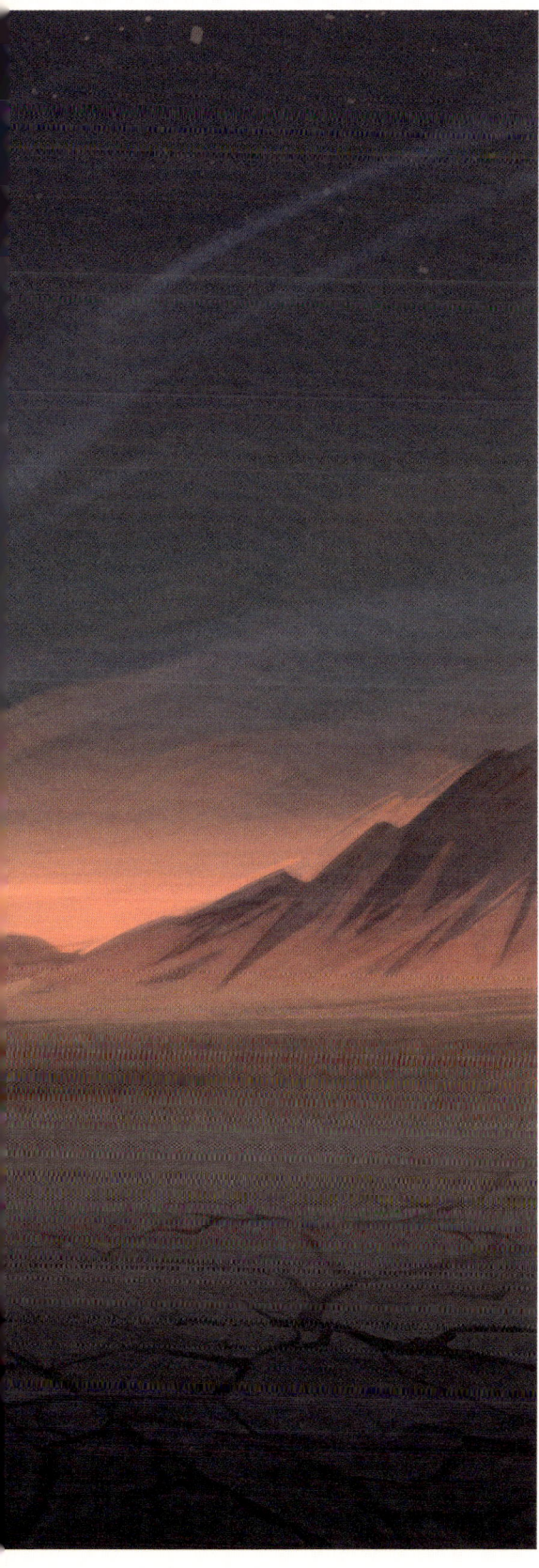

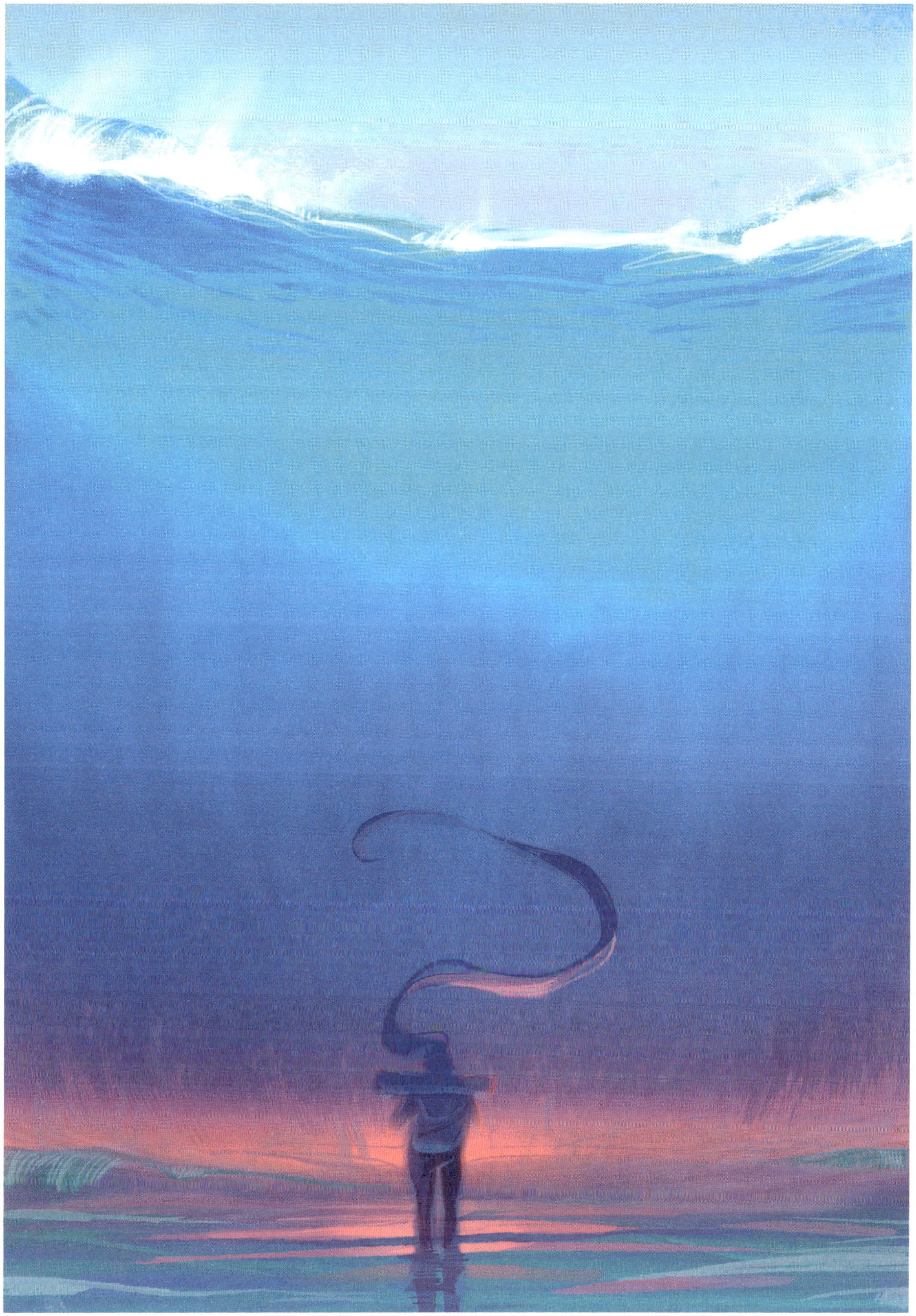

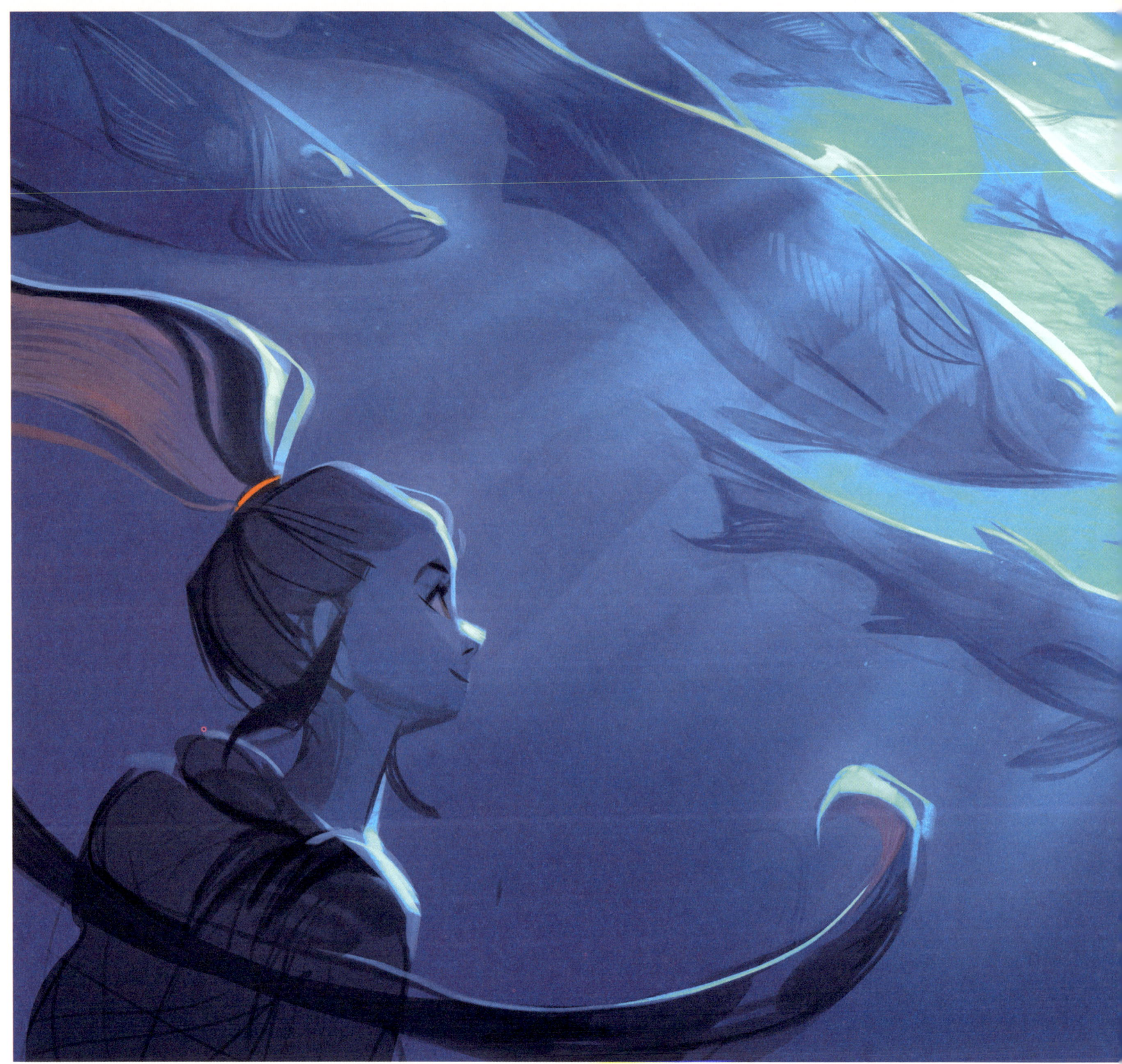

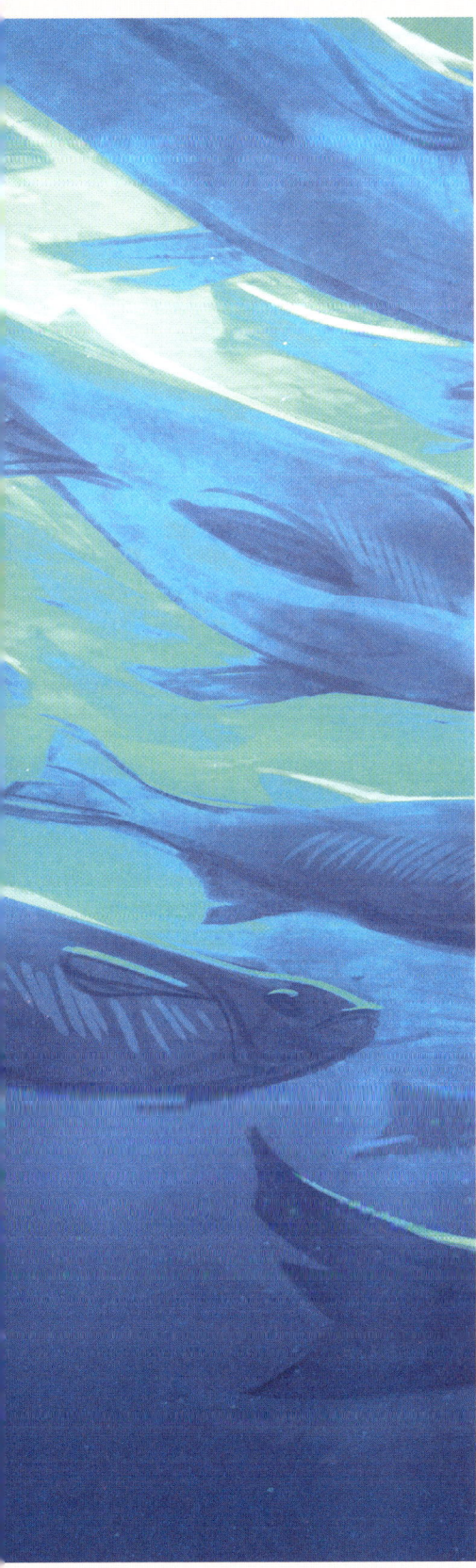

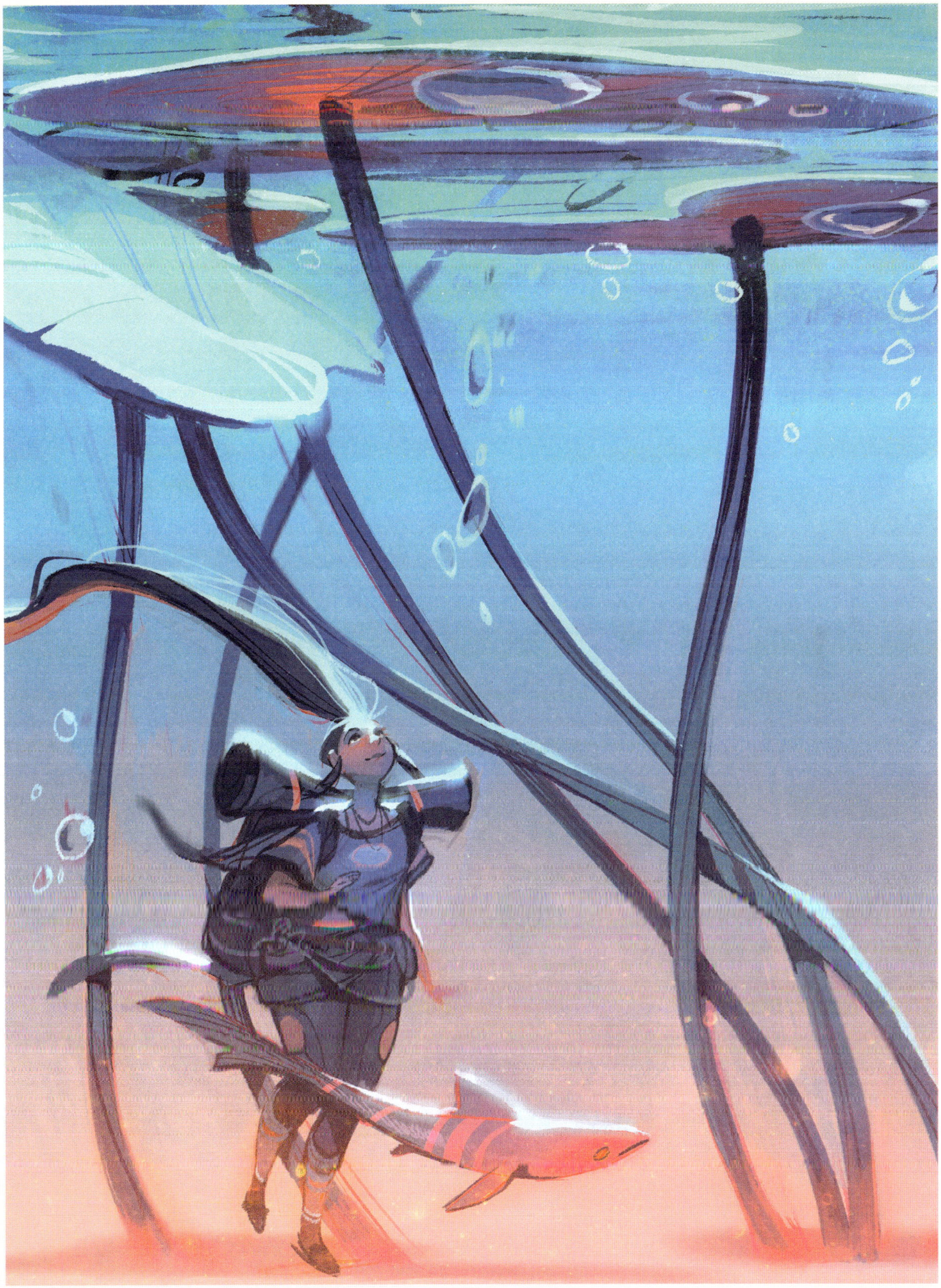

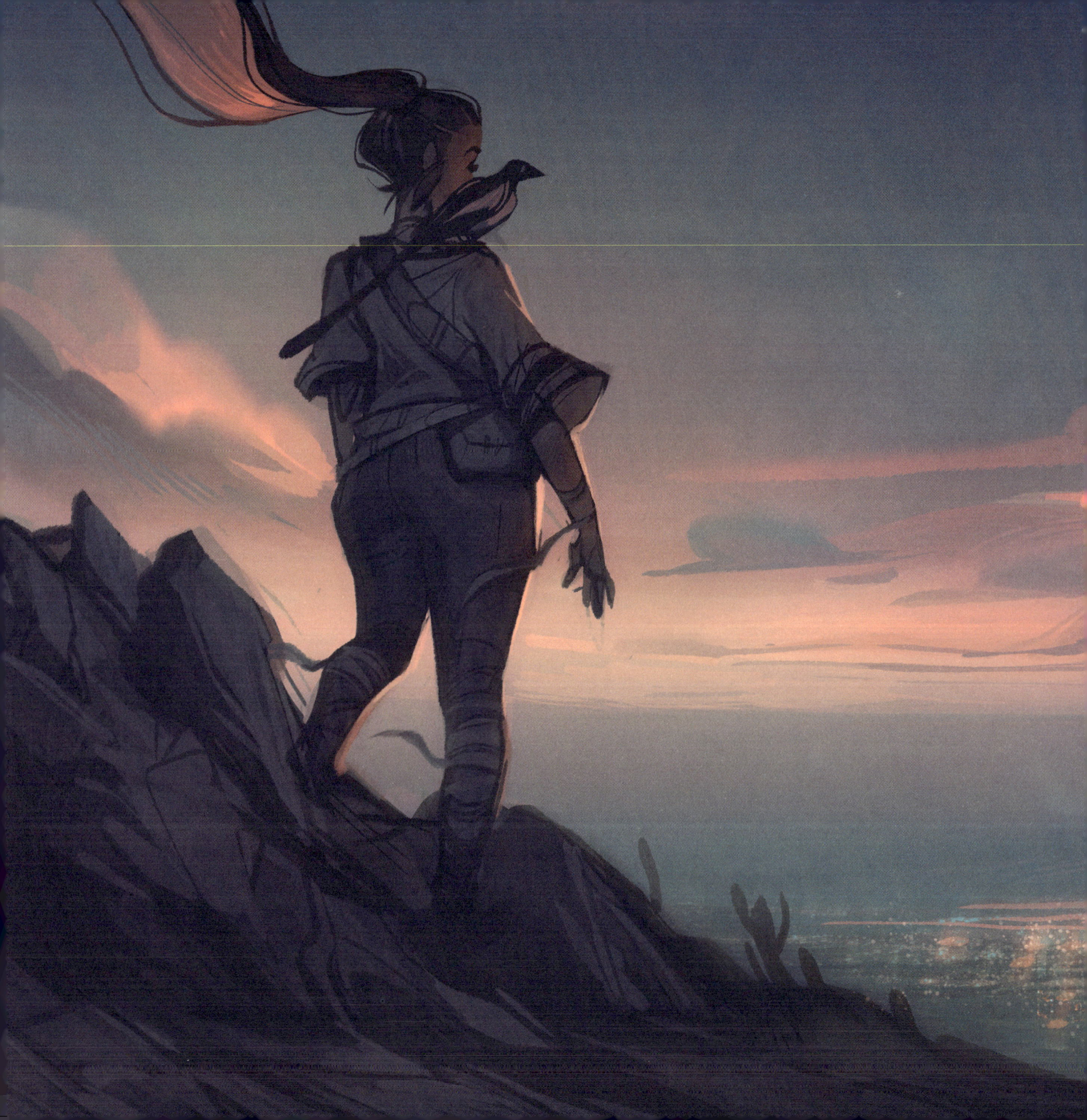

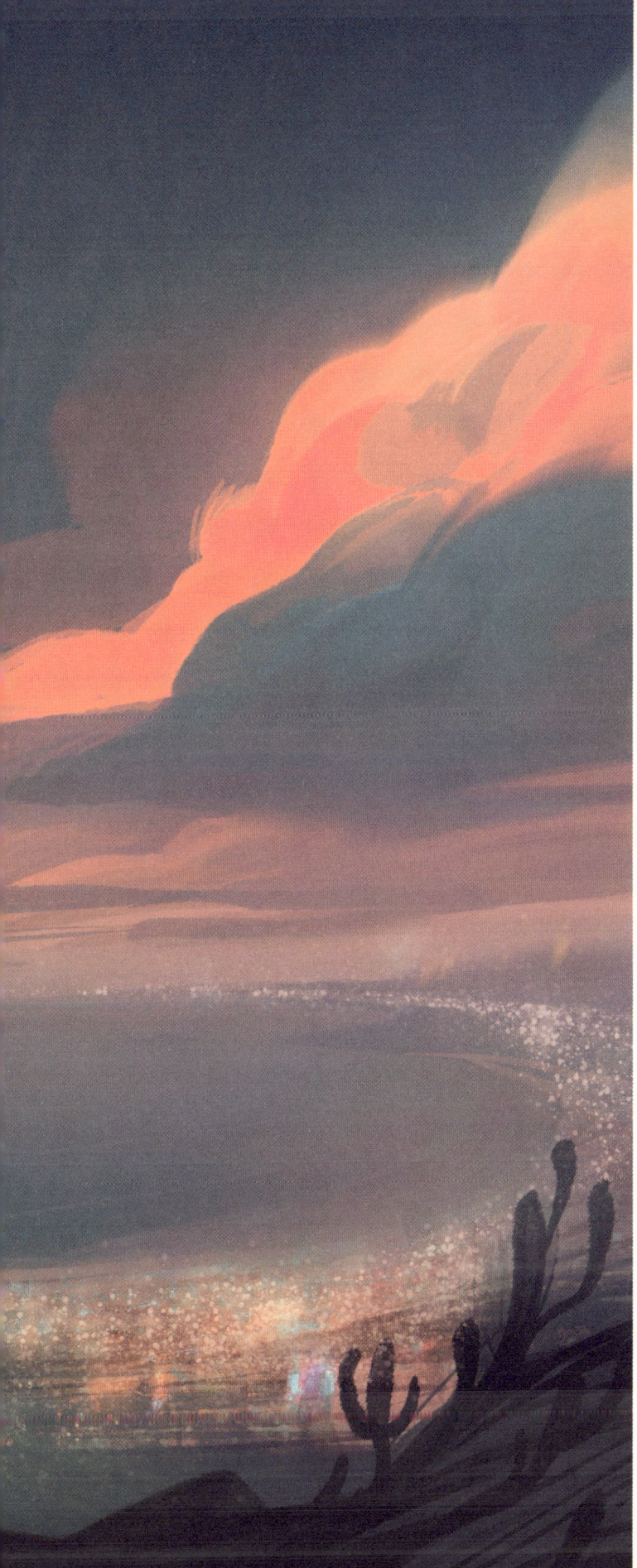

Whenever I work on an idea, I gravitate towards certain themes. I love surreal stories that feel dream-like, and convey mental states and emotional landscapes. I like settings that feel suspended in time, and of course I love underwater settings. Most importantly, I like to use color as a form of emotive expression. It is a way to not only create visual appeal but also convey a mood that resonates with the viewer.

While working on *Departure*, I allowed my thoughts and feelings to flow with whatever I was drawing at that time. I tried not to determine the nature of the concept too much beforehand. Instead I let the details form with each new drawing, and gave the concept room to change and evolve depending on what felt right. This is what I love about developing ideas: they are constantly in flux, and the meaning can change over time.

What you can see here is the foundation of my concept for *Departure*: the idea and general look have been worked out, but it can still evolve in many different directions. I hope you enjoy seeing the process of my idea growing, from simple sketch to a dream-like world.

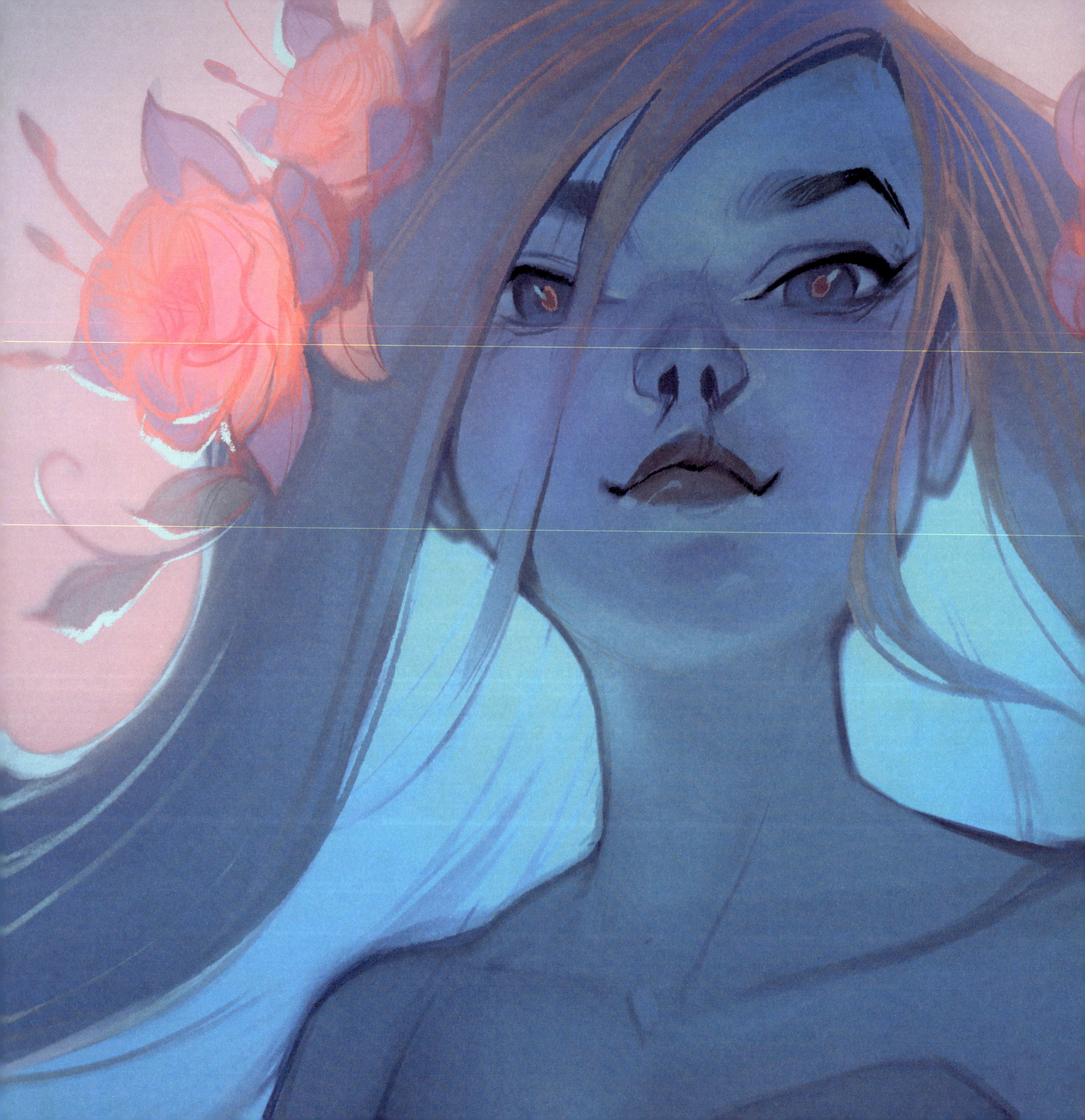

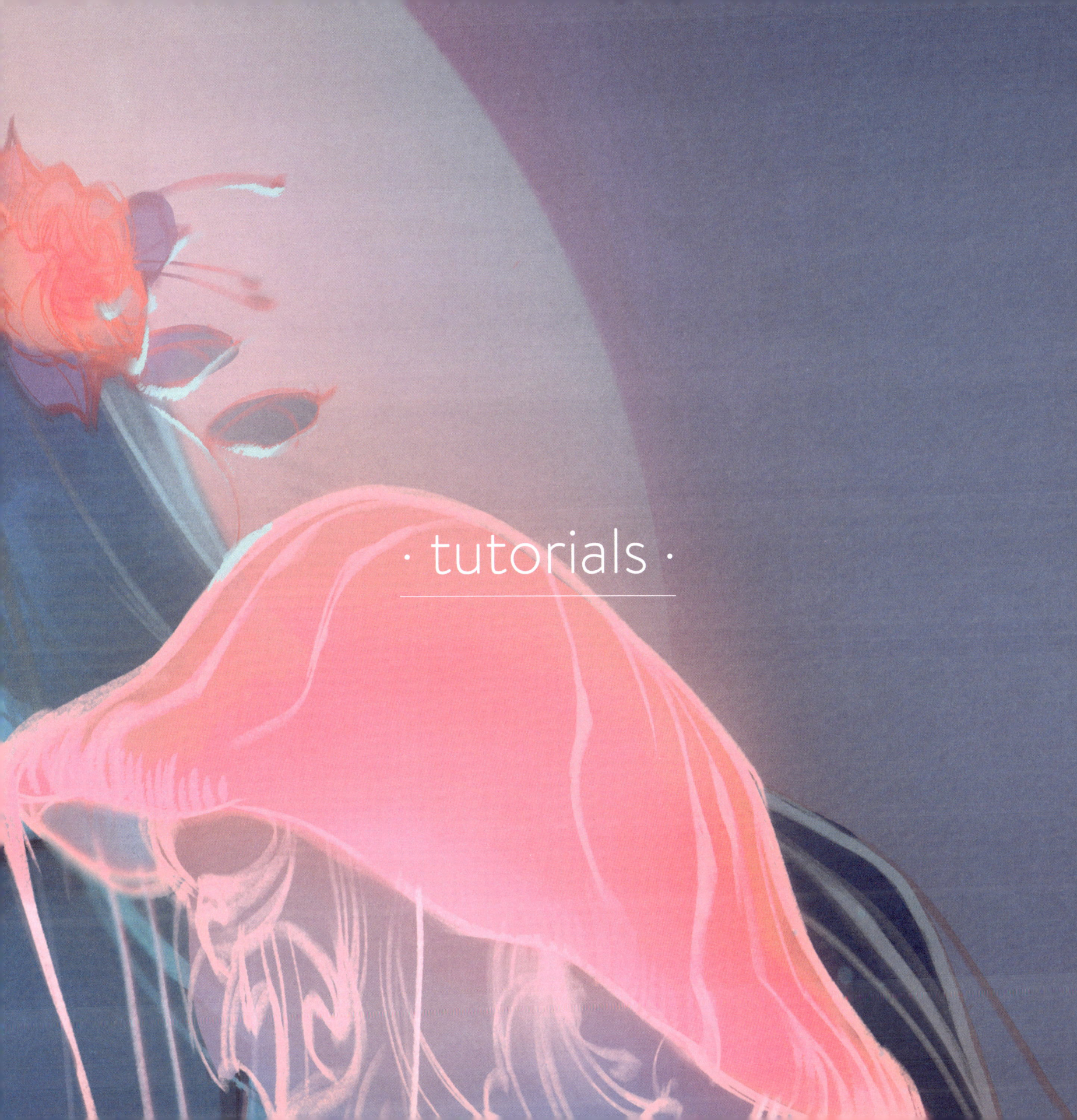

· tutorials ·

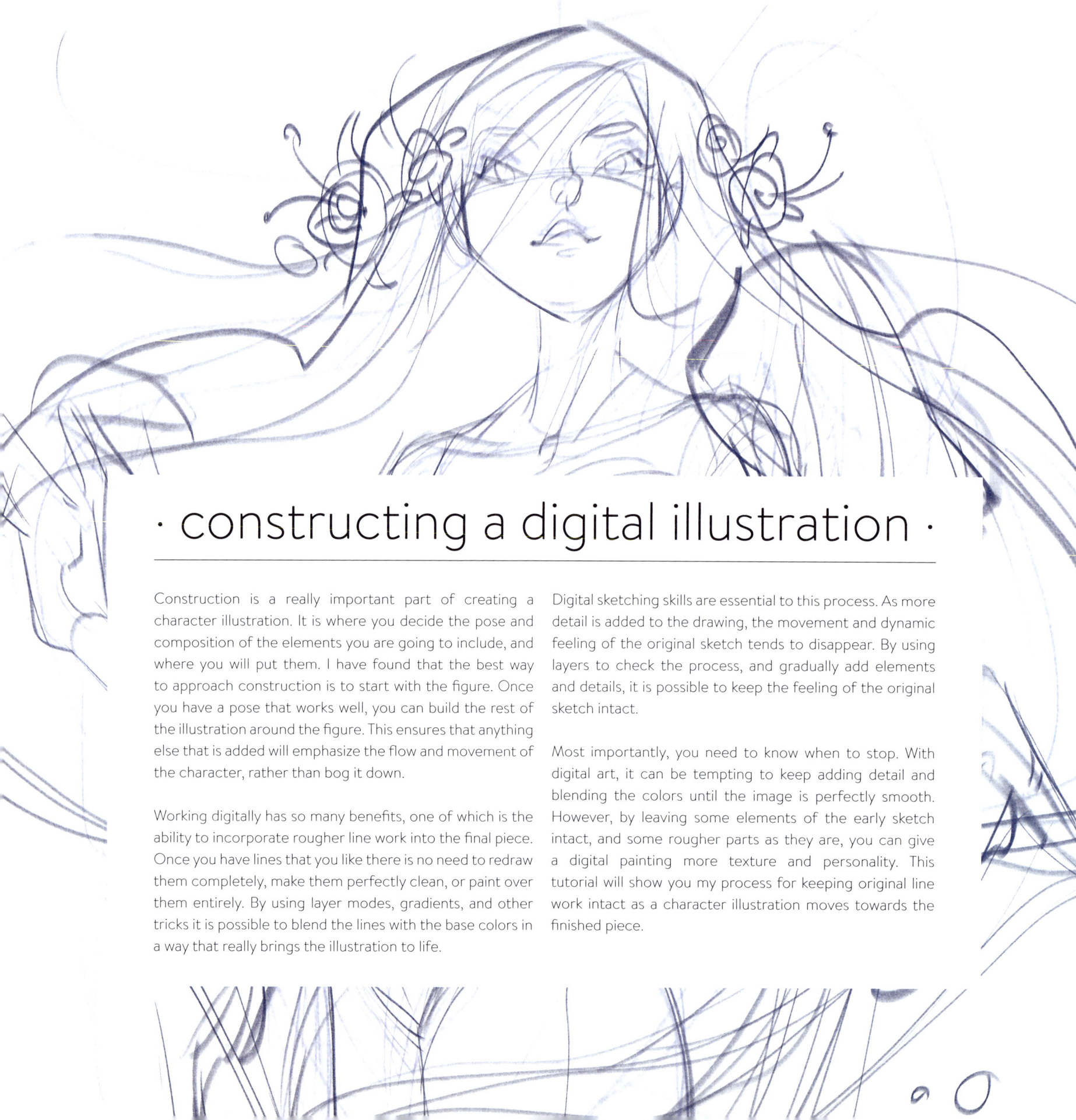

· constructing a digital illustration ·

Construction is a really important part of creating a character illustration. It is where you decide the pose and composition of the elements you are going to include, and where you will put them. I have found that the best way to approach construction is to start with the figure. Once you have a pose that works well, you can build the rest of the illustration around the figure. This ensures that anything else that is added will emphasize the flow and movement of the character, rather than bog it down.

Working digitally has so many benefits, one of which is the ability to incorporate rougher line work into the final piece. Once you have lines that you like there is no need to redraw them completely, make them perfectly clean, or paint over them entirely. By using layer modes, gradients, and other tricks it is possible to blend the lines with the base colors in a way that really brings the illustration to life.

Digital sketching skills are essential to this process. As more detail is added to the drawing, the movement and dynamic feeling of the original sketch tends to disappear. By using layers to check the process, and gradually add elements and details, it is possible to keep the feeling of the original sketch intact.

Most importantly, you need to know when to stop. With digital art, it can be tempting to keep adding detail and blending the colors until the image is perfectly smooth. However, by leaving some elements of the early sketch intact, and some rougher parts as they are, you can give a digital painting more texture and personality. This tutorial will show you my process for keeping original line work intact as a character illustration moves towards the finished piece.

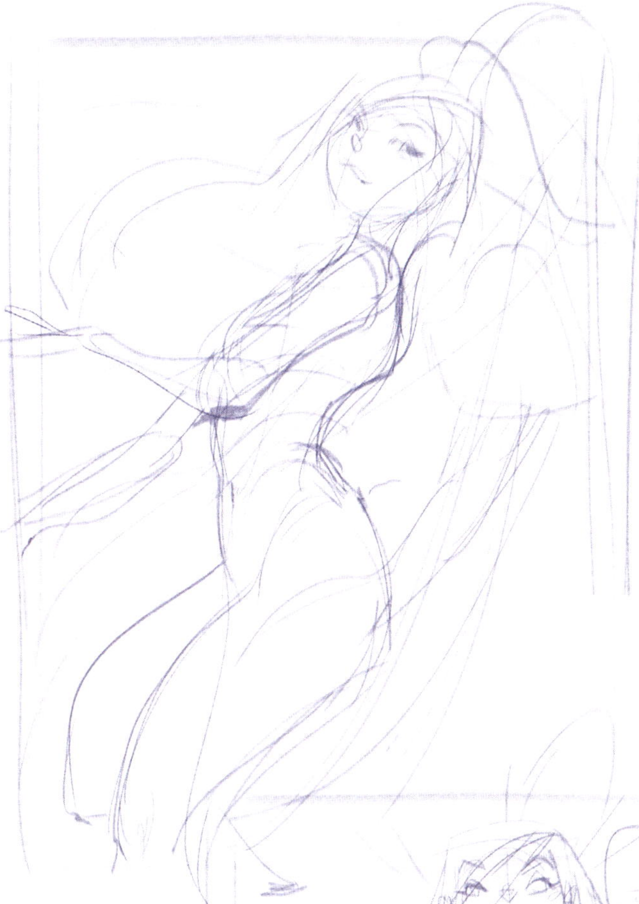

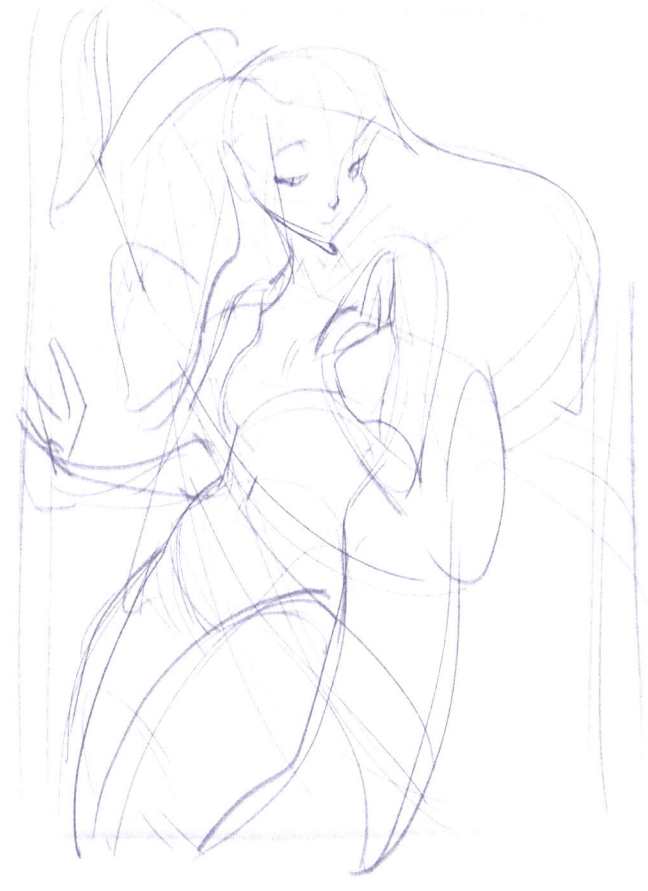

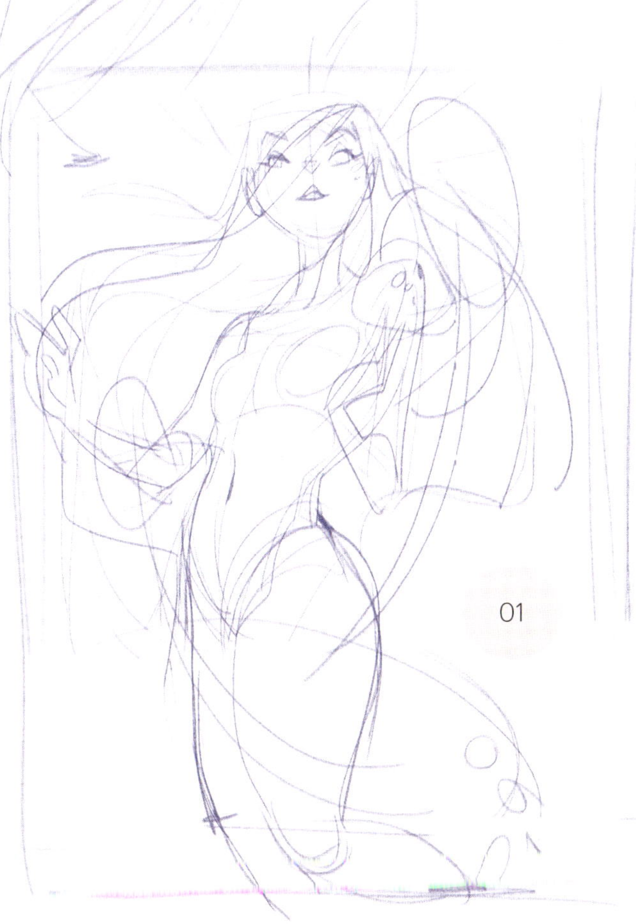

01 thumbnail sketches

I am going to show you how to create a character illustration, with an ethereal and mysterious mood, that features jellyfish. I start with three thumbnail sketches, trying out some different approaches to the theme.

At this early stage, it is important to draw in a fluid, intuitive way; the precise details are not important yet. Drawings tend to lose their sense of movement and gesture as more detail is added, so it is essential for the thumbnail drawings to be as expressive and fluid as possible. Try to work on a small scale, with a light brush color, so there is less emphasis on the details

02 construct the figure

The bottom thumbnail is the most promising I feel so I continue working on it. Now I switch from an intuitive drawing method to a more structured one: the figure forms the starting point for the rest of the image, so it needs to work well.

Copy and paste the sketch onto an A3-size canvas at 300 dpi. On a separate layer (Shift+Ctrl+N), define the basic shapes of the body – the head, torso, hips, legs, and forearms – and work out the angles of the forms

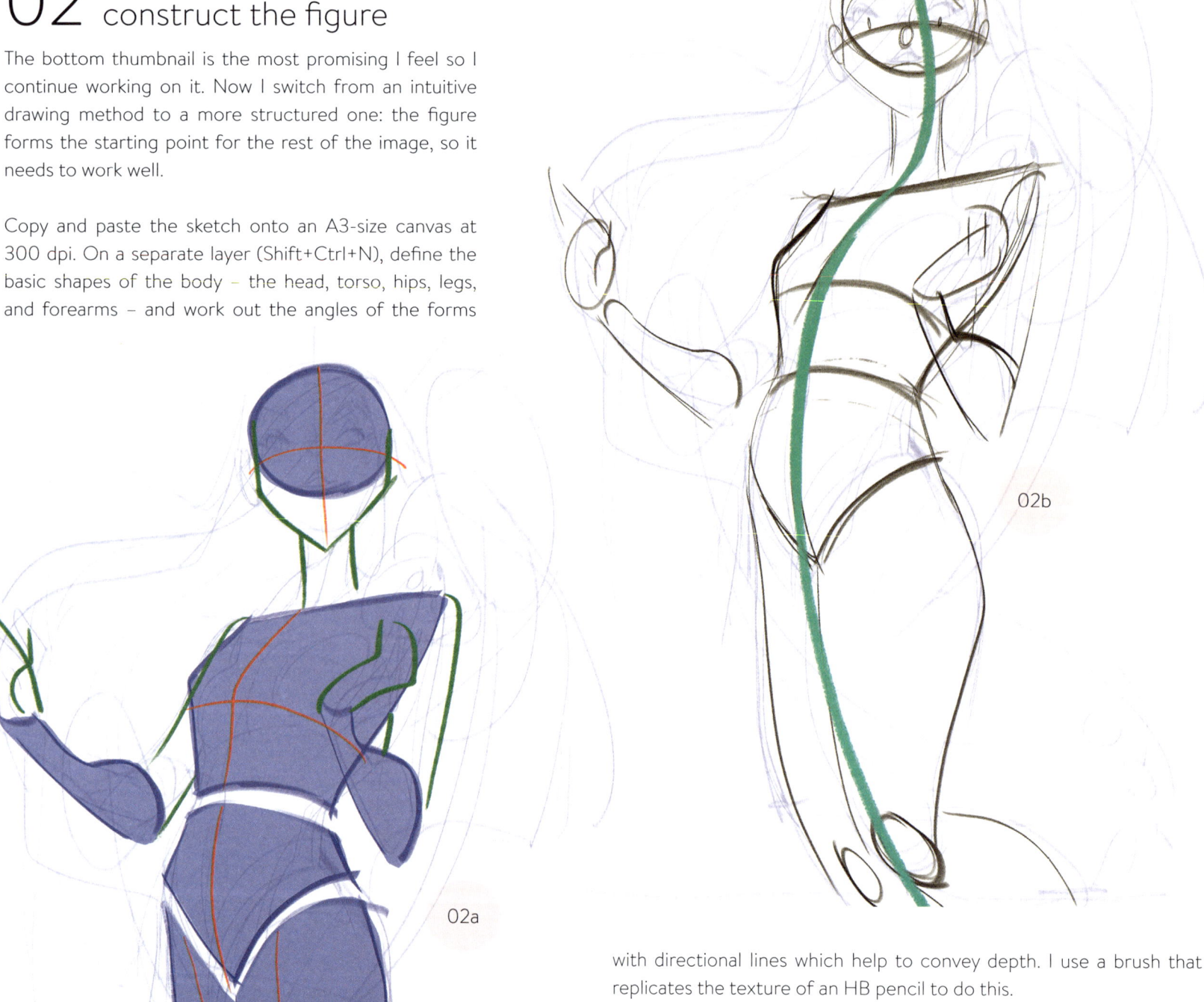

02a

02b

with directional lines which help to convey depth. I use a brush that replicates the texture of an HB pencil to do this.

Then, I connect the forms together keeping in mind the "line of action" of the figure. The line of action is a curved line that shows the direction of movement and force in a pose. You can see the line of action for this pose clearly in image 02b.

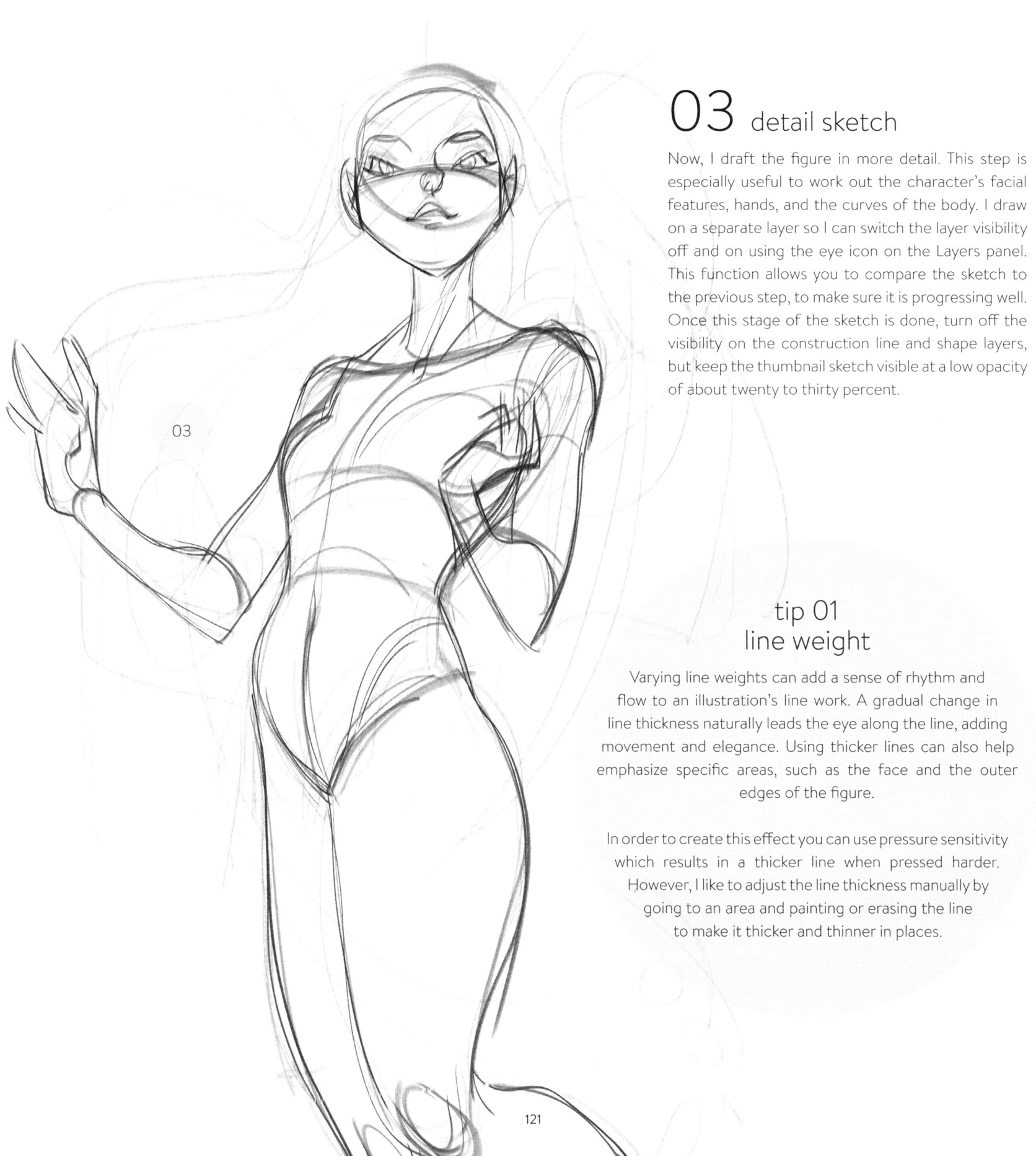

03 detail sketch

Now, I draft the figure in more detail. This step is especially useful to work out the character's facial features, hands, and the curves of the body. I draw on a separate layer so I can switch the layer visibility off and on using the eye icon on the Layers panel. This function allows you to compare the sketch to the previous step, to make sure it is progressing well. Once this stage of the sketch is done, turn off the visibility on the construction line and shape layers, but keep the thumbnail sketch visible at a low opacity of about twenty to thirty percent.

03

tip 01
line weight

Varying line weights can add a sense of rhythm and flow to an illustration's line work. A gradual change in line thickness naturally leads the eye along the line, adding movement and elegance. Using thicker lines can also help emphasize specific areas, such as the face and the outer edges of the figure.

In order to create this effect you can use pressure sensitivity which results in a thicker line when pressed harder. However, I like to adjust the line thickness manually by going to an area and painting or erasing the line to make it thicker and thinner in places.

121

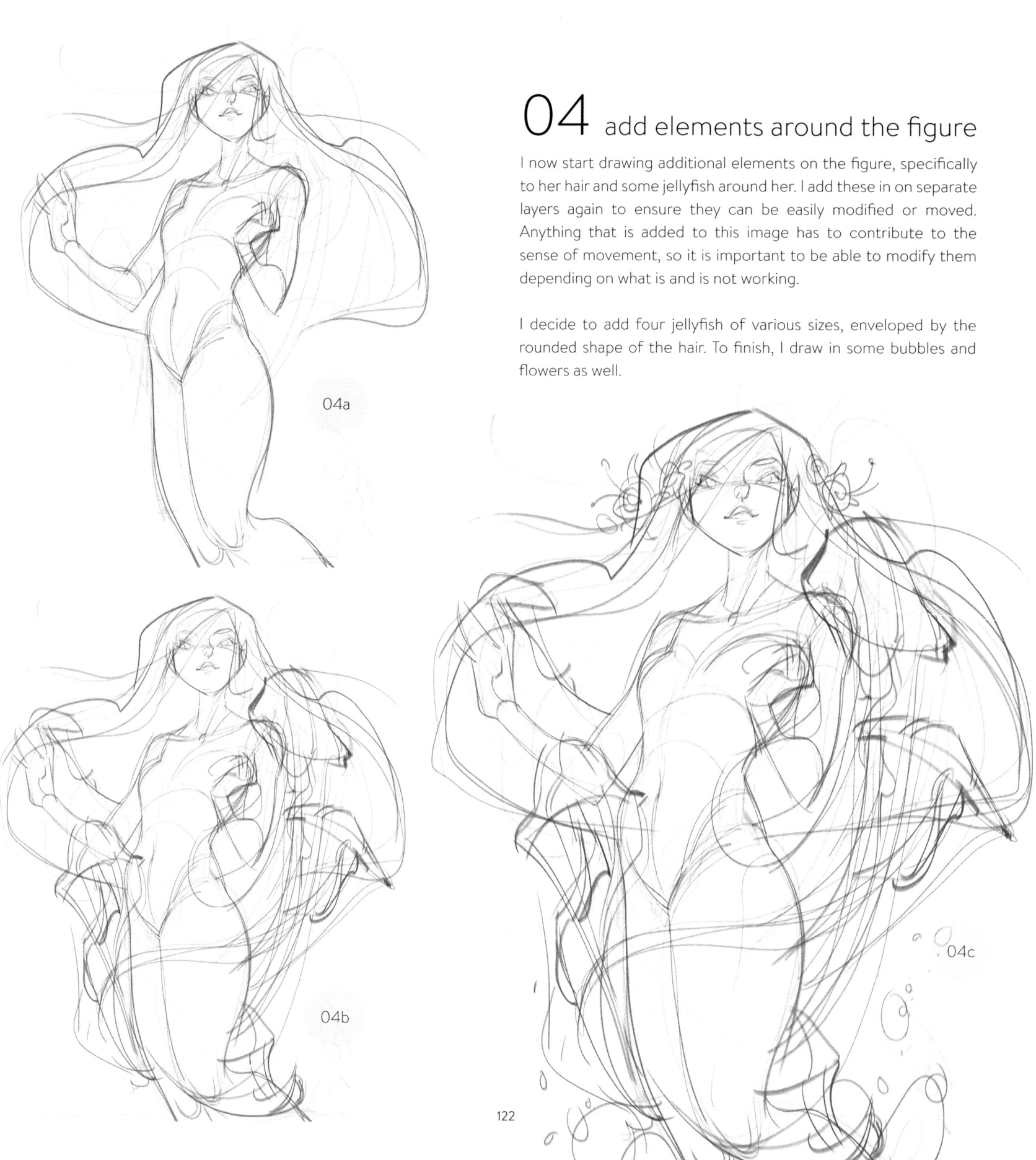

04 add elements around the figure

I now start drawing additional elements on the figure, specifically to her hair and some jellyfish around her. I add these in on separate layers again to ensure they can be easily modified or moved. Anything that is added to this image has to contribute to the sense of movement, so it is important to be able to modify them depending on what is and is not working.

I decide to add four jellyfish of various sizes, enveloped by the rounded shape of the hair. To finish, I draw in some bubbles and flowers as well.

04a

04b

04c

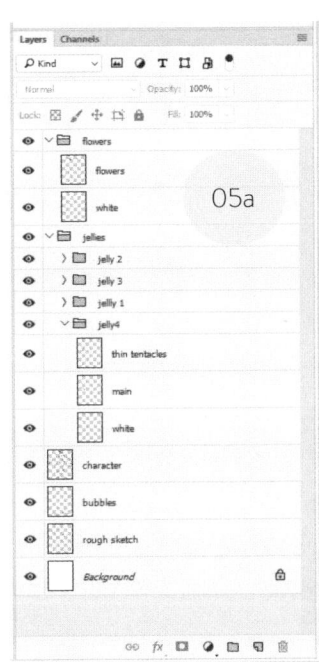

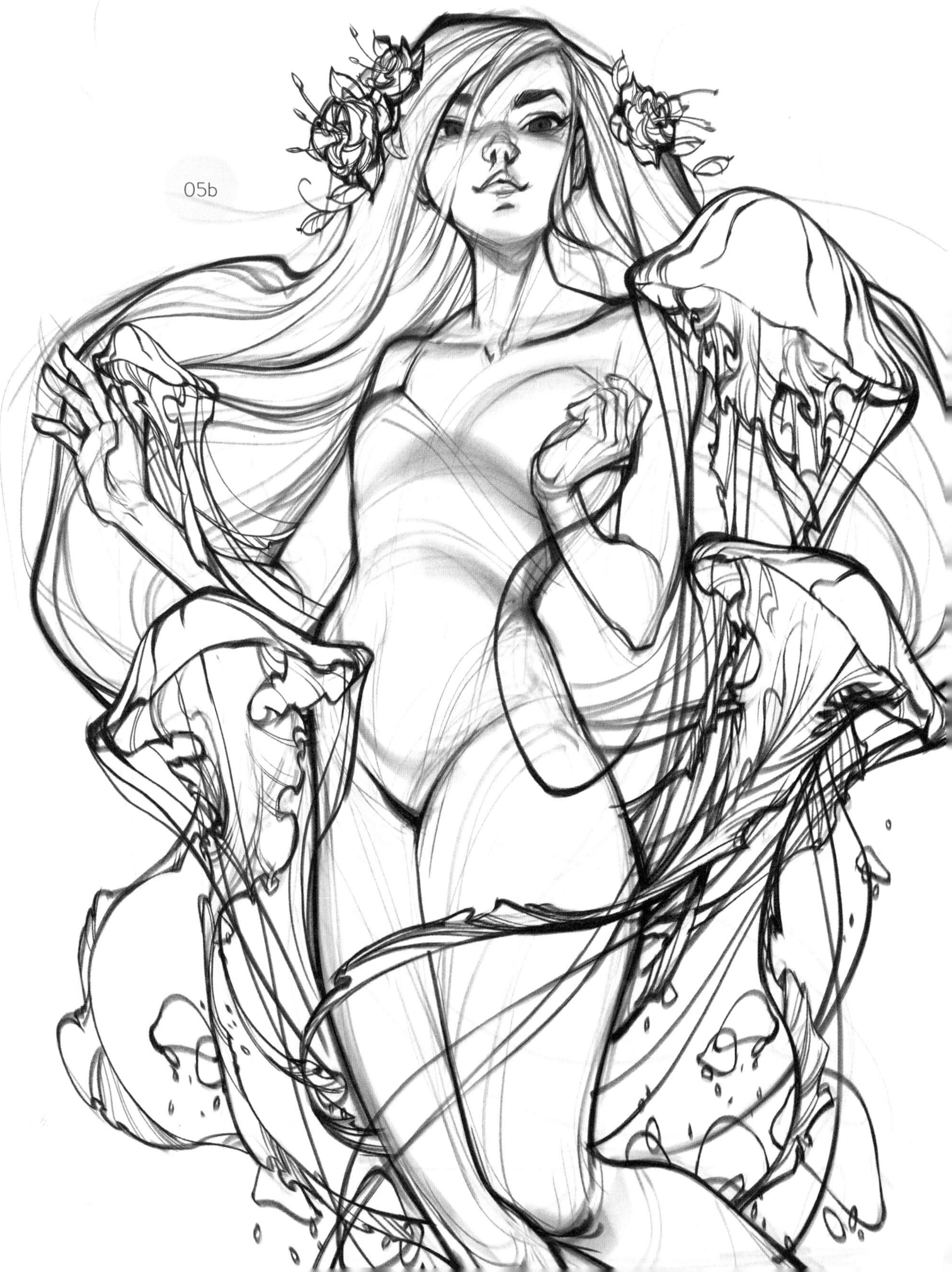

05b

05 line art

It is time to create the finalized line work. These lines will be used to create the final image, but I like to keep them somewhat sketchy and rough. They do not have to be perfect.

I draw each element on a separate layer, using the Oil Pastel brush to block in the basic form of the element in white underneath. The Oil Pastel brush is great for adding bigger blocks of color. This stops the lines of other elements from showing through and making the image too chaotic. It also makes it easier to move each element around before the positions of the jellyfish, hair, and flowers are finalized.

06 color thumbnails

Put all of the line layers in a group (Layer > Group Layers), and create a new Multiply layer on top of the group (Shift+Ctrl+N > Multiply). On this layer, I play around with some different color schemes that might work for this image.

Flood-fill the canvas with your chosen base color using the Paint Bucket tool then use a brush to block in the figure. Use the Gradient tool to add color gradations and some softness, which is important to capture a semi-translucent feel like the one I am aiming for on the jellyfish. I feel that the color scheme of 06c works best for my image, so I save this layer to reference in the next step.

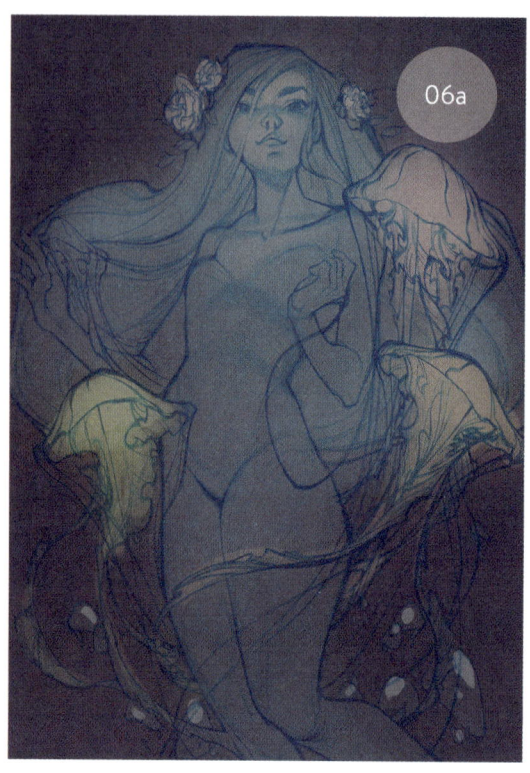
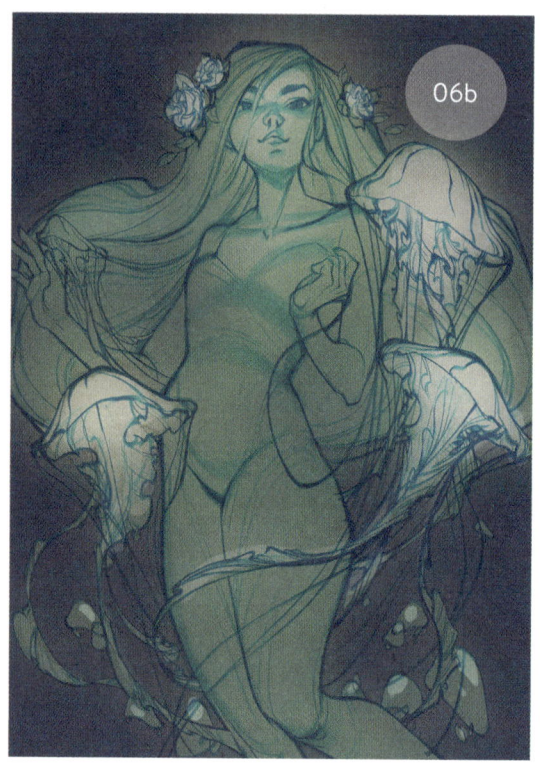

tip 02
textured brush

When I began drawing in Photoshop, I would use the standard Round brush to create line work. However, I soon discovered how difficult it can be to get the lines to look natural and flow nicely, as this brush can result in shaky and awkward lines. Using textured brushes instead can help to achieve a natural look in your line work.

I prefer texture and roughness in my digital paintings, which is an added bonus of using a textured brush. The brush I often use is the *MACALABS*GRAPHITE – HB PENCIL brush (cubebrush.co/macalabs), but you can also use the Oil Pastel brush that comes with Photoshop for some nice texture.

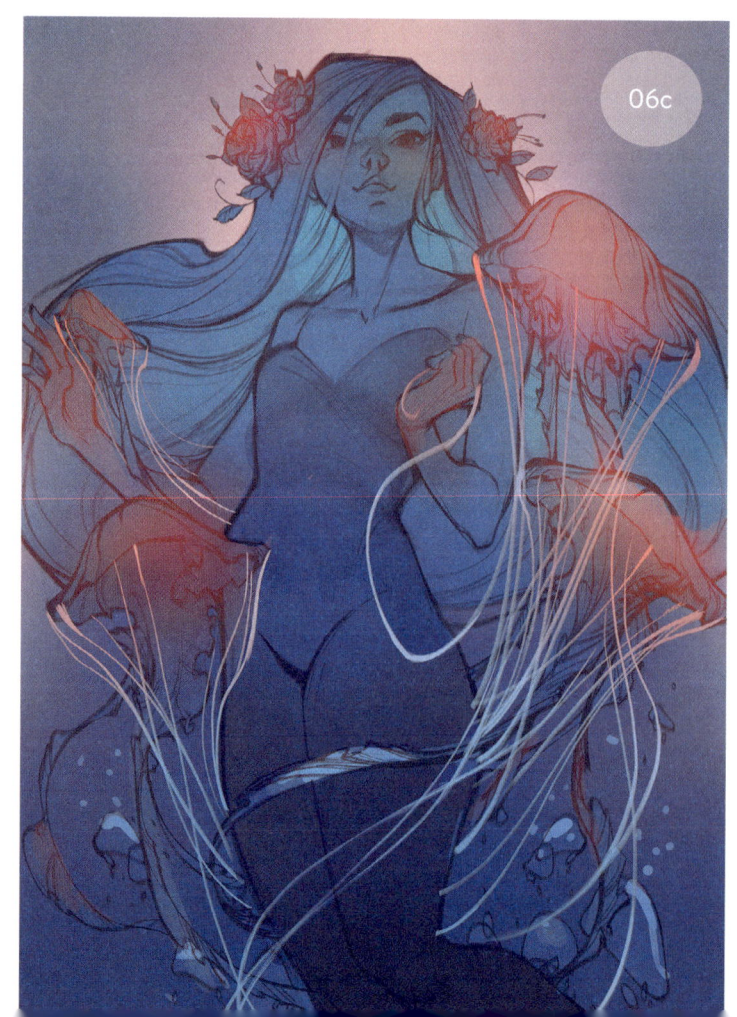

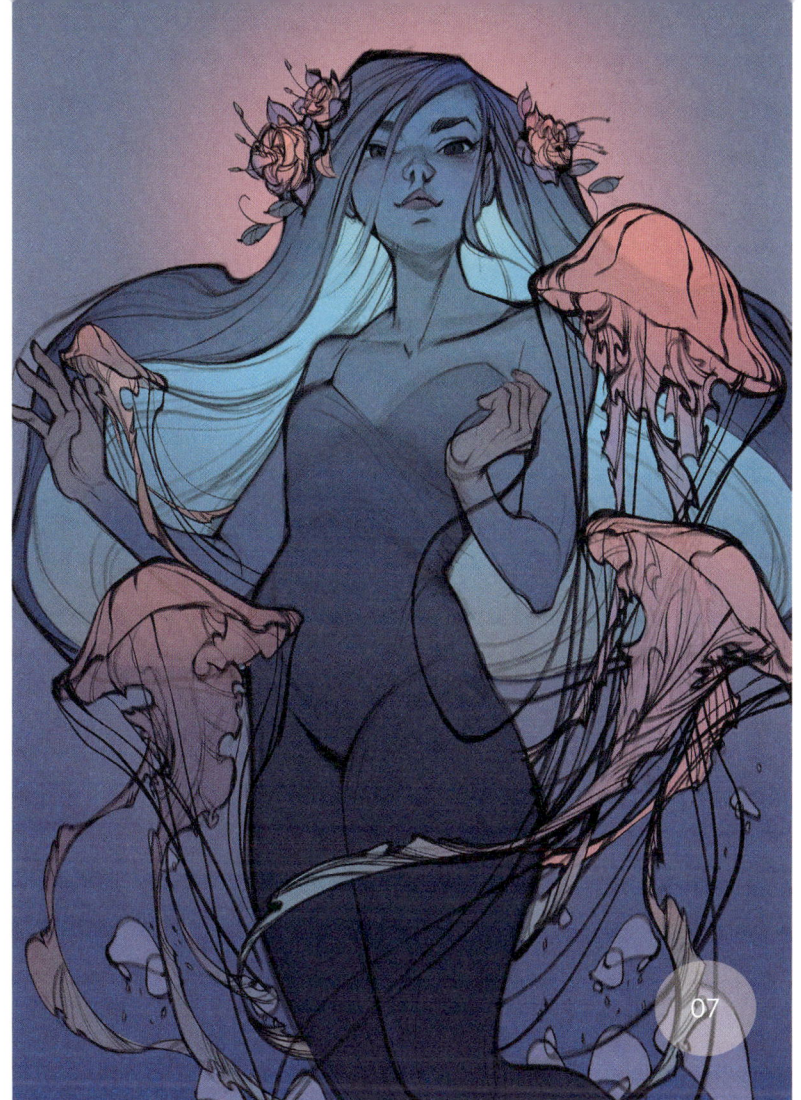

07 apply basic colors

Take the separate elements (in my case these are the figure, jellyfish, flowers, and bubbles) and block in the base color for each one. Once the basic form is blocked in, lock the layer transparency (using the checkerboard lock icon on the Layers panel) and color in specific areas such as the skin and hair.

I use the Gradient tool to add color transitions too, which help emphasize the flowing forms in the line work. Finally, I lower the opacity of the jellyfish base color layers to make them slightly see-through.

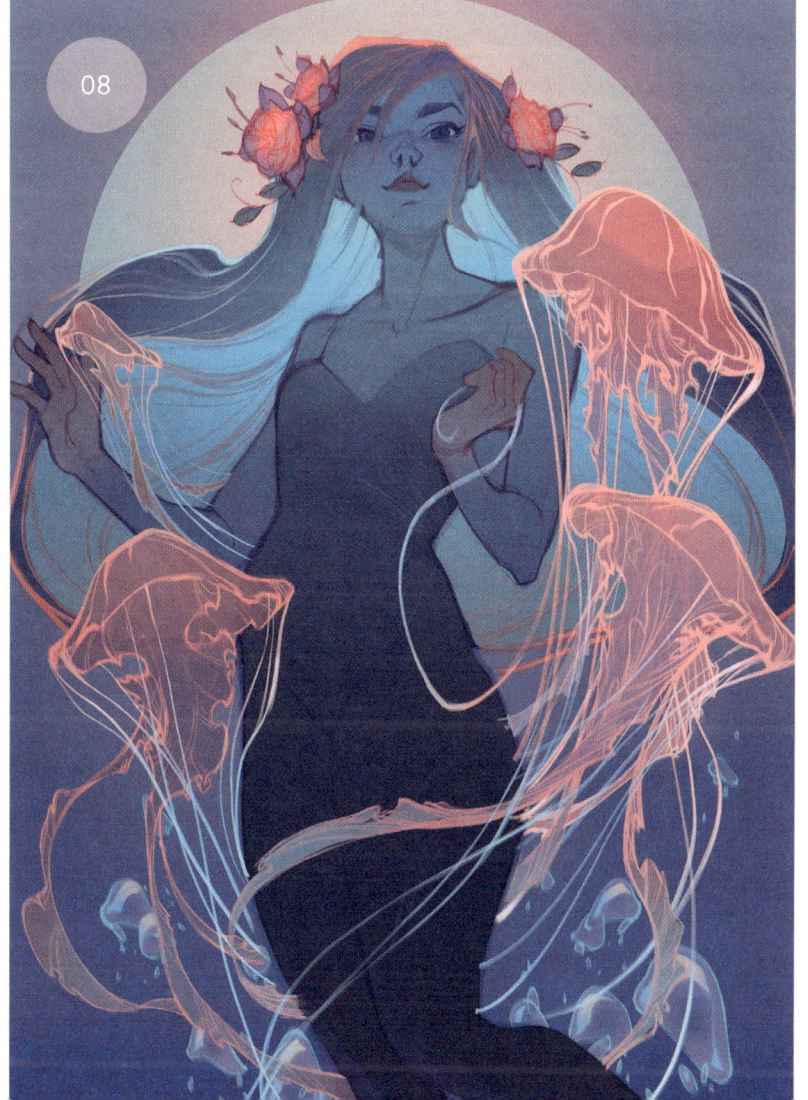

08 change line colors

Now that the base colors are set, it is useful to change the colors of the lines. I find that the details in the lines really come to life when the colors are modified to complement the base colors.

For the lines on the figure, I set the layer mode to Multiply and lighten the line color to match her base, in this case it is a bluish-purple. I also lighten the line colors of the jellyfish to a light peach, which gives them a ghostly, glowing effect.

Where needed, add color transitions to the line work by locking the transparency again and using the Gradient tool. I also decide to add a decorative circle behind the figure to bring balance to the composition. To do this, use the Elliptical Marquee tool to make a circle and then flood-fill it on a separate layer.

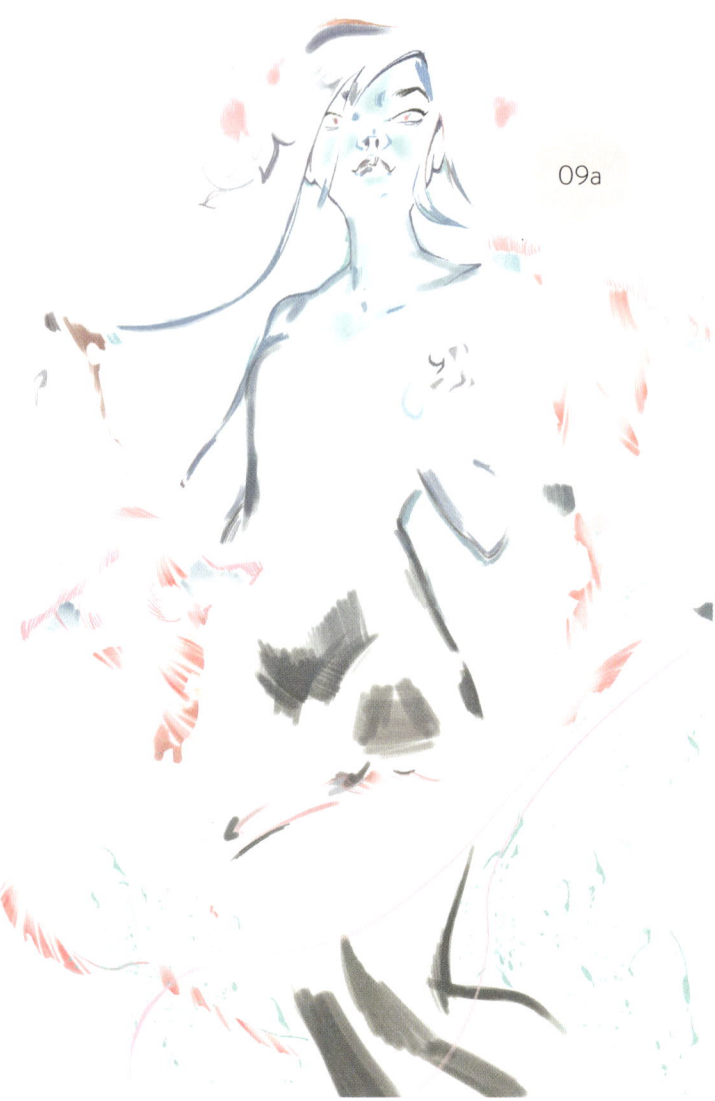

09a

tip 03
lead the eye

Digital illustrations are usually quite rich in detail, with a lot of visual information. If this information is arranged in a chaotic way, it is hard for the viewer to appreciate the complexity of the piece.

However, if the information is arranged in a way that leads the eye around the piece, it invites the viewer to enjoy the process of taking in all the details. The main way to achieve this is to pick a focal point – in this case it is the face – and make sure that the surrounding elements lead the eye to this point. Color transitions, which can be created with gradients, and flowing line work also help to lead the eye around the image.

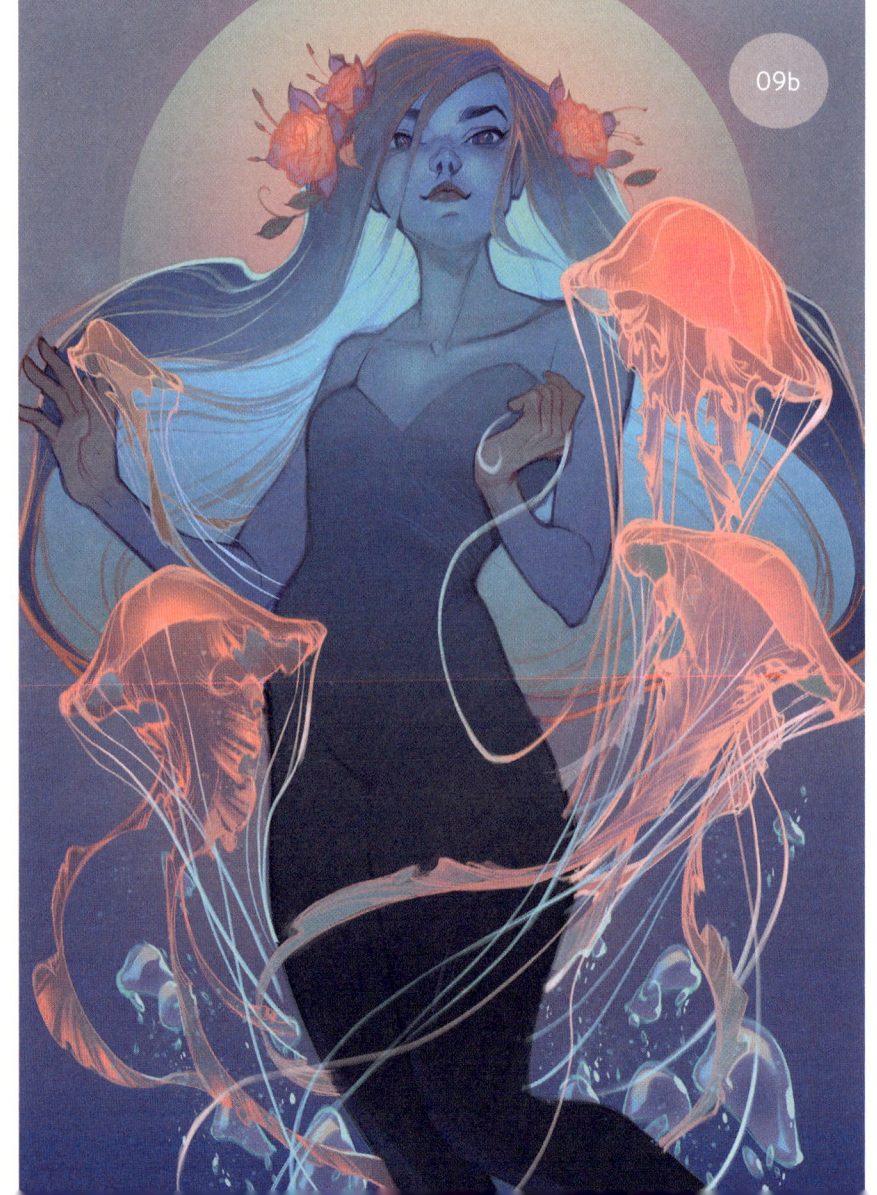

09b

09 details and polishing

On a separate layer, use a soft brush to paint in further details and clean up the illustration. Most of the detail has already been established at this point, so the image only needs a few finishing touches (shown in image 09a).

I focus on the face, adding highlights to show light coming from below and adding more detail to the eyes. I also clean up the edges of the figure, and add some highlights to the jellyfish because the face and jellyfish are elements that demand the most attention from the viewer. Then I add some sharp detail to the bubbles with a smaller brush set to a high opacity and bright color, to make them appear more realistic.

10 lighting effects

To complete the illustration, add some further lighting effects. Using a new layer set to Screen mode creates a backlit effect for the character where the light appears to pour over the edges of the hair and flowers. I duplicate the jellyfish layer too (right click > Duplicate Layer), blur it (Filter > Blur), and set it to Screen mode for a glowing effect.

I also add a sharp, subtle rim light to the flowers. I do this by painting it in on a separate layer with a smaller brush and a bright color. This layer is then duplicated, blurred, and set to Screen mode for a glowing effect.

Finally, flatten the image onto one layer (Layer > Flatten Image), duplicate it, and blur the new layer with Gaussian blur (Filter > Blur > Gaussian blur). Erasing parts of this layer with the Eraser tool mimics the way a camera lens blurs elements that are further away. Now the illustration is finished!

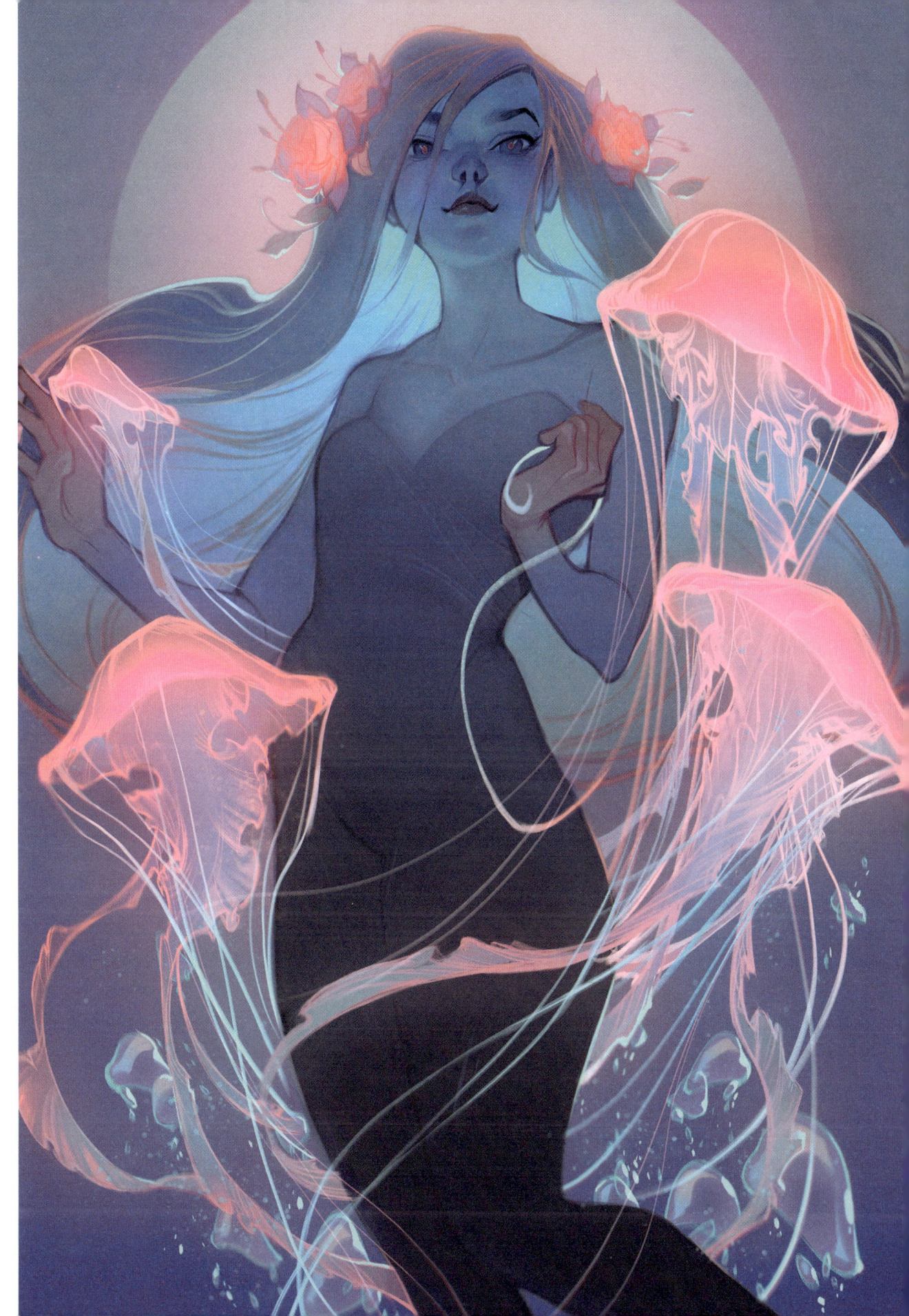

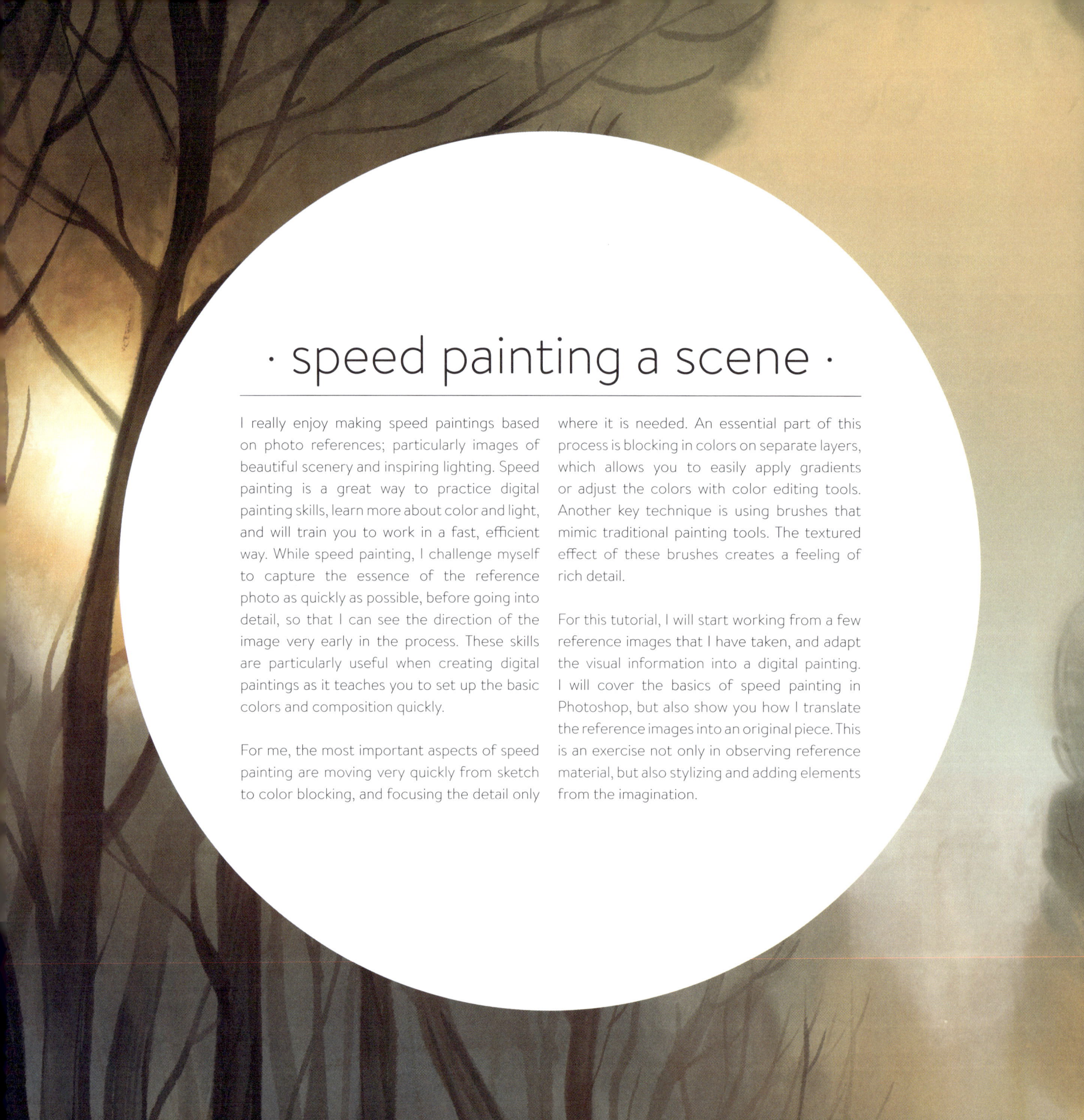

· speed painting a scene ·

I really enjoy making speed paintings based on photo references; particularly images of beautiful scenery and inspiring lighting. Speed painting is a great way to practice digital painting skills, learn more about color and light, and will train you to work in a fast, efficient way. While speed painting, I challenge myself to capture the essence of the reference photo as quickly as possible, before going into detail, so that I can see the direction of the image very early in the process. These skills are particularly useful when creating digital paintings as it teaches you to set up the basic colors and composition quickly.

For me, the most important aspects of speed painting are moving very quickly from sketch to color blocking, and focusing the detail only where it is needed. An essential part of this process is blocking in colors on separate layers, which allows you to easily apply gradients or adjust the colors with color editing tools. Another key technique is using brushes that mimic traditional painting tools. The textured effect of these brushes creates a feeling of rich detail.

For this tutorial, I will start working from a few reference images that I have taken, and adapt the visual information into a digital painting. I will cover the basics of speed painting in Photoshop, but also show you how I translate the reference images into an original piece. This is an exercise not only in observing reference material, but also stylizing and adding elements from the imagination.

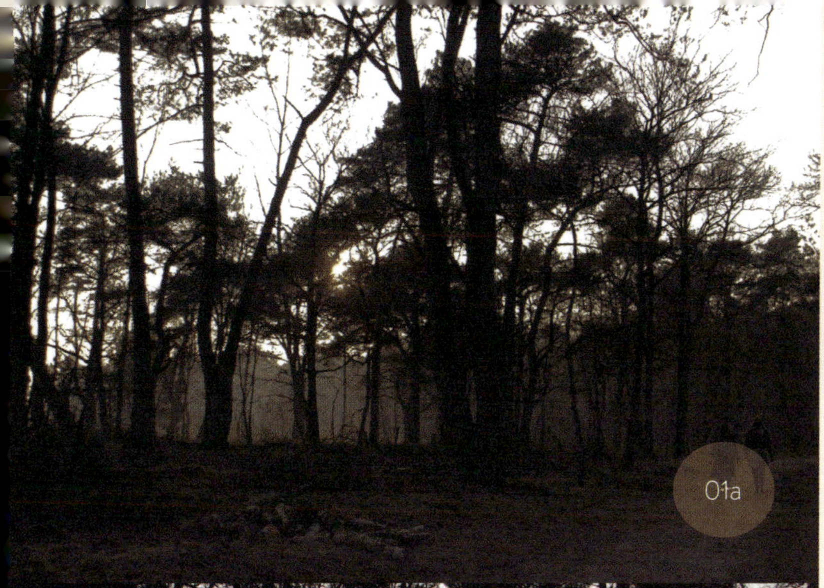

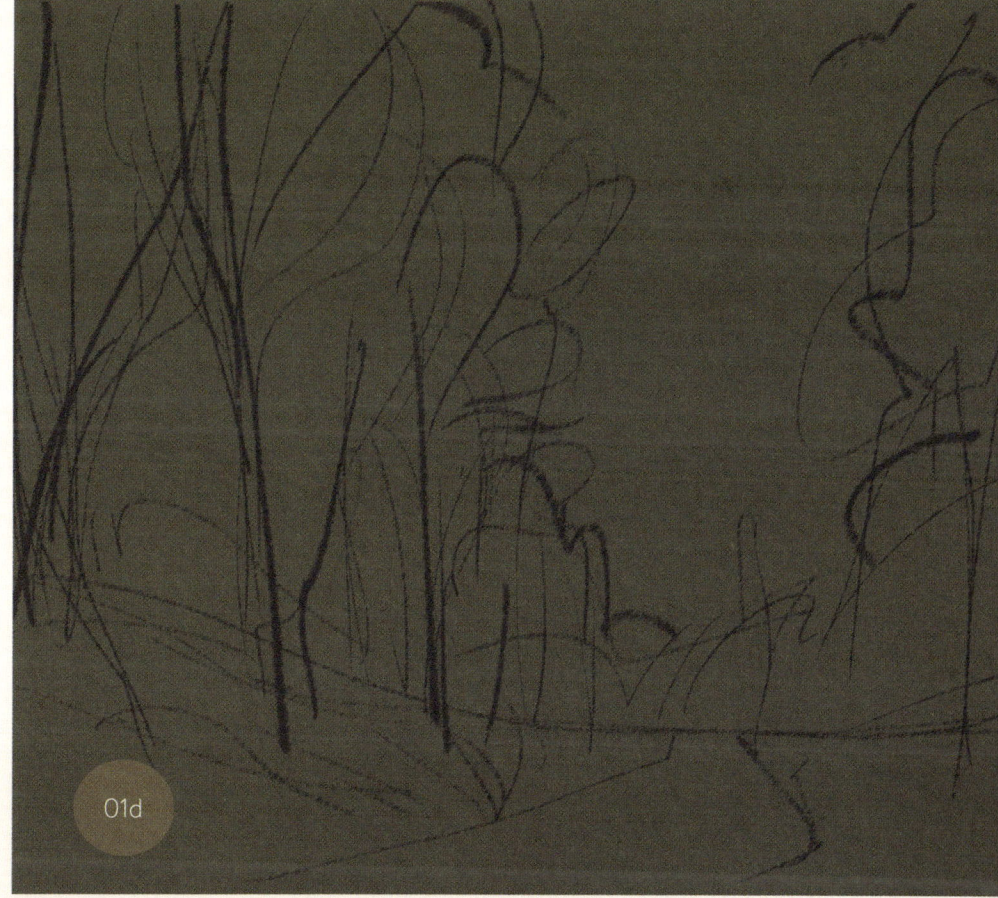
01a

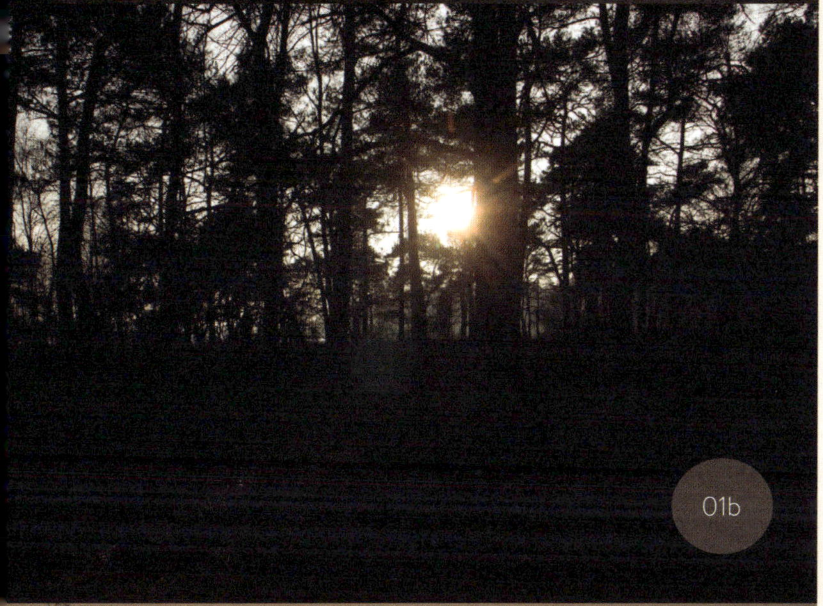

01b

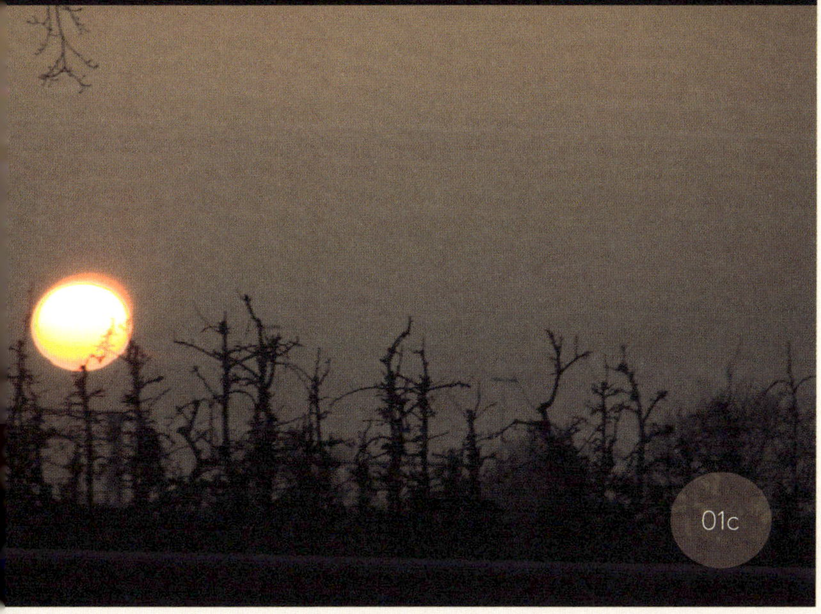

01c

01 base color & sketch

I begin by observing my three reference images. The minimalistic, almost monochromatic color scheme inspires me as well as the gentle sunlight that is shown coming from behind the trees. I decide to use one image (01a) as my main reference. This scene mostly consists of a deep green hue, so I pick this as the base color for my speed painting.

Create a canvas in Photoshop (Ctrl+N), add a new layer (Shift+Ctrl+N), and quickly use the Paint Bucket tool to fill in the base color. On another new layer, roughly sketch out the basic composition with a textured brush. I use Photoshop's Oil Pastel brush for this speed painting.

Avoid imitating the reference image too closely. Rather, use it as inspiration for a simplified composition. As a rule, I also try to avoid symmetrical compositions. Asymmetrical compositions help to lead the eye around the image, so that it is what I opt for here.

01d

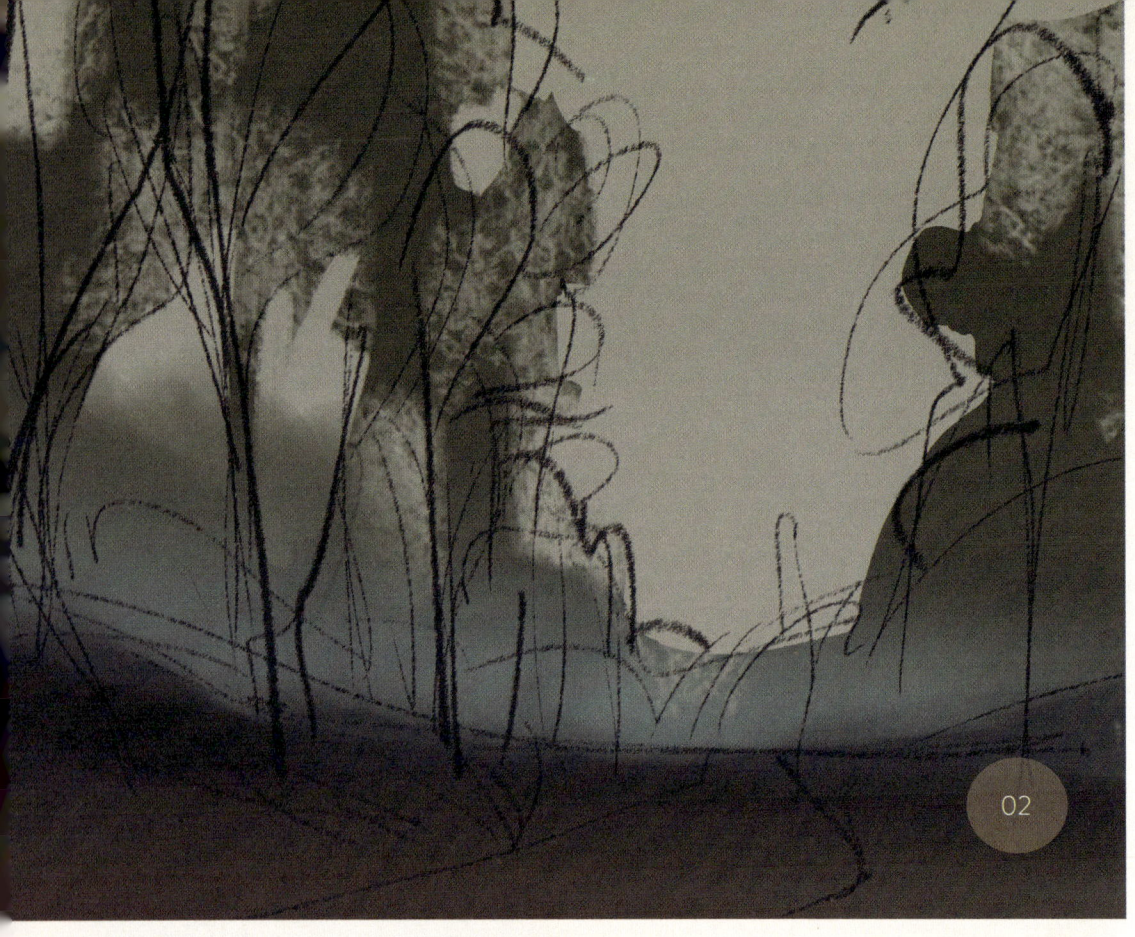

02

02 block in the main elements

Next, block in the main elements of the scene, in my case these are the sky and ground. Check your reference images to guide your color choices and draw each element on a separate layer so they can be easily modified.

I set the sketch layer from the previous step to Multiply mode, and adjust the Oil Pastel brush to a low flow of 5% for more texture. On a new layer, I block in the sky using a desaturated yellowish color. This brush allows me to paint in textured areas to suggest light scattering through the leaves. On a separate layer, I also block in the ground using a dark brown.

Now I switch to a softer brush and use a pale bluish color to paint some atmospheric mist over the ground, suggesting a distant, hazy forest. Then I use a darker brown to emphasize the horizon.

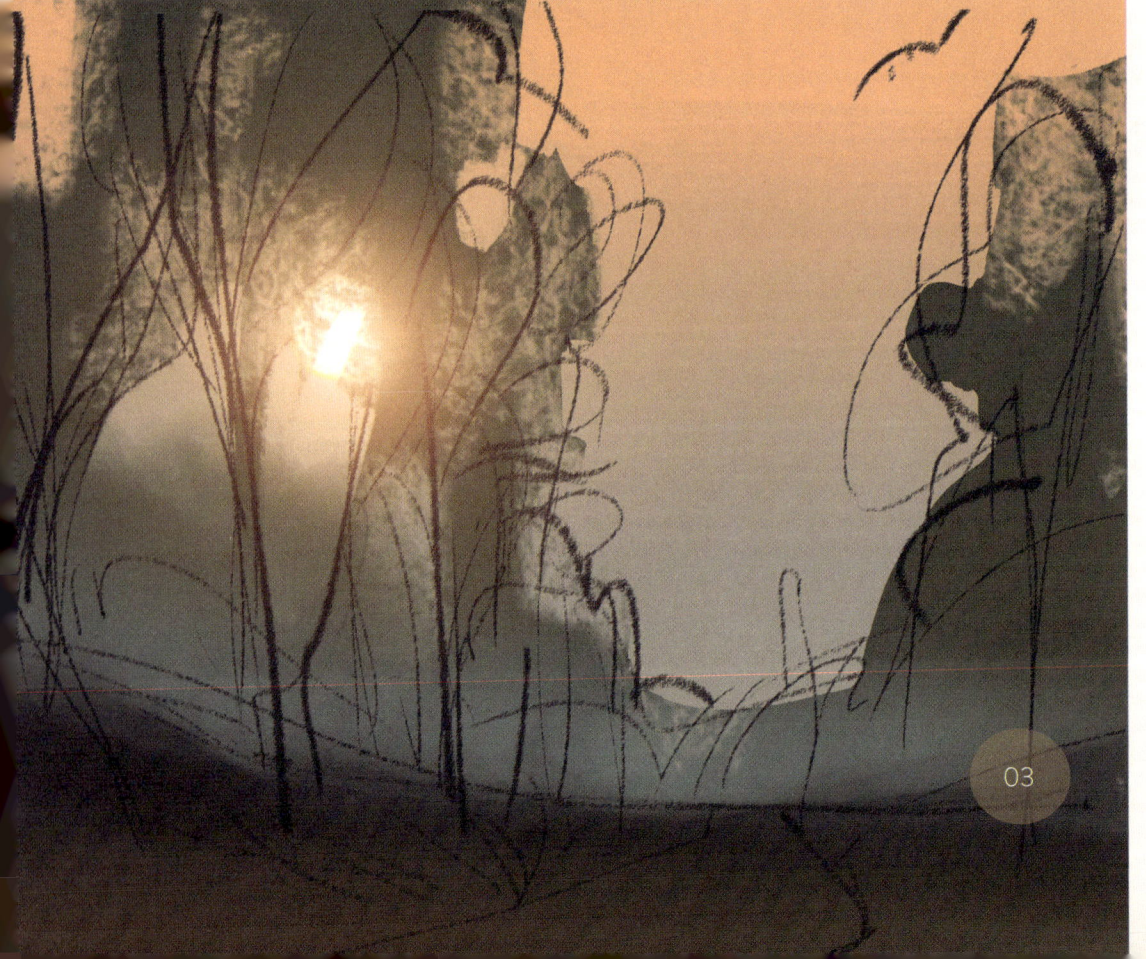

03

03 light source

It is time to add some light to the image. To start, create a new layer below the sketch layer and paint the sun as a light yellow circle with a deeper orange-yellow around it. I use another photo (01c) as a reference for these colors and make sure that the sun is hidden behind the "leaves" that I have implied during the previous step.

On a new layer set to Screen mode and placed above all the other layers, apply a circular Radial gradient to give the sun a bright glow. At this stage I also add more color to the sky by locking the transparency of that layer (using the checkerboard lock icon on the Layers panel), and adding a warm, orange gradient on top.

04 add detailed elements

Now that the basic colors have been blocked in, more detail can be added. I start with the trees, using the Oil Pastel brush to paint the main tree trunks. Rather than paint every tree individually, only paint the most important ones for now. Next, set the brush to a low flow of 5% and an opacity of 20% to block in rough shapes representing the clusters of leaves on the branches. Try to think of the leaves as bigger shapes on the trees, rather than individual leaves.

Then, on a new layer, I use the same brush to work on the ground area, adding a path and some texture details. In order to make the sketch lines blend in better with the other colors in the scene, lighten the line colors by selecting the sketch layer and adjusting the hue and saturation settings (Image > Adjustments > Hue/Saturation).

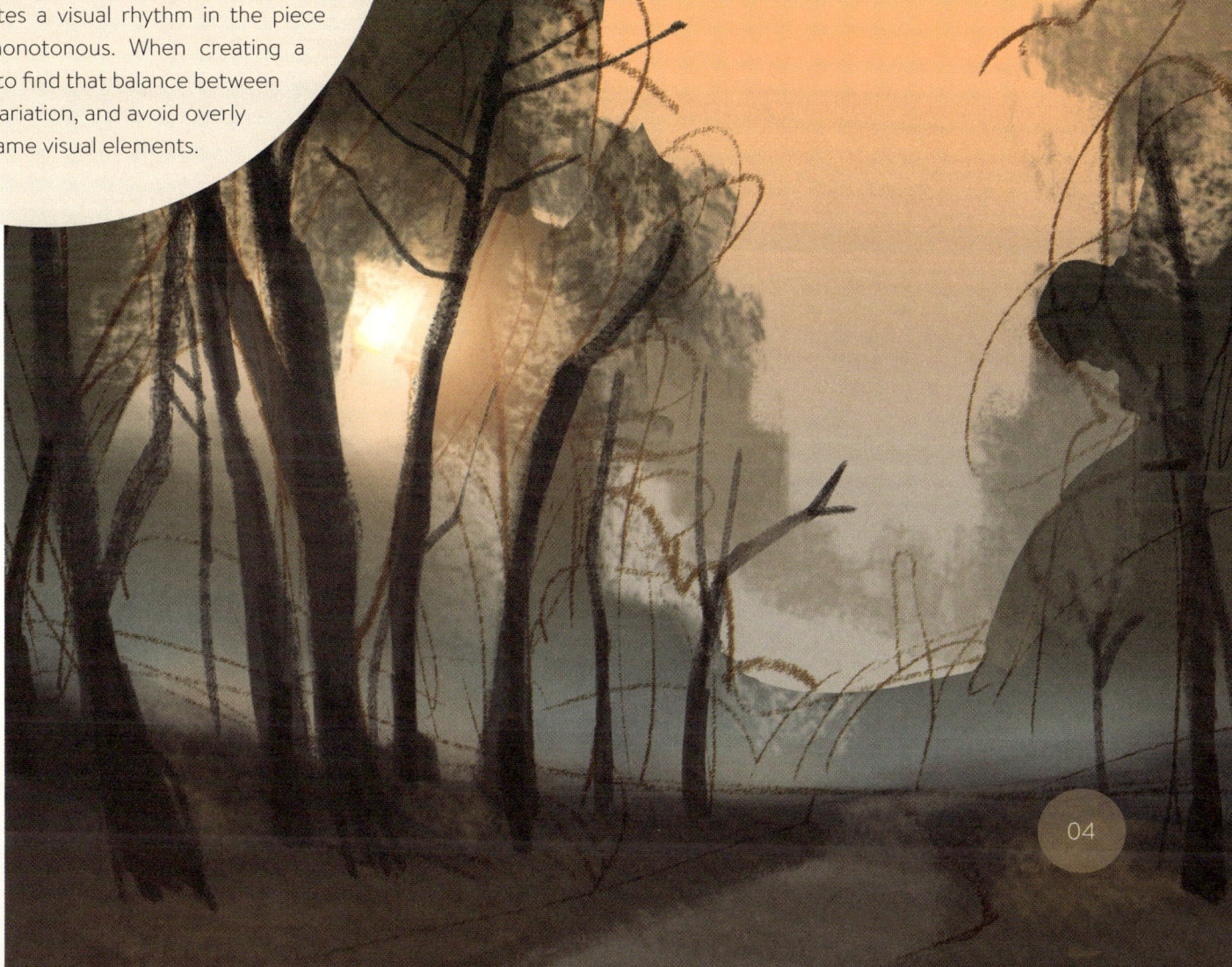

04

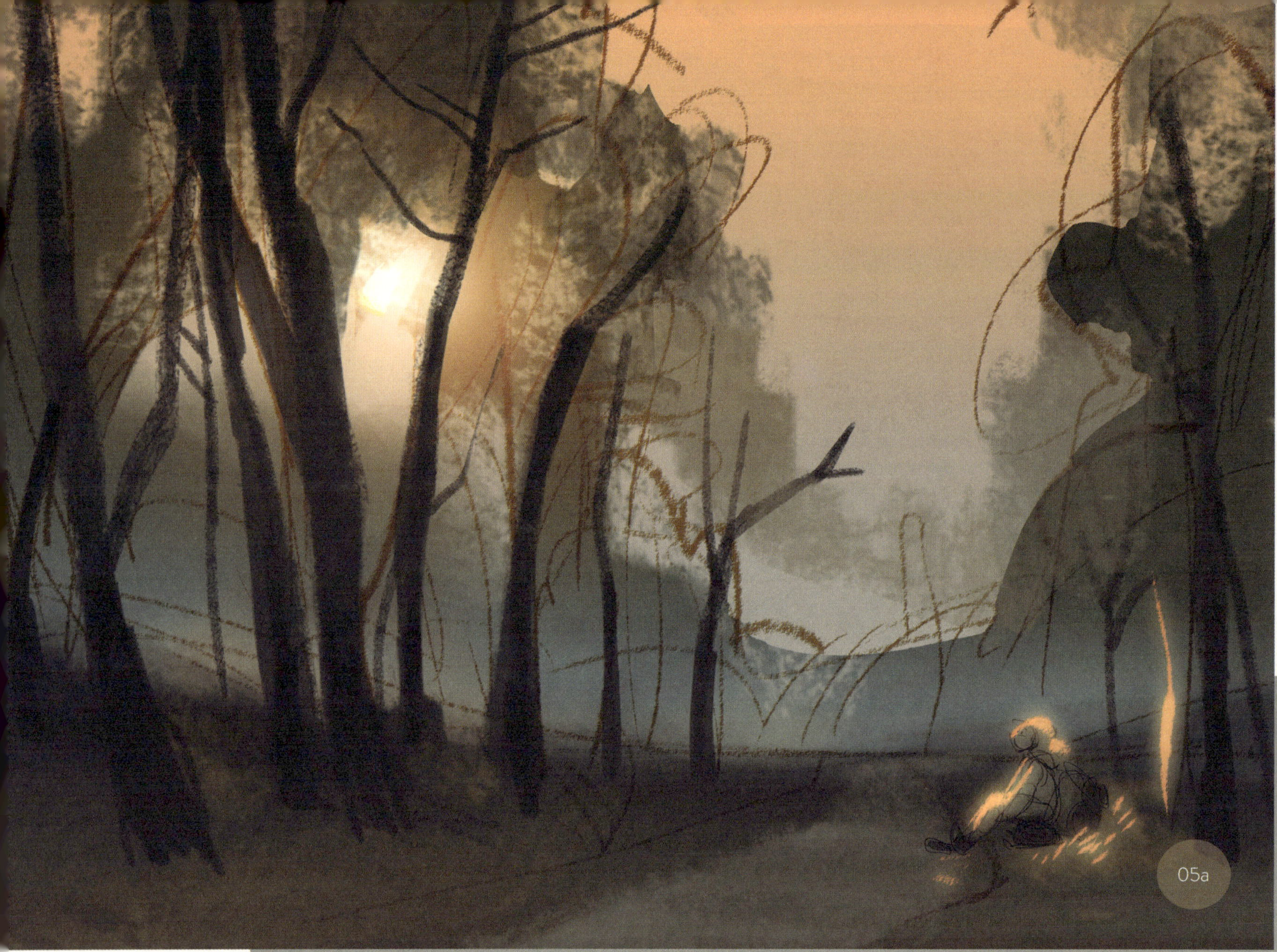

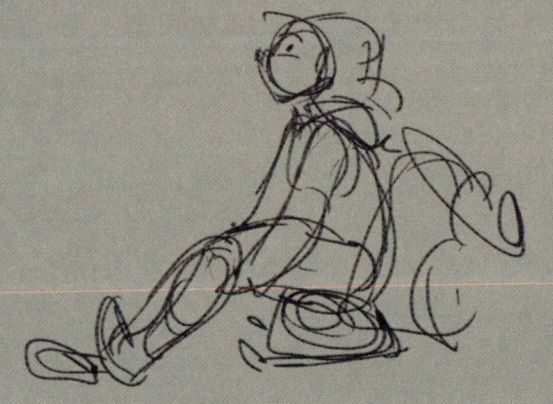
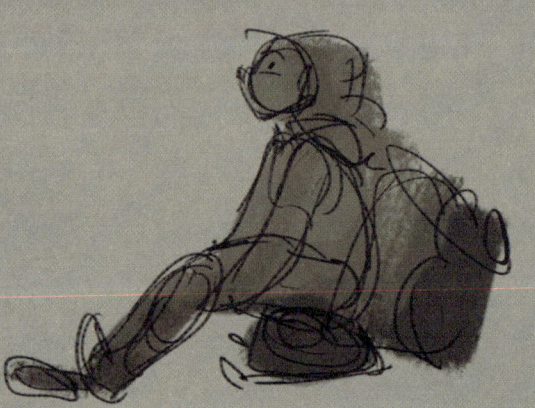

05 add a figure

I want this image to be more than just a painting of a scene. I also want to include a character from my imagination, so that the final painting has both realistic and stylized elements. I decide to add a character taking a rest from a walk and sitting peacefully in a patch of sunlight.

To start, roughly sketch a figure on a separate layer; then block in the base colors. It is important for the colors on the character to blend with the rest of the scene, so select colors that are already on the canvas using the Eyedropper tool. I also choose to add a highlight in a bright orange color so that the character is placed in a patch of sunlight.

Next, duplicate the character layer, apply Gaussian blur (Filter > Blur > Gaussian Blur), and set the layer mode to Screen. This creates a glowing effect and helps the character to stand out against the darker surroundings.

> "I also want to include a character from my imagination, so that the final painting has both realistic and stylized elements"

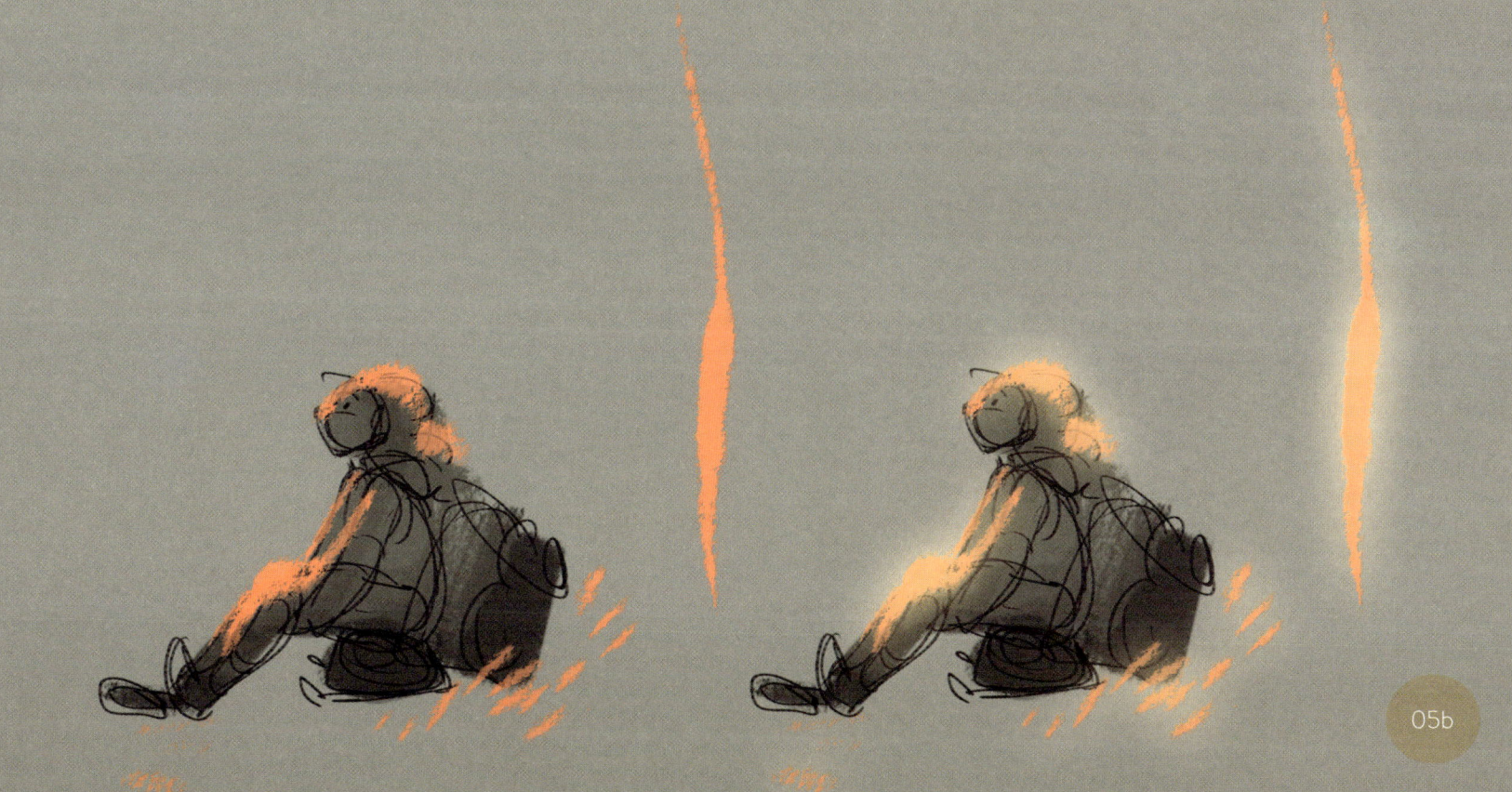

05b

133

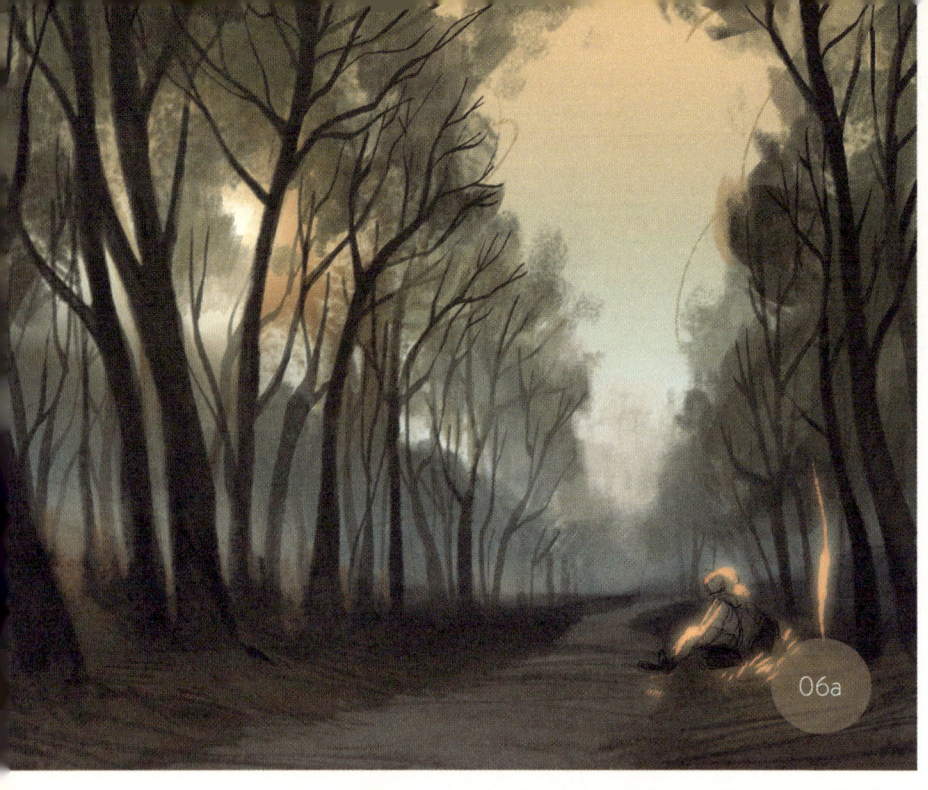

06a

06 add detail to the trees

Now I focus on the trees again. To start, I clean up the tree trunk layer using the Eraser tool to smooth the edges, and then add extra branches here and there with a brush. Next, on two separate layers, I paint a middle-ground and background layer of trees, each set at 50% opacity. This creates the illusion of depth in the forest. Elements that are closer to the viewer should be darker, and elements that are in the distance should be more hazy and light in color.

I also paint more branches towards the top of the tree trunks. The goal of this step is to refine the image and add detail without losing the rougher brushstrokes, so it is important to avoid over-smoothing the image during this step.

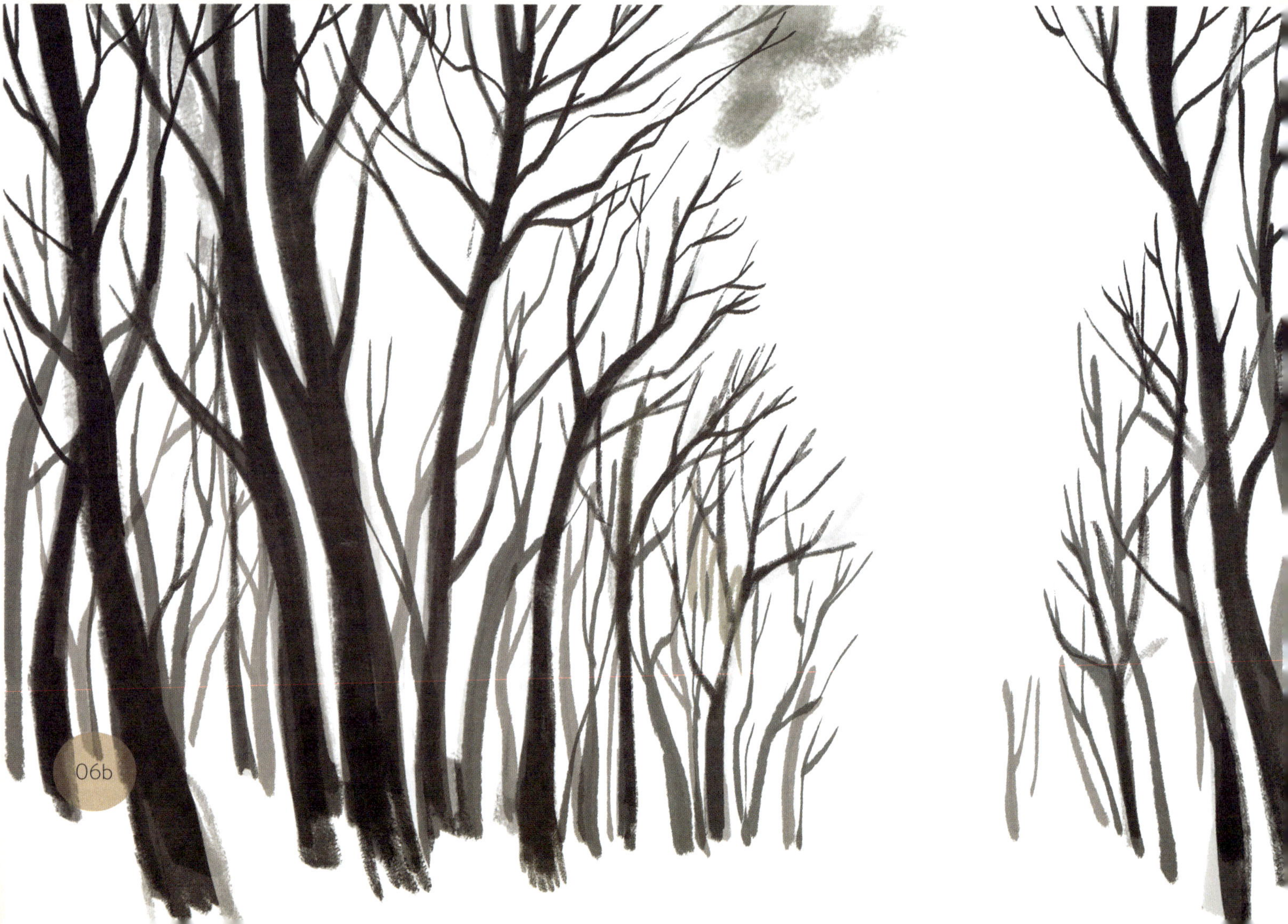

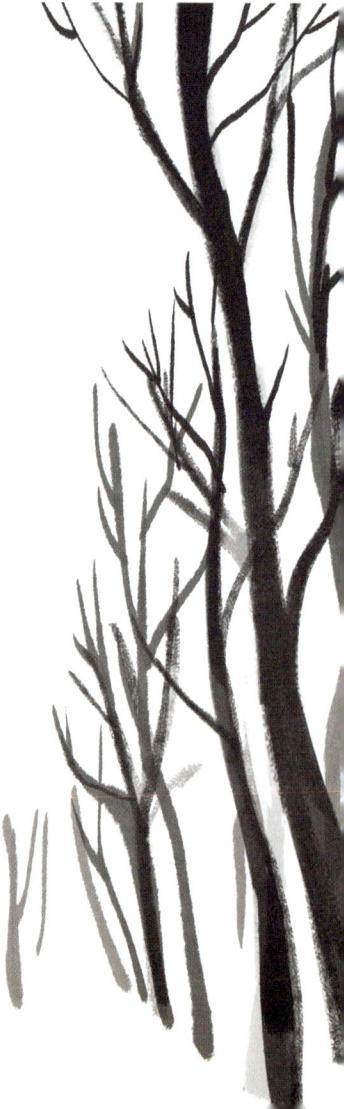

06b

07 focus on lighting

Now that there is more detail in the trees and leaves, it is good to also work out the lighting in more detail. Use two Radial gradients to intensify the glow of the sun; one set to Overlay for a more intense orange glow, and another set to Screen for some brightness.

I focus on the figure again, adding more scattered highlights to the leaves and grass blades around her. I use an orange gradient to lighten the whole area. Finally, I add more details to the figure, such as loose strands of hair and further definition to her clothing, focusing on the areas that are illuminated by the sun. The patch of sunlight around the character now looks warmer and much more inviting.

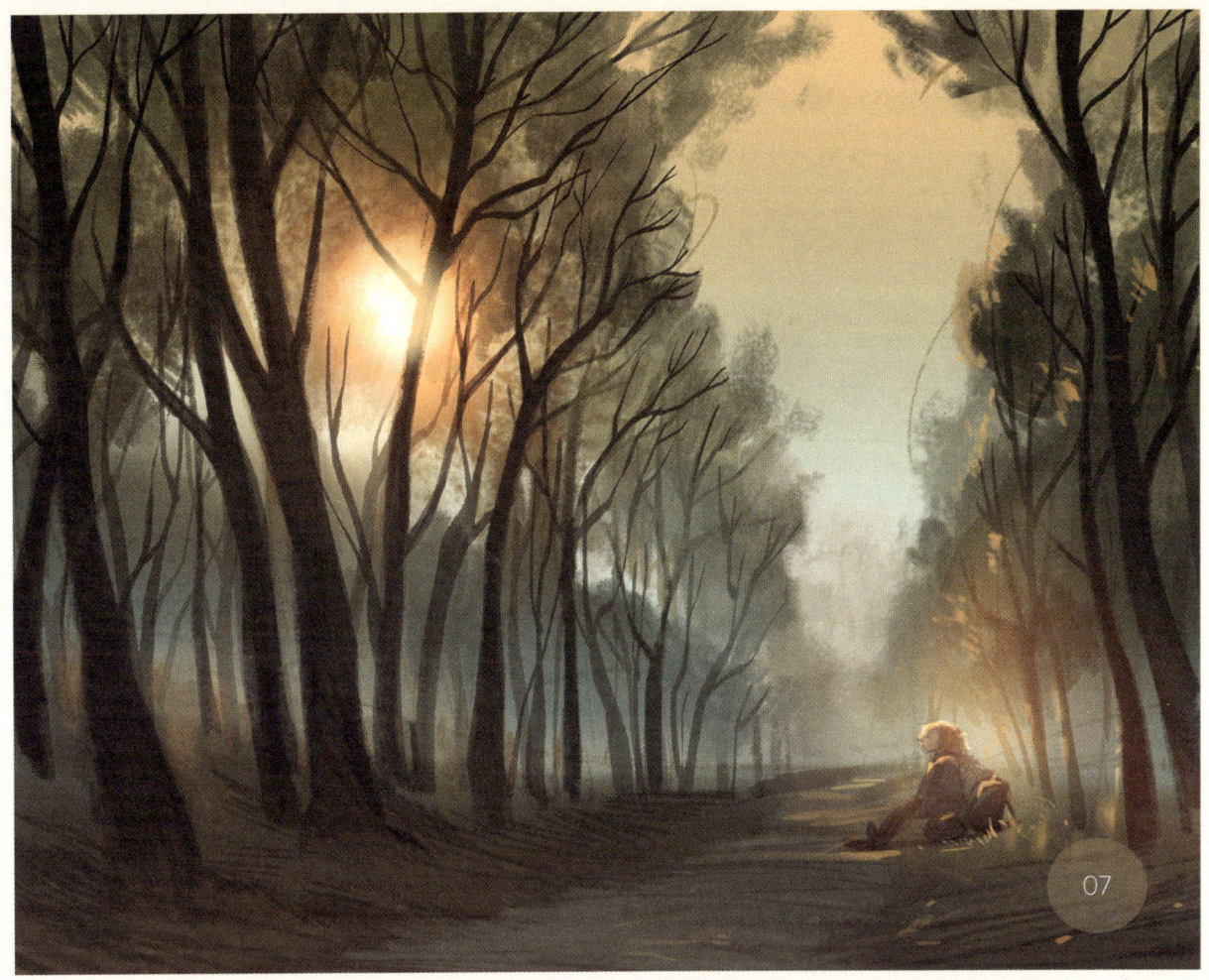

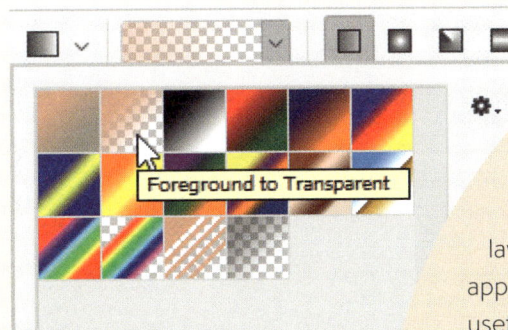

tip 02
locking layer transparency

I usually start my process by blocking in each element on a separate layer. The reason for this is that locking the layer transparency and applying gradients makes adding colors and depth very easy. This is especially useful for painting skies, which almost always require some kind of gradient.

It is also a useful technique when you are creating depth – the ground or floor of an image usually fades from dark to light. To use this technique: lock the transparency using the checkerboard lock icon on the Layers panel; set your gradient tool to "Foreground to Transparent"; and apply the gradient to your layer.

135

08 soften with gradients

I feel the image could benefit from more softness, which will create a sense
of depth as well as making the lighting appear more diffuse. To do this, use
gradients set to a low opacity, selecting sky colors with the Eyedropper
tool, and then apply them to the edges of the leaves. This creates a hazy
light effect.

I apply blue-gray gradients to the base of the trees to also make this area
seem mistier. Finally, I use a soft green hue to "fill up" the leaves of the trees a
bit more. Apply each of the gradients on a separate layer so it is easy to erase
some parts or lower the opacity on others depending on what is needed.

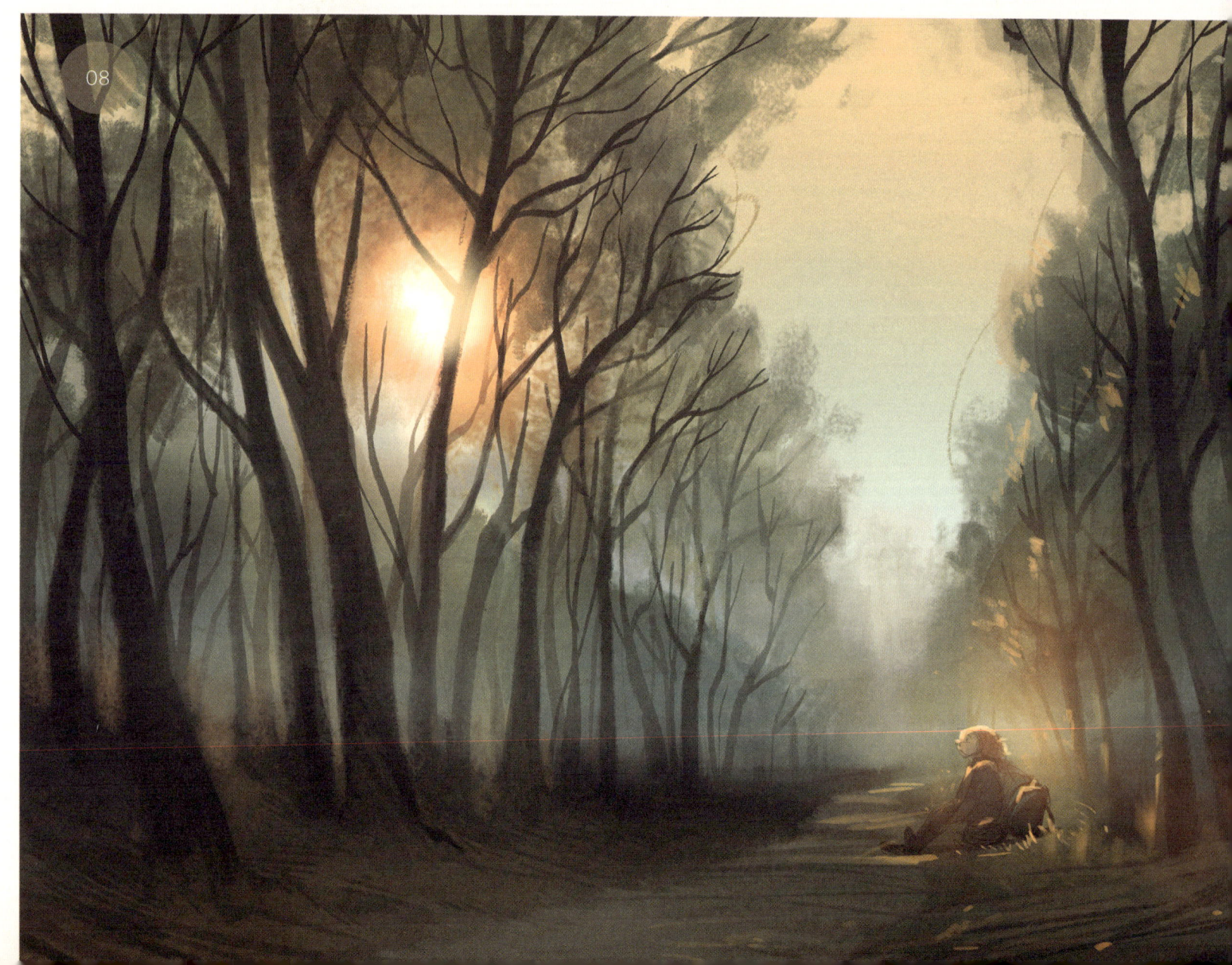

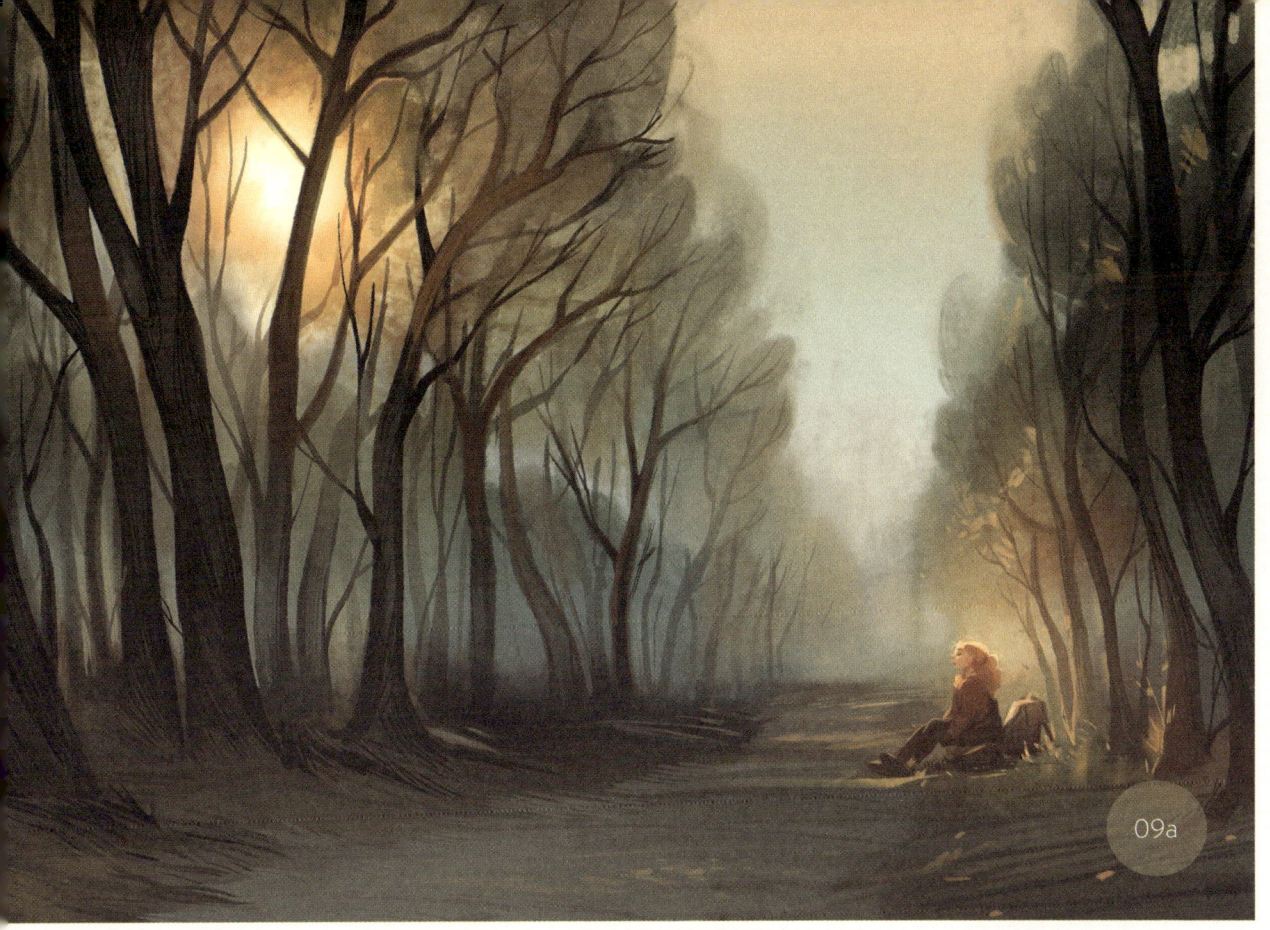

09a

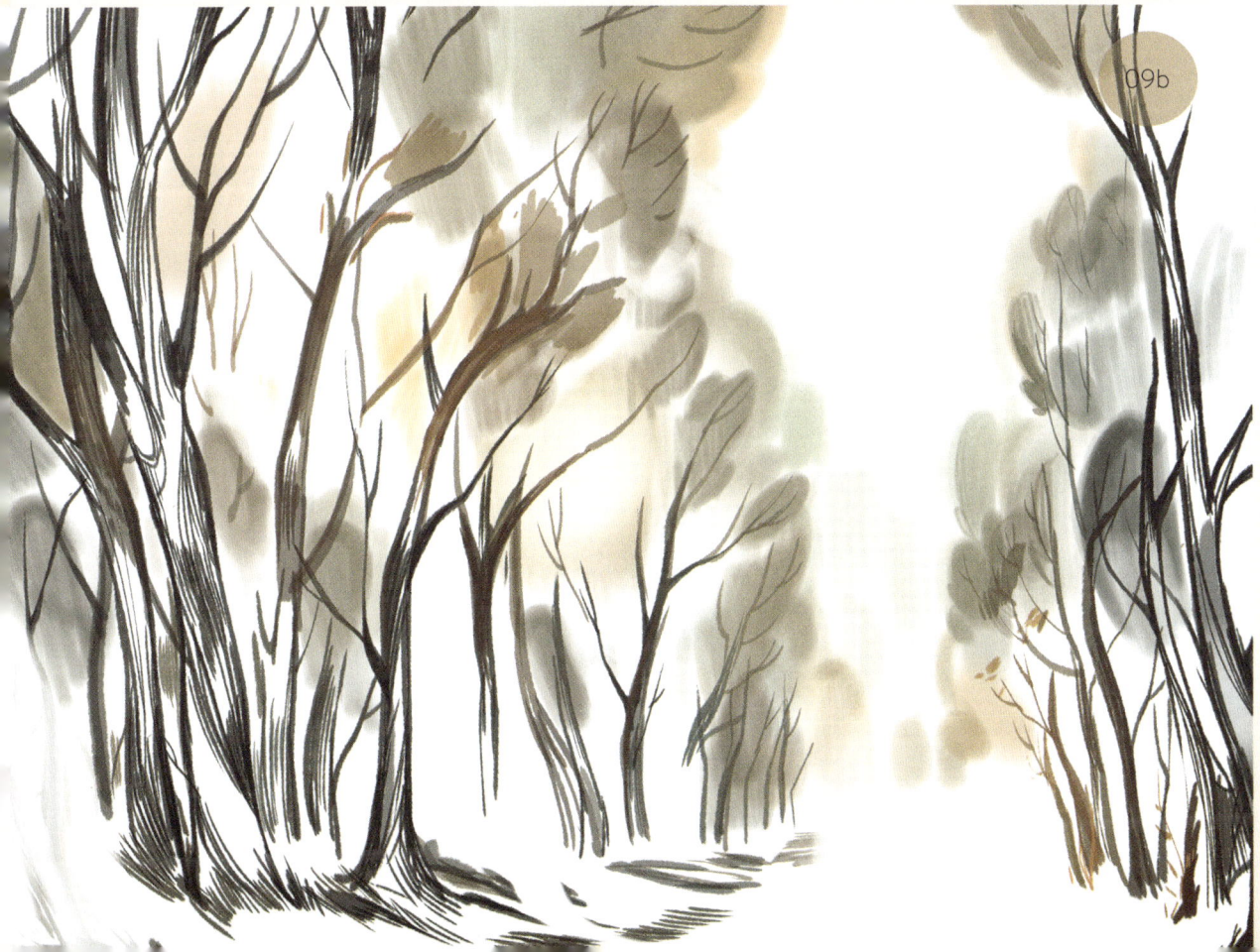

09b

09 final detail pass

I feel my image is ready for the "final pass" of detail – that is to say, the final round of paint work. For this process, create a new layer and set your brush to a smaller size. Zoom in on the image and, using the Eyedropper shortcut (hold down the letter I on your keyboard), quickly clean up some of the edges.

I work on the edges of the tree trunks and branches, and use a soft brush to soften the edges of the leaves to create gentle, rounded forms. I focus mainly on the trees in the foreground which require more detail because they are closer to the viewer. I want this image to keep some of its rough edges so I am careful not to overdo this phase.

I paint the figure in more detail, again focusing on the areas that are illuminated by the sunlight. To suit the proportions of this scene, I reduce the size of her head. To do this, use the Lasso tool with the Feather setting at 50 pixels. Then copy and paste the head, and use Transform (Edit > Transform > Scale) to shrink it down.

10 finalize the lighting

To finish the image, I want to emphasize the warm glowing light a little more. This will help to bring focus to the areas of the painting I most want the viewer to look at. Use a horizontal gradient to create a beam of light between the sun and the character – I choose a pinkish color for the beam – and set it to Screen mode. Then, lower the opacity of this layer so that it blends into the scene nicely.

In order to add contrast, I darken the lower left area of the image with a light blue Multiply layer. This not only adds darker values to the image, but also adds some cooler shades to contrast with the warm sunlight. As a final touch, I further emphasize the warm glow around the figure by painting in more highlights and adding lighter gradients. The speed painting is now complete!

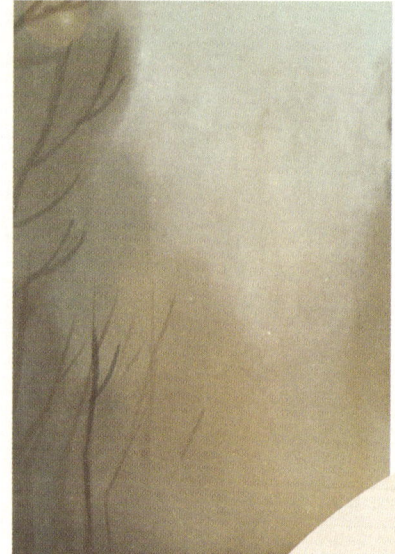
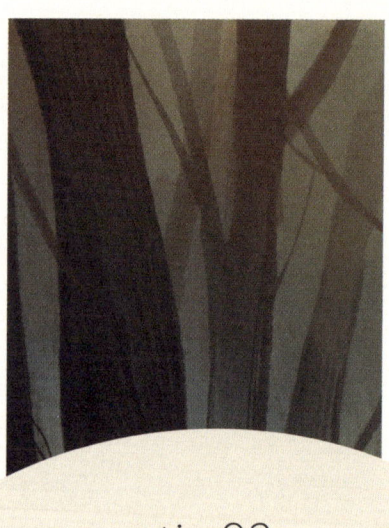
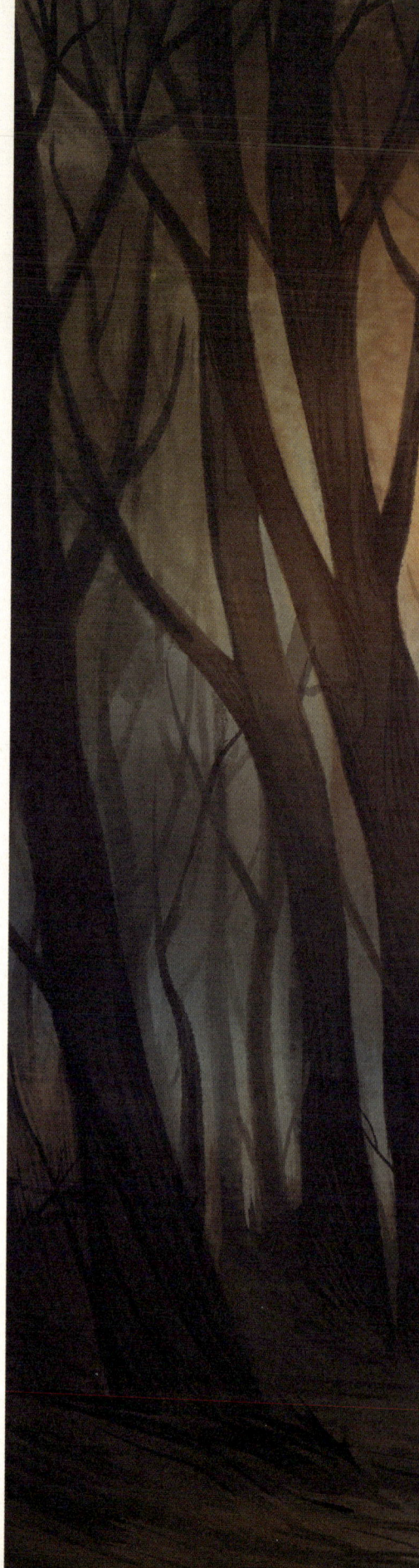

tip 03
distribution of detail

As mentioned on page 30, when drawing scenery, it is important to keep in mind how detail is distributed throughout your image. Beginners often apply the same level of detail over the whole image, believing that more detail means a stronger end result. However, this can remove the depth from your painting.

In reality, objects that are closer to you appear larger with more widely distributed details, whereas objects that are further away have denser, smaller details. Furthermore, objects that are very far away tend to appear hazy and blurred.

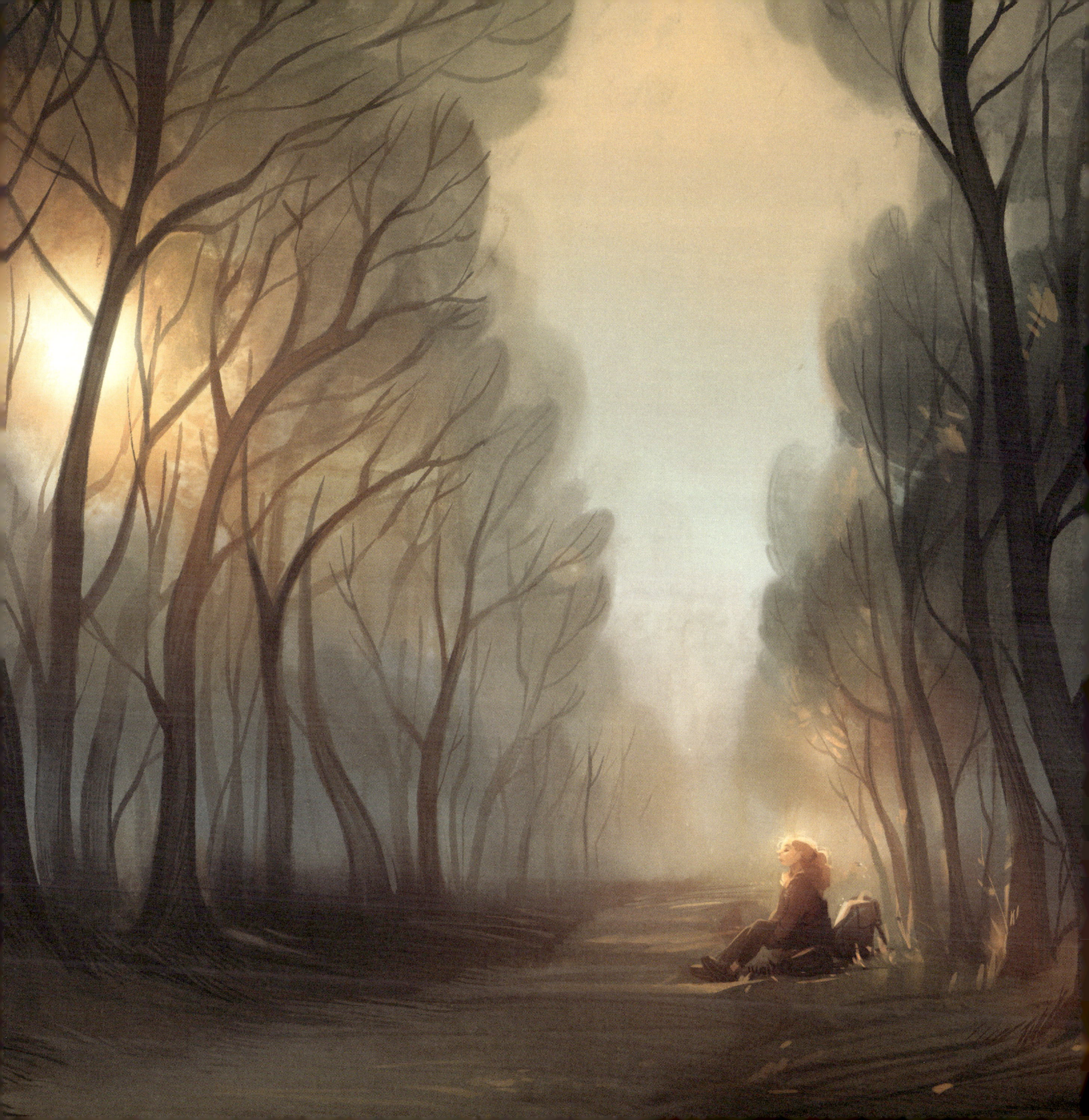

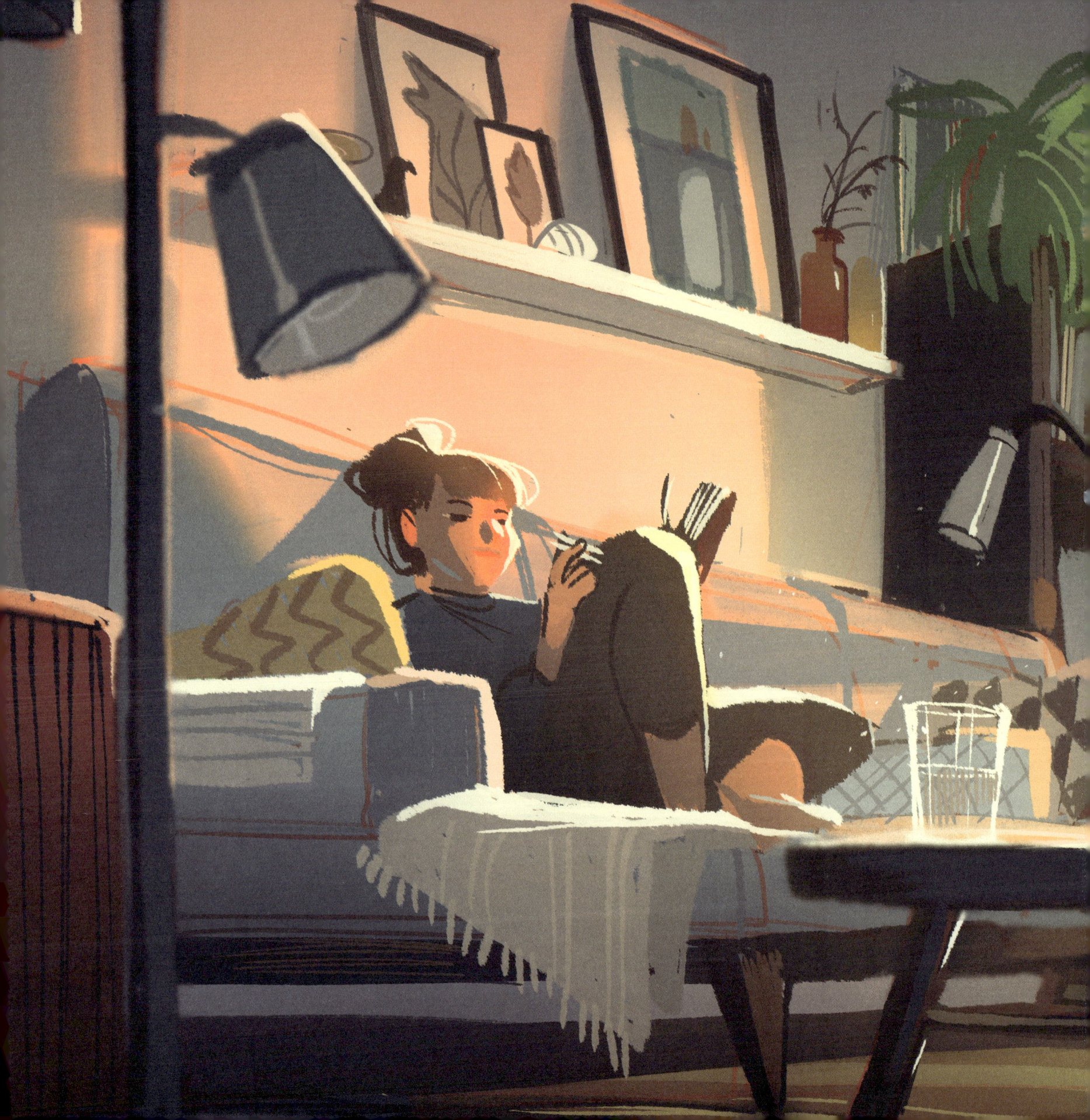

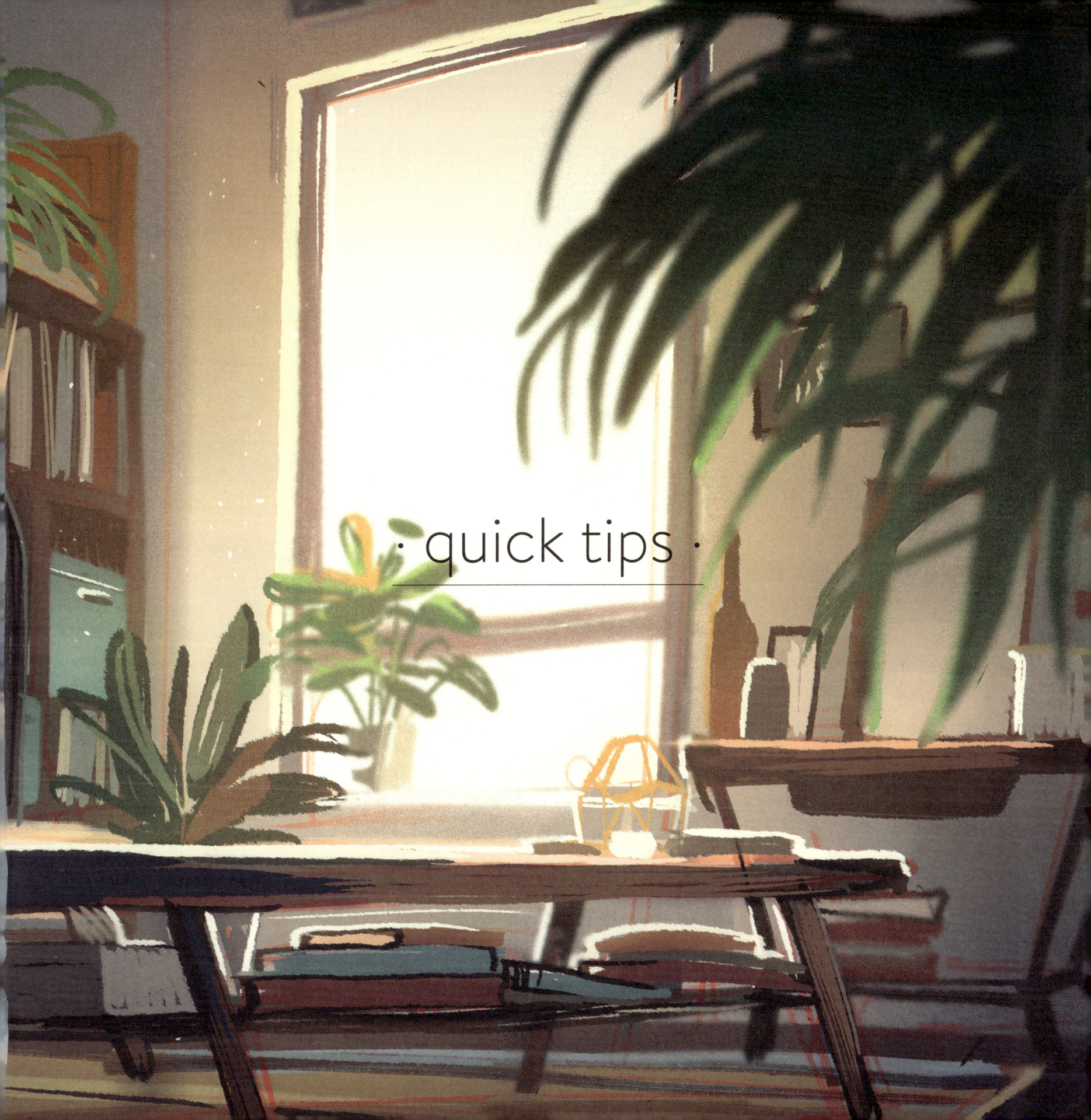

· quick tips ·

· capturing movement & gesture ·

simplify your style

Details add visual richness and appeal to a drawing, but I have learned that it is not always useful to work out every detail in the early stages. Often, these can be added later on and the early drawing style can be simplified. This maximizes gesture and movement, especially when drawing characters. Details are easy to add later, but gesture and movement are almost impossible to add if they are not present in the initial sketch.

If you struggle with movement and gesture, try to simplify your sketching process. Try not to focus on detail, but instead, focus on the "line of action" which conveys the movement of the character. I find it also helps to work in a light color which makes your lines less definite and makes the drawing process freer.

keep it simple +
don't go into too
much detail.

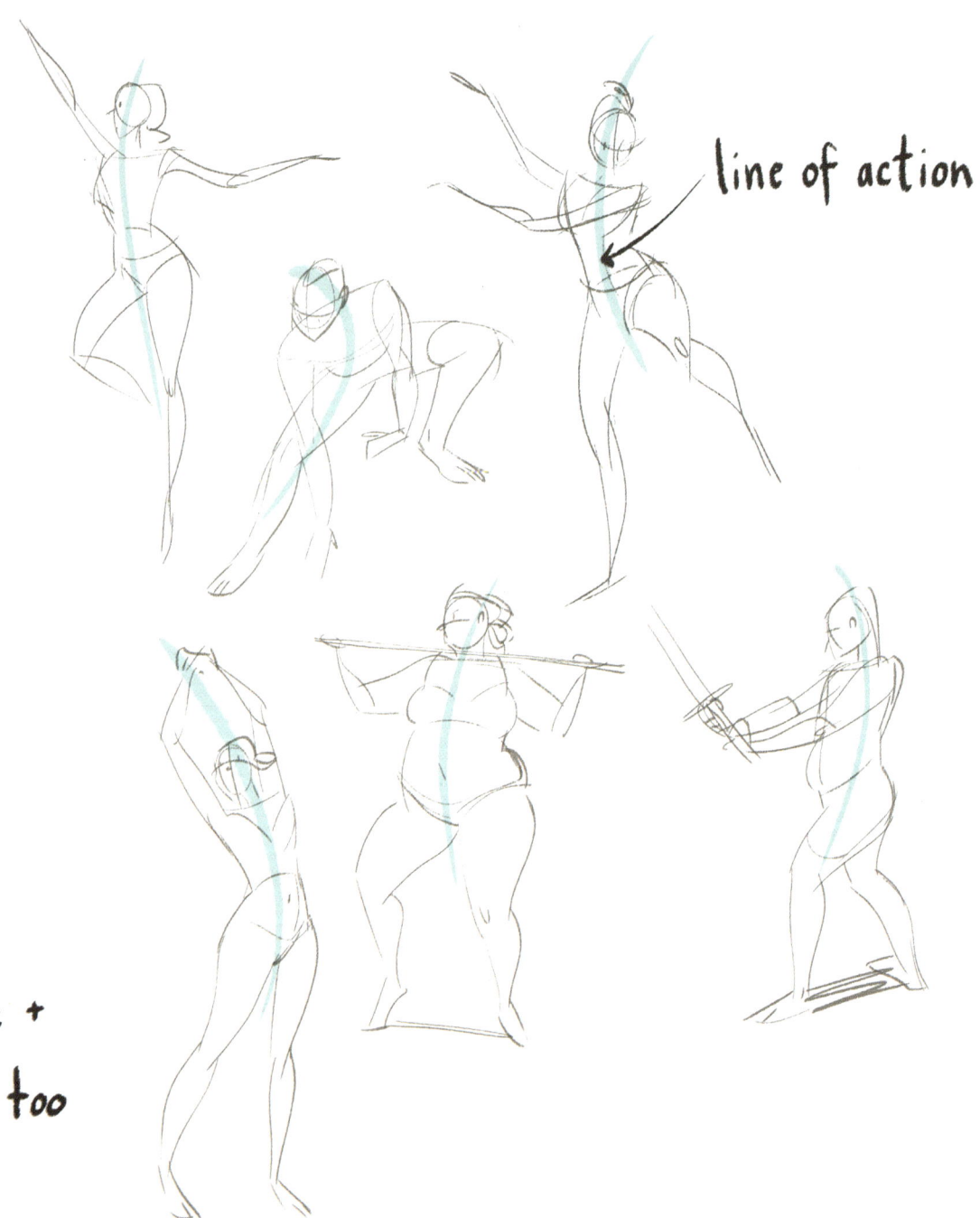

line of action

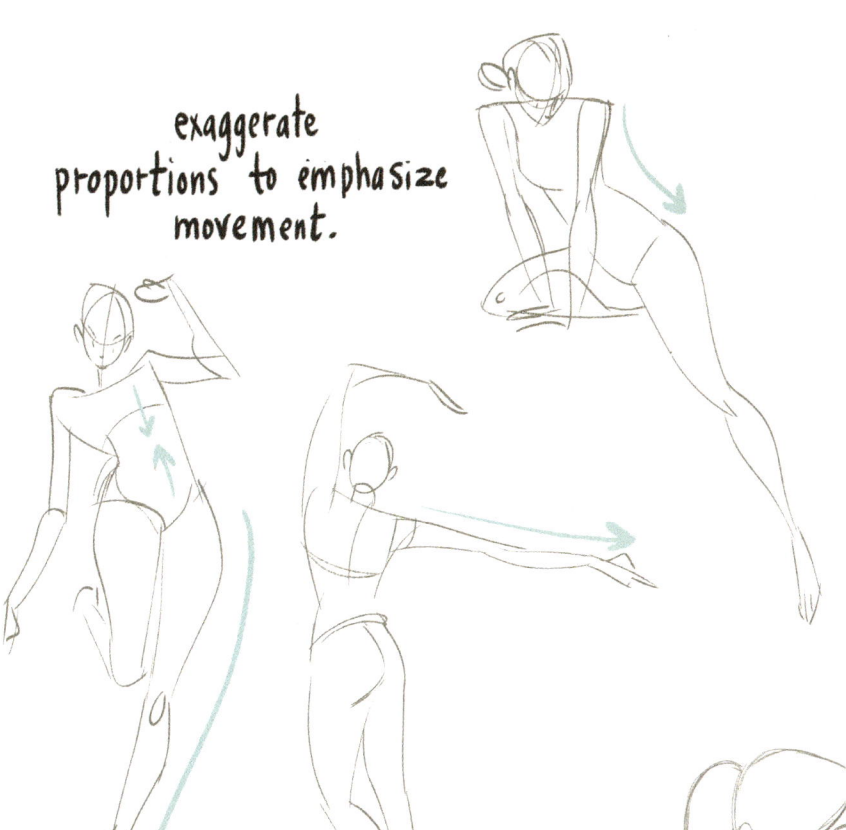

exaggerate proportions to emphasize movement.

exaggerate

It is easy to get hung up on the belief that a gesture drawing needs to be anatomically correct and have perfect proportions. However, I find that exaggerating aspects of the body shape can help to capture movement and gesture.

Although the figure might not be "correct," it is important that it is still good to look at so that the character makes sense on an intuitive level. Elongated limbs, extended body shape, and "incorrect" proportions are all okay if they help capture the movement of the figure. Challenge yourself to stylize and exaggerate the figure in order to capture this movement.

think fast!

The best way to develop a stronger sense of gesture in your sketches is to work quickly. Limit the amount of time you take to draw a certain pose to thirty seconds or less. The results might not always be perfect, but it challenges your brain to focus on the gesture rather than the details. Try to draw in smooth, confident lines and avoid overlay careful, perfect lines.

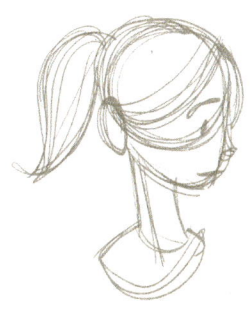

X **avoid careful scribbly lines**

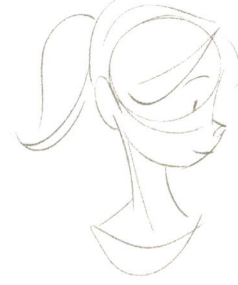

X **avoid heavy + dense sketch lines**

✓ **aim for light + simple sketch lines**

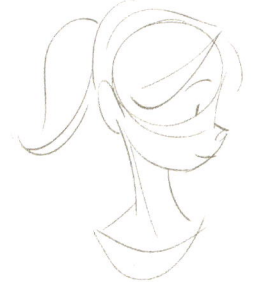
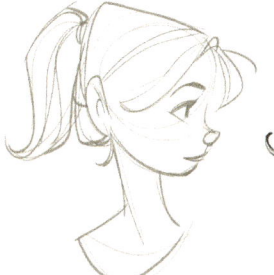
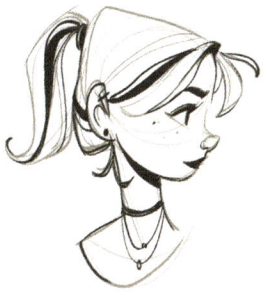

ADD DETAIL GRADUALLY

you can keep your initial sketch simple to start.

· line weight ·

flow

If you vary line thicknesses in a gradual and smooth way, the line can appear to be flowing. This is a great way to get a sense of elegance and movement in your line, especially when drawing decorative elements and hair.

Many artists create this effect by pressing down harder on the thicker parts of the line, similar to the effect of using a brush pen. Personally, I prefer to zoom in and thicken parts of the line with smaller brushstrokes, using the Eraser tool to smooth out any roughness. This gives me more control over the line weight.

for hair, lines with a thicker beginning + end add a flowing effect.

make some lines thicker than others for some nice rhythm + variation.

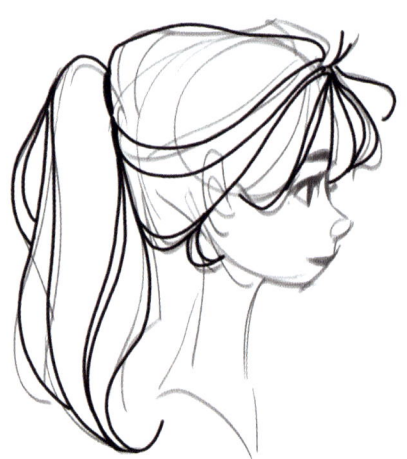

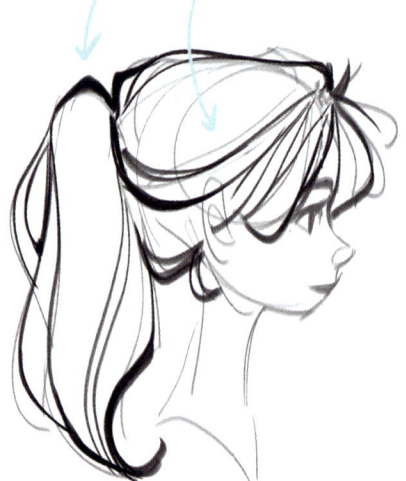

X avoid uniform line thickness

✓ use varying line weight to add movement + flow

creating movement

When working digitally, there are a lot of options in your brush settings to influence the thickness of your lines, like Pen Pressure, Tilt, and various texture options. You can draw a line that is a uniform thickness from beginning to end, or pick a brush with more variety along the length of the line.

By varying the thickness of a line at different points, you can create more movement and flow in your drawing. Variation encourages the eye to move along the line, and explore the subtle changes that occur as your eyes pass over it.

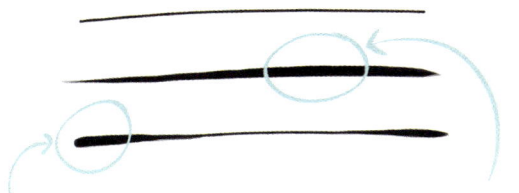

adding variation to line width adds movement, even to straight lines.

different line width gives different personality to a curved line.

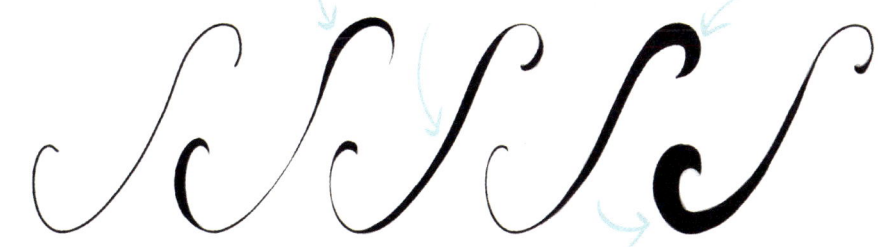

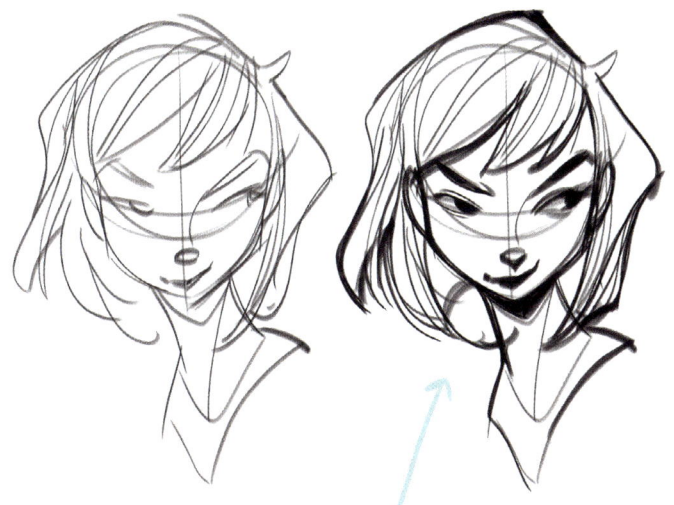

thicker lines draw attention to specific parts of the drawing.

leading the eye

With a sketch, it can be hard to draw focus towards a specific area, especially if you have a rough drawing style with many sketch lines. Rather than erasing parts of the sketch, or drawing cleaner line art on a separate layer, you can emphasize specific areas with a thicker line weight. This is a great way to draw the eye to the focal points of your sketch, such as the hair and face, without erasing or removing your rougher sketch lines. These lines often add a lot of movement and personality to your drawing, so there is no need to get rid of them!

· textured brushes ·

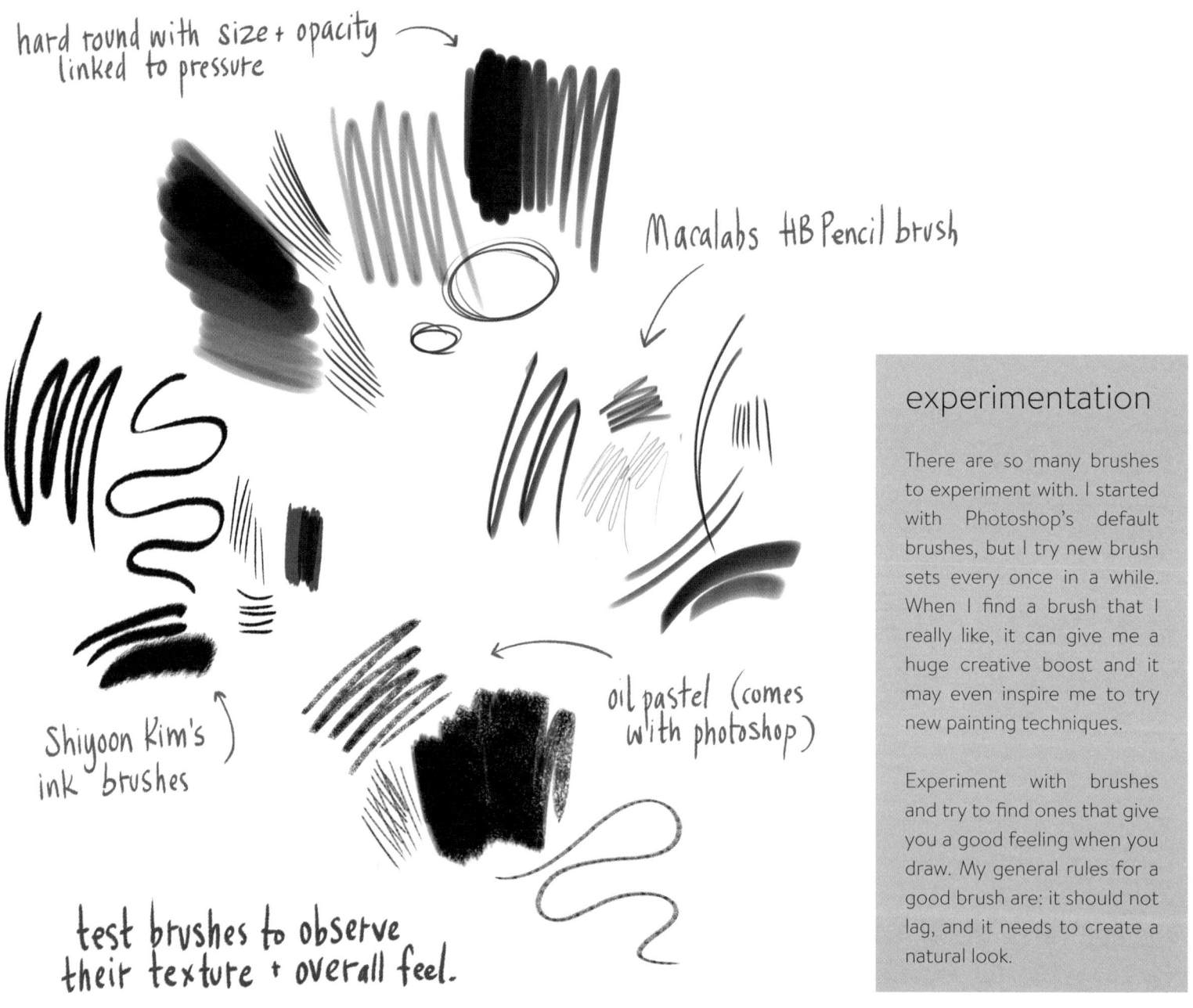

hard round with size + opacity
linked to pressure

Macalabs HB Pencil brush

Shiyoon Kim's
ink brushes

oil pastel (comes
with photoshop)

test brushes to observe
their texture + overall feel.

experimentation

There are so many brushes to experiment with. I started with Photoshop's default brushes, but I try new brush sets every once in a while. When I find a brush that I really like, it can give me a huge creative boost and it may even inspire me to try new painting techniques.

Experiment with brushes and try to find ones that give you a good feeling when you draw. My general rules for a good brush are: it should not lag, and it needs to create a natural look.

confidence in your lines

Textured brushes can also make the sketching process more pleasant. The standard round brushes that are usually the default in drawing programs can create a shaky effect, exposing mistakes. However, texture can change the feeling of the lines, leading to a more intuitive drawing experience and reducing the emphasis on the shakiness in the lines. Finding the brush that suits you can really help you get into a good creative flow.

STANDARD ROUND...
looks unnatural, exposes "mistakes" + wobbly parts.

OIL PASTEL
more organic look, but texture can be repetitive

INK BRUSH (by Shiyoon Kim)
natural look + feel, pleasant to use.

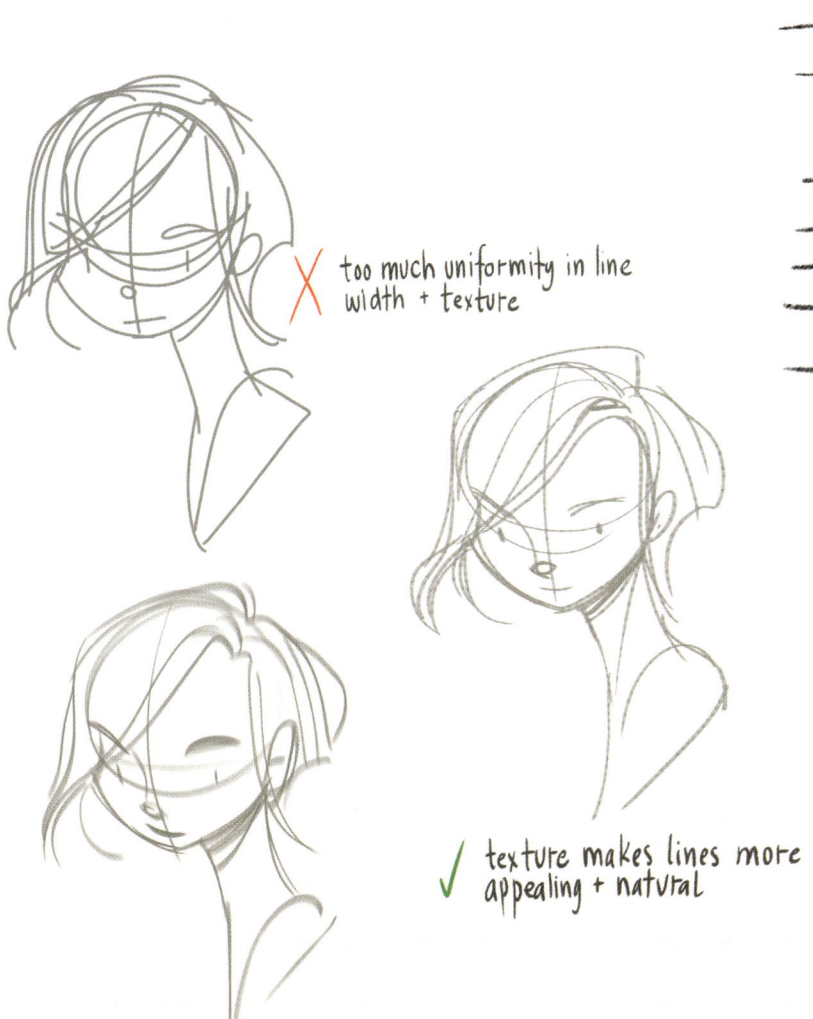

X too much uniformity in line width + texture

✓ texture makes lines more appealing + natural

✓ angled brushes add nice variation in width

getting a natural feel

Digital tools can be tough to work with as they may feel very unnatural compared to traditional tools like pencil and paper. This often prevents artists from feeling comfortable with sketching digitally, and causes them to leave the computer purely for finalizing rough work.

However, I feel that keeping a rough feel to my digital work makes it stand out and gives it added value, so I always encourage artists to sketch using digital tools, alongside the traditional pencil and paper. Exploring a variety of textured brushes that mimic real-world tools can make the learning process easier and more intuitive.

· shading & detailing ·

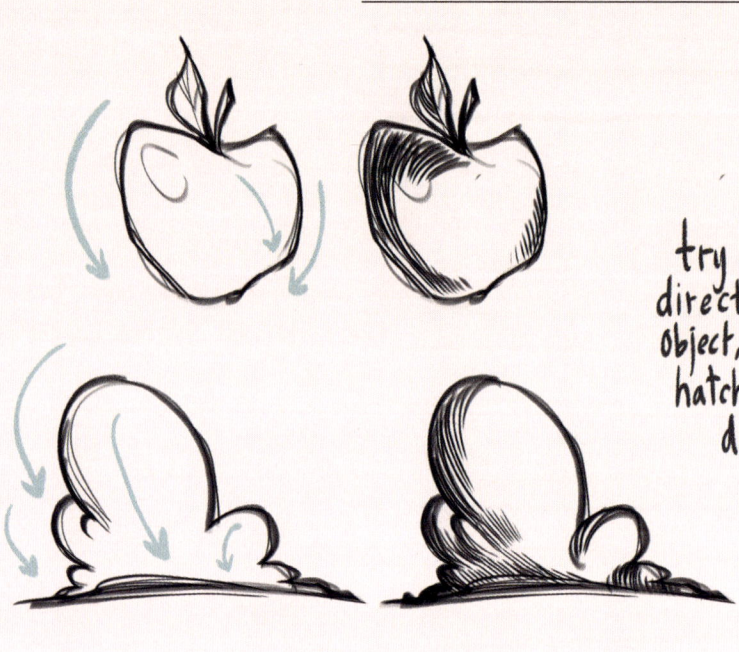

try to establish the directions + volume of the object, and draw your hatch lines in this direction.

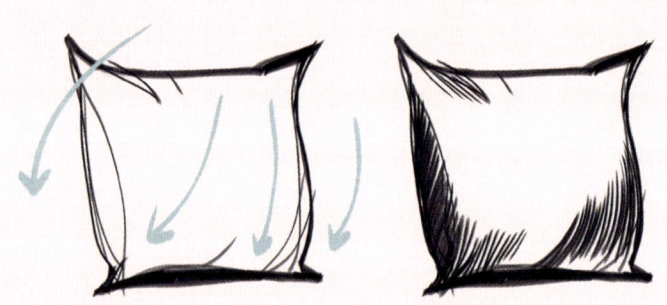

light versus direction

I used to apply shading to a sketch to convey lighting and shadows, but now I feel that direction and mass are more important. This comes from my background as an animator: I learned that everything must contribute to a sense of movement. So now, when I add shading, I try to make sure that it follows the direction and mass of the object I am drawing, and I avoid adding any details that distract from this.

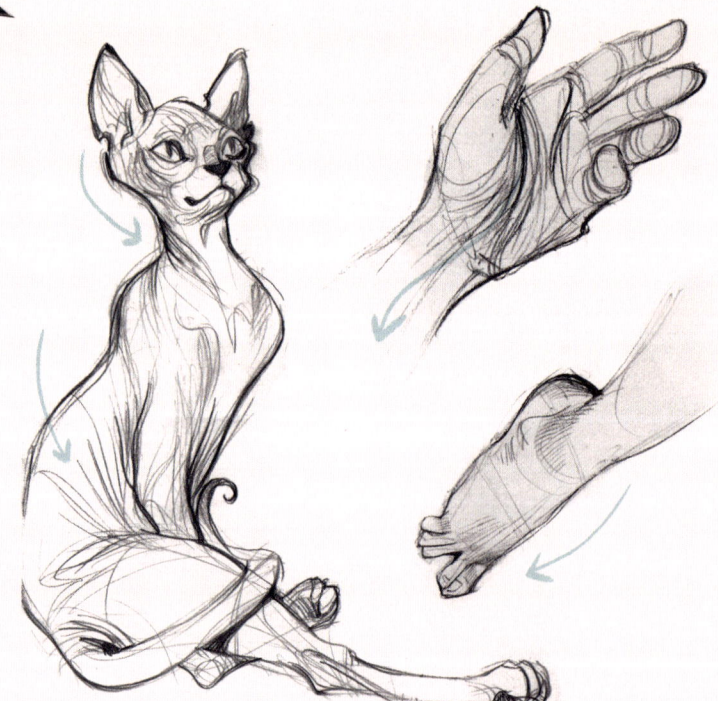

have your shading lines follow the contours of the shapes + forms.

adding depth

If you want to take your rough sketch to a more detailed level, there are different ways to give it depth and a visual richness. However, if you overdo the detail, you may lose the dynamic feeling of the sketch, so it is important to try to add detail in a way that does justice to your rough sketch lines. For this reason I prefer shading techniques that have a sketchy and rough feel.

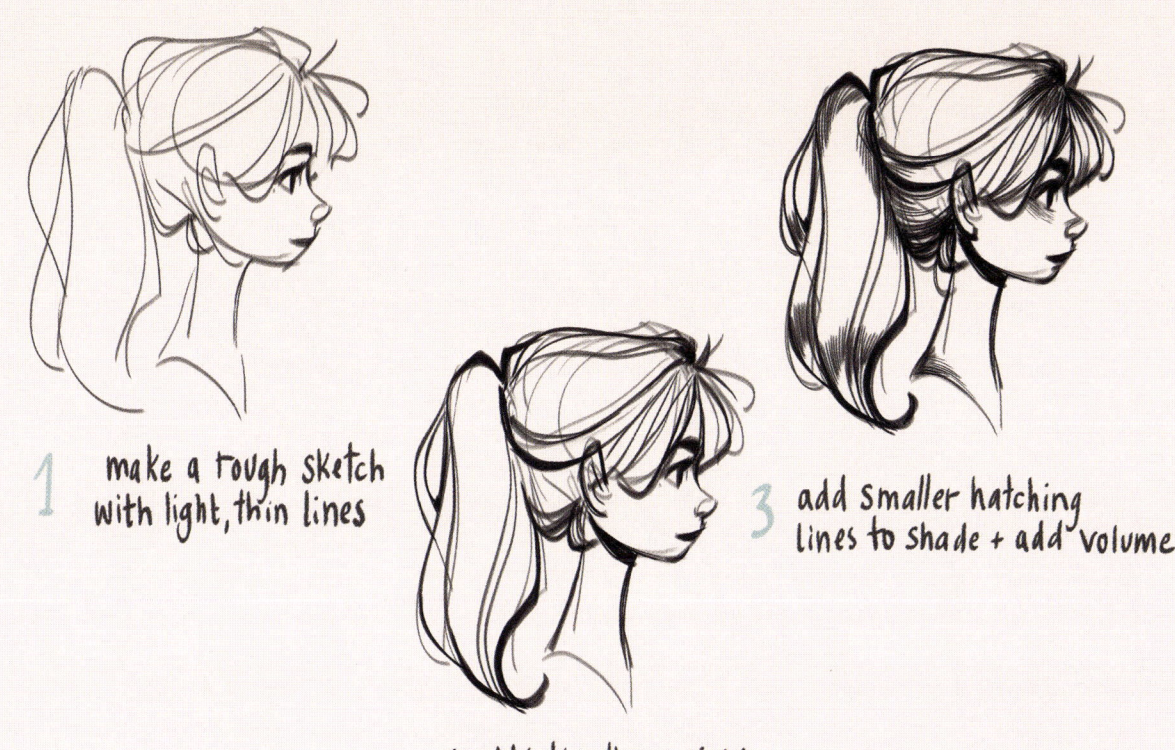

1 make a rough sketch with light, thin lines

2 use thicker line weight to add definition + detail

3 add smaller hatching lines to shade + add volume

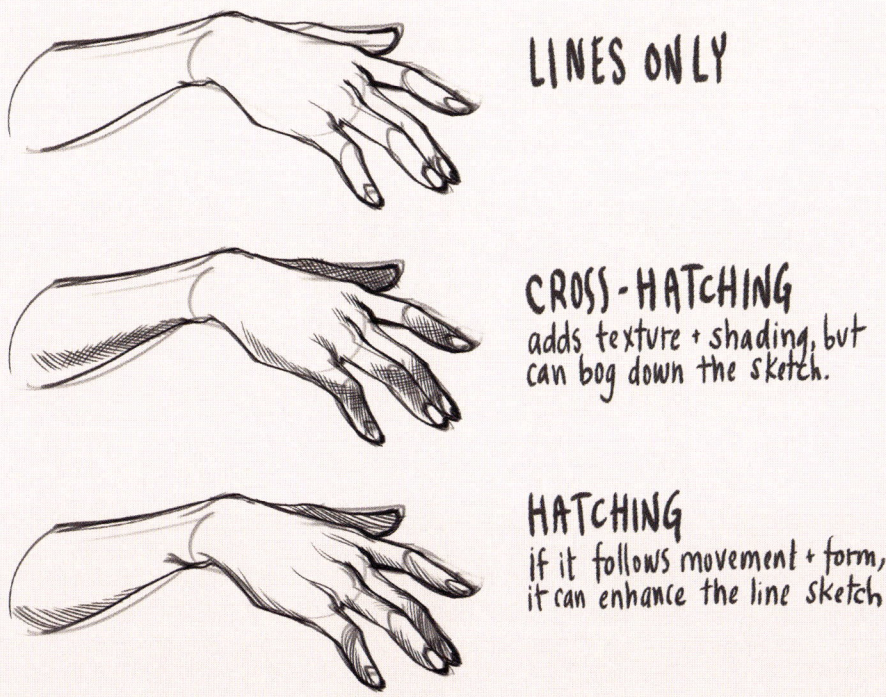

LINES ONLY

CROSS-HATCHING
adds texture + shading, but can bog down the sketch.

HATCHING
if it follows movement + form, it can enhance the line sketch

hatching

When I was learning how to draw, one of my favorite techniques was cross-hatching. This is a way of shading your sketch that involves drawing lots of smaller lines crossed over one another. As my skills improved, I was drawn to new and different techniques, but I am still a big fan of hatching.

Hatching is a shading technique like cross-hatching, but without crossing over the lines, where lots of smaller lines are used to shade. The direction of the lines adds movement to a sketch, especially if they follow the form and shape of the object being drawn. The more of these smaller lines you layer, the more complex the detail of your sketch can be.

· thank you ·

Thanks so much to everyone who helped to fund this book through Kickstarter and brought this project to life, and also to those who helped spread the word about the campaign! Your support makes so many things possible for me, and I am endlessly grateful for that. I hope I can meet all of you some day and thank you in person. Thanks also to everyone who follows my work online and supports what I do, even if it is just by following me on social media. You guys inspire and motivate me!

Thanks to 3dtotal Publishing for being the supportive, friendly, and collaborative publisher that I needed to bring my first, and now my second, art book to life.

Many thanks also to my clients who have generously allowed me to include some of the concept art for their projects in this book.

Thank you so much to all the stock photographers and models who have generously allowed me to use their images as reference for my art. Your work and willingness to share make it possible for artists to grow, improve, and learn.

Many, many thanks go to my friends and family for always helping me and cheering me on. Thanks Mama for being so supportive of my work; not only for my books, but also my career as an artist! Thanks Kaitlin for being an awesome friend and letting me use your fancy scanner. Thanks Suey for always letting me know that you are proud of me. Thanks Schoonfamilie for being my cheerleaders and enthusiastic fans. Thanks Michiel for the awesome photos you took. And most of all, thanks to Arjen, my partner in crime, for helping me through stressful times and cheering me on when I need it most!

· about the artist ·

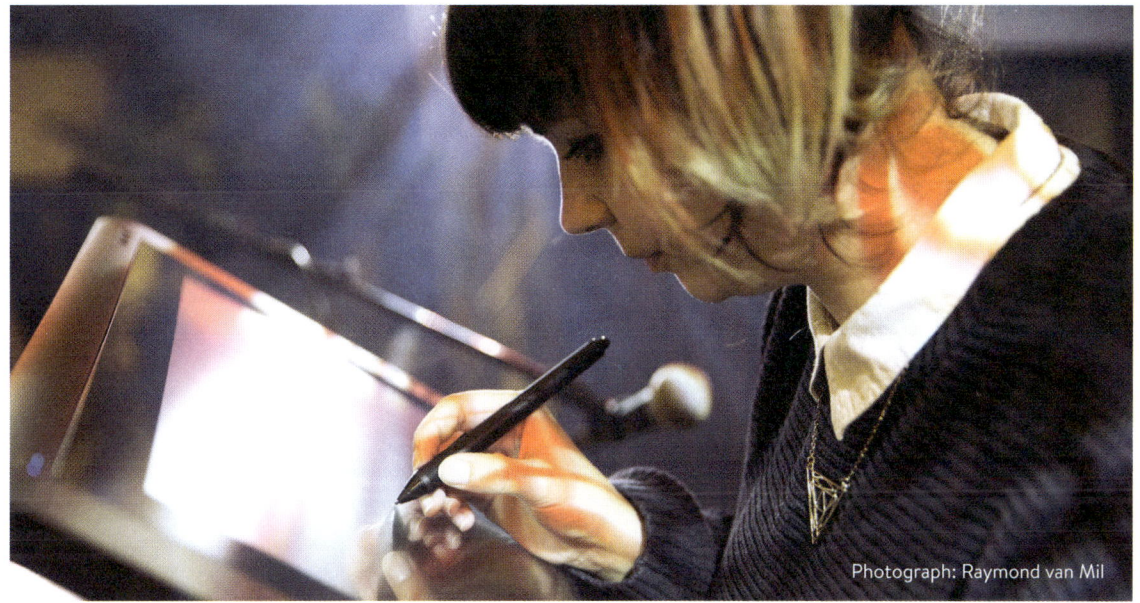

Photograph: Raymond van Mil

Lois van Baarle, otherwise known by her nickname Loish, is a digital artist and animator. She lives in Utrecht, the Netherlands, with her boyfriend Arjen Klaverstijn and her cat Charlie. She was born in the Netherlands but lived all over the world throughout her childhood, returning to the Netherlands in 2005 to study animation at the Utrecht School of the Arts.

Lois has worked as a freelance artist and animator since 2009, creating concept art and character designs for animations, games, and toy designs. She also shares her knowledge of digital art and drawing through workshops, tutorials, live demonstrations, lectures, and books.

website: loish.net | blog: blog.loish.net
facebook: @loish.fans | instagram: @loisvb | twitter: @loishh

· about 3dtotal Publishing ·

3dtotal Publishing is a small independent publisher specializing in inspirational and educational resources for artists. 3dtotal Publishing's titles proudly feature top industry professionals who share their experience in step-by-step tutorials and quick tip guides placed alongside stunning artwork to offer you creative insight, expert advice, and all-essential motivation.

Initially focusing on the digital art world, with comprehensive volumes covering Adobe Photoshop, Pixologic's ZBrush, Autodesk Maya, and Autodesk 3ds Max, 3dtotal Publishing have since expanded to offer the same level of quality training to traditional artists. Including stand-alone titles and the popular *Digital Painting Techniques*, *Beginner's Guide*, and *Sketching from the Imagination* series, their library is now comprised of over fifty titles, a number of which have been translated into different languages around the world. In 2016, 3dtotal Publishing worked with Lois van Baarle to produce her first book, *The Art of Loish: A Look Behind the Scenes*.

Based in the UK, 3dtotal Publishing is an offspring of 3dtotal.com, a leading website and resource for CG artists founded by Tom Greenway in 1999.